Peterson's

MASTER THE
NCLEX-PN

4th Edition

PETERSON'S

A **nelnet** COMPANY

About Peterson's, a Nelnet company

To succeed on your lifelong educational journey, you will need accurate, dependable, and practical tools and resources. That is why Peterson's is everywhere education happens. Because whenever and however you need education content delivered, you can rely on Peterson's to provide the information, know-how, and guidance to help you reach your goals. Tools to match the right students with the right schools. It's here. Personalized resources and expert guidance. It's here. Comprehensive and dependable education content—delivered whenever and however you need it. It's all here.

For more information, contact Peterson's, 2000 Lenox Drive, Lawrenceville, NJ 08648; 800-338-3282; or find us on the World Wide Web at www.petersons.com/about.

Stephen Clemente, President; Bernadette Webster, Director of Publishing; Jill C. Schwartz, Editor; Ray Golaszewski, Manufacturing Manager; Linda M. Williams, Composition Manager; James Holsinger, CD Producer; Jared Stein, CD Quality Assurance Analyst

ISBN-13: 978-0-7689-2818-1
ISBN-10: 0-7689-2818-4

Printed in the United States of America

10 9 8 7 6 5 4 3 2 1   11 10 09

Fourth Edition

Petersons.com/publishing

Check out our Web site at www.petersons.com/publishing to see if there is any new information, revisions, or corrections to the content of this book. We've made sure the information in this book is accurate and up-to-date; however, content may have changed since the time of publication.

Another Recommended Title:

Peterson's Nursing Programs

Contents

Contents

Contents

Contents

Before You Begin

HOW THIS BOOK IS ORGANIZED

Peterson's *Master the NCLEX-PN* provides a review of your practical nursing studies in outline form and as an overview of the Test Plan for the NCLEX-PN exam. This self-tutoring process combines the most effective practice with the content that you can expect to see on the actual exam.

Taking the NCLEX-PN is a skill. It shares some aspects with other endeavors, such as competing in athletics. It requires discipline and practice to succeed. These are skills that can be improved through coaching, but ultimately, improvement also requires practice. Peterson's *Master the NCLEX-PN* gives you both.

- "Top 10 Strategies to Raise Your Score" outlines time-tested strategies for doing your best on the exam.
- Part I includes all you need to know about the NCLEX-PN Test Plan and exam.
- Part II provides a content review that will help you do your best on the exam.
- Part III consists of two complete Practice Tests that simulate the actual exam, so you're fully prepared for test day.
- Appendixes provide information on state boards of nursing and professional organizations, as well as Web sites you can check for health, education, and job information.

SPECIAL STUDY FEATURES

Overview

Each chapter begins with a bulleted overview listing the topics that are covered in the chapter. The overviews tell you immediately where to look for a topic that you need to review.

Summing It Up

Each review chapter ends with a point-by-point summary that captures the most important information in the chapter. The summaries are a convenient way to review these points one last time before the exam.

Bonus Information

NOTE

Notes highlight critical information about the NCLEX-PN format.

TIP

Tips draw your attention to valuable concepts and advice for tackling the NCLEX-PN exam.

ALERT!

An *Alert!* warns you about a common error or makes you aware of an important nursing procedure.

ABOUT THE CD

The CD with access to two Practice Tests provides you with practice that simulates the actual NCLEX-PN exam. We suggest that you begin by taking the two Practice Tests in the book before you go on to the Practice Tests via the CD.

HOW TO GET THE MOST OUT OF YOUR REVIEW

You will need to set aside at least three weeks of study to get the most out of your exam review. Begin by reading the "Top 10 Strategies to Raise Your Score," and then plan your schedule so that you can dedicate 1 to 2 hours every day to your review.

A good plan of study is to review one chapter each day and complete the exercises that accompany it to see how well you have mastered that material. When you have finished your review of all the subjects, take the Practice Tests. This will help you assess how well you do on each Practice Test. After taking each test, review any topics with which you are still having trouble before taking the next test. This will help you sharpen your test-taking skills.

TOP 10 STRATEGIES TO RAISE YOUR SCORE

In taking the NCLEX-PN exam, some strategies are more useful than others. The following tips will help you raise your score.

1. **Create a study plan and stick to it.** The right study plan will help you get the most out of this book in the time that you have.

2. **Review key test elements daily for several weeks before the exam.** Reread the Test Plan to be sure that you understand the categories and subcategories, and reread the information about alternate test formats.

3. **Complete all the exercises in this book.** Doing so will help you recognize your areas of strength and discover which areas need improvement.

4. **If possible, visit the test center before the day of the exam.** This will help you become familiar with the location and how long it takes to travel there. On the day of the exam, leave plenty of time to get to the test center in case the buses/subways/trains are running late, the weather is bad, or parking your car is a problem.

5. **Avoid cramming the night before the exam.** This will only make you feel more nervous. It is not likely to help you learn enough to make a difference on your test score.

6. **Relax the night before the test.** Try to take your mind off the exam for a while. Go to a movie or hang out with a friend—but not with someone who will be taking the test with you.

7. **Place your Authorization to Test (ATT) and two forms of identification where you will see them in the morning before leaving for the test center.** You will not be able to take the exam without these documents.

8. **Listen to what the test administrator tells you, and pay attention to the tutorial.** Don't worry, however: You don't need to be a computer whiz to take the test.

9. **Read every word of every question on the exam.** Pay attention to details. They provide clues to the answer and help prevent you from selecting the wrong answer choice.

10. **Don't spend too much time on any one question.** You have up to 5 hours to complete your exam—but you still can't afford to spend too much time on any one question. Try to maintain a steady pace of about 1 minute per question. If you take more than 2 minutes per question, you won't get to all the questions in the allotted time.

GIVE US YOUR FEEDBACK

Peterson's publishes a full line of resources that can help guide you through the career process. Peterson's publications can be found at your local bookstore, library, and office of higher education. You can also access us online at www.petersons.com.

We welcome any comments or suggestions that you may have about this publication and invite you to complete our online survey at www.petersons.com/booksurvey. Or you can fill out the survey at the back of this book, tear it out, and mail to us at:

Publishing Department
Peterson's, a Nelnet company
2000 Lenox Drive
Lawrenceville, NJ 08648

Your feedback will help us make your education and career dreams possible.

YOU'RE WELL ON YOUR WAY TO SUCCESS!

Remember that knowledge is power. Using *Peterson's Master the NCLEX-PN* will help you become familiar with the kind of content that appears in the actual NCLEX-PN exam. We look forward to helping you obtain your PN certification. Good luck!

PART I

NCLEX-PN BASICS

All About the NCLEX-PN Exam

OVERVIEW

- About practical nursing and the job outlook
- Exam basics
- The NCLEX-PN Test Plan
- Percentage of exam items
- Integrated nursing processes
- What to expect on the exam
- Top 10 strategies for choosing the right answer
- Eight nursing areas commonly tested on the NCLEX-PN
- Summing it up

ABOUT PRACTICAL NURSING AND THE JOB OUTLOOK

The practical nursing profession began in the late 1800s. Women were trained for careers as home "attendants" caring for invalids, the elderly, and children in home settings. The profession moved outside the home during World Wars I and II, when the country had an acute need for nurses to care for wounded soldiers. In the 1940s, the National Association of Practical Nurse Education was formed. The organization developed a curriculum for Licensed Practical Nurses (LPNs), and in the late 1950s, the National League for Nursing began accrediting LPN schools in addition to those that trained registered nurses (RNs).

Today, more than 1,500 state nursing board-approved training programs for practical nurses/vocational nurses (PN/VNs) are offered through vocational and technical schools and community and junior colleges. Some high schools, hospitals, colleges, and universities also offer PN/VN programs. Most are one year long and most cost about $2,000. Admission generally requires a high school diploma or its equivalent. Programs are typically one-third class work and two-thirds clinical work, but class content is just as important as gaining clinical experience. Courses usually cover basic nursing concepts and client-care subjects, including anatomy, physiology, pediatrics, obstetrics, psychiatric nursing, drug therapy, medical-surgical nursing, nutrition, and first aid.

Becoming Licensed

A PN's scope of practice is defined by the rules and regulations of the State Board of Nursing of each state. To obtain a license, a PN/VN must pass the NCLEX-PN exam developed by the National Council of State Boards of Nursing (NCSBN), Inc. This is a national test with no state-specific sections.

chapter 1

To practice in a state other than the one in which you are originally licensed, a PN must apply to the new state's Board of Nursing for licensure. Through Interstate Endorsement, the license is usually granted after checking the PN's records, without the PN having to retake the NLCEX-PN. Requirements vary from state to state, however, so be sure to check with a state's Board of Nursing for its licensing conditions and process.

The Nurse Licensure Compact (NLC) is another means of gaining mutual recognition licensure. Through the NLC, a nurse holds a license in the state in which he or she lives but may practice, both in-person and via the Internet, in other states that belong to the NLC. Currently, twenty-three states are a part of the NLC. PN/VNs interested in obtaining information about the NLC should contact the Board of Nursing in the state in which they live. Appendix A of this book provides contact information for the Boards of Nursing for each state in the NLC.

The Job Outlook

PN/VNs work in many different settings. According to the U.S. Bureau of Labor Statistics, about 26 percent of PN/VNs work in hospitals, 26 percent in nursing care facilities, and 12 percent in doctors' offices. The remaining 36 percent work for home health-care services, employment services, residential care facilities, community care facilities for the elderly, outpatient care centers, and federal, state, and local government agencies. A PN/VN's job is to provide basic care under the supervision of doctors and RNs.

In general, a PN/VN's duties may include:

- gathering client health information
- taking vital signs
- changing dressings
- performing routine laboratory tests
- teaching clients good health habits
- teaching family members how to care for an ill relative
- helping clients with bathing, dressing, and personal hygiene

Duties may also depend on one's job setting. As a home health-care aide, a PN/VN may prepare meals for a client. In a doctor's office or clinic, a PN/VN may make appointments and keep medical records. However, as more procedures are performed in doctor's offices and outpatient facilities, PN/VNs have begun taking on direct care responsibilities for clients undergoing these procedures. PN/VNs who work in nursing homes may evaluate clients and develop care plans. In some states, PN/VNs may also administer prescribed medications and intravenous fluids.

In 2006, employment opportunities for PN/VNs numbered 749,000. The U.S. Bureau of Labor Statistics (BLS) predicts that by 2016, the nation will need another 105,000 PN/VNs: an increase of 14 percent. Practical nursing is now a fast-growing occupation in part because of the long-term care needs of a growing population of older people. Home health-care services, nursing care facilities, and doctors' offices and clinics are expected to offer an increasing number of opportunities for PV/VNs.

Salaries for PV/VNs are also rising. According to the BLS, in 2006, the median annual salary of PN/VNs was $36,500—$10,000 more than the median just five years earlier. Employment services that provide nursing staff on a contract basis offered the highest potential earnings, a median annual income, $42,110, and doctors' offices offered the lowest median annual income, at $32,710. Annual earnings are expected to continue rising as the demand for PN/VNs exceeds supply in the next five to ten years.

EXAM BASICS

NCSBN conducts periodic surveys of the tasks performed by practicing PNs and the knowledge and skills they need to perform them. This information becomes the basis of the Test Plan and the questions for the exam. Both the NCLEX-RN and NCLEX-PN exams are computer-based tests; they are not available in paper form.

You don't need to be especially computer savvy to take the test. The test administrator will show you how to use the computer, and you will be presented with sample questions to help you get a little practice before you start the actual exam. There are twenty-five pretest questions, which are not scored.

NCLEX-PN tests are administered only at Pearson Professional Centers. There is no minimum time for completing the exam, but the maximum time is 5 hours. The 5-hour limit includes time to take a tutorial, which explains the alternate item formats and provides sample questions.

Taking a Computer-Adaptive Test

The NCLEX-PN exam is a computer-adaptive test (CAT). This means that the computer program adjusts to the ability level of the candidate taking the test. As a result, no two tests are exactly alike, but each will test the range of topics and percentage of test items in the Test Plan.

All PN/VN candidates answer at least 85 questions (maximum 205). However, the number of questions you receive on your exam does not affect your score. The length of your exam is determined by your responses. The questions alternate between difficult and easy until the computer program determines your testing level—the point at which you answer approximately one half of the questions incorrectly. At this point, your exam will end. The computer then calculates with 95 percent certainty that your ability is either above or below the passing standard.

With a CAT, you see only one question at a time on the computer screen. Once you select an answer and press NEXT, you cannot return to a question to review it. You want to be sure that you've answered correctly, but try not to spend more than 1 minute on any question or you will run out of time. The average is 60 to 70 seconds per test item.

How the NCLEX-PN is Scored

According to the NCSBN, the passing standard is "the minimum level of ability required for safe and effective entry-level nursing practice." The passing standard is not based on a standard minimum number of questions answered correctly. Rather, it is reviewed every three years based on an appraisal of the previous three years of tests and on

TIP

To help you feel more at ease on the day of the exam, try a virtual tour of a Pearson Professional Testing Center online at www.vue.com/nclex.

surveys and information from the education and nursing fields. Whether a test taker passes or fails the exam depends on whether his or her ability, as demonstrated by answering questions, is above or below the passing standard.

Registering for Your Exam

To register for the NCLEX-PN, you must first check with the State Board of Nursing of the state in which you want to practice. You do not have to take the test in that state, however. States vary in procedure. Depending on your state's requirements, you may register directly at the test site, www.vue.com/nclex, or by phone or mail.

Test takers who have special needs must request testing accommodation before registering for the exam. The Board of Nursing in the state in which the exam will be taken handles these accommodations.

After you register for the exam, you will receive an Authorization to Test (ATT) form. Be sure to note the range of validity dates listed on the ATT. You must schedule and take your exam during this time period or you will need to reapply for another ATT. If you want to take the exam outside the United States, you must pay an international scheduling fee. A Value Added Tax (VAT) may also apply.

To be admitted to the test center, you need two valid forms of identification (at least one must be a photo ID) and your ATT. Both items must include your signature. Before your exam, you will be digitally fingerprinted and photographed, and you will be required to provide your signature. This information accompanies your exam results.

THE NCLEX-PN TEST PLAN

The NCLEX-PN exam is built on a Client Needs structure that provides a universal method of defining competency in all nursing settings and that corresponds to state laws and rules. The Test Plan includes the following four Client Needs categories:

1. Safe and Effective Care Environment
   - Coordinated Care
   - Safety and Infection Control
2. Health Promotion and Maintenance
3. Psychosocial Integrity
4. Physiological Integrity
   - Basic Care and Comfort
   - Pharmacological Therapy
   - Reduction of Risk Potential
   - Physiological Adaptation

Safe and Effective Care Environment

The Safe and Effective Care Environment category assesses the candidate's ability to provide "nursing care that contributes to the enhancement of the health-care delivery setting and protects clients and health-care personnel." This category includes questions about advocacy, client-care assignments, continuity of care, performance improvement, and the referral process.

The Coordinated Care subcategory is concerned with the PN's ability to collaborate with health-care team members to provide effective client care. Topics include:

- advance directives
- continuity of care
- advocacy
- establishing priorities
- client-care assignments
- ethical practice
- client rights
- informed consent
- concepts of management

- legal responsibilities and supervision
- performance improvement (quality assurance)
- confidentiality
- consultation with health-care team members
- referral process
- resource management

The Safety and Infection Control subcategory is concerned with protecting team members, clients, and clients' family members and friends from health and environmental hazards. Topics include:

- accident/error/injury prevention
- handling hazardous and infectious materials
- home safety
- safe use of equipment

Health Promotion and Maintenance

This category relates to the stages of human growth and development and with preventing health problems and early detection of health problems. The PN/VN must be familiar with the aging process, data collection methods, family planning, health promotion, screening programs, lifestyle choices, and self-care.

Psychosocial Integrity

Psychosocial Integrity is concerned with the emotional, mental, and social well-being of clients. The PN/VN is expected to aid clients and their families and significant others in coping with and solving problems such as end-of-life decisions, grief, mental illness, substance abuse, suicide, and violence.

Physiological Integrity

This category is concerned with clients' physical well-being. The PN/VN aids in promoting physical health and well-being by providing care and comfort, reducing risk potential for clients, and assisting clients with the management of health alterations.

The Basic Care and Comfort subcategory is concerned with the activities of daily living. Topics may include:

NOTE

The NCLEX-PN Test Plan document describes the scope and content of the exam. You can download a copy of the Test Plan free from the NCSBN Web site, www.ncsbn.org. Check the Detailed Test Plan (Educator Version), too. It provides more information about the test content.

- assistive devices
- nutrition and oral hydration
- elimination
- palliative/comfort care

- mobility/immobility
- personal hygiene
- nonpharmacological comfort
- rest and sleep

The Pharmacological Therapies subcategory concerns the administration of medications. Topics may include:

- adverse effects and side effects
- pharmacological actions
- pharmacological agents
- medication administration

The Reduction of Risk Potential subcategory assesses the knowledge, skills, and abilities necessary to prevent clients from developing complications or health problems related to treatments, procedures, or existing conditions. Topics may include:

- diagnostic tests
- therapeutic procedures
- laboratory values
- vital signs
- potential for alterations in body systems

- potential for complications (diagnostic tests/treatments/procedures/surgery)

The Physiological Adaptation subcategory deals with acute, chronic, and life-threatening problems related to physical health. Topics may include:

- alterations in body systems
- medical emergencies
- basic pathophysiology

- radiation therapy
- fluid and electrolyte imbalances
- unexpected response to therapies

PERCENTAGE OF EXAM ITEMS

On the NCLEX-PN, percentages are assigned to each category and subcategory of the Client Needs structure. The following table provides the specific percentages as determined by the NCSBN, which oversees the test:

Client Needs Category	Percentage of Exam Items
Safe and Effective Care Environment • Coordinated Care • Safety and Infection Control	 • 12–18 • 8–14
Health Promotion and Maintenance	• 7–13
Psychosocial Integrity	• 8–14
Physiological Integrity • Basic Care and Comfort • Pharmacological Therapies • Reduction of Risk Potential • Physiological Adaptation	 • 11–17 • 9–15 • 10–16 • 11–17

NCLEX-PN exam questions are primarily "application and analysis," which means that you need to apply what you have learned in class and in your clinical experience to make decisions based on real-life situations.

INTEGRATED NURSING PROCESSES

The NCLEX-PN is designed to assess a test taker's knowledge of the four Integrated Processes fundamental to the work of the PN/VN at the same time it evaluates his or her skills in the Client Needs categories. For example, test items that fall under the Reduction of Risk Potential subcategory of Physiological Integrity may also assess the candidate's knowledge of ways to change a client's harmful behavior (such as drinking alcohol while pregnant).

1. Clinical Problem-Solving Process (Nursing Process)—This includes data collection, planning, implementation, and evaluation of clients.
2. Caring—The PN/VN must establish an atmosphere of respect and trust with clients, their families, and their significant others to bring about the desired therapeutic outcomes.
3. Communication and Documentation—Handwritten and/or electronic records and nonverbal interactions are related to client care. Certain standards of practice and accountability apply in documenting this information.
4. Teaching and Learning—PN/VNs interact with clients, their families, and their significant others to promote positive behavioral changes in the client.

WHAT TO EXPECT ON THE EXAM

In 2003, the NSCBN added alternate formats to the standard one-answer multiple-choice format of the NCLEX-PN. This allows test takers to demonstrate what they know in ways other than answering multiple-choice questions. For example, a fill-in-the-blank question requires test takers to enter a number after performing a calculation.

NOTE

For information about the current NCLEX-PN exam, visit www.ncsbn.org.

According to the NCSBN, most candidates receive a minimum-length test that includes at least one or two alternate-format items. Let's take a look at the types of question formats you may encounter on the exam.

Multiple Choice: One Answer

Most exam questions on the NCLEX-PN are multiple-choice questions with four answer choices. You may choose only one answer for these questions. The answer choices are marked with circles.

Practice Item Type #1: Multiple-Choice Item

In this item type, you will be presented with a question and asked to select the best answer from four options. The options are preceded by circles. You can select only one option as your answer. You may use either the mouse or the number keypad to select your answer. To use the number keypad on your computer, press the appropriate number on your keyboard, either 1, 2, 3, or 4.

For the practice item below, the correct answer is option 3. Select option 3 now. If you selected a different answer, change it by selecting option 3. Note that your previous choice is deselected and that you can select only one option.

Click **Next (N)** to confirm your answer and move to the next practice item.

What color is an orange?

○ 1. Blue
○ 2. Brown
◉ 3. Orange
○ 4. Pink

Select the best response. Click the Next (N) button or the Enter key to confirm answer and proceed.   Item 1 of 6

Next (N)   Calculator (0)

Multiple Response

Multiple-response exam questions require that you select as many correct answers as apply. The answer choices are marked by boxes that you must check.

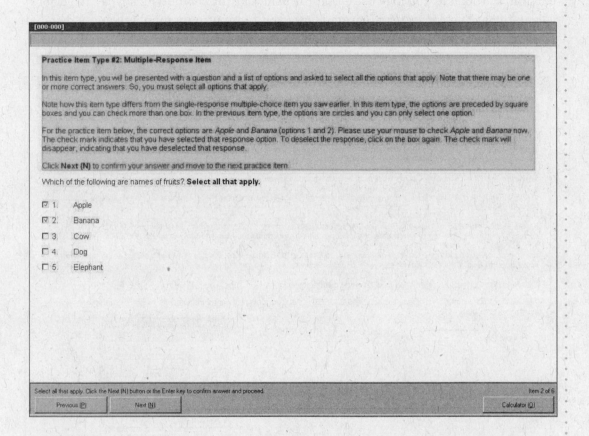

Fill in the Blank

Fill-in-the-blank exam questions require you to perform a math calculation to find the answer. A calculator button appears on the lower right corner of the screen; you must click on it to open it. You may use either the mouse or the computer's keypad to perform calculations. The computer program allows you to input only numbers and a decimal point in the answer box.

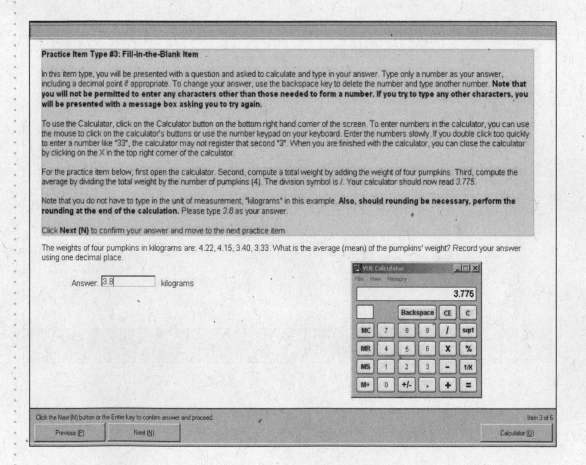

Hot Spot

Hot Spot exam questions present a problem and a figure. To answer the question, you must place the cursor on the area of the figure that corresponds to your answer choice. Clicking on the figure will place an "X" on that area as your answer.

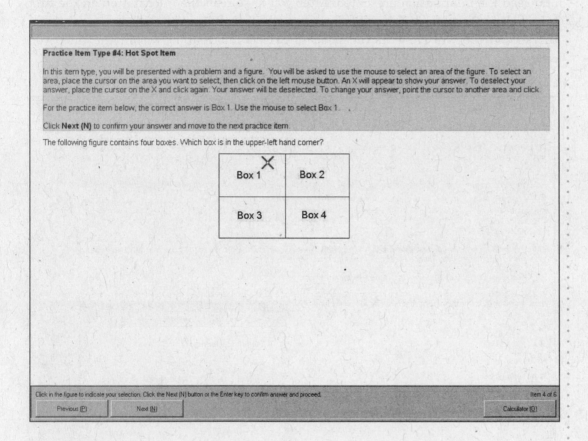

Chart/Exhibit

Chart/Exhibit exam questions require you to examine a chart or an "exhibit" on the screen that illustrates a problem. You must click on the "Exhibit" button at the bottom of the screen to open the figure. Then, click on each tab at the top of the exhibit screen and read the information presented. After you have read the information on the first tab, click on the second tab and the first one will close. When you click on the third tab, the second tab will close. If you need to reread information within the tabs, you canreopen previous tabs by clicking on them.

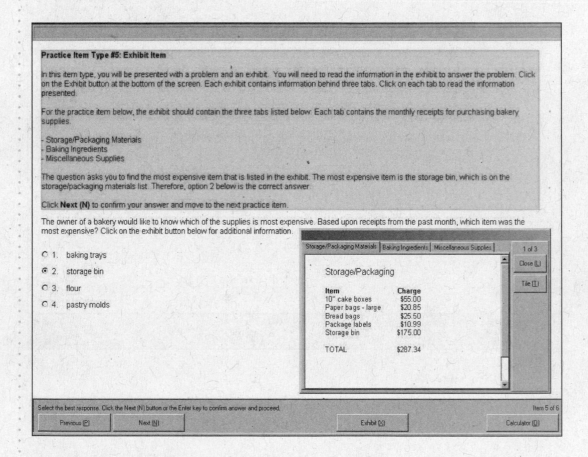

Drag and Drop/Ordered Response

Drag-and-Drop exam questions ask you to place items in a specific order, such as order of priority. Unordered items appear in a column on the left of your screen. To answer this type of question, you must move each item to the column on the right of the screen and arrange all the items in the correct order. You may either click on each item and drag it to the column on the right or highlight the item and click on the arrow key pointing to the column on the right. You can also use the keyboard arrow keys to rearrange items once you have moved all of them to the column on the right.

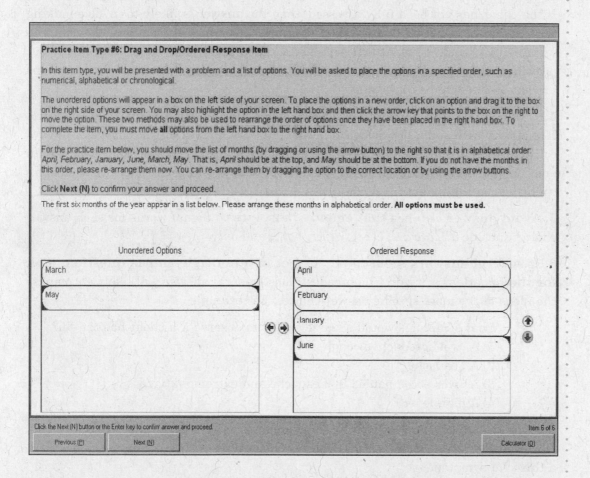

TOP 10 STRATEGIES FOR CHOOSING THE RIGHT ANSWER

Each NCLEX-PN exam includes some questions that the NCSBN is testing for validity before it places them in the official test item pool. You won't know which of the exam questions are not included in your score—so be sure that you answer all exam questions to the best of your ability.

Most exam questions consist of a case statement or situation, the question itself, and the answer choices. Here are ten time-tested techniques that will help you score high on the exam.

1. Answer only what the question asks; don't "read" information into the question. If the question asks you to identify one of the developmental stages of the physical growth of a toddler, don't become confused by an answer choice dealing with motor skills. Read each word of every case statement and question carefully, and be sure you can identify exactly what the question is asking for before you choose your answer.

2. Analyze case statements and questions for signal words that prioritize. These include *first*, *immediate*, *initial*, *next*, *primary*, *best*, *essential*, *highest priority*, and *most important*. When you see any of these words or phrases or others like them, you know that the question is asking you to indicate some type of order.

3. Use the nursing process when asked to determine what action to take first. If the client has not been fully assessed, then the answer is likely to involve making an assessment, such as taking blood pressure, assessing respirations, determining urine output, and so on. After assessing, a nurse must plan—and questions about prioritizing care often appear on the exam. Implementation and evaluation questions are not as likely to be confusing.

4. If the question relates to a client's most important needs, use Maslow's Hierarchy of Needs. Physiological needs—airways, breathing, and oxygen—always come first. If the question doesn't relate to physiological needs, then look for an answer that relates to client safety. Remember that checking the client comes before checking the equipment.

5. Avoid answer choices that employ "absolutes." Signal words for such answer choices include *all*, *always*, *every*, *never*, *none*, and *only*.

6. If several answers seem to be correct in a multiple-choice question, look for the broadest answer. The broadest, most general answer will likely encompass the ideas of the more specific answer choices. For example:

> What symptoms would a nurse expect to observe if a client has the flu?
> (1) A "wet" productive cough
> (2) A headache
> (3) A fever accompanied by headache and extreme fatigue
> (4) A high fever

Answer choices (2) and (4) are both flu symptoms, so you might choose one of them. However, the correct answer is (3), which includes both of these symptoms along with a third flu symptom.

7. In a standard multiple-choice question with similar answer choices, use the process of elimination to determine the correct answer. Let's say that three of the answer choices for a question about communicating with a mother about the care of a newborn relate to how the mother should deal with other siblings, and only one answer describes nursing the newborn. The one about nursing is most likely the correct answer.

8. Know the antidotes to common drugs. Memorize antidotes such as magnesium sulfate (calcium gluconate), heparin (protamine sulfate), and Coumadin (vitamin K or aquamephyton).

9. Memorize lab values. The exam will not provide charts of values, so take time in your test preparation to memorize them. In addition to hemoglobin (12–18 g/dl), white blood count (5000–10,000 mm^3), and platelets (150,000–400,000), make sure you know lab values for sodium, potassium, calcium, blood gases, and glucose levels. Also memorize the implications of high or low values and which diseases they are associated with.

10. If you run out of time, don't guess at answers. The NCSBN recommends against guessing when pressed for time. Unlike paper-and-pencil tests in which guessing may help your score, guessing on a CAT, such as the NCLEX-PN, may actually lower your score.

EIGHT AREAS COMMONLY TESTED ON THE EXAM

Nurses who have recently taken the NCLEX-PN list eight "hot" topics that are emphasized on the exam.

1. **Therapeutic communication**—The nurse's job is to help the client understand what his or her problem is and what options are available, not to give false reassurance or advice. It is better to ask clients to clarify what they say or what they would like than to suggest what they should do.

2. **Prioritizing care**—The nurse must be able to determine which problems are most urgent.

3. **PN/VN responsibilities**—In answering exam questions, make sure that you take into account that the nurse must make necessary assessments and meet important safety and physiological needs before an RN or MD is called.

4. **Delegation of work/responsibilities of aides, PN/VNs, and RNs**—With the growing variety of caregivers, nurses must know which kinds of care are appropriate for each category of caregiver.

5. **Age-related changes and emotions in clients**—PNs who care for older clients must be aware of problems that are specific to those clients.

6. **Signs and symptoms of serious complications**—PN/VNs must be aware of signs of serious health problems. For example, a client with hypoglycemia may have poor glucose control. This can occur with clients in a hospital or nursing care facility.

7. **Signs and symptoms of drug toxicity**—PN/VNs must be aware of signs of toxicity in clients taking medications that have serious side effects. Examples are digoxin and lithium.

8. **Pain management**—In most situations, addiction is not a concern when administering narcotics to a client for the purpose of managing pain. The client determines the level of pain he or she is experiencing; a nurse cannot decide whether a complaint of pain is valid.

SUMMING IT UP

- Practical/vocational nursing is among the fastest-growing occupations in the country.

- Check the State Board of Nursing for the state in which you want to practice to find out about licensure and taking the NCLEX-PN.

- Make your exam appointment as soon as you receive your Authorization to Test (ATT). Be sure that you make your testing appointment within the range of valid dates listed on your ATT. Remember to bring your ATT on exam day, or you will have to register and pay for the exam again.

- The Test Plan for the NCLEX-PN is built on a Client Needs approach that integrates the Nursing Process. Categories include Safe and Effective Care Environment (Coordinated Care, Safety and Infection Control), Health Promotion and Maintenance, Psychosocial Integrity, and Physiological Integrity (Basic Care and Comfort, Pharmacological Therapies, Reduction of Risk Potential, Physiological Adaptation).

- Areas that are commonly tested on the exam include therapeutic communication; prioritizing care; PN responsibilities; delegation of work and responsibilities of RNs, PNs, and aides; age-related changes and emotions; signs and symptoms of serious complications; signs and symptoms of toxicity of common drugs with serious side effects; and pain management.

- The majority of test items are the standard multiple-choice format, but test takers will also encounter Multiple-Response, Fill-in-the-Blank, Hot Spot, Exhibit, and Drag and Drop/Ordered Response question formats.

- The NCLEX-PN exam is a computerized adaptive test (CAT). With a CAT, test takers see only one question at a time on the computer screen. Once an answer is selected and entered, you cannot return to a question to review it. In order to complete the exam, you should not spend more than 60–70 seconds on each test item; however, if you are running out of time, do not guess.

PART II

NCLEX-PN REVIEW

Basic Nursing Concepts

OVERVIEW

- The nursing process
- Charting
- Role of the PN/VN
- Legal principles of PN practice
- Illegal behavior
- Risk management
- Ethical principles
- Professional organizations
- Pain management
- Nutrition
- Nutritional assessment
- Therapeutic diets
- Infection control
- Summing it up

THE NURSING PROCESS

A. Assessment
   1. The PN must collect data from the chart.
   2. The PN interviews the client for subjective information.
      a. Information not observable by another person: pain, nausea, anxiety, dizziness, tinnitus (ringing in the ears), numbness.
   3. The PN collects objective information.
      a. Information gathered through the senses: sight, hearing, touch, and smell.
      b. Information gathered with a measuring instrument: blood pressure, temperature, etc.
   4. The PN collects vital signs (objective).
      a. Temperature: normal is 97–99°F; rectal is 1° higher than normal; ear canal is roughly the same; axillary is 1° lower than normal.
      b. Pulse: normal is 60–100 beats per minute. Use apical with infants and irregular heart rates. Peripheral pulses (i.e., pedal) are used to determine adequacy of perfusion, as when there is a cast or restraint that might affect circulation.
      c. Blood pressure: normal is 100/60–139/89. 140/90 is considered hypertensive. Pulse pressure is the difference between the systolic (top) number and the diastolic (bottom) number.
      d. Respirations: normal is 12–18 breaths per minute.

B. Planning client care
1. Set priorities and determine client's needs.
2. Use data in assisting RN in formulating the nursing diagnosis.
3. Assist in determining goals/expected outcomes.

C. Implementation
1. **Preparation**—get and prepare necessary equipment, and explain care to client
2. **Performance**—follow proper procedures, infection-control guidelines, assess client's response
3. **Aftercare**—assist client in becoming comfortable after care; clean and return equipment
4. **Report and Record**

D. Evaluation
1. Assess the extent to which the need has been met.
2. Re-evaluate problem list in collaboration with RN.

CHARTING

A. Purpose
1. Continuity of care
2. Legal documentation
3. Communication between staff members

B. Entering Information
1. Use ink to note the date and time the information was entered.
2. Do not leave blank spaces.
3. Do not erase any information.
4. Do not add information after the note has been signed.
5. End note with your signature and title abbreviation (PN, VN).
6. Record the following information:
    a. Initial assessment
    b. Changes in condition
    c. Nursing care given, such as treatments or education
    d. Patient's response to care, laboratory data
    e. Physician and other health professional visits
    f. Medications after they are given to the client
7. Correct errors by drawing one line through the mistake and writing your initial beside it.

C. Care Plans—individualized or standard
1. Must be updated regularly, usually every 24 to 48 hours.
2. Cross out resolved problems using a colored felt-tip pen.

ROLE OF THE PN/VN

A. **Responsibilities**
1. Assist the RN with clients whose conditions are unstable and complex.
2. Observe, assess, record, report, and perform basic therapeutic, preventative, and rehabilitative procedures. The initial assessment is usually the responsibility of the RN.
3. Work settings include acute and long-term care hospitals, nursing homes, physicians' offices, and home health agencies.

ALERT!

Provide direct nursing care to clients in stable condition only under the supervision and guidance of a registered nurse or physician.

B. **Legislation Related to PN/VN Practice**
1. **Nurse Practice Act**
   a. Laws passed by the state's legislature pertaining to nursing are in the state's Nurse Practice Act.
   b. Nurse Practice Acts are different in each state.
   c. These acts provide for a nursing board to regulate practice and procedures for:
      (1) Nursing school approval and curriculum requirements
      (2) Licensure requirements and renewal procedures
      (3) Regulations regarding suspension and revocation of license
   d. All PN/VNs and RNs must practice nursing within the defined scope of their state's Nurse Practice Act.
2. **State Boards of Nursing**
   a. Functions
      (1) Administer the state's Nurse Practice Act
      (2) Oversee nursing schools and curriculum standards
      (3) Control licensure—administers licensure exam, renews license, revokes licenses
   b. Membership
      (1) Varies among states
      (2) Usually includes RNs, PN/VNs, and consumers appointed by the governor
3. **Licensure**
   a. Mandatory to practice nursing; it protects the public from unqualified practitioners.
   b. Qualifications vary, but most states require:
      (1) Graduation from an approved PN/VN school of nursing
      (2) Evidence of good moral character
      (3) A minimum score on the nationally administered exam
   c. License is renewed at regular intervals for a fee and may require proof of continuing education.
   d. Licenses may be revoked for misconduct or incompetence.
   e. State boards may license an individual from another state by endorsement if a review of his or her credentials indicates that the individual meets the endorsing state's requirements.
   f. Twenty-three states participate in the Nurse Licensure Compact, which allows a nurse who is licensed and lives in a Compact state to practice in other Compact states without having to obtain additional licensure.

LEGAL PRINCIPLES OF PN PRACTICE

A. **Maintaining Standards of Practice**
1. As established by the state's Nurse Practice Act, hospital policies and procedures, and the client's nursing care plan
2. As recommended by the National Association for Practical Nurse Education and Service (NAPNES)
   a. Nursing care
      (1) Follow principles of nursing process in meeting client needs
      (2) Apply skills and knowledge in providing safe, competent care
      (3) Apply principles of crisis intervention in maintaining safety and making referrals as necessary
      (4) Communicate effectively with clients and in written documentation
      (5) Serve as a client advocate
   b. Professional responsibilities
      (1) Apply ethical principles underlying the profession
      (2) Follow appropriate professional and legal requirements
      (3) Follow institutional policies and procedures
      (4) Demonstrate accountability for nursing actions
      (5) Ensure that knowledge and skills are current and regularly updated

B. **Adhering to Legal Guidelines for Health Professionals**
1. **Adhere to the state's Nurse Practice Act**
2. **Maintain Confidentiality**
3. **Understand Good Samaritan laws**
   a. Protect health professionals who give aid at the scene of an accident (not all states include nurses).
   b. Note: It is not legally necessary to help.
   c. Assistance must meet a standard of care that would be expected of the professional with a license.
4. **Child Abuse**
   a. All states require nurses to report suspected or known child abuse.
   b. Nurses and others who are required to report abuse are immune from being sued for doing so.
5. **Narcotics**
   a. Violation of the Federal Controlled Substance Act by a nurse is a felony and will result in loss of the nurse's license.

C. **Malpractice Insurance**
1. This provides insurance for any lawsuit against the nurse for damages caused by an error or negligence.
2. These policies are sold by nursing organizations, unions, and private insurance companies.
3. They will pay damages up to an amount limited by the policy.
4. An employer usually carries insurance to protect the nurse while on duty.

D. **Patient's Rights**
1. **Patient's Bill of Rights**—adapted by the American Hospital Association, must be posted on all hospital units and specify a standard of care that the client has a right to expect, including:
   a. The right to refuse treatment and be informed of the medical consequences of that act
   b. That all communication and records concerning the client's treatment be treated as confidential

  c. An explanation of the bill

  d. The client's right to examine his or her chart, if requested

 2. **Informed Consent**

  a. This is permission given by the client to be treated by health care personnel.

  b. It must be informed consent, which means that they must have been informed about the planned procedure, its risks and benefits, and any alternative treatments that might be available.

  c. Informed consent is required for most surgical and invasive procedures, but may not be necessary for minor procedures, such as putting in a foley catheter. A client may change his or her mind and refuse treatment after having giving consent.

 3. **Advance Directives**

  a. The Omnibus Budget Reform Act (OBRA) of 1990 requires hospitals to give clients the opportunity to make advance directives, which allows clients to specify plans for their care prior to such time that they may not be able to speak for themselves.

  b. Directives may include a living will, a health-care proxy, or designation of a power of attorney for health care.

  c. Check with the client's physician to determine whether advance directives are on file.

ILLEGAL BEHAVIOR

A. An Act That Injures or Results in Damage to Another Individual

 1. **Negligence** (failure to take the proper action)

  a. Performing care incorrectly

  b. Failing to prevent injury

  c. Professional misconduct

  d. Examples of the above:

   (1) Administering wrong medications; failing to ensure safety with side rails or restraints as ordered

   (2) Failing to prevent injury while applying heat

  e. Gross negligence (a client's life is put in danger) may result in criminal charges

 2. **Intentional Torts** (harming someone deliberately)

  a. May be legally liable even if there is no harm

  b. Assault—such as threatening to physically restrain a client to make him or her cooperate

  c. Battery—restraining or physically punishing a client

B. Invasion of Privacy—such as releasing private medical information

RISK MANAGEMENT

Identifying, analyzing, and controlling risks to clients.

A. Incident Report

 1. Completed whenever an unexpected adverse event occurs and turned in to the risk management department.

 2. Risk management department performs ongoing analysis to see which processes or procedures are not safe and need to be changed.

ALERT!

Consent is also required to have an autopsy performed, to dispose of body parts during surgery, and to use restraints on a client. Clients must consent to participate in medical research or to have their organs donated after death.

B. **Quality Improvement**
1. A problem is identified and a team works to generate a better method to perform tasks.
2. After this method is identified, the team implements it for a specified period and monitors the results.
3. If it results in improved efficiency or care, the method may be adopted as a new procedure.

ETHICAL PRINCIPLES

A. **Agreed-Upon Rules of Conduct**—help to make it easier for people to agree on the proper behavior for health-care workers.
1. **Ethical Principles**
   a. **Autonomy**—respecting the individual and his or her dignity and right to form judgments and take actions as long as they do not interfere with others
   b. **Beneficence**—promoting goodness, kindness, and charity, and abstaining from injuring others
   c. **Veracity**—telling the truth—on which rests the ability to trust
2. **Challenges to Ethics**
   a. **Paternalism**—the provider believes that he or she knows what is best for the client, thus robbing the client of his or her autonomy
   b. **Life**—questions about its beginning—abortion, assisted reproduction, and so on
   c. **Death**—questions about the quality of life and the definition of death and other end-of-life decisions

B. **Accountability**
1. A PN is responsible for maintaining a very high standard of responsibility and personal integrity.
2. A nurse who fails to meet this standard harms the profession.

PROFESSIONAL ORGANIZATIONS

Provide opportunities for continuing education and allow people to share professional interests.

A. **National Association of Practical Nurse Education and Service, Inc. (NAPNES)**
1. Membership open to all those interested in the education of practical nurses or the profession
2. Publication: *Journal of Practical Nursing*

B. **National Federation of Licensed Practical Nurses (NFLPN)**
1. PNs, VNs, and PN or VN students may be members
2. Official publication: *American Journal of Practical Nursing*

C. **National League for Nursing (NLN)**
1. Members can be anyone interested in nursing
2. Publications: *Nursing and Health Care*; *Nursing Research*
3. Role in nursing:
   a. Prepare and score selection and achievement tests
   b. Conduct workshops
   c. Accredit schools of nursing

PAIN MANAGEMENT

A. **Assessment**—the first step in successful pain management
   1. **Characteristics**
   2. **Onset**—when did it first begin
   3. **Duration**—how long it lasts
   4. **Location**—whether it radiates or moves
   5. **Severity**—often rated on a 0 to 10 scale
   6. **Precipitating, Aggravating, and Alleviating Factors**

B. **Nonpharmacologic Pain Treatment**
   1. **Cold**—decreases pain and swelling
   2. **Distraction**—turning the attention elsewhere
   3. **Heat**—helps decrease tension
   4. **Imagery**—uses the imagination to create positive mental pictures
   5. **Nerve blocks**—a local anesthetic injected around the nerve
   6. **Pressure**—firm, but not excessive
   7. **Relaxation**—reduces muscle tension

C. **Nursing-Care Guidelines for Pain Management**
   1. Don't argue with the client about whether he or she is in pain.
   2. Do not use a placebo to try to determine if the client has "real" pain.
   3. Offer pain relief alternatives.
   4. Assess the client for depression, anxiety, and stress.

NUTRITION

Source: Agricultural Research Service, USDA

A. **Fat-Soluble Vitamins**
   1. **Vitamin A** (retinol); **provitamin A** (carotene)
      a. Deficiency of vitamin A leads to poor night vision.
      b. Excessive intake leads to hair loss; dry, rough skin; cracked lips; and liver damage. Increased intracranial pressure can result from acute toxicity.
      c. Sources:
         (1) Retinol—liver, egg yolk, butter, milk, fortified skim-milk products
         (2) Carotene—green and yellow vegetables and fruits

2. **Vitamin D (cholecalciferol)**
   a. Helps the absorption and utilization of calcium and phosphorus .
   b. Helps the calcification of bones.
   c. Deficiency leads to rickets in children, osteomalacia in adults.
   d. Excessive intake leads to hypercalcemia, anorexia, nausea, vomiting, polyuria.
   e. Sources: fortified milk, sunshine, fish oils, butter, egg yolk, liver.
   f. Nursing note: Be alert to vitamin D deficiency in clients with dark skin, gallbladder disease, the elderly, and infants.

3. **Vitamin E** (tocopherol)
   a. Antioxidant—protects materials that easily oxidize.
   b. Deficiency leads to breakdown of red blood cells.
   c. Excessive intake leads to skeletal muscle weakness, disturbance of reproductive function, and GI upset.
   d. Sources: vegetable oils, vegetable greens, milk, eggs, meat, cereal, wheat germ.

4. **Vitamin K** (aqua mephyton)
   a. Essential for prothrombin formation and blood clotting.
   b. Deficiency leads to increased bleeding.
   c. Excessive intake leads to hyperbilirubinemia, kernicterus, and severe hemolytic anemia in newborns.
   d. Toxic in large amounts.
   e. Sources:
      (1) Green leafy vegetables, cheese, egg yolks, liver
      (2) Intestinal bacteria synthesis of *E. coli* is the body's main source
   f. Nursing implications: Be alert to vitamin K deficiency when fat intake is low; or when antibiotics, such as Neomycin, destroy intestinal bacteria. Excessive vitamin K can counteract the blood-thinning actions of coumadin.

B. **Water-Soluble Vitamins**
   1. **Vitamin B_1** (thiamine)
      a. Promotes growth, normal function of heart, nerves, and muscle.
      b. Deficiency leads to beri-beri (rare), mental confusion, polyneuritis, muscle weakness, and tachycardia.
      c. Sources: beef, liver, pork, whole grains, legumes.
      d. Thiamine needs depend on carbohydrate intake and metabolism. Alcoholics, clients on long-term IV therapy, and those with prolonged fevers may be prone to a thiamine deficiency.
   2. **Vitamin B_6** (pyridoxine)
      a. Aids in production of energy, stimulates heme production.
      b. B_6 deficiency leads to hypochromic anemia, irritability, convulsions, neuritis, and skin lesions.
      c. Sources: liver, meat, wheat germ, wheat, corn, yeast, legumes.
      d. The more protein in the diet, the greater the B_6 requirement. Such drugs as isoniazid and oral contraceptives may cause a deficiency in this nutrient.
   3. **Vitamin B_{12}** (cobalamin)
      a. Helps in red blood cell production, nerve function, and growth.
      b. B_{12} deficiency leads to pernicious anemia.
      c. Sources: liver, meat, milk, eggs, cheese, saltwater fish.
      d. After a total gastrectomy, B_{12} injections must be given to prevent pernicious anemia.
      e. Vegetarian diets, especially vegan—without any milk, eggs, or cheese—may lead to a B_{12} deficiency.

4. **Vitamin C** (ascorbic acid)
    a. Helps in iron absorption, formation of collagen, and thus capillary walls.
    b. Scurvy is caused by a vitamin C deficiency. Sore gums, hemorrhages, tendency to bruise easily, and stress reactions may be caused by a lack of vitamin C.
    c. Sources: citrus fruits, tomatoes, cabbage, potatoes, strawberries, melons, broccoli, turnip greens, green peppers.
    d. When the metabolic rate is elevated, as in hyperthyroidism, burns, fever, and neoplasms, the need for vitamin C increases.

C. **Minerals**
  1. **Iron** (Fe)
    a. Forms hemoglobin, which carries oxygen to the cells for energy production.
    b. Deficiency leads to anemia and poor growth.
    c. Excess iron can be deposited in the liver and other tissues—called hemosiderosis.
    d. Sources: liver, meat, egg yolks, whole grains, enriched bread, dark greens, vegetables.
  2. **Calcium** (Ca)
    a. Necessary for bone and tooth formation, blood clotting, and muscle contractions.
    b. Deficiency leads to rickets, osteoporosis, poor blood clotting, and tetany.
    d. Sources: milk and milk products, cheese, some green leafy vegetables (kale, collards, broccoli).

NUTRITIONAL ASSESSMENT

A. **Screening**
  1. Screen clients for nutritional risk factors.
  2. High-risk clients include those who are overweight or underweight, on long-term IV therapy, or have digestive system problems or metabolic disorders.

B. **Assessment**
  1. Includes anthropometric measurements, biochemical tests, and clinical observations.
  2. Patient gives dietary history and personal health history.

C. **Development of Appropriate Action Plan**

THERAPEUTIC DIETS

A. **Clear Liquids**
  1. **Purpose**—to provide hydration to a post-op client
  2. **Foods Allowed**—tea, coffee, fat-free broth, bouillon, fruit ices, popsicles, gelatin, soda
  3. **Foods Not Allowed**—milk products, fruit juices with pulp

ALERT!

Remember that you must assess a client's gag reflex and ability to chew and swallow before ordering his or her diet.

B. Full Liquid Diet
1. **Purpose**—after a post-op client tolerates clear liquids, this is often ordered
2. **Foods Allowed**—all foods that are liquid or are liquid at room temperature
3. **Foods Not Allowed**—nuts, beans, solid food

C. Soft Diet
1. **Purpose**—for post-op clients after full liquid or for clients with infections or GI problems
2. **Foods Allowed**—all foods that are soft, tender, minced, stewed, or creamed
3. **Foods Not Allowed**—coarse or whole grain breads, meats, sharp cheeses, dried fruits and nuts

D. Bland Diet
1. **Purpose**—to eliminate irritating foods to allow the stomach lining to heal (ulcer clients)
2. **Foods Allowed**—milk, custards, white bread, cooked cereals, creamed or pureed soups, baked or broiled potatoes
3. **Foods Not Allowed**—strongly flavored and highly seasoned foods, coffee, tea, citrus fruits, raw fruits and vegetables, whole grains, very hot or cold beverages

E. Low-Residue Diet
1. **Purpose**—to reduce fiber for clients with Crohn's disease, colon or rectal surgery, esophagitis, diarrhea
2. **Foods Allowed**—clear fluids, sugar, salt, meats, fats, eggs, some milk, refined cereals and white breads, peeled white potatoes
3. **Foods Not Allowed**—cheeses, fried foods, highly seasoned foods, high-fiber foods

F. High-Fiber Diet
1. **Purpose**—to provide bulk in the stool and bring water into the colon for clients with constipation or diverticulitis
2. **Foods Allowed**—raw fruits and vegetables, whole grains
3. **Foods Not Allowed**—minimize low-fiber foods

G. Sodium-Restricted Diet
1. **Purpose**—for clients with kidney, cardiovascular disease or hypertension to control the retention of sodium and water and thus lower blood pressure
2. **Foods Allowed**—natural foods without salt, milk, and meat in limited quantities
3. **Foods Not Allowed**—canned prepared foods, table salt, most prepared seasonings not labeled low sodium

H. Gluten-Free Diet
1. **Purpose**—eliminates gluten, a protein found in wheat products; for clients with malabsorption syndromes such as celiac disease
2. **Foods Allowed**—rice, corn, soy flour, fruits, vegetables, meat, eggs, milk
3. **Foods Not Allowed**—all wheat, rye, barley, oats; many prepared foods such as creamed sauces or breaded foods (may contain thickeners and fillers)

I. Lactose-Free Diet
1. **Purpose**—to reduce or eliminate foods with lactose; for clients who cannot metabolize it
2. **Foods Allowed**—most meats, fruits and vegetables, cereals and grains
3. **Foods Not Allowed**—foods containing lactose, such as milk, cheese, and ice cream

J. **Low-Cholesterol Diet**
1. **Purpose**—to reduce the intake of cholesterol in order to lower blood cholesterol levels
2. **Foods Allowed**—fruits, vegetables, lean meats and fish, poultry without skin, skim milk
3. **Foods Not Allowed**—organ meats, egg yolks, shrimp, beef, lamb, pork

K. **Low-Purine Diet**
1. **Purpose**—to reduce the amount of purine, which is a precursor of uric acid, in the diet; for clients who have gout or uric acid kidney stones
2. **Foods Allowed**—most vegetables (except cauliflower), spinach, asparagus, peas, fruit juices, cereals, eggs, cottage cheese
3. **Foods Not Allowed**—organ meats, fish, poultry, lentils, dried peas, nuts, beans, oatmeal, whole wheat

INFECTION CONTROL

A. **Chain of Transmission for Infectious Disease**
1. **Pathogens**—some are more toxic than others
   a. Viruses
   b. Bacteria
   c. Fungi
   d. Chlamydia
   e. Protozoa
   f. Mycoplasma
2. **Reservoir**—a place where the organism can grow and multiply
   a. Person, animal, bird, etc.
   b. Materials on which organisms may grow, like saturated wound dressings or dirty equipment
3. **Exit Port**
   a. How the infection leaves the host
   b. Feces, nasal secretions, through an intermediate carrier
4. **Route of Transmission**
   a. Way in which pathogen moves to another host
   b. Direct transmission—by direct contact, like sexual relations
   c. Indirect transmission—transmission via an indirect carrier like a mosquito, contaminated water, or food
5. **Portal of Entry**
   a. Pathogen may enter host via inhalation, ingestion, or percutaneously.
   b. Whether or not a disease will occur depends on the defense (immune) system of the invaded host. Such characteristics as age, nutritional status, stress, or illness can affect this.
6. **Control of Transmission**
   a. May be done by interfering with any link in the chain
      (1) Barrier precautions—gloves, gowns, condoms
      (2) Proper handling of food and water supplies
      (3) Avoiding high-risk behavior such as unsafe sex
      (4) Good hand-washing technique and good personal hygiene
   b. Host susceptibility can be greatly reduced by immunizations

B. Infection Control Procedures

1. **Standard Precautions**
   a. Have replaced universal precautions.
   b. Barrier (usually gloves) is worn to protect from blood, body fluids, and secretions.
   c. As always, careful hand washing is the *most important* step you can take to prevent the spread of nosocomial infections.

2. **Airborne Precautions** (tuberculosis, chicken pox)
   a. Client should be placed in a private, negative-pressure room.
   b. Wear respiratory protection (masks or face shields) when entering the room.
   c. Limit movement of client from the room.

3. **Droplet Precautions** (rubella, strep throat, pneumonia, pertussis, mumps, mycoplasma or meningococcal pneumonia)
   a. Client should be placed in a private room.
   b. A mask should be worn when working within three feet of the client.
   c. Visitors should be kept at least three feet from the client.
   d. Limit client movement from the room. If necessary to transport, have the client wear a mask.

4. **Contact Transmission–Based Precautions** (respiratory syncytial virus, shigella and other enteric pathogens; major wound infections, herpes simplex, scabies)
   a. Place the client in a private room.
   b. Wear gloves whenever entering the room. Always change gloves after contact with infectious material. Remove gloves before leaving the room, and wash your hands.
   c. Wear a gown in the room if your clothing will have contact with the client, environmental surfaces, or if the client is incontinent. Remove the gown before leaving the room.
   d. Limit movement of the client from the room.
   e. Avoid sharing any client-care equipment.

EXERCISES: BASIC NURSING CONCEPTS

1. Mr. Johnson, a 68-year-old man with congestive heart failure, has been pre-scribed a low-sodium diet. In instructing him on appropriate food choices, which would the nurse counsel him *against* eating?

    (1) Spinach salad
    (2) Canned chicken noodle soup
    (3) Whole wheat bread
    (4) Apples

2. The nurse notes that the post-operative client has been put on a clear diet. This diet could include which of the following foods? **Select all that apply.**

    ☐ (1) Apple juice
    ☐ (2) Beef broth
    ☐ (3) Orange juice
    ☐ (4) Herbal tea

3. John A. is on coumadin therapy because he has an artificial heart valve. Which meal plan would suggest the need for further teaching about the effects of diet on this medication?

    (1) Caesar salad with a spinach frittata
    (2) Steak, french fries, and a milkshake
    (3) Chicken tettrazini and fresh fruit salad
    (4) Chile con carne with garlic bread

4. A vegetarian presents with anemia, fatigue, and loss of sensation in her hands and feet. The client states that she does not eat any meat, chicken, or fish. The nurse, suspecting a vitamin B_{12} deficiency, asks whether the client includes the following in her diet:

    (1) Green, leafy vegetables
    (2) Fresh fruits
    (3) Nuts, seeds, and dried fruits
    (4) Eggs and milk

5. The nurse is counseling a 58-year-old client whose cholesterol reading was 250. She is instructing him in diet, exercise, and the avoidance of high-cholesterol foods. Which of the following food choices would indicate the need for further teaching?

    (1) Pasta primavera
    (2) Large salad with lowfat dressing
    (3) Turkey sandwich on whole-grain bread
    (4) Cheese omelet

6. A nurse is caring for an overweight 65-year-old man with gout. After discussing the need to avoid high-purine foods which promote uric acid formation, which comment by the client indicates he has understood the material?

    (1) "I will try to avoid high-carbohydrate and sugary foods."

    (2) "I will eat more foods with high fiber such as beans, oatmeal, and whole grains."

    (3) "I will avoid organ meats, alcohol, fat, beans, lentils, and bran."

    (4) "I will eat more low-fat protein and vegetables."

7. Mary J. has had a gastrectomy because of stomach cancer. To prevent anemia, the client's nurse will administer a(n)

    (1) iron supplement.

    (2) folic acid supplement.

    (3) list of foods to eat.

    (4) vitamin B_{12} injection.

8. A client has been admitted to the hospital with infectious pulmonary tuberculosis. To protect the nurse and prevent the spread of infection, which type of isolation precautions will the nurse use when caring for him?

    (1) Standard precautions

    (2) Airborne precautions

    (3) Droplet precautions

    (4) Contact precautions

9. A nurse is caring for a client who repeatedly wakes up during the night feeling disoriented to time, place, and person. The client is attempting to get out of bed and pull out his IV that is supplying hydration and necessary medication. The client has a vest restraint and bilateral soft wrist restraints. Place the actions the nurse should take in chronological order beginning with the first action.

    (1) Tie the restraints in quick-release knots. _____

    (2) Recheck and document the behavior that requires continued use of restraints. _____

    (3) Position and retie the vest restraints so that the straps cross in the front. _____

    (4) Ask the client whether he needs to go to the bathroom, and provide range-of-motion exercises (every 2 hours). _____

10. The nurse has been assigned to care for the clients listed below. For which client is it *essential* that the nurse wear a gown?

    (1) A client with measles

    (2) A client with *clostridium dificile*

    (3) A client with pertussis

    (4) A client with streptococcal pharyngitis

ALERT!

Did you notice the word *essential* in the question? This signals that you are being asked to look for the most important of the answer choices.

11. The nurse in obstetrics notes that a recently admitted client, who is expecting her first baby, has Advance Directives on file. An example would be

  (1) a birth plan.
  (2) an organ donor card.
  (3) a living will.
  (4) instructions on infant care procedures she does not want done on her baby.

12. A nurse writes "9/11 7:00 am" before describing her client's dressing change. Seven a.m. refers to the

  (1) time the dressing change was done.
  (2) time the note was written.
  (3) time the nurse's shift ends.
  (4) scheduled time for the dressing change.

13. A hospitalized client tells the nurse he wants to see his chart. The nurse correctly explains that the "Patient's Bill of Rights" gives a client the right to

  (1) have a nurse summarize his plan of care.
  (2) review the records pertaining to his or her care.
  (3) see lab reports and other data, but not narrative notes.
  (4) have the physician explain what is in the chart.

14. The nurse is caring for Mr. Smith, who has advanced lung cancer. He has been given information about Advance Directives. Which of the following comments indicates the need for further teaching?

  (1) "I don't need Advance Directives. I don't expect to get better."
  (2) "I want my nephew to make decisions for me if I am unable to."
  (3) "What if I want them to do everything they can to keep me alive?"
  (4) "I want to make a living will to specify that I don't want to be intubated."

15. An older cardiac client informs the nurse that he does not want to "be hooked up to a bunch of machines" and does not want to have CPR or other aggressive treatments done to prolong his life. The nurse tells him that the *most effective* way for him to assure that he will not have treatments he doesn't want is to

  (1) inform the hospital chaplain of his wishes.
  (2) inform his primary physician.
  (3) discuss the matter with his family.
  (4) prepare a living will.

16. The nurse-orientee asks if she may hang intravenous fluids or insert IVs after she finishes her orientation. Her preceptor replies that her scope of practice is determined by hospital policy as well as the

  (1) state's Nurse Practice Act.
  (2) nurse's association charter.
  (3) medical association guidelines for practice.
  (4) Patient's Bill of Rights.

exercises

17. You note injuries on a child admitted to the emergency room that are not consistent with the reported accident. After further discussion with the mother, she admits that her boyfriend has been beating the toddler but asks you not to tell anyone. Can you grant her request?

    (1) Yes, it is a matter of client confidentiality.

    (2) Yes, it is in the child's best interest to maintain the mother's trust in the health-care provider.

    (3) No, all client information must be reported.

    (4) No, most states have laws that require the reporting of child abuse.

18. A nurse is caring for a client who has been diagnosed with a terminal disease. The client becomes withdrawn and refuses to discuss her health issues. The client will most likely experience several stages over time while processing this news. List the characteristics of the next four stages of death and dying in ascending chronological order as described by Elisabeth Kubler-Ross.

    (1) Calmness, honesty, becomes involved in care-management decisions   _____

    (2) Negotiating, shows a new interest in healthful behaviors   _____

    (3) Irritability, complaining, adversarial   _____

    (4) Loss, grief, and intense sadness   _____

TIP

This question is an example of how NCLEX-PN test writers integrate the Nursing Process (Communication and Documentation) with the Client Needs (Health Promotion and Maintenance) structure.

19. It is helpful for a nurse to remember that the *primary* purpose of an incident report is to

    (1) identify employees who make frequent errors.

    (2) help lawyers defend the hospital against malpractice.

    (3) prevent future incidents by identifying high-risk practices.

    (4) keep accurate records on clients prone to accidents.

20. A client, who has been treated in the hospital for pneumonia, has decided to leave the hospital even though she has not been discharged. The *most important* obligation of the nurse or other medical provider on this case is to

    (1) attempt to convince the client to remain in the hospital.

    (2) notify discharge planning.

    (3) advise the client of the risks of her decision.

    (4) inform the next of kin.

ANSWER KEY AND EXPLANATIONS

1. 2	5. 4	9. 2,4,1,3	13. 2	17. 4
2. 1,2,4	6. 3	10. 2	14. 1	18. 3,2,4,1
3. 1	7. 4	11. 3	15. 4	19. 3
4. 4	8. 2	12. 2	16. 1	20. 3

1. **The correct answer is (2).** Processed and canned foods are often very high in sodium. Fresh fruits and vegetables (apples, spinach) are usually low in sodium, as are whole-grain breads.

2. **The correct answer is (1), (2), and (4).** Clear fluids are those you can see through; orange juice is among them.

3. **The correct answer is (1).** Caesar salad with spinach frittata is high in vitamin K, which is an antagonist to coumadin. The other foods listed are not high in this vitamin.

4. **The correct answer is (4).** Strict vegans eat no eggs or milk, so they are particularly at risk for vitamin B_{12} deficiency because animal foods are the only source of this vitamin.

5. **The correct answer is (4).** A cheese omelet is made up of two extremely high-cholesterol foods: eggs and cheese. The other foods are low in cholesterol.

6. **The correct answer is (3).** Organ meats, alcohol, fat, beans, lentils, and bran should all be avoided by the client with gout. Alcohol causes increased production of keto-acids, and the other foods are high in purines. Both increase uric acid levels; the pain of gout is caused by deposits of sodium urate crystals.

7. **The correct answer is (4).** Intrinsic factor, which is necessary for the absorption of B_{12}, is produced in the stomach; therefore, B_{12} injections must be given.

8. **The correct answer is (2).** Airborne precautions with specially fitted respiratory masks, and a negative-pressure room are needed to prevent the spread of *M. tuberculosis*, the causative organism of pulmonary tuberculosis. Transmission occurs when a person inhales microdroplets into the respiratory tract after someone nearby who is infected has coughed or sneezed.

9. **The correct order of answers is (2), (4), (1), (3).** The client should be checked frequently to determine whether his restraints should be removed. The nurse can assess and document this when she encounters the client initially. Toileting and range-of-motion exercises should be performed at least every 2 hours while the client is restrained. This should be handled before restraining the client again. The client's wrists should be retied in quick release knots, so that he can be freed of restraints quickly if necessary. The nurse should do this before retying the vest restraints to restrict the client's hand movement.

10. **The correct answer is (2).** *Clostridium dificile*, an enteric virus, is spread by direct contact with the

client or by indirect contact with a contaminated intermediate object. According to the Centers for Disease Control and Prevention (CDC), contact precautions, which require wearing a gown, are recommended for infection control. Transmission requires a low infectious dose, and the virus has prolonged environmental survival. Measles calls for taking airborne precautions, and streptococcal pharyngitis and pertussis require taking droplet precautions.

11. **The correct answer is (3).** All health-care institutions receiving Medicare or Medicaid funds must provide recipients with written information regarding their rights under law to make Advance Directives. These are intended to allow clients to have more control over health-care decisions at the end of life. The two main types of ADs are the living will and durable power of attorney for health care.

12. **The correct answer is (2).** The date and time preceding a nursing note refers to the time the note was written. The time of an occurrence would be mentioned in the note. Nurses' notes are legal documents, so timely documentation is important. A note that is unduly delayed must be noted as a late entry.

13. **The correct answer is (2).** The "Patient's Bill of Rights" states that the client has the right to review his or her records.

14. **The correct answer is (1).** Advance Directives are intended to give clients the right to specify how they wish to be treated when they cannot speak for themselves, and so they frequently involve end-of-life care. Since Mr. Smith says he does not expect to get better, he does need Advance Directives to express his treatment choices.

15. **The correct answer is (4).** A living will is designed to communicate a client's preferences regarding end-of-life care, and it must be noted in his or her chart. The chaplain, family members, and even the physician of the client might not be present when decisions must be made.

16. **The correct answer is (1).** Hospital policy and the Nurse Practice Act of each state determine the conditions of licensed nursing practice. The other documents listed are not legally binding.

17. **The correct answer is (4).** Nurses are legally mandated to report suspected child abuse to the proper authorities; however, most client information is regarded as confidential.

18. **The correct order of answers is (3), (2), (4), (1).** According to Kubler-Ross, the five stages of death and dying are: denial and isolation; anger; bargaining; depression; and acceptance.

19. **The correct answer is (3).** Although incident reports may be used for other purposes, their main purpose is as a risk-management tool to help avoid future accidents or problems.

20. **The correct answer is (3).** The client has the right to refuse care, but it is the health-care provider's responsibility to inform the client of any risks involved in this decision. Convincing the client to remain (1) is not necessary, nor is notifying discharge planning (2), whose role has been bypassed. Once the client has left the hospital, the hospital is not responsible for informing the next of kin (4) unless the client has a guardian or legal representative.

SUMMING IT UP

- Assessment is primarily the responsibility of the RN, but PNs must understand the process and collect data to help formulate the nursing assessment.

- The role of the PN is to provide direct nursing care to clients in stable condition under the supervision and guidance of a registered nurse or physician.

- Ethical principles include respecting the individual and his or her dignity and right to form judgments and take actions as long as they do not interfere with others; promoting goodness, kindness, and charity; abstaining from injuring others; and telling the truth.

Nursing Procedures

OVERVIEW

- Vital signs
- Hygiene
- Mobility
- Feeding the client
- Elimination—bowel
- Elimination—urinary
- Hot and cold therapy
- Wound care
- Asepsis
- Collecting specimens
- Care of the dying
- Summing it up

VITAL SIGNS

A. Temperature
    1. May be tympanic, oral, rectal, or axillary
        a. Oral—not for infants, clients with oral surgery, or clients who are unconscious or are receiving oxygen by mask
        b. Rectal—not for clients with rectal surgery
        c. Tympanic—not for clients under 3 months old
    2. Normal oral temperature range is 97–99.5 degrees. Rectal is 1 degree higher; tympanic is 0.5 degree higher; axillary is 1 degree lower.
    3. Celsius: 37 degrees Celsius equals 98.6 degrees Fahrenheit. Each Celsius degree equals 1.8 degrees Fahrenheit.

B. Pulse
    1. **Normal**—60–100 beats per minute
    2. **Radial Artery**—usually palpated
    3. **Apical Pulse**—used for babies or those with irregular heartbeats
    4. **Peripheral Pulse**—such as tibial, are used to evaluate circulation; Doppler ultrasound may be used if the pulse is not palpable
    5. **Pulse Deficit**—the apical rate is higher than the radial rate; the deficit is the apical minus the radial

C. Blood Pressure
    1. **Normal Systolic Pressure** (when the heart is contracting): 90–139 mmHg.
    2. **Normal Diastolic Pressure** (when the heart is at rest): 60–89 mmHg.

chapter 3

D. **Respirations**
   1. **Adult Respiration**—normally 12–20 breaths per minute
   2. **Assess**—depth, regularity, and rate

Normal Vital Signs

	Adult	Child 6–10	Child 2–4	Newborn
Respirations	12–18	20–26	24–32	30–60
Pulse	60–100	100	90–130	100–160
Blood Pressure	90/60–139/89	80/40–110/80		

HYGIENE

A. **Bathing**
   1. **Nursing Considerations**
      a. Provide privacy.
      b. Rinse and dry all surfaces of skin.
      c. Use a bath blanket to keep client warm—keep room temperature warm, if possible.
      d. Moisturize skin with lotion. Note: clients receiving radiation should not have soap, lotions, or powders used on the site.
   2. **Types of Care**
      a. **Complete Care**—client needs assistance with all care
      b. **Partial Care**—client can perform much of a.m. care, and a nurse usually finishes
      c. **Self Care**—client does all ADLs
   3. **Mouth and Teeth**
      a. Clean dentures, teeth, and gums every 24 hours.
      b. Dentures should be kept in the mouth as much as possible or the gums recede.
   4. **Hair**—brush daily
   5. **Bed**—a.m. care should include changing the bed linens, or at least ensuring that they are clean, and making the bed
      a. **Occupied bed:** Make with the client in bed. Turn client from side to side as bed is made.
      b. **Unoccupied bed:** Fan-fold top covers so the bed will be ready for the client.
      c. **Surgical bed:** Top covers are not tucked in, but are fan-folded to side or bottom of bed for client returning from surgery.

MOBILITY

A. **Range of Motion (ROM)**—to prevent contractures, the nurse should perform passive ROM with the client or teach the client to perform active ROM.
   1. ROM exercises consist of moving each joint through its full range of movement.
   2. Movements should never be forced.
   3. ROM should be performed twice daily on immobile clients.

B. **Body Alignment**
   1. The correct alignment in bed is in the supine position with the face looking up, arms at sides, and feet parallel with the toes pointed up and slightly outward.

NOTE

Basic Activities of Daily Living (ADLs) include bathing, dressing, eating, transferring from bed to chair and chair to bed, controlling bodily discharges, toileting, and walking.

2. Use positioning aids such as trochanter rolls by the hip to prevent abduction and external rotation of the hip.
3. The paralyzed hand may be positioned around a rolled washcloth to maintain it in a functional position.

C. Client Transfers
   1. **Bed to Stretcher**
      a. Use 2 to 3 people.
      b. Utilize a drawsheet to pull client to edge of bed with stretcher (wheels locked) beside it.
      c. Reach across stretcher and pull client toward you.
   2. **Bed to Chair**
      a. Lower bed as much as possible.
      b. Move the client to a sitting position and then to side of the bed with the legs dangling.
      c. Face client with a wide stance and her knees between your legs.
      d. Have client lean forward and place her hands on your shoulders, pull her to a standing position, and then pivot her to the chair.
      e. If possible, have client assist in lowering herself into the chair.
   3. **Pulling Client Up in Bed**
      a. Stand beside him.
      b. Lower the bed to a flat position.
      c. Have the client bend his knees and push as you pull him up (with another person if possible) by a drawsheet or by reaching under his shoulders.
   4. **Turning Client**
      a. Turn client every 2 hours while in bed.
      b. Lower bed and cross client's arms on chest.
      c. Use a drawsheet to turn client, and stabilize with pillows.

D. Assistive Devices
   1. **Cane**
      a. Stand on the affected side and stabilize client by holding the security belt and placing a hand on her shoulder.
      b. The cane should be on the unaffected side so that it can work with the weaker leg as the client steps forward.
      c. The top of the cane should reach the greater trochanter of the client's femur (where hip and thigh meet).
   2. **Crutches**
      a. Position so that you may place two fingers between the axilla and the axillary bars.
      b. Position yourself on the affected side and stabilize the client as with a cane.
      c. Instruct client not to rest underarms on the axillary bars. It could cause brachila plexus palsy.
   3. **Walker**
      a. The nurse should be positioned, as with crutches above, on the affected side.
      b. Instruct the client to move the walker forward and walk into it.

FEEDING THE CLIENT

A. Oral Feedings
   1. Place tray so client can see food being served.
   2. Check gag reflex if this is the first time client is being fed.

3. Raise head of bed to assist client in swallowing.
4. Prepare food but allow client to be as independent as possible.
5. Use straws for fluids and have client eat finger foods on his own.
6. Ask client which food he wants next.
7. Offer foods in small amounts, alternating solids and liquids.
8. Do not rush client.
9. Wash the client's hands and provide oral care before and after the meal.

B. Tube Feedings
1. Use nasogastric or gastrostomy tube for clients who cannot swallow.
2. Feedings may either be continuous or intermittent.
3. Feeding solution should always be at room temperature to avoid cramping.
4. Flush tube with water before and after each feeding and each medication.
5. Raise head of bed during feedings, and maintain 45-degree angle for 45 minutes afterwards.
6. Give feedings by gravity infusion; do not force.
7. Aspirate stomach contents before feeding or one hour after to assess for residual left in stomach.
8. Give mouth care every 2 hours.
9. Provide emotional support.

ELIMINATION—BOWEL

A. Enema (must be ordered)
   1. **Cleansing Enema**
      a. Use tap water, soap and water, or saline.
      b. Solution should be no hotter than 105 degrees.
      c. Position client in left lateral Sims position.
      d. Administer 500–1000 mL of fluid.
      e. Insert lubricated tube approximately 3–4 inches; hold fluid about 18 inches above rectum.
      f. If cramping occurs, stop and have client take several deep breaths until it passes.
      g. Observe results and record amount of feces expelled. If ordered "to clear," do not give more than three enemas, unless specifically requested.
   2. **Oil Retention Enema**
      a. Given to soften stool.
      b. Warm oil to about 100 degrees.
      c. Give about 100 cc and encourage client to retain it for about 30 minutes.

B. Manual Extraction of Impaction
   1. Order required for cardiac clients.
   2. Put gloves on and lubricate index finger.
   3. Position client in left lateral Sims position.
   4. Insert finger and gently break off and remove hard pieces of stool.
   5. Stop if vital signs change or client becomes uncomfortable.
   6. Give client a bedpan after procedure to allow to evacuate rest of stool.

C. Colostomy Irrigation
   1. Done to regulate passage of stool and empty bowel.
   2. Not all clients perform this.
   3. Done every other day or every day.

4. Use a special ostomy pouch for irrigation to collect feces.
5. Use warm saline or tap water.
6. Record results.

ELIMINATION—URINARY

A. **Assistance**
1. Offer bedpan at regular intervals or leave nearby.
2. Provide privacy.
3. Encourage client to assume position of choice.
4. If client has difficulty voiding, try running water, placing the client's hand in warm water, or pouring warm water over the perineum.

Urinary Problems

Incontinence: client is unable to control urination
Retention: client is unable to void
Dysuria: painful urination
Polyuria: excessive urination
Oliguria: output less than 400 mL/day
Anuria: no urine output

B. **Catheters**
1. **Straight Catheters**—are inserted to empty the bladder and then removed
2. **Foley Catheters**—are inserted and left in for variable lengths of time
3. **Procedure**
   a. Sterile technique.
   b. Explain procedure, provide privacy, and position client.
   c. Put on sterile gloves and open sterile kit.
   d. Cleanse the urinary meatus front to back.
   e. Lubricate catheter and insert about 3–4 inches in women, and 6–8 inches in men.
   f. If using a Foley catheter, inflate the balloon, which is in the bladder, with 5–10 cc of water. Tape tube to the thigh, connect to tubing and bag.

C. **Catheter Irrigation**
1. **Sterile Technique**
   a. Obtain an irrigation kit, or 50–60 mL syringe, pad, and drainage tray.
   b. Explain procedure, open the irrigation tray, and pour the sterile irrigant into the syringe.
   c. Instill the irrigant and allow it to drain. Record amount of irrigant and output.

D. **Removal of Foley Catheter**
1. Provide privacy and position client.
2. Use a syringe to withdraw water from the inflated balloon.
3. Gently withdraw tube. Discard tubing and bag.
4. Monitor client for voiding within 8 hours of removal.
5. Encourage fluid intake to improve output.

HOT AND COLD THERAPY

A. Heat Therapy
1. **Indications**—stiffness, arthritis, pain. **Contraindications:** trauma, edema, malignant tumors, burns, testes, sensory impaired or confused clients, due to increased possibility of burn
2. **Local Effects**
   a. Vasodilation, increased oxygen and blood flow to the area
   b. Muscle relaxation
   c. Decreased stiffness, spasm

B. Cold Therapy
1. **Indications**—sprains, fractures, swelling, bleeding. **Contraindications:** open wounds, impaired circulation, sensory-impaired, or confused clients, due to greater possibility of injury
2. **Local Effects**
   a. Vasoconstriction—decreases O_2 to area—increased cell death
   b. Decreased metabolism
   c. Decreased pain, decreased fluid, and thus less swelling

WOUND CARE

A. Purpose—to protect from infection and further damage as well as promote healing

B. Speed of Healing—affected by nutritional status, circulation, location and type of wound, and underlying disease, such as diabetes

C. Nursing Care
1. **Sterile Dressing**
   a. Wash hands, assemble equipment.
   b. Remove old dressing using clean gloves; assess drainage on dressing, status of wound.
   c. Dispose of dressing in closed container.
   d. Put on sterile gloves and clean wound from clean area (center) to dirty area. Do not go back over an area previously cleaned. Discard cleansing swab after each stroke.
   e. Apply sterile dressing, and tape or anchor securely with binder.
   f. Chart color, amount and odor of drainage, as well as the status of the wound.
2. **Wet-to-Dry Dressing**
   a. Follow steps above, except sterile saline is used to moisten dressing; acts to help clean wound and remove necrotic tissue.
   b. After applying wet dressing, cover with dry sterile dressing and secure. Allow to dry for 4–6 hours. Don't get the dressing too wet; it should be allowed to dry between dressing changes.
3. **Obtaining a Wound Culture**—must be done before antibiotics are given or antimicrobial agent is applied to wound
   a. Gently take a sterile swab and roll it in the purulent drainage.
   b. Put swab in culture tube or sterile container for culture and analysis.
4. **Jackson-Pratt Drainage System**—prevents excessive buildup of drainage
   a. Consists of a bulb that must be compressed to allow air to escape.
   b. Bulb is then recapped to maintain suction.

5. **Hemovac**—also intended to remove drainage from wound
   a. This drainage device must be compressed every 4 hours to maintain suction.
   b. Empty drainage from pouring spout.

ASEPSIS

A. **Procedures Requiring Sterile Technique**
   1. **Surgical**
   2. **Catheterization of Body Cavities**
   3. **Injections, Infusions**
   4. **Dressing Changes**—usually the first: dressings over catheters that go into body cavities
   5. **Dressings of Immune-Compromised Clients or Burn Clients**

B. **Sterile Field**
   1. The sterile field must be within your view at all times.
   2. Below the waist is not a sterile field since it is not within your view.
   3. Moisture will carry bacteria through a cloth barrier, so wet areas are not sterile.
   4. The edges (the one-inch border) of a sterile field are unsterile.
   5. Talking over a sterile field will contaminate it.
   6. Setting up a sterile field
      a. Wash hands; open pack on a clean, dry surface.
      b. Position outer flap away from you. Lift it up and away from you. Try to keep your arms at your sides so you don't reach over the sterile area.
      c. Open side flaps.
      d. Open flap closest to you—step back so your clothing won't touch it.
      e. Peel the outer flaps of sterile supplies apart like a banana, and drop the inner sterile package onto the sterile field. Do not touch the inside of the sterile packaging, and prevent the unsterile container from contaminating the sterile field by holding the container at least 6 inches above the field.

C. **Putting on Sterile Gloves**
   1. Wash hands, open the outer wrap of the sterile glove package, and remove the inner wrap.
   2. Place the inner wrap on a clean, dry surface.
   3. Unfold the inner wrap, touching only the edges.
   4. Once open, use your dominant hand to grasp the opposite glove on the inner fold of the cuff, and carefully slip your nondominant hand into it.
   5. Pull the glove up, still holding the inner cuff.
   6. With your sterile gloved hand, slip your fingers under the folded cuff of the remaining glove.
   7. Slip the glove over your fingers and pull the glove over your hand.

COLLECTING SPECIMENS

A. **Urine Specimens**
   1. **Sterile Specimen**
      a. Collected by straight catheterization
      b. Can also withdraw urine from a Foley catheter through the access port with a sterile needle after wiping the port with alcohol

2. **Voided "Clean Catch"**
   a. Wash perineal area.
   b. Collect midstream specimen by having client start to void, stop, then void into a sterile container.
   c. Clean specimens are used for urinalysis.
   d. May be a single specimen or a 24-hour cumulative specimen.
   e. With a 24-hour specimen, discard first void and record the time. Collect all urine for the next 24 hours.
3. **Double Voided Specimen**—assures fresh urine for testing
   a. Client voids as usual.
   b. Client then collects next voided specimen—used for acetone and glucose.

B. **Culture and Sensitivity Specimens**
   1. Identifies organisms causing an infection as well as drugs that may be used to treat it.
   2. Collect specimen before any antibiotics have been given topically or orally or by IV.
   3. Sterile technique is used to collect and store the specimen.
   4. The results are used to determine the antibiotics to be used.

C. **Sputum Specimen** (often used to test for TB)
   1. Used to inspect sputum for infectious agent or malignancy.
   2. Best to obtain it in the morning prior to breakfast.
   3. Have client breathe deeply to induce a cough.
   4. Use a sterile container with the correct cytology preservative.

D. **General Principles**
   1. Use the correct container for each specimen. The container must be sterile.
   2. Be sure to use universal (or standard) precautions.
   3. Properly label the specimen with the client's name, date and time, and your name or initials.

CARE OF THE DYING

A. **Physical Care**
   1. Provide comfort measures including:
      a. Good mouth care
      b. Skin care
      c. Artificial tears if eyes are dry
      d. Suctioning if needed to ease breathing
      e. Adequate hydration
      f. Frequent position changes to keep client comfortable
      g. Clean linens and gown
      h. Maintain adequate pain management

B. Spiritual/Cultural Care
1. Provide support to family and client.
2. Continue to observe any religious customs.
3. Help to open communication with the client and family.
4. Allow family time alone with the client if desired.
5. Be honest with the family, and keep them informed of the client's status.

C. After Death (must be after a physician pronounces client dead)
1. Position body in natural position—place a pillow under the head and close eyes.
2. Place dentures in the mouth as soon as possible and close mouth.
3. Clean body and remove all IV's, tubing, dressings, etc.
4. Allow family time alone with the client after completing the preparations above.
5. Wrap body in shroud and label with tags according to agency policy.
6. Gather and label client's belongings.
7. Record observations, procedures, disposition of valuables, and time of death.

NOTE

Different religions have varying customs related to the end of life. For example, Roman Catholics anoint the dying and perform the sacraments of reconciliation and communion; most Protestant denominations do not anoint the sick. Muslims may wish to face Mecca, recite verses from the Qur'an over the dying, and may consent to autopsies only when absolutely necessary. The practice of routine autopsies is contrary to Jewish law (autopsies are believed to desecrate the body); however, an autopsy may be performed in certain situations. If you're unsure about a client's religious wishes, it is best to ask the client's family.

EXERCISES: NURSING PROCEDURES

1. A nurse needs to perform the following procedures on her older client. For which procedure is it *essential* that she use surgical asepsis?

    (1) Intramuscular injection

    (2) Removal of an indwelling catheter

    (3) Colostomy irrigation

    (4) Gastric tube feeding

2. The nurse observes an aide putting on sterile gloves. When putting on the first glove, the aide indicates that she is following the *correct* technique by grasping it

    (1) at the top edge of the cuff.

    (2) under the folded cuff.

    (3) with a 2 × 2 sterile gauze.

    (4) by the tip of the middle finger.

3. A nurse must obtain a clean-catch urine specimen. He or she is responsible for which of the following?
    Select all that apply.

    ☐ **(1)** Instructing the client in the proper technique for obtaining a clean-catch specimen.

    ☐ **(2)** Determining whether the test is necessary.

    ☐ **(3)** Preventing contamination of the specimen.

    ☐ **(4)** Labeling the specimen and sending it to the lab.

4. A nurse is preparing the room for a sterile procedure. He opens a sterile drape and places it over the top and sides of the table, and carefully peels back the wrapping of several syringes and drops them on the table. He then pours 1–2 mL of sterile water into a waste receptacle and the remainder into a sterile bowl he has previously placed on the table. Some of the water splashes onto the table. The nurse, who is wearing a sterile gown and gloves, realizes that he may only touch *one* of the following to maintain sterility:

    (1) The water in the bowl

    (2) The border of the sterile drape

    (3) The spot where the water splashed

    (4) The part of the drape covering the sides of the table

5. A nurse documents the characteristics of wound drainage after he changes the dressing. He includes which of the following observations?
    Select all that apply.

    ☐ **(1)** Color

    ☐ **(2)** Amount

    ☐ **(3)** Odor

    ☐ **(4)** Temperature

6. A nurse knows to maintain *medical* asepsis when performing the following procedure:

   (1) Insertion of an IV catheter

   (2) Endotracheal suctioning

   (3) Gastric tube feeding

   (4) Foley catheter insertion

7. A nurse is preparing to catheterize her client before surgery. After gathering all of the necessary equipment, the nurse will open the sterile pack containing the catheter set. What is the correct order for implementing this aseptic procedure?

   (1) Putting on sterile gloves.   ____

   (2) Opening the side flaps of the sterile pack.   ____

   (3) Opening the flap of the sterile pack closest to the nurse.   ____

   (4) Opening the flap of the sterile pack farthest from the nurse. ____

8. Ann Taylor has just been transferred to her postpartum room after delivering a stillborn infant. Her husband is with her, and they ask if they may see the baby. Which is the *best* response by the nurse?

   (1) Offer to bring them a photo of the infant.

   (2) Bring them a hospital bereavement package—a lock of hair, ID bands, footprints, and other keepsakes.

   (3) Suggest that it would be best not to see the baby, since they don't want to remember him that way.

   (4) Bring the baby to the parents and allow them to spend time alone with him.

9. A nurse is caring for a 62-year-old woman who is dying of gastric cancer. The woman's daughter tells the nurse that they do not want her to be told that she is dying because she "would not be able to handle it." The nurse is concerned that this approach will hurt the family because

   (1) the older woman might learn the truth from someone else and feel betrayed.

   (2) she might not be as cooperative with the medical plans if she feels it is useless.

   (3) it prevents open discussion about what is happening to the dying woman and her loved ones and doesn't allow her to express her feelings.

   (4) it is difficult to conceal the truth from someone who knows you well.

10. The doctor has ordered a urinalysis with C & S (culture and sensitivity) on a client in your care. She has an indwelling Foley catheter to bedside drainage. The best way to obtain the specimen is to:

    (1) open the port on the holding bag and obtain approximately 100 cc to use for both tests.

    (2) separate the catheter from the drainage bag tubing and drain only from the catheter.

    (3) empty the collecting bag and collect the next 100 cc that drains into the bag.

    (4) use a sterile needle and withdraw urine through the rubber port on the drainage tubing.

ANSWER KEY AND EXPLANATIONS

1. 1	3. 1,3,4	5. 1,2,3	7. 4,2,3,1	9. 3
2. 1	4. 1	6. 3	8. 4	10. 4

1. **The correct answer is (1).** Surgical asepsis is needed for administering an intramuscular injection because it involves intentional perforation of a client's skin. Procedures requiring surgical asepsis include those involving broken skin or which involve insertion of catheters or surgical instruments into sterile body cavities. None of the other procedures fit these categories.

2. **The correct answer is (1).** When putting on sterile gloves, the first glove is grasped by the folded edge of the cuff with the nondominant hand. The dominant hand is then slipped into it. The second glove is then picked up by slipping the fingers of the gloved hand under the cuff and inserting the nondominant hand. The other options are incorrect.

3. **The correct answers are (1), (3), and (4).** The nurse is responsible for actions related to obtaining an adequate specimen. She cannot decide whether or not a test is appropriate; that is the provider's responsibility.

4. **The correct answer is (1).** The water in the bowl is sterile, but the one-inch border of the drape (2), the spot where the water splashed (3), and the sides of the table (4) are all considered unsterile, according to current practice guidelines.

5. **The correct answers are (1), (2), and (3).** When changing a dressing, the nurse should chart the color, amount, and odor of any discharge present. Charting the temperature is not feasible or needed.

6. **The correct answer is (3).** Insertion of an IV catheter (1), endotracheal suctioning (2), and Foley catheter insertion (4) all involve inserting something into a normally sterile body cavity and require surgical asepsis. Gastric tube feeding, however, merely requires clean technique, or medical asepsis.

7. **The correct order of answers is (4), (2), (3), (1).** Opening the side farthest from the nurse (4) first prevents contamination of the sterile field by reaching over it to open it after the sides (2) and front (3) have been opened. The sterile gloves (1) should be put on after the pack is opened because the outside of the pack is not sterile.

8. **The correct answer is (4).** Part of the grieving process involves confirmation and validation of the parents' feeling of loss, and it is helpful for the parents to hold the baby and spend time alone with the infant to do this.

9. **The correct answer is (3).** Denial of an older person's impending death makes it impossible for the dying person to talk about what is happening to her and for the family to fully take advantage of their last opportunity to communicate.

10. **The correct answer is (4).** The first three options do not guarantee a sterile specimen. Only by entering the port with a sterile needle will a sterile specimen be obtained.

answers exercises

SUMMING IT UP

- Vital signs—temperature, pulse, blood pressure, respirations
- Hygiene—bathing
- Mobility—range of motion, body alignment, client transfers, assistive devices
- Feeding the client—oral feedings, tube feedings
- Elimination—bowel, urinary
- Hot and cold therapy
- Wound care—speed of healing, nursing care
- Asepsis—procedures that require sterile technique, sterile field
- Collecting specimens
- Care of the dying—physical care, spiritual/cultural care, after death

Pharmacology

OVERVIEW

- Basic concepts
- Drug legislation
- Drug names
- Drug actions
- Drug metabolism (pharmacokinetics)
- Drug forms
- Nursing responsibilities in medication administration
- Drug interactions
- Legal aspects of drug administration
- Routes of medication administration
- Calculation of medication dosages
- Drugs that require specific nursing actions or considerations
- Summing it up

BASIC CONCEPTS

A basic knowledge of pharmacology—the study of how substances interact with living organisms to produce a change in function—is central to nursing. The field includes drug composition and properties, interactions, toxology, therapy, and medical applications.

DRUG LEGISLATION

A. **Pure Food and Drug Act (1906)**—U.S. government set standards for drug quality and purity
   1. The *United States Pharmacopeia (USP)* and the *National Formulary* set standards for strength, quality, safety, labeling, and dosage forms.

B. **Food, Drug, and Cosmetic Act (1938)**
   1. Regulations to ensure safety and effectiveness were developed.
   2. A physician's prescription was needed to purchase a drug.

C. **Controlled Substances Act (1970)**
   1. Drug dependency and addiction were defined.
   2. Drugs were classified according to potential for abuse.
   3. Methods were determined for regulating the manufacture, distribution, and sale of controlled substances.
   4. Education and treatment programs for drug abuse were established.

TIP

Drugs that have important
nursing implications (such as
those that increase bleeding)
and require a specific
assessment before
administration often appear in
questions on the exam.

D. Schedule of Controlled Substances
   1. **Schedule I**—drugs that have a high potential for abuse and have no currently accepted medical use in the United States (such as cocaine)
   2. **Schedule II**—drugs with a high potential for abuse but which currently have an accepted medical use for treatment or a currently accepted medical use with severe restrictions
   3. **Schedule III**—drugs that have a lower potential for abuse than those in Schedules I and II; abuse may lead to high psychologic and moderate-to-low physical dependence
   4. **Schedule IV**—drugs with low potential for abuse relative to those on Schedule III—use may lead to limited psychologic or physical dependence
   5. **Schedule V**—drugs with lower potential for abuse than those on Schedule IV; may be dispensed by pharmacists without a prescription, but should have some restrictions, such as record-keeping

DRUG NAMES

A. Generic Name—the official name of a drug listed in publications
   1. Meperidine is the generic name for the pain medication Demerol.

B. Trade Name—the name given to a drug by a drug company
   1. Trade name is Demerol.
   2. NCLEX exam will use both generic and trade names for medications.

DRUG ACTIONS

A. Drugs have one or more desired actions; responses
   1. Usually predictable but undesirable (side effects).
   2. May be unexpected, such as an allergic reaction or idiosyncratic response of an individual.

B. Factors that determine an individual's response to a drug
   1. Infants and the elderly are usually more susceptible to drug actions. They are also subject to cumulative effects of drugs in which more medication is being administered than is being removed.
   2. History of drug use may also affect response. A tolerance may have developed for certain types of drugs, or interactions may increase or decrease the response of more than one medication. Drugs may have a cumulative effect when they are not excreted as rapidly as they are given.
   3. Interactions may alter the effects of one or both of the drugs, increasing, decreasing, or eliminating some responses altogether.
   4. Alterations in kidney or liver function affect drug metabolism.
   5. Administration method (IM, p.o., IV, etc.) affects absorption.
   6. Emotional factors may also play an important part. A client who has confidence in his or her doctor and expects benefits from the medication is more likely to experience those benefits.

DRUG METABOLISM (PHARMACOKINETICS)

A. **Absorption**—movement of the dissolved drug from the site of administration to the bloodstream. Affected by
   1. Rate drug is dissolved
   2. Surface area exposed to the dissolved drug
   3. Blood flow to the site of drug absorption
   4. Fat solubility—more fat soluble, the faster the absorption of the drug
   5. Route of administration
   6. Client's health condition

B. **Distribution**—movement of the drug throughout the body. Affected by
   1. Blood flow through tissues
   2. Ability of drug to leave the vascular system
   3. Ability of the drug to enter cells
   4. Chemical properties of the drugs

C. **Metabolism**—enzymatic alteration of drug structure; also known as biotransformation
   1. Primarily occurs in the liver
   2. Prepares the drug for action or excretion
   3. Affected by age of client, liver function, nutritional status, and competition of two drugs for the same enzymes
   4. The time the drug is administered

D. **Excretion**—removal of drug from the body
   1. Usually occurs through the kidneys and urine
   2. Affected by renal function
   3. Some excretion through nonrenal sources such as bile and feces, lungs, skin, tears, and saliva

---

Drug Metabolism in Older Clients

Absorption: Drugs are absorbed more slowly due to decreased GI motility and blood flow.

Distribution: Less body fluid, more relative fat and lower serum protein result in a greater concentration of drugs in the fluid, buildup of drugs in fat, and, in protein-bound drugs, more free drug due to fewer protein binding sites.

Metabolism: Decreased liver function and blood flow lead to a reduction in the metabolism of a drug, which leads to a longer half-life and drug accumulation.

Excretion: Decreased kidney blood flow and lower filtration rate prolong drug excretion, which, again, leads to drug accumulation.

DRUG FORMS

A. **Liquid**
   1. **Solution**—drug dissolved in a liquid, usually water
   2. **Suspension**—drug in small particles suspended in liquid
   3. **Emulsion**—suspension of fat globules in water
   4. **Tincture**—drugs dissolved in alcohol
   5. **Lotion**—liquid dispersion of drug for topical use
   6. **Liniment**—drug in oily, soapy, or alcohol mixture applied to soothe skin

ALERT!

Antacids can affect the absorption rate of medications.

B. Transdermal
   1. Fat-soluble form of medication
   2. Applied to skin or on a covered patch
      a. Longer absorption and duration of action

C. Solid or Semisolid Drug Forms
   1. **Capsule**—liquid or solid drug inside gelatinous capsule that dissolves after swallowing
      a. Sustained release—drug in small particles with different coatings to dissolve at different speeds (slow release, should not be crushed)
   2. **Tablet**—solid form of drug pressed into various sizes and shapes
      a. Buccal—solid form dissolves when held between cheek and gum (directly absorbed by oral mucosa)
      b. Sublingual—solid form that dissolves when held under tongue (absorbed by oral mucosa)
      c. Enteric-coated—drug coated with substance that delays release of drug until it reaches the intestine (should not be crushed)
   3. **Suppository**—drug made of a material that melts at body temperature when inserted
   4. **Ointment**—semisolid, oily substance for external application
   5. **Lozenge** (troche)—drug incorporated into a sugar or fruit base that will dissolve in the mouth

NURSING RESPONSIBILITIES IN MEDICATION ADMINISTRATION

A. Observe the Five Rights
   1. "**R**ob **T**o **P**ay **D**rug **D**ealer"
      a. Right *r*oute of administration
      b. Right *t*ime
      c. Right *p*atient
      d. Right *d*rug
      e. Right *d*osage and documentation

B. Be Familiar with the Medication
   1. The reason it is being administered
   2. Side effects
   3. Typical dose and range of safety, if applicable
   4. Specific safety regulations before administering:
      a. Heparin—check clotting times
      b. Digitalis—check apical pulse
   5. Check the compatibility of the medication with other drugs and infusions the client is receiving
   6. Do not administer any medication that you have not prepared

C. Assess the Client
   1. Food or drug allergies
   2. Past medical history and present condition
   3. Knowledge deficits and teaching needed.

D. **Evaluate Response**
   1. Evaluate client for his or her response to the medication, and document if appropriate.
   2. Report any unfavorable or unexpected response.
   3. Report allergic responses. Allergic responses include difficulty breathing, rashes, nausea, vomiting, pruritis, wheezing, and palpitations.

DRUG INTERACTIONS

A. **Drug-Drug Interactions**
   1. **Additive Effect**—1 + 1 = 2
      a. Diuretic plus a beta blocker increases antihypertensive effect
   2. **Synergistic Effect**—1 + 1 = 3
      a. Vistaril potentiates the effect of Demerol
   3. **Antagonistic Effect**—1 + 1 = 0
      a. Beta blocker plus a beta stimulant cancel each other out

B. **Drug-Food Interactions**
   1. Food may bind with a drug to delay drug absorption (tetracycline + dairy product = a decrease in circulating tetracycline).
   2. Food may increase the absorption of a drug (lopressor + food = an increase in circulating lopressor).
   3. MAO inhibitors (antidepressants), when taken with foods containing tyramine, such as cheese, beer, or yogurt, can lead to a hypertensive crisis.

LEGAL ASPECTS OF DRUG ADMINISTRATION

A. **Physician or Other Authorized Practitioner's Order Required**
   1. The nurse is responsible for verifying that the dose is within the normal range and that the route is appropriate. The provider should be consulted if there are any questions.
   2. The nurse must positively identify the client before giving medication by checking the ID band and asking the client his or her name.
   3. The nurse is responsible for assessing the client before and after drug administration.
   4. The medication should be charted on the Medication Administration Record (MAR) as soon as possible after administration.
   5. Carefully repeat orders to the provider to verify their correctness when taking telephone orders. These must be signed by the provider as soon as possible.
   6. Medication errors should be reported immediately to the physician. The client should be carefully assessed for detrimental effects, and an incident report should be filled out.
   7. Medications should never be left at the client's bedside.

ROUTES OF MEDICATION ADMINISTRATION

A. **Oral (P.O.)**
   1. **Swallowed**
   2. **Sublingual** (under the tongue)
   3. **Buccal** (allowed to dissolve on mucous membrane of cheek)

B. Rectal (P.R.)
1. **Suppository**
2. **Liquid** (as in enema)

C. Parenteral
1. **Intravenous (IV)**
   a. Must be given slowly in diluted form
   b. Immediate response
   c. Over 5 mL may be given IV
2. **Intradermal (ID)**
   a. Usually used for allergy or TB tests
   b. Inner aspect of arm is usual site
   c. Use 26-gauge needle, bevel up, inserted at approximately a 15-degree angle
   d. Normally should not be over 0.1 mL
3. **Subcutaneous (SC or SQ)**
   a. Injection into the fatty layer under the skin
   b. Use 25-gauge needle
   c. Sites include upper abdomen, upper thigh, or lateral upper arm
   d. Medication is to be absorbed slowly with prolonged effect
   e. Rotate sites with insulin or another drug that must be given repeatedly
   f. Amounts are usually 0.5–1.5 mL
4. **Intramuscular (IM)**
   a. Needle gauge and length will vary with site
      (1) Deltoid—use 25–26-gauge needle, no more than 2 mL
      (2) Thigh and buttock—longer needle needed to reach muscle, approximately 1–3 inches
      (3) Needle gauge is approximately 20–22, no more than 5 mL
   b. IM is usually for an irritating drug
   c. Systemic effect; rate of absorption depends on the client's circulation
   d. Infants are given IM medications in the vastus lateralis muscle: anterior and mid-thigh

D. Ocular
1. OD = right eye; OS = left eye; OU = both eyes
2. Instill drops or ointment into lower conjunctival sac while client looks up

E. Otic Medications
1. Warm solution to body temperature.
2. Adult ear canal pulled up and back, child's pulled down and back.
3. Have client tilt head while instilling, and leave head tilted for a few minutes afterwards.

F. Transdermal Medications
1. Apply measured amount or premeasured pad to intact skin.
2. Leave covered medication in place for specified time.
3. Use upper back, upper chest, or upper arms.

G. Suppositories
1. Rectal
   a. Client assumes Sims position.
   b. Lubricate and insert suppository past rectal sphincter.
   c. Client may take deep breaths if tense.
2. Vaginal
   a. Have client lie on back with knees bent and separated.
   b. Insert into vagina and have client lie down for required length of time.

CALCULATION OF MEDICATION DOSAGES

NOTE

Remember that during the actual NCLEX-PN exam, you will be able to use the calculator on the computer if a question requires you to calculate a dosage.

Formulas for Calculations

- Calculate drip rate for an IV infusion:

  Volume of solution = drops/minute

  Time interval in minutes × drop factor

  Example: A physician asks you to hang a bag of Lactated Ringers to infuse over 8 hours. The bag contains 1,000 mL of fluid. The drop factor, which is printed on the infusion set box, is 10 drops per cc (the factor for most sets except microdrips).

  $$\frac{1,000}{8 \times 10} = 125 \text{ drops (gtt) per minute}$$

- Oral medication calculation

  $$\frac{\text{Dose desired}}{\text{Dose on hand}} = \text{amount to give}$$

  Example: The order on the MAR is for 150 mg of amoxicillin, which comes in 75 mg tablets.

  $$\frac{150}{75} = 2$$

  Another way to set up this calculation is by algebraic ratios:

  $$\frac{150}{75x} = 1$$
  $$75x = 150$$
  $$x = 2$$

  Calculate IM medications as follows:

  $$\frac{\text{Dose desired}}{\text{Dose on hand}} \times \text{quantity of solution} = \text{amount to give}$$

  Example: An order for 75 mg Demerol, which comes in vials of 100 mg per cc.

  $$\frac{75}{100} \times 1 = \frac{3}{4}$$

  You would draw up $\frac{3}{4}$, or 0.75, of a cc of the Demerol.

  Another way to set up this calculation is by algebraic ratios:

  $$\frac{75}{100x} = 1$$
  $$100x = 75$$
  $$x = \frac{3}{4} \text{ or (0.75)}$$

DRUGS THAT REQUIRE SPECIFIC NURSING ACTIONS OR CONSIDERATIONS

Check or Order Blood Levels per Protocol

Drugs that require serum blood levels drawn to determine therapeutic dosages:

Antibiotics: gentamicin, amikacin, netilmicin, tobramycin, vancomycin

Anticonvulsants: carbamazepine (Tegretol), phenobarbitol, phenytoin (Dilantin), valproic acid (Depakote)

Cardiovascular Drugs: digoxin (Lanoxin), lidocaine (Xylocaine), procainamide (Pronestyl), quinidine, warfarin

Respiratory: theophylline, aminophyllin

Antirejection Drug: cyclosporine

Psychiatric: lithium

Antidotes

Magnesium Sulfate: Calcium gluconate is the antidote in case of respiratory depression.

Heparin: The antidote in case of excessive bleeding is protamine sulfate.

Warfarin (Coumadin): The antidote in case of excessive bleeding is vitamin K.

Cogentin and Benadryl: Treat movement disorders caused by antipsychotic drugs.

Narcan: Reverses the effects of narcotics

Precautions

MAO Inhibitors: Marcan, Nardil, Parnate—If tyramine-containing foods are eaten, the patient may have a hypertensive crisis. Foods to avoid are cheese, yogurt, red wine, and beer.

Digoxin: Withhold if pulse rate is below 60 bpm.

Antibiotics: Clients must be instructed to finish the prescription, even if they feel better.

Morphine: A respiratory depressant. It should be withheld if the respirations are below 10.

Medication Abbreviations

a.c.	before meals	qd	every day
ad lib	as desired	qh	every hour
bid	twice a day	qid	four times a day
gt or gtt.	drop(s)	qs	quantity, sufficient
IM	intramuscular	q2h	every 2 hrs
npo	nothing by mouth	q3h	every 3 hrs
oob	out of bed	stat	immediately
p.c.	after meals	tid	three times a day
p.o.	by mouth	WBC	white blood cells/ white blood count
prn	whenever needed		

EXERCISES: PHARMACOLOGY

1. The physician orders penicillin for a client with streptococcal pharyngitis. The nurse administers the drug as ordered, and the client has an allergic reaction. The nurse checks the medication order sheet and finds that the client is allergic to penicillin. Legal responsibility for the error is

   (1) only the nurse's—she should have checked the allergies before administering the medication.

   (2) only the physician's—she gave the order, the nurse is obligated to follow it.

   (3) only the pharmacist's—he should alert the floor to possible allergic reactions.

   (4) the pharmacist's, physician's, and nurse's, as they are all liable for the mistake.

2. A nurse is administering Augmentin to her client with a sinus infection. Which is the *best* way for her to ensure that she is giving it to the right client?

   (1) Call the client by name.

   (2) Read the name of the client on the client's door.

   (3) Check the client's wristband.

   (4) Check the client's room number on the unit census list.

3. Tom R., a newly admitted client, has a seizure disorder that is being treated with medication. Which of the following drugs would the nurse question if ordered for him?

   (1) Phenobarbitol, 150 mg hs

   (2) Amitriptylene (Elavil), 10 mg qid

   (3) Valproic acid (Depakote), 150 mg bid

   (4) Phenytoin (Dilantin), 100 mg tid

4. When counseling a client who is starting to take MAO (monoamine oxidase) inhibitors such as Nardil for depression, it is *essential* that the client is warned not to eat foods containing tyramine, such as

   (1) Roquefort, cheddar, or Camembert cheese.

   (2) grape juice, orange juice, or raisins.

   (3) onions, garlic, or scallions.

   (4) ground beef, turkey, or pork.

5. The nurse is administering an antibiotic to her pediatric client. She checks the client's wristband and verifies the correct medication by checking the physician's order, medication Kardex, and vial. Which of the following are considered among the Five Rights of Medication Administration?
   Select all that apply.

   ☐ **(1)** Right procedure

   ☐ **(2)** Right route

   ☐ **(3)** Right frequency

   ☐ **(4)** Right time

6. A physician orders an intramuscular injection of Demerol for the postoperative client's pain. When preparing to draw up the medication, the nurse is careful to remove the correct vial from the narcotics cabinet. It is labeled

   (1) simethicone.
   (2) albuterol.
   (3) meperidine.
   (4) ibuprofen.

NOTE

Question 7 is an example of how NCLEX-PN test writers integrate Clinical Problem-Solving (Nursing Process) with Coordinated Care, a subcategory of Safe and Effective Care Environment.

7. Mrs. Garvey has been dealing with uterine cancer for several months. Pain management is the primary focus of her current admission to your oncology unit. Her vital signs on admission are BP 110/64, pulse 78, respirations 18, and temperature 99.2 F. Morphine sulfate 6 mg IV, q 4 hours, prn has been ordered. During your assessment after lunch, your findings are: BP 92/60, pulse 66, respirations 10, and temperature 98.8. Mrs. Garvey is crying and tells you she is still experiencing severe pain. Your action should be to

   (1) give her the next ordered dose of MS.
   (2) give her a back rub, put on some light music, and dim the lights in the room.
   (3) report your findings to the RN, requesting an alternate medication order be obtained from the physician.
   (4) call her daughter to come and sit with her.

8. A client is receiving medication intravenously in a saline solution. The IV is set to deliver 8 units of the drug per hour. The solution in the IV bag contains 40 units of drug per 100 mL of normal saline solution. The PN should calculate the rate of infusion to be how many mL/hr?

   Answer: _____ mL/hr

9. Frank Jones, a nurse on a geriatric floor, is administering a dose of digoxin to one of his clients. The woman asks why she takes a different pill than her niece, who also has heart trouble. Frank replies that as people get older, liver and kidney function decline, and if the dose is as high as her niece's, the drug will tend to

   (1) have a shorter half-life.
   (2) accumulate.
   (3) have decreased distribution.
   (4) have increased absorption.

10. A pediatric nurse is putting erythromycin ointment in a newborn's eyes to prevent infection. In which area of the eye does the nurse place it?

    (1) Under the eyelid

    (2) On the cornea

    (3) In the lower conjunctival sac

    (4) By the optic disc

exercises

ANSWER KEY AND EXPLANATIONS

1. 4	3. 2	5. 1,3	7. 3	9. 2
2. 3	4. 1	6. 3	8. 20	10. 3

1. **The correct answer is (4).** The physician, nurse, and pharmacist all are licensed professionals and share responsibility for errors.

2. **The correct answer is (3).** The correct way to identify a client before giving a medication is to check the name on the medication administration record with the client's identification band. The nurse should also ask the client to state his or her name. The name on the door or the census list are not sufficient proof of identification. Calling the client by name is not as effective as having the client state his or her name; a client may not hear well or understand what the nurse is saying, and may respond to a name that is not his or her own.

3. **The correct answer is (2).** Elavil is an antidepressant that lowers the seizure threshold, so it would not be appropriate for this client. The other medications are anti-seizure drugs.

4. **The correct answer is (1).** Monoamine oxidase inhibitors react with foods high in the amino acid tyramine to cause dangerously high blood pressure. Aged cheeses are all high in this amino acid; the other foods are not.

5. **The correct answers are (1) and (3).** The Five Rights of Medication Administration are: right drug, right dosage and documentation, right route, right time, and right client. Procedure and frequency are not among these rights.

6. **The correct answer is (3).** The generic name for Demerol is meperidine.

7. **The correct answer is (3).** Morphine sulfate depresses the respiratory center. When the rate is less than 10, the physician should be notified.

8. **The correct answer is 20.**
$$\frac{8 \text{ units}}{\text{hr}} = \frac{100 \text{ mL}}{40 \text{ units}} = \frac{800 \text{ mL}}{40 \text{ hr}} = 20 \text{ mL/hr}$$

9. **The correct answer is (2).** The decreased circulation to the kidney and reduced liver function tend to allow drugs to accumulate and have toxic effects.

10. **The correct answer is (3).** The ointment is placed in the lower conjunctival sac so it will not scratch the eye itself and will get well distributed.

SUMMING IT UP

- There will be questions on the exam about drugs that have important nursing implications (such as those that increase bleeding) and require a specific assessment before administration with special client education.

- Drugs have one or more desired actions for which they are administered.

- Drug forms—liquid, transdermal, solid, or semisolid drug forms.

- Observe the five rights: right route of administration, right time, right client, right drug, right dosage and documentation.

answers exercises

Maternal/Newborn Nursing

OVERVIEW

- Basic concepts
- Anatomy
- Physiology
- Childbearing
- Maternal changes during pregnancy
- Signs of pregnancy
- Antepartum care
- Labor and delivery
- Postpartum
- Newborn
- Summing it up

BASIC CONCEPTS

Maternity care today is client- and family-centered, offering choices to mothers about their delivery and including the father, siblings, and grandparents as part of the family unit. This care is sensitive to the cultural background of the family and takes into account practices and preferences that stem from their cultural background.

In pregnancy, preventive care is emphasized due to the importance of prenatal care in preventing poor pregnancy outcomes. Scientific advances have brought ethical questions about the status of surrogate parents and assisted reproductive technologies to the forefront, as well as the problem of the long-term outlook for extremely premature infants who are resuscitated.

ANATOMY

A. **External structures**
   1. **Visible Organs of the Vulva**
      a. Mons pubis—covered with pubic hair—located over pubic bones, serves a protective function
      b. Labia major and labia minora—two pairs of tissue surrounding the outer part of the vulva
      c. Vestibule—surrounded by the labia, it contains the vaginal opening and urethra
      d. Vaginal opening
      e. Clitoris—erectile tissue analagous to the penis

    f. Urethral orifice
    g. Perineum—the region of the genital area between the vulva and the anus; this
        is the location of an episiotomy if performed during birth
2. **Breasts**—mammary glands
    a. Function is to secrete milk for infant—lactation
    b. After delivery, the withdrawal of estrogen and progesterone due to the expul-
        sion of the placenta cause prolactin to be produced, which stimulates milk
        formation; oxytocin is a hormone that stimulates the release of milk

B. Internal Reproductive Organs
    1. **Located in the Pelvic Cavity**
        a. Ovaries—female gonads located on each side of the uterus. Functions include
            (1) Development and release of the ovum (egg)
            (2) Secretion of the hormones estrogen and progesterone
        b. Fallopian tubes
            (1) Carry the ovum from the ovary to the uterus
            (2) Fimbriae sweep ovum into the tube
        c. Uterus
            (1) Hollow pear-shaped organ that stretches and enlarges during pregnancy to
                 support the fetus
            (2) Other functions include menstruation and expelling of the fetus during
                 labor
            (3) Divisons of the uterus are: fundus—uppermost portion; corpus—the body;
                 cervix—lower third that exits into the vagina through the cervical os
        d. Vagina
            (1) Curved tube leading from the uterus to the vestibule
            (2) Functions as a passageway for menstrual flow, organ of copulation, and
                 birth canal

C. Pelvis
    1. **Bones**—support and protect pelvic contents
        a. Sacrum—wedge-shaped bone formed by the fusion of five vertebrae
        b. Coccyx—small triangular bone at bottom of the vertebral column
        c. Innominate bones
            (1) Ilium—upper prominence of the hip
            (2) Ischium—L-shaped bone below the ischium. Distance between the ischial
                 spines is the shortest diameter of the pelvic cavity.
            (3) Pubis—slightly bowed front portion of the innominate bone. The pubis
                 meet at the front of the pelvis to make up the joint called the symphysis
                 pubis. Below the symphysis is a triangular space called the pubic arch,
                 under which the fetal head passes during birth.
    2. **Pelvic floor**—muscular floor of bony pelvis, supports pelvic contents
        a. Levator ani—major portion, made up of four muscles
            (1) Ileococcygeus
            (2) Puboccygeus
            (3) Puborectalis
            (4) Pubovaginalis
        b. Coccygeal muscle—underlies sacrospinous ligament, a thin muscular sheet that
            helps the levator ani support the pelvic contents
    3. **Pelvic shapes**—vaginal birth is never ruled out because of pelvic type without a
        trial of labor
        a. Android—narrow, heart shaped, similar to shape of male pelvis—not favorable
            for vaginal birth
        b. Anthropoid—widest from front to back—usually adequate for vaginal birth

    c. Platypelloid—widest from side to side—not favorable for vaginal birth

    d. Gynecoid—"classic" female pelvis—approximately 50 percent of women and the best for vaginal birth

PHYSIOLOGY

A. Menstrual Cycle—during puberty, menarche, the beginning of menstruation occurs; consists of two interrelated cycles: the menstrual cycle and the ovarian cycle

  1. **Four Phases of the Menstrual Cycle**

    a. Menstrual Phase (days 1–5)—shedding of the endometrium; low estrogen levels, scanty cervical mucus

    b. Proliferative phase (days 6–14)—endometrium thickens, increasing estrogen, and cervical mucus becomes more clear, thinner, and more elastic. It is favorable to sperm.

    c. Secretory phase (days 15–26)—Estrogen levels fall and progesterone increases. Endometrium becomes thicker and secretes glycogen to prepare for the fertilized ovum.

    d. Ischemic phase—Levels of estrogen and progesterone fall. Spiral arteries, which nourish the endometrium, vasoconstrict causing the endometrium and blood to be shed, which begins the next menstrual phase.

  2. **Ovarian Cycle**

    a. Follicular phase (days 1–14)—Ovarian follicle (and ovum) mature under the influence of FSH and LH. At first, several follicles develop, but eventually one outgrows the others. The follicles secrete estrogen, which accelerates maturation. Estrogen affects endometrium, and ovulation occurs after the LH surge.

    b. Luteal phase (days 15–28)—After ovulation, the ovarian follicle becomes the corpus luteum and produces progesterone, which suppresses the growth of other follicles. The corpus luteum degenerates after a week or so, and, if fertilization doesn't occur, the hormone levels drop, the endometrium is shed, and the menstrual flow starts.

B. Sexual Response—Four Phases

  1. **Excitement**—vaginal lubrication and vasocongestion of external genitals

  2. **Plateau**—vagina lengthens, cervix and uterus become elevated, clitoris retracts

  3. **Orgasm**—multiple contractions of pelvic muscles

  4. **Resolution**—body gradually returns to unaroused state

CHILDBEARING

A. Conception

  1. One ovum is fertilized by one sperm (although approximately 300 million are deposited in the vagina), and a fertilized ovum—zygote—results. Each gamete (sperm or ovum) has 23 chromosomes (due to meiosis or reduction division). The zygote contains 46 chromosomes, half from the maternal gamete and half from the sperm.

  2. Sex of child determined at time of fertilization by male gamete, or sperm, depending on whether it carries an X or Y chromosome. The ovum only has X chromosomes.

  3. After fertilization, the fertilized egg travels through the fallopian tubes to the uterus.

B. Fetal Development

1. **Implantation**—occurs approximately seven days after fertilization
   a. Membranes called the chorion and amnion form at implantation.
   b. Embryo floats in a cavity formed by the amnion.
   c. The chorion encloses the amnion, and later fuses with it.
2. **Embryo**—from time of implantation to eight weeks from last menstrual period
   a. Period of organogenesis.
   b. Most vulnerable time to teratogens, which can result in birth defects.
3. **Fetus**—from nine weeks to term
   a. By nine weeks major organ systems have formed.
   b. They continue to develop and mature during the fetal stage.
4. **Amniotic fluid**—forms in the amniotic cavity. By term, there will be 500–1,000 mL of fluid.
   a. Contains fetal urine, lanugo, epithelial cells.
   b. Functions to protect fetus from injury and maintain optimal temperature.

Development of Fetus (lunar months)

1 month
- Body systems have rudimentary form.
- Cardiovascular system is functioning.

2 months
- Head appears large.
- Facial features are becoming distinct.
- Some fetal movement is noticeable.

3 months
- Fingers and toes are formed.
- Eyes are fused.
- Fetus swallows.
- Sex is distinguishable.

4 months
- Lanugo is over body.
- Face has human appearance.
- Intestine contains meconium.

5 months
- Permanent teeth buds develop.
- Fetal movements are felt by mother.
- Fetal heart rate can be heard with fetoscope.

6 months
- Eyebrows and eyelashes are formed.
- Fat is being deposited.
- Head is more in proportion to body.

7 months
- Immature, but may be viable if born now.
- Skin is covered with vernex.

8 months
- Nails are firm.
- Lanugo begins to thin.
- Fetus is likely to survive if born now.

9 months
- More fat is present.
- Weight is about 5 pounds, length is about 18 inches.

10 months
- Fetus is full term.
- Skin is pink and smooth.
- Fetus is approximately 20 inches long and 7 pounds.

C. **Fetal Circulation**
1. **Fetal Arteries**—carry unoxygenated blood—two arteries in the umbilical cord
2. **Fetal Veins**—carry oxygenated blood—one vein in the umbilical cord
3. **Ductus Venosus**—is a passage between the umbilical vein and the inferior vena cava, bypassing the fetal liver, which is not used to exchange waste
4. **Ductus Arteriosus**—blood passes from pulmonary artery to the descending aorta, without passing through the lungs
5. **Foramen Ovale**—an opening between the right and left atrium that lets blood flow from the right atrium to the left without going to the lungs
    a. After birth, when the lungs become functional, the ductus venosus, ductus arteriosus, and umbilical vein and arteries close and become ligaments, and the foramen ovale closes.

D. **Due Date Calculation**
1. **EDC** (estimated date of confinement)
    a. 280 days from last menstrual period (LMP)
    b. 266 days from the time of ovulation
    c. 40 weeks
    d. 9 calendar and 10 lunar months
2. **Nageles Rule**—to obtain due date, count back three months from LMP and add seven days: LMP—January 1; EDC—October 8

E. **Pregnancy Tests**
1. **HCG**
    a. Blood test that measures human chorionic gonadotropin, a hormone secreted by the placenta
    b. Can be positive two days after missed period
    c. Radioimmunoassay (RIA)—positive eight days after ovulation or six days before scheduled menses; results in one hour

MATERNAL CHANGES DURING PREGNANCY

A. **Physiological**
1. **Cardiovascular**
    a. Blood volume increases 50 percent.
    b. Pulse rate increases 10 bpm.
    c. Blood clotting factors increase.
    d. White blood cell count increases to an average of 15,000.
    e. BP lowers 5–10 mmHg in first and second trimesters, returns to prepregnancy. in third
2. **Respiratory**
    a. Oxygen consumption increases during second half of pregnancy.
    b. Enlarging uterus presses on diaphragm, causing shortness of breath near term.
3. **Gastrointestinal**
    a. Nausea and vomiting in first trimester are common.
    b. Progesterone slows GI transit time; constipation and heartburn are common.
    c. Gums swell and bleed easily.
4. **Urinary**
    a. Frequency is typical during first and third trimester.
    b. Kidney filtration rate increases approximately 50 percent.
    c. Water retention increases as pregnancy progresses.
    d. Dilation of ureters increases susceptibility to urinary tract infections.

5. **Skin**
   a. Increased pigmentation
      (1) Areola, nipples, vulva, and linea nigra
   b. Chloasma (mask of pregnancy) may develop.
   c. Stretch marks are common.
6. **Musculoskeletal**
   a. Pelvic joints relax due to relaxin and progesterone.
   b. Posture changes—exaggerated lumbosacral curve.
7. **Metabolism**
   a. Average weight gain 25–35 pounds.
   b. Pattern of weight gain
      (1) First trimester—3–4 pounds
      (2) Second and third trimesters—1 pound/week
8. **Reproductive**
   a. External
      (1) Increased vascularity and enlargement
      (2) Vulvar varicosities and hemorrhoids possible
   b. Uterus
      (1) Enlarges and thickens
      (2) Braxton-Hicks contractions—irregular and painless
      (3) Softening of lower uterine segment (Hegar's sign)
   c. Cervix
      (1) Softening (Goodell's sign)
      (2) Formation of mucus plug to provide a barrier against ascending infection
   d. Vagina
      (1) Increased vaginal secretions
      (2) Color changes to bluish tone (Chadwick's sign)
   e. Breasts
      (1) Increase in size, tingling, tenderness, feelings of fullness
      (2) Superficial veins prominent, darkening of areola
      (3) Leakage of colostrum by third trimester

B. Psychological
   1. Ambivalence common in early pregnancy
   2. Acceptance gives increased sense of well-being, fewer physical discomforts
   3. Introversion typical of second trimester—focus on self and baby
   4. Mood swings due to hormone changes common throughout pregnancy
   5. Body image changes—woman's view of herself and how others see her

SIGNS OF PREGNANCY

A. Presumptive (subjective)
   1. **Amenorrhea**
      a. Breast tenderness and enlargement
   2. **Nausea and Vomiting**
   3. **Urinary Frequency**
   4. **Quickening**
   5. **Increased Skin Pigmentation**

B. Probable (objective)
   1. **Hegar's Sign**—softening of lower uterine segment
   2. **Chadwick's Sign**—bluish vaginal color

3. **Goodell's Sign**—softening of cervix
4. **Ballottement**—feeling the fetus rebound when pushed
5. **Enlarged Abdomen**
6. **Braxton-Hicks Contractions**
7. **Positive Pregnancy Test**

C. **Positive (diagnostic)**
   1. **Fetal Heartbeat Heard**—Doppler (10–12 weeks)
   2. **Fetoscope** (18–20 weeks)
   3. **Fetal Movements Palpated**
   4. **Ultrasound Visualization of Fetus**
   5. **Fetal Heart Tracing by EKG**

Terms

Gravida: A pregnancy, regardless of duration
Para: Pregnancy that continues to period of viability
Primigravida: Pregnant for the first time
Multigravida: Pregnant more than once
Multipara: Given birth to more than one child (Twins count as one in this system, because it refers to the pregnancy, not the fetus.)

GTPAL Recording Method
   G = number of pregnancies
   T = number of infants born at term (over 37 weeks)
   P = number of infants born preterm (less than 37 weeks)
   A = number of miscarriages or abortions
   L = number of living children

ANTEPARTUM CARE

A. **Initial visit**
   1. **Medical History**
      a. Social habits
      b. Communicable disease history
      c. Previous pregnancies and outcome
      d. Menstrual history
      e. Surgical history
      f. Family health history
   2. **Physical Exam**
      a. Vital signs, blood pressure
      b. Pelvic exam
      c. Breast exam
      d. Speculum exam and cultures
   3. **Laboratory Tests**
      a. Urine for glucose, protein
      b. Routine prenatal labs: usually include blood type, antibody screen, hemoglobin and hematocrit, VDRL, HIV, hepatitis

B. Subsequent Care
  1. **Follow-Up Schedule**
    a. Monthly exams for first seven months
    b. Every two weeks until week 36
    c. Weekly until term
  2. **Follow-Up Routine for Prenatal Visits**
    a. Urine dip test for protein and glucose
    b. Vital signs, including blood pressure
    c. Weight
    d. Fundal height measurement
    e. Listen to fetal heart tones
    f. Answer questions and provide teaching
  3. **Health Teaching**
    a. Elimination of harmful substances and medications (includes alcohol and cigarettes)
    b. Nutrition—increase diet by approximately 300 calories from nutritious sources; protein increase to 60 grams; prenatal vitamins
    c. Exercise—avoid becoming overheated, moderation important
    d. Work—avoid long periods of standing, severe physical strain, heavy lifting

---

Tests of Fetal Well-Being

Ultrasound: Uses high-frequency sound waves to assess fetal heart, growth, movement, breathing activity, location of placenta, anomalies, etc. (done any time in pregnancy)

Nonstress Test: Monitor response of the fetal heart rate to fetal movement (third trimester)

Contraction Stress Test: Monitor response of the fetal heart rate to contractions (37+ weeks)

Amniocentesis: Analyze fetal chromosomes and determine fetal lung maturity (after 14th week)

Triple-Screen: Screen for the presence of neural tube defects or Down's syndrome (15–18 weeks)

Biophysical Profile (BPP): Ultrasound evaluation of fetal tone, movement, breathing, amniotic fluid, plus a nonstress test (two points each)

---

    e. Discuss common discomforts of pregnancy and measures for relief
      (1) **Heartburn:** Eat small, frequent meals, sit up for an hour after eating, avoid fatty foods
      (2) **Varicose veins:** Avoid standing for long periods, use support hose
      (3) **Hemorrhoids:** Walk, increase fiber and fluids in diet, take warm sitz baths
      (4) **Backache:** Wear low-heeled shoes, use proper posture, do pelvic-tilt exercise
      (5) **Leg cramps:** Dorsiflex the foot to stop, take magnesium
      (6) **Nausea and vomiting:** Small frequent meals, dry crackers in the morning
  4. **Teach Client Danger Signs to Report**

Danger Signs of Pregnancy

1. Escape of fluid from the vagina or bleeding
2. Visual disturbances
3. Swelling of face or hands
4. Severe headache, abdominal pain
5. Absence of fetal movement
6. Persistent vomiting
7. Fever and chills

C. Pregnancy Complications

1. **Abortion**—expulsion of the fetus before it is viable; may be spontaneous or induced
   a. Risk factors for spontaneous abortion: fetal abnormalities, maternal structural problems of the reproductive tract, infection, endocrine disturbances
   b. Treatment
      (1) Assess bleeding, contractions, passage of tissue, provide emotional support
      (2) Administer Rhogam if mother is Rh negative
   c. Aftercare—assess for infection and increased bleeding
2. **Ectopic Pregnancy**—a pregnancy that develops outside of the uterus; 90 percent are tubal
   a. Assessment—ultrasound or quantitative hCG. Ruptured tube causes sudden severe abdominal pain, possible referred shoulder pain as abdomen fills with blood.
   b. Treatment: laparoscopy, laparotomy, methotrexate
   c. Nursing care: provide care for shock, prepare for surgery (permit, IV, O_2, blood)
   d. Administer Rhogam if mother is Rh negative
3. **Hyperemesis Gravidarum**—severe, persistent vomiting during pregnancy
   a. Assessment—weight loss, dehydration, electrolyte imbalances, increased BUN, possible ketoacidosis; often, psychological component
   b. Treatment—frequent small feedings, dry foods preferred; antiemetics, may require hospitalizattion with IV hydration
   c. Nursing care—careful I & O, dipstick urine for ketones, reduce stimuli and restrict visitors if needed. Monitor fetal heart tones.
4. **Placenta Previa**—the placenta partially or completely covers the internal os of the cervix
   a. Assessment—ultrasound diagnosis, painless vaginal bleeding after the seventh month without known cause
   b. Treatment—hospitalization, assessment of fetal maturity, betamethasone injections to accelerate fetal lung maturation, no vaginal exams, cesarean delivery
   c. Nursing care—antepartum: count perineal pads, monitor for hemorrhage. Provide emotional support and explain procedures, monitor for fetal heart tones. Postpartum as for C-Section (C/S) delivery.
5. **Abruptio Placentae**—separation of the placenta from the uterus before the baby's birth.
   a. Assessment—main sign is vaginal bleeding with abdominal pain. May be concealed signs—cramp-like pain, uterine tenderness, absence of normal contraction pattern. Fetal heart tones may indicate bradycardia or be absent.
   b. Treatment—for blood loss and shock. If bleeding moderate, rupture membranes

to hasten delivery and monitor bleeding. Immediate C/S if severe bleeding. Bedrest.

c. Nursing care—monitor contractions, fetal heart tones, vital signs, I & O. After delivery, monitor closely for hemorrhage, observe for anuria (a sign of acute tubular necrosis).

6. **Pregnancy-Induced Hypertension**

a. Assessment—symptoms vary with the severity of the disease. Presence of the three symptoms (see NOTE); elevated liver enzymes, oliguria, headache, blurred vision, epigastric pain, vomiting, hyperreflexia

b. Treatment

(1) Mild: usually remains at home, extra rest, increased fluid intake, weight checks, BP checks

(2) Moderate: antihypertensive, sedative drugs, increased protein, attempt to increase diuresis by promoting adequate perfusion, bed rest, $MgSO_4$

c. Monitor vital signs, BP, deep tendon reflexes, observe for CNS irritability. Record I & O, weight checks, test urine for protein, limit visitors, maintain seizure precautions. If client is on $MgSO_4$, keep the antidote, calcium gluconate, in the room.

> **NOTE**
>
> Triad of Symptoms: Hypertension, Edema, Proteinuria

Pregnancy-Induced Hypertension

Mild Preeclampsia	Severe Preeclampsia	Eclampsia
Increased BP (systolic increase 30 mmHg convulsions over baseline; diastolic ↑15	BP 160/110	Tonic-clonic
	Proteinuria—3–4+	Possible coma
	Very edematous	Renal shutdown
1+ proteinuria	Elevated BUN, serum creatinine, uric acid	
Edema, especially of hands and face	Oliguria (> 400 cc/24 hrs)	
	Cerebral or visual disturbances	
	Epigastric pain, vomiting	

7. **Gestational Diabetes**—diabetes diagnosed during pregnancy. Hormonal changes of pregnancy cause increased resistance to insulin.

a. Assessment—woman may be asymptomatic or have the following:

(1) Polyuria, polydipsia, weight loss, polyphagia

(2) Elevated blood and urine glucose levels

(3) GCT (glucose challenge test) and GTT (glucose tolerance test)

b. Between 24–28 weeks of pregnancy, women are screened for diabetes. They are given a 50 g glucose load and then tested in 1 hour—if the serum glucose is over 140 mg/dL, a diagnostic GTT is given.

c. For the GTT, a fasting blood glucose is drawn when the woman arrives. She then drinks a 100 g glucose solution and her blood sugars are tested at 1, 2, and 3 hours. If the client's blood sugar is equal to or higher than the following readings, she is diagnosed as a gestational diabetic.

(1) Fasting—105 mg/dL

(2) 1 hour—190 mg/dL

(3) 2 hours—165 mg/dL

(4) 3 hours—145 mg/dL

    d. Treatment
       (1) An 1,800- to 2,200-calorie diabetic exchange diet
       (2) Regular planned exercise
       (3) Blood sugar monitoring, three to four times a day
       (4) Insulin injections if blood sugar is not maintained between 60–120. Human insulin should be used. Oral hypoglycemics cannot be used during pregnancy or lactation.
       (5) Diabetic control plan must be changed periodically, since insulin requirements, which are low during the first trimester, increase in the second and third.
    e. Nursing care
       (1) Inform client of increased risk of PIH, infection, polyhydramnios, and measures to decrease risk.
       (2) Discuss possibility of macrosomic infant, hypoglycemic infant, and increased risk of respiratory distress. Emphasize that blood sugar control will help protect her and her baby.
       (3) Monitor fetal well-being frequently, nonstress tests, kick counts, and biophysical profile.

LABOR AND DELIVERY

A. Beginning of Labor
  1. **Early Signs**
    a. Lightening—fetal head descends into the pelvis. Mother can breathe easier, but urinary frequency is more problematic. May be two weeks to a few days before labor for primips, usually not until labor begins for subsequent births.
    b. Increased Braxton-Hicks contractions may be confused with labor but do not dilate cervix.
       (1) Braxton-Hicks are usually not painful.
       (2) They often stop or start with a change in activity.
       (3) They do not continue to get stronger and closer together.
    c. Weight loss often occurs near term, due to a change in hormones.
    d. Cervix becomes softer and somewhat dilated and may be 1, 2, or more centimeters dilated by the start of labor.
    e. A discharge of blood and mucus from the mucus plug usually occurs within one to two days of labor.
    f. Many women report a sudden burst of energy one or two days before labor (said to be nesting instinct by some).
    g. Spontaneous Rupture of Amniotic Membranes (SROM). Gush or trickle of fluid. Loss of a barrier to infection. Many physicians will induce labor within 24 hours of SROM.
  2. **First Stage** (dilatation of the cervix)
    a. Begins with labor contractions and ends with full (10 cm) dilatation of the cervix
       (1) Unlike Braxton-Hicks, labor contractions are regular, increase in intensity and frequency, and the pain tends to radiate from the back to the abdomen.
       (2) The contractions often increase in intensity with walking.
       (3) They result in cervical dilatation.
    b. Three phases of first stage
       (1) Latent phase (0–3 cm)
         (a) Mild to moderate intensity pain

       (b) Contraction duration 30–60 seconds; start approximately 10–15 minutes apart, and end 5 minutes apart

       (c) Mood often excited

       (d) Most variable duration, usually 6 to 8 hours for primips

     (2) Active phase (3–7 cm)

       (a) Pain is moderate to strong intensity

       (b) Contractions last approximate 60 seconds at decreasing intervals—from 5 minutes apart to about every 2 to 3 minutes

       (c) Serious mood

       (d) Duration approximately 2 to 3 hours

     (3) Transition phase (7 cm to full dilatation)

       (a) Intense contractions

       (b) Contractions last 60–90 seconds, frequency increasing from every 3 minutes to every 90 seconds

       (c) Phase usually lasts 1 to 2 hours

       (d) Mood is irritable, restless, feeling out of control

3. **Second Stage** (delivery of baby)

  a. Starts at 10 cm cervical dilatation

  b. Ends with delivery of baby

  c. May be short—one contraction/push to several hours in length

  d. Typical primip duration is 1 hour to 2 hours. Contractions are further apart—from 2–5 minutes

  e. Mother is serious, working hard to push baby through the birth canal—effort is more prominent than pain during this stage

4. **Third Stage** (delivery of placenta)

  a. Starts with baby's birth

  b. Ends with delivery of placenta

  c. Lasts 5–30 minutes—contractions are milder and the mother is usually so involved with the baby that they are barely noticed

  d. Mother is usually excited and happy

5. **Fourth Stage** (maternal stabilization)

  a. Begins with delivery of placenta

  b. Ends with maternal stabilization—approximately 1 to 4 hours

  c. The first hour is most critical in terms of possible complications/bleeding

  d. Best time for interacting with infant—breastfeeding should be initiated at this time unless mother plans to formula-feed

B. Nursing Care During Labor

  1. **First Stage**

    a. Admission—check vital signs, fetal heart tones, and frequency of contractions (often 20-minute monitor strip done), dilatation of cervix, determine if membrane is intact (amniotic fluid turns nitrazine paper blue, exhibits ferning on microscopic exam), encourage woman to void—check for protein and glucose, draw admission bloodwork, complete forms; start IV if ordered, usually npo with ice chips.

    b. Check client every 15 to 30 minutes or more often depending on progress of labor. Monitor frequency of contractions, fetal heart tones, blood pressure. Check temperature every 4 hours if intact membranes, 2 hours if ruptured. Evaluate labor progress—dilatation and effacement prn. (Hospital protocols may vary for these evaluations—administration of pitocin increases their frequency.)

    c. If membranes rupture, note time, color, and odor; check fetal heart tones.

    d. Encourage client to ambulate unless membranes are ruptured, and encourage voiding q 1 to 2 hours.

e. Keep client and support person informed of progress, provide comfort measures.

f. Administer analgesia or assist with administration of anesthesia as ordered/requested.

2. **Second Stage**

a. Check FHR q 5 minutes or after each push.

b. Check BP q 15 minutes.

c. Support client's efforts; keep her and partner informed of progress.

d. Position instrument table. Assist physician or midwife.

e. Note time and position of birth.

3. **Third Stage**

a. Note time of delivery of placenta.

b. Administer pitocin if ordered.

c. Assist MD with stitching episiotomy, infant care, prn, etc.

d. Assign APGAR score.

Infant Sign	0	1	2
Heart rate	None	<100	>100
Respirations	Absent	Slow, irregular	Good, crying
Muscle tone	Flaccid	Some flexion	Active motion
Reflexes	No response	Grimace	Cry
Color	Blue, pale	Pink, extremities blue	Pink

4. **Fourth Stage**

a. Palpate fundus and check blood pressure q 15 minutes and prn for the first hour. Massage uterus if not firm. (Uterus displaced to one side—often accompanied by increased bleeding and less uterine tone—usually means a full bladder.) Catheterize or have client void prn.

b. Check vital signs.

c. Check lochia for color, amount, and characteristics of flow.

d. Check episiotomy and perineum for bleeding, unusual redness, and swelling.

e. Ice pack to perineum, warm blankets.

f. Transfer to postpartum floor (if applicable) when stable.

g. Assess intake and output for first 24 hours until mother voiding well.

C. Obstetrical Monitoring

1. **Electronic Fetal Monitor**

a. Provides continuous readout of fetal heart rate and contraction pattern

b. Ultrasound transducer picks of motion of fetal heart valves ⇒ external recording of fetal heart rate

c. External pressure—sensitive monitoring of uterine fundus ⇒ external monitoring of contractions

(1) Internal monitoring with fetal scalp electrode and intrauterine pressure monitor may be done in high-risk situations

2. **Monitoring Fetal Heart Rate** (FHR)

a. Normal rate is 120–160 bpm. Baseline FHR is rate between contractions.

b. Variability (desirable)

(1) Irregularity of fetal heart rate over 10 minutes ⇒ long-term variability

(2) Fluctuations of FHR from beat to beat ⇒ short-term variability

(3) Variability greater than 6–10 bpm is good; 3–5 is minimal; 0–2 is absent. (Classification may vary by institution and by new terminology instituted over time.)

(4) *Early deceleration:* 10–20 beat deceleration that mirrors a contraction; caused by head compression

(5) *Late deceleration:* 10–0 beat deceleration that begins after a contraction has started and ends after it is finished; usually indicates uteroplacental insufficiency—fetal distress

(6) *Variable deceleration:* Non-uniform in shape and irregular timing—usually indicates cord compression

(7) *Bradycardia:* a persistent (greater than 10-minute) drop of 20 bpm or under 110 bpm may indicate fetal distress

(8) *Tachycardia:* a FHR of greater than 160 bpm for 10 minutes or more; may indicate fetal distress or maternal or fetal infection

(9) *Acceleration:* a FHR increase of 15 bpm for at least 15 seconds; considered a "reassuring" sign indicating fetal well-being

D. Complications of Labor and Delivery

1. **Dystocia/Dysfunctional Labor**—can be caused by large baby; cephalopelvic disproportion—head is too large for the pelvis; an unusual presentation—breech; abnormalities of the pelvis, uterus, or cervix; or ineffective contractions

   a. If the signs of abnormal labor persist, or if fetal distress occurs, a cesarean section is usually performed.

   b. This is the most common reason given for an unplanned C/S.

2. **Premature Labor and Delivery**—when infant is delivered after the age of viability but before 37 weeks. Incidence between 5–10 percent of pregnancies.

   a. Causes may be cervical incompetence, infection, multiple births, preeclampsia, or placental disorders. Many are for unknown reasons.

   b. Medical management

      (1) Attempt to arrest labor by Ritodrine, Brethine, or $MgSO_4$. Often put client on bed rest.

      (2) Administration of betamethasone, if labor progresses, to help accelerate fetal lung maturation

   c. Nursing interventions

      (1) Monitor client with electronic fetal monitor, as ordered.

      (2) Help client maintain bed rest on left side, if possible.

      (3) Monitor client for signs and symptoms of labor and fetal movement.

      (4) Administer medications, as ordered, and inform client of expected side effects.

      (5) Help client with diversional activities and other means of tolerating prolonged bed rest, if indicated.

3. **Prolapsed Umbilical Cord**

   a. Cord displacement near or in front of presenting part; may occur when membranes rupture or after

   b. More common in premature labor, unengaged fetus, breech presentation

   c. Emergency—cord compression leads to fetal hypoxia, CNS damage, and death

   d. Nursing interventions

      (1) Monitor FHR after membrane ruptures; assess for prolapsed cord if bradycardia present.

      (2) If prolapsed cord present, press presenting part farther into vagina to reduce pressure on the cord. Place client in knee-chest or high Trendelenburg position.

      (3) Administer oxygen and prepare for emergency C/S.

      (4) If cord is outside vagina, cover with sterile gauze moistened with sterile saline.

      (5) Notify or have someone else notify RN and provider.

ALERT!

If signs of fetal distress occur, the nurse should change the mother's position, stop pitocin if it is being administered, increase the IV rate, and administer oxygen. The occurrence of these signs and corrective measures taken must be charted and reported to the RN at once and to the provider immediately if unchanged, or later if improved by nursing actions taken.

4. **Premature Rupture of Membranes**
   a. Loss of amniotic fluid prior to the onset of labor
   b. Associated dangers include prolapsed cord, infection, potential for preterm delivery
   c. Nursing interventions
      (1) Monitor maternal/fetal vital signs.
      (2) Observe for signs of infection, signs of labor
         (a) If signs of infection, administer antibiotics.
         (b) Induction of labor not necessary if no infection present.
         (c) If fetus is close to term, labor may be induced within 24 hours of membrane rupture to minimize the chance of infection, which is more common more than 24 hours after membranes have ruptured.

5. **Amniotic Fluid Embolism**
   a. Amniotic fluid escaping into the maternal circulation—may happen during period of intense contractions
   b. Emergency—maternal and fetal death likely
   c. Assessment—sudden onset of respiratory distress, hypotension, chest pain, signs of shock, bleeding, cyanosis, pulmonary edema
   d. Nursing interventions
      (1) Life support—oxygen, CPR if cardiac arrest, insert IV, administration of medications as ordered
      (2) Prepare for emergency C/S to deliver infant

6. **Induction of Labor**
   a. Reasons—postmature pregnancy, preeclampsia, eclampsia, premature rupture of membranes, maternal or fetal condition that would make continuation of pregnancy dangerous
   b. Methods
      (1) Amniotomy—may work if labor is imminent anyway
      (2) Pitocin—to induce contractions
      (3) Prostaglandin in gel or suppository form to "ripen" cervix and induce contractions
   c. Nursing interventions
      (1) Assist with amniotomy, if performed.
      (2) After prostaglandin administered, monitor for contractions, diarrhea, and other side effects.
      (3) Administer pitocin and monitor mother and fetus continuously. Discontinue pitocin if signs of fetal distress.
      (4) Notify RN and/or provider of any complications.

E. **Analgesia and Anesthesia in Labor**
   1. Systemic *analgesics* given in labor are primarily narcotics, such as Demerol, and medications to potentiate their effect, such as Vistaril and Phenergan. Both Vistaril and Phenergan are antihistamines that have a sedating effect, as well as antiemetics, which help to counteract the nausea many people experience as a side effect of narcotics.
      a. Given IM or IV. Excessive dosages or administration close to delivery can cause the infant to be depressed at delivery.
      b. A narcotic antagonist such as Narcan may be given to reverse these effects.
   2. The most common and popular form of *anesthesia* in labor is the epidural. It is a regional anesthetic administered into the epidural space of the spine in the lumbar area.
      a. Typical ingredients are a local anesthetic, such as Marcaine, and a narcotic to help augment the pain relief with less numbness and paralysis
      b. Side effects and nursing considerations

(1) Client must receive 1 to 2 liters of fluid prior to administration, because the epidural has a hypotensive effect.

(2) If given too early the epidural may slow labor (may slow labor even if not given too early). Pitocin is often given to counteract this effect.

(3) It is often allowed to wear off before the time for the mother to push, since it is more difficult for her if she is numb. If it has not worn off, she may require a lot of coaching and/or forceps or vacuum assistance to deliver the baby.

(4) A "spinal" headache is possible if there is any leakage of spinal fluid during insertion. Measures to help alleviate this are bed rest (the headache worsens when the client sits up), caffeine for vasoconstriction, fluids, and analgesics. If necessary, a "blood patch" may be administered in which some of the client's blood is withdrawn from a vein and inserted into the spine to restore volume. This eliminates the pain almost immediately.

F. Operative Obstetrics
1. **Episiotomy**
   a. Incision into perineum to enlarge the vaginal opening; lidocaine or other local anesthetic usually given
   b. Two types
      (1) Midline or median—from posterior vaginal opening toward anal sphincter
         (a) Most common, less discomfort
         (b) Problem: extension into anal sphincter
      (2) Mediolateral—posterior vaginal opening to left or right at 45-degree angle
         (a) More uncomfortable
         (b) Can extend without damaging anal sphincter
   c. Side-lying position minimizes strain on the perineum and may reduce need for episiotomy
   d. Nursing interventions
      (1) Apply ice packs to perineum first 24 hours.
      (2) Observe for signs of infection.
      (3) Suggest kegel exercise to promote healing.
      (4) Administer warm sitz baths.
      (5) Teach client hygiene with peri bottle.
2. **Cesarean Birth**—delivery of the baby through an incision in the abdomen and uterus
   a. Indications
      (1) Cephalopelvic disproportion (most frequent reason)
      (2) Fetal distress
      (3) Breech presentation—especially in primip
      (4) Placenta previa, abruption of placenta
      (5) Prolapsed cord
      (6) Previous C/S with vertical incision
      (7) Obstetric emergencies
   b. Types of incisions
      (1) Vertical or Classic
         (a) Used when speed is important
         (b) Greater amount maternal bleeding
         (c) Increased chance of scar rupture during a subsequent labor or pregnancy
      (2) Low cervical transverse incision above pubic hairline
         (a) Most common method—takes longer (need to deflect bladder)
         (b) Less maternal bleeding
         (c) Possibility of vaginal birth

  c. Nursing interventions
   (1) Preoperative care: shave/prep, insertion of foley catheter, IV insertion
   (2) Documentation including consent
   (3) Postoperative care (general surgical care and postpartum care)

POSTPARTUM

A. Physical Changes—Reproductive System
1. **Uterus**
   a. Involution—returns to pre-pregnant state. Fundus descends by one finger-breadth each day after delivery. By six weeks, it is close to pre-pregnant size.
   b. Lochia—uterine discharge of blood and waste from decidua. May persist for three or more weeks.
   c. Placental site—blood vessels become compressed/thrombosed.
2. **Cervix**
   a. Internal os closes by two weeks
   b. External os remains more open—looks like a slit
3. **Vagina**
   a. Rugae reappear in two weeks
   b. Remains slightly larger—close to prepregnant size six to eight weeks after delivery
   c. Normal mucus production returns with ovulation
4. **Perineum**
   a. Episiotomy initial healing by two to three weeks; may take four to six months to heal completely.
   b. Hemorrhoids are common.
   c. Muscle tone restored by Kegel exercises.
5. **Menstruation**
   a. Time of return is variable.
   b. Lactating women resume menses within twelve weeks to eighteen months.
   c. Nonlactating women begin to menstruate from six weeks to six months.
6. **Breasts**
   a. Vascularity and size increased approximately day 3—milk "comes in."
   b. If not breastfeeding, engorgement subsides in 24–36 hours.
   c. Secrete colostrum first two to three days, becomes transitional and then "true" milk after this.
   d. Oxytocin releases milk, prolactin produces more milk. Both are secreted in response to suckling.

B. Physiological Changes—Other Systems
1. **Cardiovascular**
   a. Cardiac output returns to normal in two to four weeks.
   b. Cardiac load increases.
2. **Hematologic**
   a. Average blood loss at delivery less than 500 mL—more is considered hemorrhage.
   b. Blood volume returns to pre-pregnant within three to four weeks.
   c. Hematocrit increases immediately after delivery, returns to pre-pregnant level in four to five weeks.
   d. White blood cell count may increase during first ten days.

NOTE

Lochia changes from rubra (first three days), to serosa (ten days), to alba (two weeks). May temporarily go back to rubra with increased activity.

        e. Clotting factors, which were elevated, return to normal in four to five weeks. Increased risk of thrombophlebitis and thromboembolism after delivery.

        f. White blood cells 20–30,000/mm.

    3. **Renal**

        a. Urinary retention may occur after birth.

        b. Increased renal blood flow returns to normal within first six weeks postpartum.

        c. Diuresis 8–12 hours postpartum.

    4. **Gastrointestinal**

        a. Decreased motility after delivery.

        b. Normal bowel elimination returns after two to three days.

    5. **Integumentary System**

        a. Abdominal skin and muscle is flabby—tone regained gradually after several months.

        b. Skin discolorations fade gradually, although some mild changes may persist.

        c. Stretch marks gradually fade and turn silvery color.

    6. **Weight Loss**

        a. Initial 10–12-pound loss due to infant, amniotic fluid, and placenta.

        b. Diuresis leads to an additional 5-pound weight loss.

        c. By six to eight weeks, if 25–35-pound weight gain, return to pre-pregnant weight.

C. Psychological Responses

    1. **Phases After Delivery** (Rubin, 1961)

        a. Taking-in phase

           (1) First few postpartum days

           (2) Mother passive, dependent, preoccupied with own needs

           (3) Talkative

        b. Taking-hold phase

           (1) Two to three days postpartum

           (2) Increase in sense of well-being

           (3) Mother takes hold of the task of parenting—receptive to teaching

    2. **Attachment Behavior**

        a. Touch (extremities first)

        b. Eye-to-eye contact (en face position)

    3. **Postpartum Blues**

        a. Transient depression—insomnia, tearfulness, let-down, sad feeling

        b. May be due to fatigue, sensory overload, hormonal changes

        c. Needs support and reassurance that feelings are transitory

D. Nursing Care of the Postpartum Mother

    1. **Assessment**

        a. Vital signs

        b. Breasts (engorgement), nipples (soreness, cracks)

        c. Uterine fundus—height and firmness

        d. Bladder—assess for distention, especially first 24–48 hours; report to RN if present

        e. Perineum—check episiotomy, approximated, swelling, hematoma; comfort measures—ice, sitz bath. Hemorrhoids—comfort measures, hydrocortisone cream.

        f. Lochia—record color, odor, amount. Report increased bleeding to RN.

        g. Lower extremities—assess for Homan's sign. Report positive finding to RN.

        h. Abdomen and perineum—initiate exercises: Kegel and pelvic tilt

2. **Comfort Measures**
   a. Analgesics for uterine afterpains
   b. Episiotomy—ice, sitz baths
   c. Perineal care—peri bottles for cleansing
   d. Hemorrhoids—sitz baths, anesthetic ointment, stool softeners, Tucks, rectal suppositories, hydrocortisone cream
   e. Breast engorgement—warm compresses before a feeding, cold compresses after, Acetominophen, well-fitting bra

3. **Promoting Attachment**
   a. Encourage parents to care for infant.
   b. Point out unique features (i.e., dimples, long lashes, etc.).
   c. Use infant's name when discussing baby.
   d. Help parents accept and adjust to older sibling's behavior.

4. **Infant Care and Feeding**
   a. Nonlactating mother
      (1) Teach how to bottle feed and burp.
      (2) Discuss types of formulas, emphasize importance of following mixing. instructions exactly.
      (3) Teach typical feeding schedules, amounts of formula usually taken.
   b. Lactating mother
      (1) Teach proper latch-on and positioning.
      (2) Discuss nipple soreness and measures for relief.
      (3) Teach mother ways to assess adequacy of feedings—after milk has come in, six to eight wet diapers plus two or more stools.
      (4) Feed baby on demand, 8–12 times per day.
      (5) Discuss need for mother to avoid recreational drugs, excessive alcohol, or caffeine; inform MD she is breastfeeding when receiving medication for illness.
   c. Diapering
      (1) Diaper changes frequently to avoid diaper rash
      (2) Petroleum jelly or diaper ointment to protect skin
   d. Bathing
      (1) Sponge bathe until cord falls off
      (2) Every other day is often enough
      (3) Mild soap, lotion if desired, no talc powder
   e. Cord care
      (1) Alcohol to cord three to four times a day
      (2) Report redness, discharge, foul odor to provider
   f. Sleep
      (1) Position on back or side (protective against SIDS)
      (2) Sleep when the baby sleeps
   g. Illness
      (1) Teach parent how to take infant's temperature.
      (2) Inform parent to call provider if infant has fever, is lethargic, or unusually irritable. Other signs to report include projectile vomiting, poor appetite, yellow skin tone indicating jaundice.
   h. Health measures
      (1) Need for car seat
      (2) Importance of follow-up well-baby care and immunizations

E. Postpartum Complications
1. **Infection**
   a. Risk factors
      (1) Premature rupture of the membranes
      (2) Prolonged labor
      (3) Anemia, postpartum hemorrhage
      (4) Frequent vaginal exams, poor aseptic technique
   b. Assessment
      (1) Temperature elevation 38 degrees Centigrade (100.4 degrees Fahrenheit) after the first 24 hours
      (2) Tachycardia, chills, abdominal tenderness, headache, and malaise
      (3) Foul-smelling lochia
      (4) Infection usually endometrial, may have urinary tract infection
   c. Interventions
      (1) Administer antibiotics, antipyretics, as ordered
      (2) Encourage increased fluid intake, adequate diet, as tolerated
      (3) Obtain cultures
      (4) Check vital signs every 2 to 4 hours
   d. Evaluation
      (1) Vital signs within normal limits
      (2) Signs and symptoms of infection resolve
2. **Hemorrhage**
   a. Blood loss of over 500 cc
   b. Assessment
      (1) Uterine atony, cervical or vaginal lacerations
      (2) Retained placental parts
      (3) Confusion and restlessness
   c. Interventions
      (1) Massage uterus, assess amount of bleeding
      (2) Monitor vital signs
      (3) Increase IV fluids
      (4) Empty bladder
      (5) Administer methergine, hemabate
      (6) Assist with transfusion, if needed; D & C or hysterectomy, if required
      (7) Treat shock
   d. Evaluation
      (1) Fundus firm and midline
      (2) Vaginal bleeding moderate
      (3) Vital signs within normal limits
      (4) Laboratory values are stable
3. **Hematoma**
   a. Assessment
      (1) Visible vaginal hematoma
      (2) Large blood-filled sac visible
   b. Interventions
      (1) Ice to area for 24 hours
      (2) Analgesics
      (3) Incision or ligation, if necessary
      (4) Comfort measures such as sitz bath
4. **Thrombophlebitis**
   a. Assessment
      (1) Formation of a thrombus when a vein wall is inflamed
      (2) Occurs in leg or pelvis vein
      (3) Pain in area of thrombus

(4) Edema, redness over area

(5) Positive Homan's sign

b. Interventions

(1) Bed rest with leg elevated on pillow

(2) Apply moist heat

(3) Administer analgesics, as ordered

(4) Administer anticoagulant therapy, as ordered

(5) Apply elastic support hose, if ordered

(6) Teach client not to massage legs

NEWBORN

A. Physiological Response to Birth

1. **Circulatory**

a. The structures in the heart that are necessary for fetal circulation (ductus venosus, foramen ovale, ductus arteriosus) close after birth—closure may not be immediate, but rather gradual over several days.

b. Peripheral circulation is established slowly, and the infant may have a mottled appearance, or acrocyanosis, for 24 hours.

2. **Respiratory**

a. Often established immediately after birth.

b. Should not be excessive respiratory effort, noise, or retractions.

c. Newborns are nose-breathers; nasal obstruction can lead to respiratory distress.

d. Normal respiratory rate is 30–60. Over 60 can occur during the first hour or so after birth, but should not persist. Short periods of apnea (less than 20 seconds) are normal.

3. **Renal**

a. Urine in bladder at birth, but infant may not void for first 12–24 hours. Later on, 6–10 voids per day indicate adequate fluid intake.

b. Infants cannot concentrate urine for the first three months and are more prone to dehydration.

c. Initial voidings may leave brick red spots—uric acid crystals.

4. **Gastrointestinal**

a. Stomach capacity varies—between 50 and 60 cc.

b. First stool is meconium (black, tar-like), usually passed within first 24 hours and followed by transitional stool (between second and fourth day).

c. After three days, stools become loose and golden yellow for breastfed infant, formed and pale yellow for formula fed. Number of stools per day varies from one every feeding to one to two per day.

5. **Hepatic**

a. Newborns have increased numbers of red blood cells that are both more fragile than those of adults and have a shorter life span. Thus, destruction occurs the first few days after birth—the byproduct of RBC destruction being bilirubin. The liver is responsible for conjugating and excreting bilirubin.

b. Jaundice is probably related to several factors, including increased red blood cell destruction, as with bruising or cephalhematoma, and an immature liver.

c. Neonatal bilirubin levels below 12 mg/dL on the second to seventh day of life are considered within the range of normal—visible jaundice occurs at 4 to 6 mg/dL.

d. The liver synthesizes clotting factors, which are prolonged for the first week or so of life. This is due to the baby's inability to synthesize and use vitamin K.

NOTE

Progression of stool is often tested.

This is now administered to all newborns, which has eliminated hemorrhagic disease of the newborn.

6. **Immunologic**
   a. Newborns are less able to concentrate anti-inflammatory cells and thus localize infection. Local infections are more likely to become systemic in infants than older children.
   b. IgG is passed to an infant through the placenta at 33 weeks' gestation, which protects infant from organisms to which the mother is immune.
   c. IgM and IgA are large molecules and do not cross the placenta. However, secretory IgA is present at high levels in colostrum and provides immunity to respiratory and gastrointestinal infections. IgM is produced by the newborn; IgA is not.

7. **Neurologic**
   a. By 26 weeks' gestation, all of the neurons of the brain are formed.
   b. Brain development, branching, and myelination are not complete until the end of the second year.

8. **Thermoregulation**
   a. Infants lose heat faster than adults because of large skin surface relative to body mass.
   b. Four mechanisms of heat loss
      (1) *Conduction*—when baby is on a cold surface
      (2) *Convection*—heat is transferred to cool air moving across the surface of the infant's skin
      (3) *Evaporation*—evaporation of moisture from wet hair or body surfaces dissipates heat
      (4) *Radiation*—heat from infant's body radiates to a colder surface, such as cold incubator wall
   c. Brown fat is the primary way newborns produce heat.

B. **Sensory**
   1. **Vision**
      a. Infants can fixate on an object 8–10 inches away and prefer to focus on complex patterns such as a human face
      b. Infants can distinguish one visual stimulus from another—can appear puzzled if mother changes her appearance
   2. **Hearing**
      a. Well-developed at birth
      b. Prefer voice of mother over that of another woman
   3. **Smell**
      a. Can distinguish odor of mother's body at six days
   4. **Taste**
      a. Show pleasure at sweet taste—sucking behavior
      b. Displeasure at salty, bitter, or acid—turn away and protrudes tongue

C. **Nursing Assessment and Care of Newborn**
   1. **Post-Delivery Care**
      a. Suction to maintain client airway
      b. Apply cord clamp—check vessels (cord should have two arteries and one vein)
      c. Wrap in pre-warmed blanket and place in preheated crib or on radiant warmer
      d. Erythromycin ointment to each eye
      e. Vitamin K IM
      f. Complete identification bands and footprint sheet
      g. Apgar score documented
      h. Encourage bonding and initiate breastfeeding, if mother plans to breastfeed

2. **Vital Signs/Measurements**
   a. Axillary temperature—normal 96 to 99 degrees Fahrenheit
   b. Pulse 120–160 bpm, normally irregular
   c. Respirations—30–60 per minute, irregular, abdominal
   d. Blood pressure—normal is 60–90 mmHg systolic, 40–50 mmHg diastolic
   e. Length—18–22 inches (45–55 cm)
   f. Head circumference—13–14 inches (33–35 cm)
   g. Chest circumference—12–13 inches (30–33 cm)
   h. Weight—newborns should not lose more than 10 percent of birth weight and should regain birth weight by 7–10 days of life; after that, gain approximately 1 ounce a day for the first six months

3. **Skin/Birth Marks**
   a. Milia—small white sebaceous glands
   b. "Stork bites" telangiectasis or capillary hemangiomas—fade
   c. Red nevi—circumscribed, blanch on touch, disappear in six months to a year
   d. Mongolian spots—bluish, bruise-like spots on buttocks, backs, shoulders, disappear by preschool; most common in African American, Hispanic, and Asian babies
   e. Erythema toxicum—newborn rash—goes away, no treatment needed
   f. Strawberry mark—usually disappear by 5 or 6 years
   g. Port-wine stain—doesn't blanch, may not go away
   h. Lanugo—soft, downy hair on ears, forehead, shoulders, neck; disappears in weeks

4. **Reflexes**

Newborn Reflexes		
Reflex	**How to Test**	**Age of Disappearance**
Tonic neck	Turn supine infant's head to one side—arm and leg extend on the side the head is turned	Six months
Sucking	Touch or stroke lips ⇒ infant sucks	Twelve months
Stepping	Have sole of infant's foot touch flat surface ⇒ will make stepping movement	Eight weeks
Rooting	Stroke cheek—infant will turn toward side touched	Eight months
Moro	Loud noise disturbs baby's equilibrium ⇒ startle response	Eight months
Grasp—palmar	Finger pressed against baby's palm ⇒ fingers close around it	Three to four months
Plantar grasp	Object pressed against ball of baby's foot—toes curl around it	Ten months
Babinski	Stroke lateral side of foot ⇒ toes fan and great toe dorsiflexes	One year

5. **Gestational Age Assessment**—Ballard/Dubowitz
   a. Physical changes as gestational age is greater
      (1) Skin thickens, may be dry or peeling
      (2) Lanugo disappears
      (3) Plantar (sole of foot) creases increase
      (4) Areola of breast enlarges
      (5) Ear cartilage stiffens
      (6) Male genitalia—testes descend, more scrotal rugae
      (7) Female genitalia—labia majora covers the labia minora and clitoris
   b. Neuromuscular changes
      (1) Increased flexion of resting posture
      (2) Increased angle of hand flexion—square window
      (3) Angle of arm recoiling decreases
      (4) Popliteal (knee) angle decreases
      (5) Resistance to drawing arm across body increases (scarf sign)
      (6) Raising heel to ear—resistance increases

D. **High-Risk Newborn**
   1. **Premature Infant**
      a. Born before 37 weeks of gestation
      b. Weight usually less than 5 pounds
      c. Major associated problems
         (1) Respiratory distress syndrome—need for CPAP or respirator
         (2) Thermoregulatory problems—must be kept warm
         (3) Infection—give baby mother's milk when possible, strict asepsis
         (4) Hemorrhage (intraventricular)—trauma, other factors being researched
   2. **Small for Gestational Age (SGA)**—term birth weight is in bottom 10 percent.
      a. Causes may be IUGR, infection, malformations
      b. Treat according to problems exhibited
   3. **Hyperbilirubinemia**
      a. Elevated serum bilirubin due to increased red blood cell destruction or decreased ability of newborn to process bilirubin
      b. Kernicterus—major complication that causes brain damage due to very high levels of unconjugated bilirubin
      c. Jaundice usually progresses from head to toe
      d. Phototherapy helps increase conjugation of bilirubin
      e. Increased intake of calories—breastmilk or formula (bilirubin is excreted through the stool)
      f. Exchange transfusion if necessary
   4. **Neonatal Sepsis**
      a. Due to pathologic organisms in the blood
         (1) Prolonged rupture of membranes, maternal infection, nosocomial infection, meconium aspiration
      b. Blood cultures done
      c. Antibiotics given
   5. **Hypoglycemia**
      a. Due to maternal diabetes, stress
      b. Early feeding and blood glucose monitoring

EXERCISES: MATERNAL/NEWBORN NURSING

1. The nurse admits the pregnant woman, who is a 36-week primipara. Her blood pressure is 145/96, and her hands and face are swollen. What other finding would the nurse expect when assessing this preeclamptic woman?

    (1) Oligohydramnios
    (2) Proteinuria
    (3) Polyuria
    (4) Irregular contractions

2. A nurse is evaluating the prenatal client. The client asks when she can expect to feel the baby move. The nurse replies:

    (1) "You can expect to begin to notice movement during the first trimester."
    (2) "By the end of the sixth month, you may feel some kicking."
    (3) "It is unusual to feel the baby move until two weeks before your due date."
    (4) "Most women can feel fetal movement at approximately 16–20 weeks gestation."

3. Susan Miller is seven-and-a-half months' pregnant. She has a number of physical discomforts to report to the nurse. Which of these symptoms should be reported to the physician?

    (1) Shortness of breath when climbing up the stairs
    (2) Heartburn
    (3) Constipation
    (4) Headaches and "spots" before her eyes

4. A young woman is planning to become pregnant. She asks the nurse whether she should be careful about taking medications before becoming pregnant. The nurse replies that the fetus is most susceptible to teratogens during the third to eighth week after conception, often before women know they are pregnant. The nurse explains that this part of pregnancy is called the:

    (1) fetal period.
    (2) embryonic period.
    (3) mesodermic period.
    (4) phase of the zygote.

5. A first-time mother who is eight months' pregnant tells the nurse that she learned in Lamaze class that her water might break before she goes into labor. She asks whether this might hurt the baby. The nurse explains that unless the membrane ruptures before the baby is due, it is not usually a problem. This response is based on the nurse's knowledge of the functions of the amniotic fluid. Those functions include which of the following?
Select all that apply.

    ☐ **(1)** Protection of the fetus from injury
    ☐ **(2)** Protection of the fetus from infection
    ☐ **(3)** Temperature maintenance
    ☐ **(4)** Providing adequate oxygenation

6. A nurse assists in the delivery of a 34-week-old male infant weighing 5 pounds, 4 ounces. Because the baby is premature, the nurse called respiratory in advance to set up Continuous Positive Airway Pressure (CPAP) equipment in the special-care nursery. Soon after birth, the infant, as expected, has respiratory distress. He is tachypneic and has substernal retractions. He is transferred to the special-care nursery for CPAP therapy. The nurse knew that the CPAP might be needed because premature infants often have

   (1) insufficient development of the respiratory accessory muscles.
   (2) inability of the fetal hemoglobin to bind to oxygen.
   (3) insufficient surfactant.
   (4) minimal cardiac reserve.

7. While assessing the newborn, a nurse checks the umbilical cord and counts the vessels present. The nurse notes one artery and one vein. Which of the following actions would be *most* appropriate for the nurse to take in response to this finding?

   (1) Chart the assessment along with any other normal findings.
   (2) Inform the physician or RN that the baby only has one vein.
   (3) Inform the physician or RN that the baby only has one artery.
   (4) Chart the assessment as a normal variation in the newborn.

8. A nurse offers the pregnant client an HIV test. The client acts offended, but the nurse explains that all prenatal clients are offered this test because

   (1) it gives the medical team an idea of her lifestyle choices.
   (2) they will then be able to notify her partner if she is positive.
   (3) if she is positive, the baby is likely to present with HIV syndrome, which needs prompt treatment.
   (4) if the mother is positive, she and the baby can be treated with zidovudine, which greatly reduces the chance of the baby becoming infected.

9. A 34-year-old client is pregnant with her third child. She complains to the nurse that her varicose veins are feeling worse than in her previous pregnancies and asks whether she can do anything herself to relieve the discomfort. The nurse correctly suggests which of the following recommendations?
   Select all that apply.

   ☐ (1) Elevate the legs while sitting.
   ☐ (2) Stand for long periods of time.
   ☐ (3) Exercise the calf muscles.
   ☐ (4) Wear support stockings.

10. The nurse weighs a newborn boy at 4,200 grams. The most appropriate nursing intervention for this large-for-gestational-age baby would be to

   (1) monitor blood glucose levels frequently.
   (2) delay feeding longer than usual to allow the infant's glucose level to decrease.
   (3) bottlefeed instead of allowing infant to breastfeed until glucose levels are normal.
   (4) provide respiratory support to the newborn.

11. A nurse is taking the vital signs of a new labor client. The nurse notes that the woman's blood pressure is 146/94, her face is edematous, and she is complaining of a headache. Her urine is 2+ protein. The physician orders an infusion of $MgSO_4$ (magnesium sulfate) to be administered. The nurse will monitor the client by assessing the client's vital signs and

    (1) urine for glucose.

    (2) deep tendon reflexes.

    (3) calf tenderness.

    (4) abdominal distention.

12. The weight of a newborn at the time of delivery is 3,860 grams (g). The delivery nurse announces the baby's weight to the parents in pounds (lbs) and ounces (oz). What weight does she announce to the new parents?
    Round your answer to one decimal point.

    Answer: _____ / _____ (lbs/oz)

13. The nurse is teaching a first-time mother what signs of approaching labor she should report to the physician. The nurse correctly tells the client she should *immediately* contact the physician if she experiences

    (1) vaginal bleeding.

    (2) loss of the mucus plug.

    (3) irregular contractions for over an hour.

    (4) ripening of the cervix.

14. Nancy, a primipara who is due to deliver next week, calls and tells a nurse she has been having contractions every 4 minutes for an hour. Before the nurse asks any further questions, she confirms that Nancy knows how to time contractions correctly, which is from the

    (1) end of one contraction to the beginning of the next.

    (2) beginning of one contraction to the end of the next.

    (3) end of one contraction to the end of the next.

    (4) beginning of one contraction to the beginning of the next.

15. A woman is recovering in the hospital 8 hours after delivering her baby. The nurse comes in to the client's room to check on the new mother and begins to palpate the uterine fundus of the client. Identify with an "X" the area of the abdomen where the nurse should expect to feel the fundus.

16. Ingrid, a 29-year-old mother of two, is in active labor with her third baby, and the nurse checks the fetal monitor tracing. The baby's heart rate is going down with each contraction. It starts to get lower after the peak of the contraction and slowly returns to baseline. Which of the following would be appropriate action(s) for the nurse to take?
    Select all that apply.

    ☐ **(1)** Positioning the client in the left lateral position
    ☐ **(2)** Administering oxygen at 7–8 liters/minute
    ☐ **(3)** Increasing the rate of Pitocin to hasten the delivery
    ☐ **(4)** Notifying the physician of fetal status while the RN remains with the client

17. The nurse knows that the most likely cause of Ingrid's fetal monitor tracing pattern is

    (1) head compression.
    (2) uteroplacental insufficiency.
    (3) cord compression.
    (4) maternal hyperglycemia.

18. A first-time expectant mother is experiencing regular contractions, approximately 6 to 8 minutes apart. She is uncomfortable and has just ruptured her amniotic membranes. The resident did a vaginal exam and said she was 2 to 3 centimeters dilated. She asks the nurse if that means that she will deliver soon. The nurse correctly replies:

    (1) "Your membranes have ruptured, so it should not be more than an hour."
    (2) "You are in active labor, but it will take at least 2 to 3 more hours."
    (3) "You are still in the early phase of labor, so it is difficult to predict how fast you will progress once your labor gets more active."
    (4) "You are in the second stage of labor, so it should not be long."

19. After the baby has been born, the nurse tells the mother that the staff will watch her carefully for the first 2 to 4 hours. Which of the following findings should be immediately reported to the RN in charge or the physician?

    (1) Increased bleeding and a boggy uterus, despite massage
    (2) Systolic blood pressure of 100
    (3) Shaking chills
    (4) Uterus displaced to the right

20. As Linda, the antepartum client, was going to the bathroom, she suddenly noticed a looped cord coming out of her vagina. She quickly rang the emergency call bell, and the first nurse to arrive explained that her baby had a prolapsed cord and quickly did the following:

    (1) Placed her in a trendelenberg or knee chest position to relieve pressure on the cord
    (2) Ruptured her membranes to help speed the labor
    (3) Called ultrasound to get a stat biophysical profile
    (4) Performed a vaginal exam to determine cervical dilatation

TIP

Question 18 is an example of a test item containing similar information in two or more answer choices. Remember to look for the broadest, or most general, answer: It is very likely to be the correct one.

ANSWER KEY AND EXPLANATIONS

1. 2	5. 1,2,3	9. 1,3,4	13. 1	17. 2
2. 4	6. 3	10. 1	14. 4	18. 3
3. 4	7. 3	11. 2	15. umbilicus	19. 1
4. 2	8. 4	12. 8/8	or belly-	20. 1
			button area	
			16. 1,2,4	

1. **The correct answer is (2).** Pregnancy-induced hypertension, which is often referred to as preeclampsia, is characterized by hypertension, edema, and proteinuria.

2. **The correct answer is (4).** Between sixteen and twenty weeks, most women feel some fetal movement. Multiparas are more likely to notice it sooner, because they are familiar with the sensation, while first-time mothers often don't realize what they are feeling until later.

3. **The correct answer is (4).** Shortness of breath (1), heartburn (2), and constipation (3), unless severe and accompanied by other signs or symptoms, are normal pregnancy discomforts. Headaches and "spots" before the eyes are ominous symptoms of preeclampsia, which signal neurological involvement and may precede a seizure.

4. **The correct answer is (2).** The embryonic period, which begins after implantation and ends by week nine, is the time when most major body systems are formed, and the fetus is most susceptible to the action of teratogens.

5. **The correct answers are (1), (2), and (3).** The amniotic fluid is not involved in oxygenation (4), which is done through the umbilical vein. The functions of the amniotic fluid include temperature regulation (3), protection from injury (1), and, in addition, the membranes act as a barrier to infection (2). Once the membranes rupture, if the baby is term, there is no problem and labor often begins spontaneously. If the baby is premature, however, there is a risk of infection and miscarriage or premature delivery.

6. **The correct answer is (3).** There is no problem with the respiratory accessory muscles in premature babies (1), fetal hemoglobin binds well with oxygen (2), and, at any given oxygen tension, the fetal blood has a higher oxygen saturation than does adult blood. Cardiac problems are usually not involved (4). Surfactant reduces the surface tension of the alveoli and reduces the effort needed to expand the lungs. It only begins to be manufactured at 32–33 weeks and is rarely adequate before 35 weeks.

7. **The correct answer is (3).** The newborn should have two arteries and one vein, and the absence of an artery can indicate other congenital problems, especially with the kidneys. This is not a normal finding and should be reported to the RN or physician.

8. **The correct answer is (4).** Many states are urging prenatal clients to

be tested for HIV now that there is a treatment, zidovudine, which greatly reduces the possibility of transmission of the virus to the baby, if given to the mother antepartum and intrapartum, and to the baby after delivery. Transmission to the baby is reduced from up to 33 percent to approximately 8 percent.

9. **The correct answers are (1), (3), and (4).** Elevating the legs (1), exercising the calf muscles (3), and wearing support stockings (4) may all help relieve the discomfort of varicose veins. Standing for long periods tends to make them ache more.

10. **The correct answer is (1).** A large-for-gestational age baby is at risk for hypoglycemia, because increased size is often due to high maternal blood glucose, which the baby adjusts to by producing more than the usual amount of insulin. After the baby is born, the insulin levels are still high, but the maternal glucose source is absent, so the baby often becomes hypoglycemic.

11. **The correct answer is (2).** $MgSO_4$, magnesium sulfate, is often given to preeclamptic women to prevent seizures. Some of its side effects are respiratory depression and decreased deep tendon reflexes. Respiratory rate and reflexes should be assessed regularly while it is being infused. Urine glucose levels (1) are not affected, nor is the likelihood of calf tenderness (3), or phlebitis. Abdominal distention (4) does not result from this treatment.

12. **The correct answer is 8/8 (8 lbs/8 oz).** Use the following conversions to determine the baby's weight in pounds and ounces:

1000 g = 1 kilogram (kg)
1 kg = 2.2 lbs
16 oz = 1 lb

$$\frac{x \text{ kg}}{3860 \text{ g}} = \frac{1 \text{ kg}}{1000 \text{ g}}$$

Solve for x:
$x = 3.86$ kg

Convert kg to lbs:
$3.86 \times 2.2 = 8.5$ lbs
(rounded to the nearest one tenth)

Next, convert this answer into pounds and ounces:
0.5 lbs $\times$ 16 oz = 8.0 oz

Baby's weight = 8 lbs, 8 oz

13. **The correct answer is (1).** Vaginal bleeding is a potentially dangerous symptom that could indicate placenta previa, placental abruption, uterine rupture, or other serious complications. Loss of the mucous plug (2) is normal and can occur several days before labor starts. Irregular contractions (3) may precede active labor by hours or even days. Ripening of the cervix (4) is not noticed by the client and indicates readiness of the cervix to dilate.

14. **The correct answer is (4).** The frequency of labor contractions are assessed by monitoring the time from the beginning of one contraction to the beginning of the next contraction.

15. **The correct answer is the umbilicus.** You should have put an "X" over the umbilicus. The nurse should be able to feel the uterus at the level of

the umbilicus ("belly button") from 1 hour after birth to approximately 24 hours after birth.

16. **The correct answers are (1), (2), and (4).** This heart-rate pattern is called late decelerations, which indicates uteroplacental insufficiency. To counteract fetal distress and increase oxygenation, the nurse places the client in the left lateral position to maximize blood flow to the fetus (1), administers oxygen (2), and notifies the physician (4). Pitocin (3) would be shut off because it adds to fetal stress by increasing the strength and frequency of the client's contractions.

17. **The correct answer is (2).** As mentioned above, this tracing pattern is caused by uteroplacental insufficiency. Head compression (1) causes early decelerations, cord compression (3) causes variable decelerations, and maternal hyperglycemia (4) does not cause decelerations.

18. **The correct answer is (3).** At 2 to 3 centimeters with contractions 6 to 8 minutes apart, the woman is in the early phase of the first stage of labor, which has a more variable duration than when the contractions become regular and closer together.

19. **The correct answer is (1).** A boggy uterus with increased bleeding could lead to postpartum hemorrhage if not corrected. A systolic blood pressure of 100 (2) is not unusual, nor are shaking chills (3). A uterus that is displaced to the right (4) usually indicates a full bladder.

20. **The correct answer is (1).** A prolapsed cord is an obstetrical emergency, and the first priority is to relieve pressure on the cord to maintain circulation to the baby. Rupturing membranes (2) are irrelevant, since they must be ruptured for this to happen. A biophysical profile (3) is a somewhat lengthy evaluation of fetal status and would not be done at this time. A vaginal exam (4) would not be done since it would further press on the cord, and a stat C-section is usually performed.

answers exercises

SUMMING IT UP

- Maternity care today is client- and family-centered. This care is sensitive to the cultural background of the family and takes into account practices and preferences that stem from their cultural background.

- Preventive care is emphasized due to the importance of prenatal care in preventing poor pregnancy outcomes.

Pediatric Nursing

OVERVIEW

- Basic concepts
- Nursing care of sick children
- Child development
- Toddler development
- Preschool-aged child development (3 to 6 years)
- School-aged child development (6 to 12 years)
- Adolescent development (12 to 20 years)
- Respiratory disorders
- Gastrointestinal disorders
- Genitourinary disorders
- Endocrine disorders
- Cardiovascular disorders
- Hematopoietic disorders
- Neurological disorders
- Musculoskeletal disorders
- Cognitive and sensory disorders
- Skin disorders
- Growth and development disorders
- Summing it up

BASIC CONCEPTS

A basic knowledge of growth—in physical terms, developmental terms, and functional terms—is central to pediatric nursing. In addition, children are prone to developing a number of disorders that are fairly unique to this period of development, in part due to physiological differences and to an immature immune system.

As you read through this chapter, keep in mind the four major Client Needs categories as they relate to children:

chapter 6

1. **Safe, Effective Care Environment**
   - Accident prevention
   - Prevention of the spread of communicable diseases

2. **Health Promotion and Maintenance**
   - Stages of development
   - Immunizations
   - Programs for good health habits

3. **Psychosocial Integrity**
   - Awareness of child abuse and neglect
   - Play

4. **Physiological Integrity**
   - Nutrition
   - Exercise
   - Rest and sleep
   - Prevention of infectious diseases

NURSING CARE OF SICK CHILDREN

A. **Child's View of Illness**
   1. **Infant**
      a. Change in routine
      b. Change in familiar surroundings, toys
   2. **Toddler**
      a. Separation anxiety at its peak in this group
      b. Feels responsibility for illness
   3. **Preschool**
      a. Fear of pain, bleeding, injury
      b. Less separation anxiety; may consider illness as punishment for wrongdoing
   4. **School-Aged**
      a. Fear of consequences of illness
      b. Dislikes separation from peers
   5. **Adolescent**
      a. Anxiety related to loss of control, independence
      b. Privacy concerns
      c. Understands illness at this time

B. **Separation response**
   1. **Greatest Impact**—between the ages of 1 and 3
   2. **Three Phases**
      a. *Protest:* cries, wants parents back, refuses care from others
      b. *Despair:* stops crying, acts depressed, "settles in"
      c. *Detachment:* superficially appears to adjust, ignores parents to avoid feelings of loss

C. **Response to Pain**
   1. **Infant** (0–1 year)
      a. Generalized body response—sometimes local response, withdrawal on stimulation
      b. Crying, skin color changes

    c. Vital sign fluctuations

    d. Change in eating and sleeping patterns

  2. **Older Infant/Toddler** (1–3 years)

    a. Localized pain response

    b. Crying, facial expression of pain

    c. Physical resistance, tries to push away

  3. **Young Child/Preschooler** (3–6 years)

    a. Loud crying

    b. Verbal expressions, physical resistance

    c. May need physical restraints

    d. Clings to parent

    e. If pain continues, restless and irritable

  4. **School-Aged Child** (6–11 years)

    a. Same as above

    b. May stall in anticipation of procedure

    c. Often anticipates with muscular rigidity

  5. **Adolescents**

    a. Less vocal protest/physical activity

    b. More verbal comments on pain

    c. Increased tension

D. Nursing interventions

  1. **Infant**

    a. Promote interaction between parent and infant.

    b. Provide appropriate activities and toys.

    c. Allow parents to accompany and comfort child as much as possible.

    d. Keep staff as consistent as possible.

    e. Do not perform procedures in room or crib if possible.

  2. **Toddler**

    a. Encourage parent to visit.

    b. Have consistency in staffing.

    c. Play hide-and-seek, peek-a-boo—play at disappearing and returning.

    d. Have parent bring items from home.

    e. Use comfort measures child is used to—blanket, bottle.

    f. Explain procedures honestly before doing them.

    g. Allow child to handle and play with hospital supplies when possible.

    h. Avoid painful procedures in room.

  3. **Preschool Child**

    a. Assure child that she isn't responsible for illness.

    b. Before leaving, have parents tell child in understandable terms when they will return—before bedtime, for dinner, etc.

    c. Allow play with hospital supplies when possible.

    d. Explain procedures honestly, as above.

  4. **School-Aged Child**

    a. Encourage frequent visits by parents.

    b. Incorporate home routine into hospital routine as much as possible.

    c. Allow continuation of school if possible.

    d. Encourage expression of feelings through drawing, acting out with doll, etc.

  5. **Adolescent**

    a. Allow participation in care decisions.

    b. Encourage visits from friends and family.

    c. Provide privacy as much as possible.

CHILD DEVELOPMENT

A. **Infant (1 month to 1 year)**
1. **Physical Development**
   a. Height increases by 50% at 1 year
   b. Newborn loses 5–10% of birth weight; it is usually regained by 2 weeks
   c. Birth weight doubles by 5 months, triples by 1 year
   d. Anterior fontanelle closes at 12 to 18 months
2. **Health Maintenance**
   a. Feeding
      (1) Breast or formula feeding for first year
      (2) Introduce solid foods at four to six months
      (3) One food at a time, often starting with rice or other iron-fortified cereal, then fruits
3. **Safety**
   a. *Suffocation*—no plastic bags, don't prop bottles, no small objects in reach
   b. *Falls*—crib rails up, don't leave unattended on a raised surface, use infant seat with belt; gates on stairways
   c. *Car safety*—approved car seat, rear facing, in back seat
   d. *Poisons*—keep out of low cupboards; don't put toxic substances in food containers; use childproof caps on all medications; keep poison control number posted
   e. *Burns*—keep hot water down to 120 degrees; use flame-retardant pajamas; keep electrical wires and appliances out of reach; use a smoke alarm
4. **Immunizations**
   a. Contraindications to vaccines.
      (1) Delay if child is sick with anything more than a cold.
      (2) Omit if there was an allergic response to a previous vaccination or is allergic to vaccine components (e.g., eggs for MMR).
      (3) OPV—contraindicated if their there is someone in the household with an altered immune system; IPV—inactivated polio vaccine can be substituted.
      (4) History of seizures may make the pertussis vaccine contraindicated.

First-Year Growth and Development

Age	Fine/Gross Motor	Play/Speech/Social	Activities	Safety
0–3 months	Head lag when pulled to sitting	Reflexes; social smile	Talk and sing to baby; hang mobile with black and white designs; cuddle, rock	Don't put baby unattended on raised surface; no plastic bags near baby; use car seat
3–6 months	Sits with support; rolls over; reaches for objects	Knows image in mirror; recognizes familiar faces	Rattle, soft squeeze toys, swing, cradle gym; floor play	Prevent choking by not leaving small objects near baby
6–9 months	Sits without support; can feed self a cracker	Says "mama" and "dada" without attaching meaning; stranger anxiety	Play pat-a-cake, peek-a-boo; likes to look in the mirror	Fence top and bottom of stairways, avoid walkers
9–12 months	Creeps, then crawls; stands with support; picks up and releases objects; median age for walking is 12 months	Feeds self finger foods; says a few words with meaning; knows own name	Large pictures in books, simple nursery rhymes; push/pull toys	"Childproof" home—put covers on electrical outlets; move all dangerous chemicals and medicines out of reach

Recommended Childhood Immunization Schedule—United States (2009)

(Department of Health and Human Services—Centers for Disease Control and Prevention)

Vaccine ▼ Age ▶	Birth	1 month	2 months	4 months	6 months	12 months	15 months	18 months	19–23 months	2–3 years	4–6 years	
Hepatitis B[1]	HepB	HepB		see footnote 1		HepB						Range of recommended ages
Rotavirus[2]			RV	RV	RV							
Diphtheria, Tetanus, Pertussis[3]			DTaP	DTaP	DTaP		DTaP				DTaP	
Haemophilus influenzae type b[4]			Hib	Hib	Hib	Hib						
Pneumococcal[5]			PCV	PCV	PCV	PCV				PPSV		Certain high-risk groups
Inactivated Poliovirus			IPV	IPV		IPV					IPV	
Influenza[6]						Influenza (Yearly)						
Measles, Mumps, Rubella[7]						MMR					MMR	
Varicella[8]						Varicella					Varicella	
Hepatitis A[9]						HepA (2 doses)				HepA Series		
Meningococcal[10]											MCV	

This schedule indicates the recommended ages for routine administration of currently licensed vaccines, as of December 1, 2008, for children aged 0 through 6 years. Any dose not administered at the recommended age should be administered at a subsequent visit, when indicated and feasible. Licensed combination vaccines may be used whenever any component of the combination is indicated and other components are not contraindicated and if approved by the Food and Drug Administration for that dose of the series. Providers should consult the relevant Advisory Committee on Immunization Practices statement for detailed recommendations, including high-risk conditions: http://www.cdc.gov/vaccines/pubs/acip-list.htm. Clinically significant adverse events that follow immunization should be reported to the Vaccine Adverse Event Reporting System (VAERS). Guidance about how to obtain and complete a VAERS form is available at http://www.vaers.hhs.gov or by telephone, 800-822-7967.

TODDLER DEVELOPMENT

A. **Physical Growth**
   1. **Grows Taller in Proportion to Weight**—boys taller
   2. **Adult Height**—can be estimated by multiplying 2-year length by 2
   3. **Rate of Weight Gain Declines**
   4. **Vital Signs Change**
      a. Pulse—80 to 120
      b. Respirations—20 to 40
   5. **Teeth**
      a. Primary teeth in by 2 to 3 years

B. **Motor Skills**

---

1 to 3 Years

Gross Motor Skills

24 months: Walks steadily, walks up and down stairs, throws ball, kicks ball forward

36 months: Rides a tricycle, balances 2 seconds on one foot, hops on one foot

Fine Motor Skills

24 months: Drinks from cup with one hand, turns page of a book, turns door knobs, takes off clothes

36 months: Copies circle and cross, draws recognizable figures, builds tower with seven or eight blocks

---

C. **Social Skills: Erikson—*Autonomy* vs. *Shame and Doubt***
   1. **15 Months**—Less stranger anxiety, more independent
   2. **18 Months**—Imitates housework, temper tantrums emerge, hugs and kisses familiar people, has bedtime rituals, says "no"
   3. **24 Months**—Peak of tantrums, separation anxiety high, can begin to toilet train
   4. **30 Months**—Likes rituals, resists going to bed, can separate from mother for 3- to 4-hour time spans, has "security" toys or blankets; everything is "mine"; shares nothing
   5. **36 Months**—Interactive play, daytime training complete, less negative, imitates adult behavior

D. **Cognitive Development—Piaget**
   1. **Sensorimotor Period** (newborn to age 2)
      a. Starts to explore relationships between shapes; beginnings of memory development
      b. Ages 18–24 months: Cause and effect, "make-believe," some sense of time; totally egocentric
   2. **Preoperational Thought** (ages 2 to 4)
      a. "Magical thinking," increased sense of time and space
      b. Animistic thought—teddy bears talk

Language and Developmental Tasks—1 to 3 years

15 months—10–15 single words, understands "no," imitates simple activities, indicates when diaper is wet.

18 months—Uses phrases.

24 months—Approximately 300-word vocabulary. Uses short sentences and phrases. Obeys simple commands.

36 months—900-word vocabulary, uses plural forms of words. May take turns and share. Goes to the toilet by himself or herself, often needs help wiping.

Toys—Push-pull, balls, puzzles with large pieces, thick crayons, blocks, musical/talking toys.

Food—Can feed self by 18 months. May be picky eater. Give small servings, don't force child to eat.

Safety—To prevent falls, keep windows and doors screened or closed, supervise child. Car seats are mandatory. Swimming pools need childproof locks. Teach swimming and water safety; don't leave child unsupervised near water. Childproof home as much as possible.

PRESCHOOL-AGED CHILD DEVELOPMENT (3–6 YEARS)

A. **Physical**
   1. **Taller**—gains about 5 lbs. per year
   2. **Increasing Agility**—5-year-old can jump rope, use roller skates
   3. **More Skills**—such as dressing, tying shoelaces, printing a few letters, use of simple tools

B. **Language/Social**
   1. **By 5 Years**—has a 2,100-word vocabulary. Correct grammar (unless word is an exception to rules, as "three tooths"). Knows colors and money, counts to 10.
   2. **Dramatic and Imitative Play**—dress-up, playing house. Often has imaginary friends.
   3. **Playground Equipment**—tricycles, electronic games, books, dolls, simple board games.

C. **Nutrition**
   1. **Caloric Intake**—approximately 90 calories per kg per day
   2. **Can Be Finicky**—they feed themselves at this stage

D. **Safety**
   1. **Education and Role-Modeling**—important
   2. **Less Risk-Taking**
   3. **Parents**—should teach and use seat belts themselves

E. **Sleep**
   1. **Bedtime Fears**—often resists bedtime
   2. **May Give Up Nap**
   3. **Establish Consistent Bedtime Routine**

F. **Sex Education**
   1. **Aware of Differences**—by age 5. Curiosity about differences as well as sex.

2. **"Doctor play"**—child may masturbate. Parents should emphasize privacy issue and not punish.
3. **Answer Questions**—answer questions about sex honestly, but don't overwhelm child with details.

SCHOOL-AGED CHILD DEVELOPMENT (6–12 YEARS)

A. **Growth**
   1. **Usually a Steady 2 Inches Per Year**—boys taller until age 10, then girls taller until age 14
   2. **Average Weight**—weight-gain 5 to 7 lbs. per year
   3. **Eyes**—acquire 20/20 vision
   4. **Permanent Teeth Acquired**
   5. **Secondary Sex Characteristics May Begin to Develop**

B. **Motor Skills**
   1. **Strength Doubles**—refine and expand skills
   2. **Regular Exercise Important**—swimming, games, skating, biking
   3. **Growth Spurt**—as growth spurt begins, may become more awkward
   4. **Hand Preference**—definite by now
   5. **Engages in Craft Projects**

C. **Social Development: Erikson**—*Industry* vs. *Inferiority*
   1. **Peer Relationships Important**
   2. **Peer Pressure**
   3. **Teacher Approval Important**
   4. **Increased Cooperation**

D. **Cognitive Skills: Piaget**—*Concrete Operations (7–11 years)*
   1. **Can Organize and Classify Objects**
   2. **Symbolic Thinking**
   3. **Conservation**—amount same in different containers
   4. **Reversibility**—mentally reverse a process
   5. **Time Recognition**—clock, seasons, months

E. **Play**
   1. **Team Sports, Scouts, Computer Games, Books**
   2. **Quiet Play**—an important balance; likes to collect things

F. **Nutrition**
   1. **Caloric Needs Increase**—junk foods prevalent
   2. **Childhood Obesity**—incidence higher
   3. **Influence of Advertisements**—education important

G. **Safety**
   1. **Seat Belts, Street, and Bicycle Safety Important**
   2. **Teach Water Safety**

H. **Sex Education**
   1. **Parents and School Involved**
   2. **Mass Media Affects Perceptions**

I. **Drugs/Alcohol/Smoking**
   1. **Peer Pressure**—earlier start more likely to cause problems
   2. **Parents and Teachers**—important as role models

ADOLESCENT DEVELOPMENT (12–20 YEARS)

A. **Physical Growth**
   1. **Boys and Girls Grow Approximately One Fourth of Adult Height During Their Growth Spurt**
   2. **Girls**—gain approximately 15–55 lbs.; average menarche (start of menstruation) is 12 to 13 years
   3. **Boys**—gain 15–65 lbs.; spermatozoa production, male secondary sex characteristics

B. **Social—Erikson:** *Identity* vs. *Role Confusion*
   1. **Trying Various Roles Searching for a Fit**
   2. **Peer Relationships Very Important**
   3. **Must "Fit In" and Look the Same**
   4. **Intimate Sexual Relationships Begin**
   5. **Detaches from Parental Supervision**—may develop relationships with adults other than parents
   6. **Recreation**—school dances, boy-girl parties, music, and concerts; organized sports

C. **Cognitive: Piaget**—*Formal operations stage (11 years and older)*
   1. **Thinks Abstractly, Forms Hypotheses, Deductive and Inductive Reasoning**
   2. **Egocentric**

D. **Health Maintenance**
   1. **Nutrition**—increased calorie needs, fast foods common. Some anorexia, also obesity beginning.
   2. **Safety**—accidents leading cause of death, especially car accidents. Education important.
   3. **Sex Education and Education About Contraception Is Needed**
   4. **Physical Activity and Sports Help Promote Sense of Physical and Emotional Well-Being**
   5. **Smoking, Drugs**—adolescent smoking can lead to a habit that can shorten lives by many years. Providing education and a positive role model can help counteract advertising and peer pressure.

RESPIRATORY DISORDERS

A. **Croup**—inflammation of larynx, trachea, bronchi; viral illness, most common between the ages of 3 months to 3 years
   1. **Assessment**
      a. "Barking" cough; inspiratory stridor, respiratory distress
      b. Low-grade fever
      c. Usually occurs suddenly at night
   2. **Medical Treatment**
      a. Hospitalize if severe
      b. Give O_2, IV, humidity, corticosteroid therapy; epinephrine for transient relief
      c. ET equipment nearby

3. **Nursing Interventions**
    a. Monitor vital signs frequently, including oxygen perfusion and breath sounds.
    b. Provide humidified oxygen with croup tent or similar device.
    c. Teach parents about emergency care at home; inhaling humidified air from steamy bathroom shower may relieve symptoms.

B. **Epiglottitis**—bacterial infection of epiglottis and surrounding structures; the cause is usually *H. influenzae*, type B. Often preceded by a URI, *can result in total obstruction of airway*. Most often occurs in 3–7-year-olds.
    1. **Assessment**
        a. Fever, toxic appearance, temperature
        b. Inspiratory stridor, labored respirations, retractions, sore throat, dysphagia, drooling
        c. Classic posture: sitting up, leaning forward, chin out, tongue protruding, mouth open; irritable, anxious; froglike sound on inspiration; cherry-like epiglottis (only a qualified examiner should check)
    2. **Medical Treatment**
        a. Provider must examine throat with extreme care with intubation equipment available
        b. Antibiotics plus corticosteroids to reduce edema
    3. **Nursing Interventions**
        a. Provide mist tent with oxygen.
        b. Administer IV antibiotics, as ordered.
        c. Provide endotracheal tube care.
        d. Evaluate for pallor, tachycardia, tachypnea, and diminished breath sounds.
        e. Suction if needed.
        f. Provide reassurance, involve parents in care.

C. **Pneumonia**—localized inflammation of lung tissues caused by bacteria, viruses, or aspiration. Usually viral cause in children.
    1. **Assessment**
        a. Dry cough, fever 103–104 degrees
        b. Shallow, rapid respirations; tachycardia; sternal retractions and nasal flaring possible
    2. **Medical Treatment**
        a. Treat viral with riboviran, bacterial with antibiotics
        b. Antipyretics (not aspirin, which may lead to Reye's Syndrome)
    3. **Nursing Inteventions**
        a. Humidified O_2, chest PT, and postural drainage
        b. Monitor intake and output
        c. Bed rest until fever diminishes, then activity as tolerated
        d. Frequent vital signs
        e. Administer antipyretics and antibiotics as ordered

D. **Tonsilitis and Adenoiditis**—inflammation of tonsils and adenoids, caused by bacteria or viruses
    1. **Assessment**
        a. Difficulty swallowing and breathing
        b. Nonproductive cough; possible temperature
        c. Hoarseness
        d. Visualization of throat shows presence of redness and swelling of tonsils and adenoids
    2. **Medical Treatment**
        a. Antibiotics, if indicated
        b. Surgical removal of tonsils and adenoids if chronic infections present

3. **Nursing Interventions**
   a. Postoperative: Observe for *signs of bleeding*—increased pulse, restlessness, frequent swallowing, nausea and vomiting
   b. Position on side or stomach
   c. Monitor vital signs
   d. Encourage cool, nondairy liquids
   e. Instruct child and parents on diet, fluids, activity, prevention of infections, and delayed hemorrhage

E. **Acute Otitis Media**—infection of middle ear, frequently caused by nose/throat infections that travel through the child's shorter, wider eustachian tube; usually follows upper respiratory infection. Most common in infants and preschoolers.
   1. **Assessment**
      a. Earache, fever, possible drainage, hearing loss in affected ear
      b. Otoscope exam—red or opaque, bulging or retracting tympanic membrane
   2. **Medical Treatment**
      a. Antibiotics to treat infectious organism
      b. Possible myringotomy, if infections are chronic
   3. **Nursing Interventions**
      a. Administer antibiotics, analgesics, decongestants, as ordered.
      b. Encourage fluid intake.
      c. Observe for ear drainage.
      d. Teach child and family about cause and treatment of otitis media.
      e. Teach precautions, importance of avoiding water in ear, if myringotomy tubes.

F. **Asthma**—obstructive airway disease caused by spasms of bronchioles due to hypersensitive airways. Most common in school-aged children.
   1. **Assessment**
      a. Bronchospasm, increased mucus secretion, edema, decreased diameter of air passage
      b. Shortness of breath, tachycardia, prolonged expiratory phase—wheezing
   2. **Medical Treatment**
      a. Identify and eliminate irritants and allergens.
      b. Treat with bronchodilators and cromolyn sodium to prevent repeat attacks.
   3. **Nursing Interventions**
      a. Administer and teach client about bronchodilators and corticosteriods
         (1) Monitor for side effects of bronchodilators—tachycardia, restlessness, heart palpitations, and nausea, and vomiting.
         (2) Educate client and family about short- and long-term care.
         (3) Maintain hydration by encouraging fluid intake.

G. **Cystic Fibrosis**—multisystem disorder primarily affecting exocrine (mucus-producing) glands. Body produces thick mucus, which accumulates and obstructs small ducts and passages. Pancreatic ducts become blocked—enzymes don't reach duodenum, impairment in digestion and absorption of nutrients. Males usually don't produce sperm. Sweat glands don't reabsorb sodium. *High levels of sodium and chloride present in the sweat*. It is inherited as an *autosomal recessive trait*.
   1. **Assessment**
      a. The newborn may have a meconium ileus—abdominal distention; vomiting; no passage of stool; bulky, frothy stools; weight loss; tissue wasting; failure to thrive
      b. Frequent upper respiratory infections
      c. Chronic cough, barrel chest, and dyspnea
      d. Delayed puberty

ALERT!

Sudden Infant Death Syndrome (SIDS) occurs more frequently in male babies than in female babies; it also occurs more frequently among Native American, African American, and Hispanic children, and more frequently in children between 2 and 4 months old. To help prevent SIDS, place infants in the supine position to sleep, and remove any soft bedding and stuffed toys.

2. **Medical Treatment**
    a. Nutrients should include pancreatic enzymes with food intake, vitamins, high protein, and high-salt diet during summer
    b. Respiratory therapy
    c. Antibiotics, mucolytics, expectorants
    d. Genetic counseling
    e. Diagnosis by sweat chloride test over 60 mEq/L

3. **Nursing Interventions**
    a. Teach about dietary requirements.
    b. Provide inhalation therapy, postural drainage, breathing exercises, and mucolytic drugs, as ordered.
    c. Prevent respiratory infection.
    d. Administer antibiotics, other medications, as ordered.
    e. Provide emotional support to family and refer to Cystic Fibrosis Foundation and other community agencies.

GASTROINTESTINAL DISORDERS

A. **Cleft Lip and/or Cleft Palate (congenital malformation)**—clefts in upper lip and/or palate.
  1. **Assessment**
    a. Facial malformations including a defect in the lip and/or palate
    b. Incidence higher in Caucasians, affects approximately 1 in 1,000 births
    c. Causes predisposition to infection because of communication between nose and mouth
  2. **Medical Treatment**
    a. Surgical correction
      (1) Lip repair done at approximately 2 months
      (2) Cleft palate repair done at 18 months
    b. Referral to speech therapist, dentist, orthodontist
  3. **Nursing Interventions**
    a. Use special nipple or appliance when feeding. Keep head upright to prevent aspiration. Burp frequently.
    b. After lip surgery, protect operative site—don't position on stomach, apply elbow restraints; maintain metal appliance, avoid straining on suture line by anticipating needs.
    c. After palate surgery, avoid placing object in mouth, use elbow restraints.

B. **Tracheoesophageal Fistula (TEF)**—malformation in which the esophagus and trachea do not separate. Similar anomalies occur in which the esophagus ends in a blind pouch.
  1. **Assessment**
    a. Drooling, coughing, cyanosis, feedings returning through the nose
    b. Gastric distention due to air entering stomach through the fistula
  2. **Medical Treatment**
    a. Antibiotics for respiratory infections
    b. Surgery
      (1) Placement of gastrostomy tube for feedings
      (2) Corrective surgery to correct the defect
  3. **Nursing Interventions**
    a. Before surgery
      (1) Maintain patent airway, position with 30-degree head elevation.

(2) Provide nasal suctioning as needed, keep NPO, administer IV fluids as ordered.
  b. After surgery
    (1) Gastrostomy tube feedings until surgical site is healed
    (2) Promote respiratory function, position properly, suction, as needed
  c. Teach parents alternative feeding methods, signs of respiratory distress, and suctioning techniques.

C. Pyloric Stenosis—malformation of the pyloric sphincter (the stomach outlet) that makes it difficult for food to enter the small intestine
  1. **Assessment**
    a. Forceful to projectile vomiting shortly after a feeding
    b. Weight loss, signs of dehydration
    c. Olive-sized bulge under right rib cage
  2. **Medical Treatment**
    a. Diagnosis by upper GI series
    b. Surgery—pyloromyotomy
  3. **Nursing Interventions**
    a. Assess for dehydration, monitor electrolytes (at risk for metabolic alkalosis due to vomiting and loss of stomach acid).
    b. Monitor weight and urine-specific gravity daily.
    c. Administer thickened feedings.
    d. Keep on right side after feedings.
    e. After surgery (usually done at two months)—advance diet as tolerated, place on right side after feedings, monitor weight, intake and output, observe for signs of infection.
    f. Teach parents how to feed and position infant prior to discharge.

D. Intussusception—part of intestine falls forward into an adjoining part, causing edema, obstruction, and possible bowel necrosis
  1. **Assessment**
    a. Currant jelly–like stools
    b. Vomiting of bile-stained fluid
    c. Severe abdominal pain
  2. **Medical Treatment**
    a. Barium enema to release telescoping by pressure
    b. Surgery if barium is unsuccessful
  3. **Nursing Interventions**
    a. Preoperative and postoperative care for abdominal surgery.
    b. Monitor for fluid and electrolyte balance.
    c. Assess for signs of peritonitis.

> **NOTE**
> Know intussusception is characterized by currant jelly–like stools.

E. Imperforate Anus—congenital malformation in which the rectum has no exterior opening
  1. **Assessment**
    a. Meconium is not passed within 24 hours of birth
    b. Stool passage from another opening
    c. Absence of anus
  2. **Medical Management**
    a. Surgery to reconstruct opening (may only be covered by a membrane)
    b. Temporary colostomy if necessary
  3. **Nursing Interventions**
    a. If imperforate anus suspected, no rectal temperatures.
    b. Assist in diagnostic procedures.

      c. Perform manual dilatation, as ordered.

      d. Monitor intake and output; weigh daily.

      e. Support parents and provide teaching about diet and postoperative care.

F. Hirschsprung's Disease—enlargement of lower colon due to lack of nerve cells in area

  1. **Assessment**

      a. Failure or delay in passage of meconium

      b. Constipation and abdominal distention

      c. Impaction results in only loose stools being passed

      d. Nausea and anorexia

      e. Failure to grow, loss of weight

  2. **Medical Treatment**

      a. Stool softeners, isotonic enemas

      b. Low residue diet

      c. Surgery—colostomy or bowel reconstruction

  3. **Nursing Interventions**

      a. Administer stool softeners and enemas, as ordered.

      b. Administer TPN, as ordered.

      c. Provide support to parents and teach about low-residue diet and colostomy care.

      d. Postoperative care and teaching after reconstructive surgery.

G. Celiac Disease—malabsorption syndrome characterized by intolerance of gluten (found in wheat and other grains); familial, cause unknown; flat mucosal surface and lack of villi in intestine, causing malabsorption of fats; onset between ages 1 to 5

  1. **Assessment**

      a. Steatorrhea: frothy, pale, bulky, foul-smelling, greasy stools

      b. Failure to thrive and muscle wasting; distended abdomen

      c. Abdominal pain, irritability, apathy

  2. **Medical Treatment**

      a. Dietary elimination of wheat, barley, rye, and oats

      b. Supplemental vitamins and minerals

      c. TPN in extremely malnourished children

  3. **Nursing Interventions**

      a. Teach and monitor gluten-free diet.

      b. Administer supplemental vitamins, as ordered.

      c. Provide family/client teaching prior to discharge

        (1) Gluten-free diet and importance of reading labels

        (2) Avoiding infraction

        (3) Importance of long-term management

GENITOURINARY DISORDERS

A. Epispadias and Hypospadias—congenital malformation of penis in which urethra opens on dorsal surface (epispadias) or ventral surface (hypospadias)

  1. **Assessment**

      a. Often picked up by pediatric nurses when stream of urine is off-center

      b. Urinary meatus is misplaced

      c. May be associated with chordee—ventral curvature of penis—causing constriction

  2. **Medical Treatment**

      a. If defect minimal, intervention may not be necessary.

      b. Neonatal circumcision is delayed because tissue may be needed for repair.

    c. Corrective surgery usually performed between 6 and 18 months—may be several surgeries.

  3. **Nursing Interventions**

    a. Provide emotional support to parents, as well as teaching about corrective surgery.

    b. Postoperative care: monitor urinary catheter drainage, change dressing.

B. Cryptorchidism (absence of testes in scrotal sac on one or both sides)—unilateral is most common. Normally, testes descend at eight months' gestation (premature infants' testes will not be descended). Testes may descend spontaneously within first year. Risks of cryptorchidism are sterility and increased incidence of testicular cancer.

  1. **Assessment**

    a. Unable to palpate testes in scrotal sac

  2. **Medical Treatment**

    a. Usually treated before age 1 or 2

    b. May be given human chorionic gonadotropin to promote descent of testes

    c. Orchipexy: surgical treatment to bring testes down the inguinal canal

  3. **Nursing Interventions**

    a. Parental support and teaching

    b. If surgery, routine preoperative and postoperative care

C. Wilms Tumor (nephroblastoma)—fast-growing malignant tumor of the kidney; most common in children under 2

  1. **Assessment**

    a. Mass palpable on either side of abdomen or costovertebral area

    b. Possible hematuria, fever, and hypertension

  2. **Medical Treatment**

    a. Surgery to remove the tumor within 48 hours of diagnosis

    b. Postsurgery radiation, possibly chemotherapy

  3. **Nursing Interventions**

    a. Don't palpate abdomen or mass to prevent spreading.

    b. Preoperative and postoperative care.

    c. Monitor bowel sounds following surgery.

    d. Provide support and information to family (prognosis is good with early diagnosis and treatment for children under 2 years old).

D. Enuresis—involuntary passage of urine (usually at night) after usual age of continence, approximately 4 years old; familial tendency, most common in boys

  1. **Assessment**

    a. Rule out organic cause

    b. Physical exam normal

  2. **Medical Treatment**

    a. Bladder retention exercises

    b. Behavior modification—bed alarm devices

    c. Drug therapy—Tricyclic antidepressants (Tofranil) or anticholinergics

  3. **Nursing Interventions**

    a. Reassure parents that this is not misbehavior or due to an emotional disturbance.

    b. Most often due to incomplete neuromuscular maturation of the bladder.

    c. Involve child in care and use praise and support.

ENDOCRINE DISORDERS

A. **Congenital Hypothyroidism (Cretinism)**—absent or nonfunctioning thyroid. Newborns have maternal thyroid that may last up to three months or after weaning in breastfed infants.

   1. **Assessment**

      a. PKU newborn screening test will give results on thyroid function and can prevent problems

      b. Prolonged physiological jaundice, lethargy, feeding difficulties, large protruding tongue, hypothermia, and hypotension

      c. Low levels of T3 and T4

   2. **Medical Treatment**

      a. Lifetime thyroid hormone replacement therapy

   3. **Nursing Interventions**

      a. Administer oral thyroxine and vitamin D, as ordered, to prevent mental retardation.

      b. Provide client teaching and instruction regarding medication administration, side effects, and importance of continued therapy.

B. **Juvenile Diabetes Mellitus**—most common endocrine disorder of children, onset at any age. All are insulin dependent. Cause may be genetic, and/or possible autoimmune response to a virus.

   1. **Assessment**

      a. Polyuria, polydipsia, polyphagia

      b. Weight loss

      c. Hyperglycemia: blood sugar level over 140 mg/dL

   2. **Medical Treatment**

      a. Diet appropriate for age and growth requirements

      b. Insulin replacement

   3. **Nursing Interventions**

      a. Routine assessments: blood sugar, glycosylated hemoglobin (to determine glucose concentration over time).

      b. Teach client (parent and child) about the need for monitoring blood sugar, symptoms of hyperglycemia and hypoglycemia.

      c. Teach administration of insulin.

      d. Discuss effect of exercise and infection on blood glucose levels.

      e. Importance of a medical alert bracelet.

CARDIOVASCULAR DISORDERS

Defect	Description	Surgical Correction
Acyanotic Defects		
Patent ductus arteriosus	Failure of fetal ductus arteriosus to close after birth—increases pulmonary circulation	Ligation of the ductus arteriosus
Coarctation of the aorta	Narrowing of the aorta, leading to decreased circulation	Removal of the narrowed area, attaching the two other segments
Atrial septal defect	Abnormal opening between the left and right atria	Closure or patching of the defect
Ventricular septal defects	Abnormal opening between the right and left ventricle	Closure or patching of the defect
Cyanotic Defects		
Tetralogy of Fallot	Four defects: pulmonic stenosis, ventricular-septal defect, overriding aorta, and hypertrophy of the right ventricle	Correction of pulmonic stenosis, closure of the ventricular septal defect, movement of the aorta to the left ventricle
Transposition of the Great Vessels	Aorta originates from the right ventricle, the pulmonary artery from the left ventricle	Switching of vessels to correct their anatomic position
Tricuspid atresia	Small right ventricle, large left ventricle, and diminished pulmonary circulation	Glenn anastomosis or bidirectional Glenn shunt
Truncus arteriosus	Pulmonary and systemic circulation are made up of one arterial trunk—no separation of pulmonary artery and aorta	Pulmonary arteries are excised from the common trunk and attached to the right ventricle.

NOTE

All cyanotic defects begin with a "T."

A. **Congenital Heart Disease**—occurs in approximately 8 in 1,000 births; thought to be due to combined genetic and environmental factors; classified into acyanotic defects, which typically lead to congestive heart failure, and cyanotic defects, which have a worse prognosis

    1. **Assessment**

        a. Cyanosis at rest or during exertion; shortness of breath

        b. Fatigue, failure to thrive, tachypnea

        c. With coarctation of the aorta, there is a significant difference in pulse and blood pressure between the upper and lower extremities

    2. **Medical Treatment**

        a. Most defects must be corrected by surgery.

        b. Some symptoms may be treated with medications.

    3. **Nursing Interventions**

        a. Preoperative—provide support and teaching to family.

        b. Postoperative—monitor vital signs, dressing, neurologic status.

c. May give oxygen, suction, perform postural drainage.

d. Provide client teaching and discharge planning.

B. **Rheumatic Fever**—an inflammatory disorder preceded by an infection of group A beta-homolytic streptococcus; usually school-aged child; antibodies against the strep also attack heart valves

  1. **Assessment**

     a. Lethargy, low-grade fever, anorexia

     b. Muscle and joint pain, carditis

     c. Subcutaneous nodules—usually associated with carditis and severe disease

  2. **Medical Treatment**

     a. Antibiotics

     b. Salicylates for joint pain

     c. Steroids for inflammation

  3. **Nursing Interventions**

     a. Maintain client on bed rest.

     b. Administer antibiotics.

     c. Encourage age-appropriate sedentary play.

     d. Support parents and client and provide discharge teaching.

C. **Kawasaki Disease**—a systemic inflammation of the small vessels, affecting primarily children under 3 years; no known cause; pericarditis and aneurysms may develop, as well as thrombus formation

  1. **Assessment**

     a. High fever, unresponsive to antipyretics

     b. Strawberry tongue, inflammation of the pharynx and oral mucosa

     c. Rash, lymphadenopathy

     d. Edematous extremeties with erythema of palms and soles of feet

     e. Symptoms of congestive heart failure

  2. **Medical Treatment**

     a. IV gamma globulin

     b. Salicylates

     c. Coumadin if aneurysms are present

  3. **Nursing Interventions**

     a. Monitor cardiac status.

     b. Weigh daily and monitor intake and output.

     c. Provide range-of-motion exercises to prevent stiffness from arthritis.

     d. Support and teach client and family; educate about providing home care.

HEMATOPOIETIC DISORDERS

A. **Sickle Cell Anemia**—an autosomal recessive genetic disorder most common among African Americans (if both parents are carriers, 1 in 4 children will have sickle cell disease, 2 in 4 will be carriers, 1 in 4 will be free of the disease). Normal adult hemoglobin (HbA) is replaced by hemoglobin S (HbS). HbS hemoglobin assumes a rigid sickle shape and has a shorter life and decreased oxygen-carrying capacity.

  1. **Assessment**

     a. Chronic anemia, growth retardation, and delayed puberty

     b. Sickle cell crisis occurs when client is ill or stressed and involves painful swelling of areas involved—such as joints, hands

     c. Hemoglobin electrophoresis determines the type and extent of abnormal hemoglobin

2. **Medical Treatment**
   a. Promote adequate oxygenation and adequate hydration to prevent sickling.
   b. Treat crisis with bed rest, fluids, analgesics, transfusions, oxygen.
   c. Splenectomy may be needed for recurrent pooling of blood in spleen.
3. **Nursing Interventions**
   a. Administer oxygen, analgesics, and IV therapy, as ordered.
   b. Warmth provides comfort to affected areas.
   c. Teach family preventive care and how to manage client at home.

B. **Leukemia**—most common childhood cancer, highest incidence between ages 3 and 5; involves unrestrained growth of abnormal, immature white blood cells
   1. **Assessment**
      a. Weight loss, fatigue, weakness
      b. Abdominal and joint pain
      c. Petechiae and bruises
      d. Enlarged liver and spleen
   2. **Medical Treatment**
      a. Chemotherapy
      b. Prevent infection
      c. Reverse isolation, if very low white blood count
   3. **Nursing Interventions**
      a. Administer antiemetic 30 minutes before eating.
      b. Offer high-calorie, cold liquids as diet supplements.
      c. Provide emotional support to child and parents.

C. **Hodgkins Disease**—malignancy of the lymph system, involving a proliferation of lymphocytes; most commonly occurs between 15 and 29 years of age
   1. **Assessment**
      a. Major symptom is enlarged nodes in lower cervical region—nontender, firm, and movable
      b. Recurrent fever, night sweats
      c. Weight loss, lethargy
      d. Pruritis
   2. **Medical Treatment**
      a. Staging of disease: up to 98% survival if stage I, single lymph node involvement
      b. Radiation and chemotherapy
   3. **Nursing Interventions**
      a. Administer chemotherapy, as ordered, and take measures to help alleviate side effects.
      b. Protect client from infection.
      c. Provide support and teaching for child and parents.

D. **Hemophilia**—bleeding disorders in which there is a defect in part of the clotting mechanism
   1. **Assessment**
      a. Prolonged bleeding after minor injury—circumcision, IM immunizations
      b. Easy bruising, hematomas
      c. Bleeding into a joint may cause contractures
   2. **Medical Treatment**
      a. Diagnostic testing to determine type of disorder
      b. Administration of clotting factors, as appropriate
      c. Genetic counseling
      d. Control of acute bleeding episodes

3. **Nursing Interventions**
   a. Help protect client from environment and teach parents how to do this—padding crib rails, etc.
   b. Monitor transfusions and observe for signs of reactions.
   c. Apply cold compresses and pressure to stop bleeding.

E. **Infectious Mononucleosis**—an infection caused by the Epstein Barr virus; it is thought to be only mildly contagious—causes an increase in mononuclear white blood cells and symptoms of a generalized infection
   1. **Assessment**
      a. Fatigue, sore throat, enlarged lymph glands
      b. Red, flat rash on the body
      c. Tonsillitis
   2. **Medical Treatment**
      a. Diagnosis based on symptoms and a positive Monospot blood test
      b. Rest and symptomatic treatment
      c. Acyclovir given to immunosuppressed clients
   3. **Nursing Interventions**
      a. Provide teaching about disease and method of transmission—"kissing disease."
      b. Maintain bed rest as needed.
      c. Provide diet and hydration.
      d. Maintain medical asepsis, reverse isolation usually not needed.

NEUROLOGICAL DISORDERS

A. **Spina Bifida**—neural tube defect in which the vertebra fail to fuse, and part of the meninges and spinal cord protrude through the spinal column; often familial, insufficient folic acid is thought to be one of the causes. Severity varies; the most common site for the lesion is the lumbosacral area.
   1. **Assessment**
      a. Findings depend on the site and severity of the defect
      b. Skin may be intact, covering the sac, or may be leaking fluid
      c. Motor/sensory—low (lumbosacral) lesion results in minimal weakness of legs
      d. Possible incontinence, loss of bowel control, and loss of feeling below the lesion
   2. **Medical Treatment**
      a. Surgery to cover skin and protect lesion.
      b. Correct associated abnormalities, if possible.
      c. Monitor for hydrocephalus, infections, renal problems.
      d. Colostomy or urinary diversion for incontinence.
      e. Shunt procedure, if accompanied by hydrocephalus.
   3. **Nursing Interventions**
      a. Maintain integrity of sac and protect from infection or further damage.
      b. Preoperative care—optimal nutrition, hydration, skin care.
      c. Postoperative care—prevention of infection, hydration, nutrition.
      d. Provide bladder care and perform and teach family Crede maneuver to expel urine.
      e. Administer antibiotics, as ordered.
      f. Provide emotional support to parents and family.

B. Hydrocephalus—increased amount of cerebrospinal fluid in the ventricles of the brain
1. **Assessment**
   a. Enlarging head size, bulging fontanelles
   b. "Sunset sign"—sclera visible above iris
   c. Poor neck control
   d. Feeding problems
2. **Medical Treatment**
   a. Insertion of shunt to drain fluid
3. **Nursing Interventions**
   a. Preoperative care—emotional support and optimal nutrition.
   b. Postoperative care—observing neurologic and vital signs; supporting head and neck during movement; preventing infection; assessing for proper function of shunt.
   c. Support family and teach strategies to prevent or decrease long-term complications.

C. Meningitis—viral or bacterial infection of the meninges and cerebrospinal fluid
1. **Assessment**
   a. Fever, irritability, high-pitched cry
   b. Nuchal (neck) rigidity
   c. Seizures are likely
   d. Bulging fontanelles in infant
2. **Medical Treatment**
   a. Lumbar puncture to determine causative organism
   b. Antibiotics or antivirals
3. **Nursing Interventions**
   a. Assist with lumbar puncture. Have client lie flat for several hours after the puncture to prevent spinal headache.
   b. Administer antibiotics or antiviral medication.
   c. Monitor vital signs, frequent neurological checks.
   d. Seizure precautions.
   e. Restrict fluids to prevent increased intracranial pressure.
   f. Maintain quiet environment and support client and family.

D. Epilepsy—recurrent, transient, unprovoked seizure activity; may be absence seizures, which can be confused with inattentiveness or tonic-clonic seizures; most common during first 2 years
1. **Assessment**
   a. Family history for seizures
   b. Age at onset of seizures, detailed description of seizures
   c. Presence of aura
   d. Behavior after seizure
2. **Medical Treatment**
   a. Anticonvulsants
   b. Determine cause and correct, if possible
   c. Promote as normal a lifestyle as possible
3. **Nursing Interventions**
   a. Administer anticonvulsants, as ordered.
   b. Protect child from injury during seizure.
   c. Do not place anything in child's mouth.
   d. Comfort child after seizure.
   e. Support and help child and family deal with problems related to the disorder.

MUSCULOSKELETAL DISORDERS

A. **Talipes**—a deformity in which the foot is twisted out of its normal position; most common is talipes equinovarus, with the foot pointing downward and inward; a congenital defect that is usually unilateral
   1. **Assessment**
      a. Foot cannot be moved into correct position
   2. **Medical Treatment**
      a. Correct deformity by successive casts until normal muscle balance
      b. Use of Denis Browne splint to normalize position (less severe defects)
      c. Surgical correction
   3. **Nursing Interventions**
      a. Teach family cast care.
      b. Preoperative and postoperative care.
      c. Support and educate family about continuing care after discharge.

B. **Congenital Dislocation of the Hip**—familial congenital deformity, more common in girls. Defect involves displacement of the head of the femur from the acetabulum.
   1. **Assessment**
      a. Asymmetrical gluteal and thigh folds
      b. Limitation of movement on affected side
      c. Ortolani maneuver—performed by experienced practitioner—is positive (click heard)
   2. **Medical Treatment**
      a. Goal is to maintain hip abduction
         (1) Newborn—triple diapering
         (2) Immobilization devices: splints, casts (often spica cast), abduction braces
      b. Older child (over 18 months)—surgical reduction
   3. **Nursing Interventions**
      a. Maintain cast, if present.
      b. Careful skin care to prevent breakdown near corrective device.
      c. Range-of-motion exercises to unaffected limbs.
      d. Check circulation, sensation, and motion every 4 hours.

C. **Scoliosis**—lateral curvature of the spine, most common in adolescent girls. Two types: *Nonstructural* (functional)—may be corrected by stretching exercises; *Structural*—brace/surgery needed.
   1. **Assessment**
      a. Curvature of spine noted when standing or bending
      b. Uneven shoulders, waist, hips
      c. X-ray confirmation
   2. **Medical Treatment**
      a. External (Milwaukee) brace
      b. Casting
      c. Skeletal traction
      d. Surgical internal fixation—Harrington rod or spinal fusion
      e. Electrical stimulation
   3. **Nursing Interventions**
      a. Screen school-aged children.
      b. Teach and encourage prescribed exercises.
      c. Monitor pressure points of brace.
      d. Promote positive body image with brace.
      e. Cast care or preoperative and postoperative care, if applicable.

D. Juvenile Rheumatoid Arthritis—chronic, systemic disorder of the connective tissue due to an autoimmune reaction; leads to eventual joint destruction and is most common in pre-adolescent girls

  1. **Assessment**
    a. Joint swelling, limitation of movement
    b. Morning stiffness, pain on motion
    c. Intermittent macular rheumatoid rash

  2. **Medical Treatment**
    a. Suppress inflammatory response (NSAIDs, corticosteroids, cytotoxic drugs).
    b. Preserve form and function with physical therapy.
    c. Reduce pain with analgesia.

  3. **Nursing Interventions**
    a. Administer anti-inflammatory and pain medications, as ordered.
    b. Provide heat to affected joints.
    c. Help with range-of-motion exercises.
    d. Teach client and family to follow up with treatments at home.

E. Fracture—a break in bone continuity, usually caused by a traumatic injury. Children's bones are more easily injured than adults' but often do not completely break because of their flexibility.

Types of Fractures	
Simple (closed):	Fracture of bone with no external skin wound
Compound (open):	Break with external wound present at site
Comminuted:	Bone is splintered into fragments
Greenstick:	One side of the bone is broken, the other side is bent

  1. **Assessment**
    a. Pain, tenderness, and muscle spasm over fracture site
    b. Deformity
    c. Diminished function
    d. Diagnosis by X-ray

  2. **Medical Treatment**
    a. Regain correct alignment through reduction
      (1) Open—surgical incision used to align
      (2) Closed—bone brought into alignment by external manipulation
    b. Stabilization of corrected alignment
      (1) Open—metallic pins, wires, screws, rods
      (2) Closed—cast, splint, and/or traction

  3. **Nursing Interventions**
    a. Monitor for complications by frequent (at least every 4 hours) assessments distal to the injury.

Five P's of Neurovascular Assessment
① Pain
② Peripheral pulses
③ Pallor of skin
④ Paresthesia
⑤ Paralysis

    b. Complications include:

      (1) Infection, especially with open fractures

      (2) Compartmental syndrome—fascia between compartments in the extremities does not expand with increase in contents, due to bleeding or swelling, and may cause permanent damage to the nerves or blood vessels

      (3) Volkmann's contracture—crippling hand injury in which circulation is compromised following casting of an elbow or forearm injury

      (4) Venous stasis and thrombus formation

    c. Assess skin for breakdown.

    d. Cast—do not apply heat to dry quickly and don't let it get wet. Elevate extremity for the first day after casting.

    e. Traction—maintain proper alignment, assess pin sites.

    f. Instruct client and family on home care, including signs and symptoms to report to provider.

Types of Traction

Countertraction: A force pulling against the traction.

Suspension Traction: Suspension of a body part with frames, slings, pulleys, and weights.

Skin Traction: Attaching weights to bands on the skin.

Buck's Traction (skin): Applying a straight pull on an extremity—such as immobilizing a leg.

Russell's Traction (skin): In addition to a straight pull, has a sling suspending the knee joint; may be used with a femur fracture, since it allows some knee flexion.

Skeletal Traction: Traction is affixed directly to the bone by a wire or pin, not externally as with skin traction. An example is cervical tongs used to maintain alignment of the spine.

F. Cerebral Palsy—a neuromuscular disorder resulting from damage to the part of the brain that controls motor function. Treatment focuses on optimizing function, since the disorder cannot be cured. Most commonly found in premature infants, it is associated with anoxia during pregnancy, labor and delivery, or post-birth.

  1. **Assessment**

    a. Abnormal muscle tone and coordination

    b. Seizures

    c. Problems with speech, hearing, or vision

  2. **Medical Treatment** (primarily supportive)

    a. Maximize mobility with physical therapy and orthopedic devices

    b. Skeletal muscle relaxants

  3. **Nursing Interventions**

    a. Assist child in becoming as independent and self-sufficient as possible.

    b. Encourage age-appropriate play.

    c. Provide parent and family support as well as referral to community resources.

COGNITIVE AND SENSORY DISORDERS

A. **Strabismus**—the eyes are not directed and focused on the same object. One eye deviates to the center (esotropia) or to the outer corner (exotropia). May result in *amblyopia,* "lazy eye," in which there is reduced visual acuity in one eye.
   1. **Assessment**
      a. Apparent deviation of an eye
      b. Possible decreased visual acuity or double vision
   2. **Medical Treatment**
      a. Surgical correction
      b. Patching of one eye to force child to use and strengthen the other eye
      c. Corrective lenses to help focus object on retina
   3. **Nursing Interventions**
      a. Assist in implementing therapies such as patching.
      b. Teach preoperative and postoperative care.
      c. Support and educate child and family.

B. **Down's Syndrome (trisomy 21)**—a chromosomal disorder that causes multiple defects as well as mental retardation; incidence increased in mothers who are over 35 years old
   1. **Assessment**
      a. Protruding tongue
      b. Short hands and fingers
      c. Simian crease (transverse palmar crease)
      d. Decreased muscle tone
      e. Often associated with cardiac anomalies
   2. **Medical Treatment**
      a. Correction of associated anomalies
      b. Encourage genetic counseling and prenatal screening (amniocentesis and triple screen), as appropriate
   3. **Nursing Interventions**
      a. Assist family in optimizing child's development through infant stimulation and special education.
      b. Support and educate child and family.

SKIN DISORDERS

A. **Pediculosis capitis (head lice)**—a parasitic infestation that is particularly common among school children. The louse is spread by close physical contact (sharing combs, hats, etc.).
   1. **Assessment**
      a. Itching of scalp
      b. White eggs (nits) visible on hair shaft
      c. Nits most commonly found at the nape of the neck and behind the ears
   2. **Medical Treatment**
      a. Treat with shampoo designed to kill lice.
      b. Administer antipruritics.
   3. **Nursing Interventions**
      a. Teach family how to apply shampoo and remove nits with fine-toothed comb.
      b. Educate client and family about means of transmission and teach not to share combs, etc.
      c. Instruct family to wash all bedding, clothing, hats, towels, etc., in hot water to destroy lice and eggs.

B. Ringworm—fungal infection spread by direct contact; called tinea capitis (affects scalp), tinea corporis (on body), tinea pedis (feet)
1. **Assessment**
   a. Itching
   b. Presence of papules or dry scales
   c. Spreads in a circular pattern
   d. Detected by Wood's lamp—turns green at base of affected hair shaft
2. **Medical Treatment**
   a. Antifungal ointment
   b. Oral griseofulvin
3. **Nursing Interventions**
   a. Teach family how to administer medications.
   b. Educate client and family to prevent by isolation from known sources of infection.

C. Impetigo—bacterial infection of the outer layers of the skin. Agent is usually staphylococcus or streptococcus. It is common in toddlers and preschoolers. The infection is very contagious and related to poor sanitation.
1. **Assessment**
   a. Macules, papules, and vesicles that rupture, causing a moist erosion
   b. Drying of moist area leaves a honey-colored crust
   c. Usually found on face, axillae, and extremities
   d. Itching
2. **Medical Treatment**
   a. Topical and systemic antibiotics
3. **Nursing Interventions**
   a. Gently soften (with Burrow's solution compresses) and remove crusts.
   b. Cover and isolate infected areas.
   c. Teach client and family about medication administration and proper hygiene.

GROWTH AND DEVELOPMENT DISORDERS

A. Failure to Thrive—a condition in which a child fails to gain weight and is persistently below the 5th percentile on growth charts. If it is not due to an organic reason, it may be caused by a disrupted maternal-child relationship.
1. **Assessment**
   a. Physical exam indicates delayed growth and development—physical, social, etc.
   b. Listlessness, poor appetite, unresponsive to being cuddled.
   c. Assess parenting skills and possibility of abuse or neglect.
2. **Medical Treatment**
   a. Assess for disease or other physical problem.
3. **Nursing Interventions**
   a. Provide child with sensory stimulation.
   b. Give family emotional support and encourage parents to participate in care.
   c. Provide small, frequent feedings to promote weight gain.
   d. Teach parenting skills.
   e. Assess home situation.

EXERCISES: PEDIATRIC NURSING

1. When teaching clients to prevent the recurrence of scabies, the nurse would include which of the following instructions?

   (1) "Discard all makeup and skin lotions after six months of use."

   (2) "All clothing and linens must be washed in hot water and dried in the hot cycle."

   (3) "Wear absorbent materials such as cotton underwear and socks."

   (4) "Use an antibacterial soap whenever there is a possibility of exposure."

2. The nurse answers a call bell and finds a frightened mother whose child, the client, is having a seizure. Which of these actions should the nurse take?

   (1) A nurse should insert a padded tongue blade in the client's mouth to prevent the child from swallowing or choking on his tongue.

   (2) The nurse should help the mother restrain the child to prevent him from injuring himself.

   (3) The nurse should call the operator to page for seizure assistance.

   (4) The nurse should clear the area and position the client safely.

3. A 12-month-old girl is diagnosed with otitis media for the third time. The mother is concerned that her child is catching too many colds and that this is leading to the infections. The nurse explains that the anatomy of a child's ear differs from that of an adult, and that this difference in structure can cause children to develop otitis media after having a cold. Identify with an "X" the portion of a child's ear that differs from an adult ear.

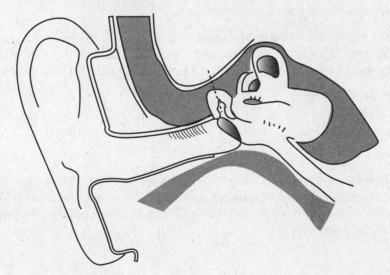

4. At the community center, a nurse leads an adolescent health information group, which often expands into other areas of discussion. She knows that these youths are trying to find out "who they are," and the discussion often focuses on which directions they want to take in school and life, as well as peer relationships. According to Erikson, this stage is known as

   (1) identity vs. role confusion.
   (2) adolescent rebellion.
   (3) career experimentation.
   (4) relationship testing.

Question 5 has three answer choices that are similar to one another. Remember that the answer choice that differs most from the others is likely to be the correct one.

5. The young mother tells the nurse that she is concerned about the safety of her 15-month-old son, who seems to be "getting into everything" and needs to be watched constantly. The nurse responds that the most important consideration in accident prevention with toddlers is

   (1) teaching them the meaning of "no."
   (2) buying only age-appropriate toys.
   (3) not allowing them to play with dangerous items.
   (4) ensuring a safe environment by childproofing.

6. A nurse is assessing a 9-month-old boy for a well-baby check up. Which of the following observations would be of most concern?

   (1) The baby cannot say "mama" when he wants his mother.
   (2) The mother has not given him finger foods.
   (3) The child does not sit unsupported.
   (4) The baby cries whenever the mother goes out.

7. A new mother asks the nurse whether she should pick up the baby when he cries. According to Erikson's theory of psychosocial development, the nurse's most appropriate reply should take into consideration his developmental task, which is

   (1) trust vs. mistrust.
   (2) intimacy vs. isolation.
   (3) autonomy vs. doubt and shame.
   (4) identity vs. role confusion.

8. Karen, the mother of an 11-month-old girl, Shannon, is in the clinic for her daughter's immunizations. She expresses concern that Shannon cannot yet walk. The nurse correctly replies that, according to the Denver Developmental Screen, the median age for walking is

   (1) 12 months.
   (2) 15 months.
   (3) 10 months.
   (4) 14 months.

9. The school nurse is explaining physical development to a class of 11-year-old girls. She states that most girls begin their periods between ages 10 and 18, with the average age being 12. This event is called

   (1) ovulogenesis.
   (2) menorrhagia.
   (3) menarche.
   (4) puberty.

10. Morgan B., age 13, has had a lumbar puncture to examine the CSF to determine whether she has a bacterial infection. The best position in which to keep her after the procedure is

    (1) prone for 2 hours to prevent aspiration, should she vomit.
    (2) semi-Fowler's, so she can watch TV for 5 hours and be entertained.
    (3) supine for several hours, to prevent headache.
    (4) on her right side to encourage return of CSF.

11. Johnny has a short leg cast for a fractured ankle he sustained while playing football. You instruct him to

    (1) use a hair dryer to finish drying the cast when he gets home or after showering.
    (2) try not to wiggle his toes, but keep them warm and covered.
    (3) keep his leg elevated for the first day.
    (4) not to worry if his toes feel numb—that it is to be expected.

12. Buck's traction with a 10-lb. weight is securing a client's leg while she is waiting for surgery to repair a hip fracture. It is important to check circulation-sensation-movement every

    (1) shift.
    (2) day.
    (3) 4 hours.
    (4) 15 minutes.

13. Adam W., age 15, is an insulin-dependent diabetic and has been taking insulin injections for four years. Adam calls the clinic to report that he is beginning a martial arts program tomorrow and needs to know if he should adjust his insulin in any way before he goes. Your best answer is

    (1) "Take the same dose as usual and see how it goes."
    (2) "Exercise may change your insulin requirements. You should speak to your physician to determine if you should make any changes."
    (3) "Take 5 units less than usual because the increased exercise will use up your glucose and you won't need as much."
    (4) "Ask to speak with the instructor to determine how much added activity will be involved."

14. A 10-year-old child is suspected of having leukemia. He is admitted to a hospital for a bone marrow aspiration. Below are several interventions that the nurse on his case should perform. Place them in the chronological order in which the nurse should perform them.

    (1) Reassure the child that the pain will pass quickly.   _____

    (2) Explain that he will feel pressure and discomfort during the procedure.   _____

    (3) Check the biopsy site for bleeding and inflammation; observe the child for signs of hemorrhage or infection.   _____

    (4) Discuss the procedure with the child's parents and explain how they can help prepare him for it.   _____

15. A nurse working in a college health center admits a young woman who complains of a severe headache, fever, and neck stiffness. The nurse's care is based on the knowledge that these symptoms are characteristic of

    (1) mononucleosis.

    (2) meningitis.

    (3) rheumatic fever.

    (4) Asian flu.

16. The adolescent client has symptoms of meningitis: nuchal rigidity, fever, vomiting, and lethargy. The nurse knows to prepare for which test?

    (1) Blood culture

    (2) Throat and ear culture

    (3) CAT scan

    (4) Lumbar puncture

17. A nurse is caring for a client who has been newly diagnosed as diabetic. The care plan includes careful monitoring of intake and output. The nurse will expect to find which of the following that is a typical presentation of diabetes?

    (1) Anuria

    (2) Polyuria

    (3) Hematuria

    (4) Oliguria

18. A nurse is drawing blood from the diabetic client for a glycosolated hemoglobin test. She explains to the woman that the test is used to determine

    (1) the highest glucose level in the past week.

    (2) her insulin level.

    (3) glucose levels over the past several months.

    (4) her usual fasting glucose level.

19. A nurse is caring for a young man who is in traction with skeletal tongs. She knows that the client most likely is suffering from a

    (1) fracture of the cervical vertebrae.

    (2) spiral fracture.

    (3) tibial fracture.

    (4) displaced fracture.

20. A 12-year-old boy has fractured his arm after falling from his bike. After the injury has been casted, the nurse on this case knows that it is most important to assess the area distal to the injury. Which of the following assessments should the nurse perform?
Select all that apply.

- ☐ **(1)** Capillary refill
- ☐ **(2)** Radial and ulnar pulse
- ☐ **(3)** Finger movement
- ☐ **(4)** Skin integrity

21. Lisa Brown is using bronchodilators for asthma. The side effects of these drugs that you need to monitor this client for include

(1) tachycardia, nausea, vomiting, heart palpitations, inability to sleep, restlessness, and seizures.

(2) tachycardia, headache, dyspnea, temp > 101° F, and wheezing.

(3) blurred vision, tachycardia, hypertension, headache, insomnia, and oliguria.

(4) restlessness, insomnia, blurred vision, hypertension, chest pain, and muscle weakness.

22. The nurse is caring for a client with an arm fracture. The client complains of numbness and tingling of the hand, pain unrelieved by analgesics, and the radial pulse is diminished. The nurse realizes the client may have which of the following complications that requires prompt intervention?

(1) Fat embolism

(2) Infection

(3) Compartment syndrome

(4) Venous stasis

exercises

ANSWER KEY AND EXPLANATIONS

1. 2	6. 3	11. 3	15. 2	19. 1
2. 4	7. 1	12. 3	16. 4	20. 1,2,3
3. Eustachian tube	8. 1	13. 2	17. 2	21. 1
4. 1	9. 3	14. 4,2,1,3	18. 3	22. 3
5. 4	10. 3			

1. **The correct answer is (2).** Scabies is an infestation of the itch mite, Sarcoptes scabiei. It is transmitted sexually through skin-to-skin contact or through household contact. After treatment with permethrin cream or lindane, clients are advised to wash and dry clothing and bedding on the hot cycles.

2. **The correct answer is (4).** The primary role of the nurse when a client has a seizure is to protect the client from harming him- or herself. Forcing an object into the client's mouth (1) could cause injury, as could restraining the client (2). Calling the operator for seizure assistance (3) is unnecessary, since the primary intervention is to protect the client from self-injury.

3. **The correct answer is the Eustachian tube.** In young children, the Eustachian tube is straighter and shorter than in older children and adults. This allows fluid to stagnate at times, and the fluid can act as a medium for bacteria.

4. **The correct answer is (1).** During this period, which lasts up to the age of 18–21 years, the individual develops a sense of "self." Peers have a big influence over behavior, and the decision is to determine a vocational goal.

5. **The correct answer is (4).** Toddlers are too young to be relied upon to remember rules, and they move quickly. The best way to keep them safe is to make sure that their play area is childproofed as much as possible.

6. **The correct answer is (3).** Over 90 percent of babies can sit unsupported by 9 months. Most babies cannot say "mama" in the sense that it refers to their mother at this time (1). Finger foods are not essential at this time (2). It is a good sign that the baby cries when his mother leaves, because he is developing stranger anxiety and his mother is important to him (4).

7. **The correct answer is (1).** The infant develops trust by parents' meeting their needs for love, security, and food.

8. **The correct answer is (1).** By twelve months, 50 percent of children can walk well.

9. **The correct answer is (3).** Menarche is defined as the beginning of

the menstrual cycle and reproductive function in the female.

10. **The correct answer is (3).** Lying flat keeps the client from having a "spinal headache." Increasing the fluid intake will assist in replenishing the lost fluid during this time.

11. **The correct answer is (3).** The leg should be elevated to prevent edema resulting in decreased circulation to the foot and toes. The other choices are wrong; moving the toes will encourage circulation, and numbness is an indication of neuropathy or decreased circulation.

12. **The correct answer is (3).** The client can lose vascular status without the nurse being aware if left for more than 4 hours, yet checks should not be so frequent that the client becomes anxious. Vital signs are generally checked q 4h, at which time the CSM checks can easily be performed.

13. **The correct answer is (2).** Nurses do not prescribe medication doses. You understand that increased exercise would lessen that need for insulin, but it is not within the scope of nursing to make that decision.

14. **The correct order of answers is (4), (2), (1), (3).** The nurse must first discuss the procedure with the child's parents and instruct them on how best to prepare their child. Next, the nurse should explain to the child what he will be experiencing during the procedure. She should be honest and let the child know that although he might be uncomfortable at times, the pain will go away quickly. Finally, after the procedure is completed, the nurse must check for

bleeding, inflammation, and signs and symptoms of pain and infection.

15. **The correct answer is (2).** A severe headache, fever, and neck stiffness are characteristics of meningitis.

16. **The correct answer is (4).** Meningitis is an infection of the meninges, the outer membrane of the brain. Since it is surrounded by cerebrospinal fluid, a lumbar puncture will help to identify the organism involved.

17. **The correct answer is (2).** Polyuria is one of the "three P's" of diabetes: polyuria, polyphagia, and polydipsia.

18. **The correct answer is (3).** The glycosolated hemoglobin test measures glucose levels for the previous three to four months.

19. **The correct answer is (1).** Skeletal tongs are used to stabilize the spine in a client suffering from a cervical fracture (1).

20. **The correct answers are (1), (2), and (3).** Capillary refill (1), pulses (2), and skin temperature and color (3) are indicative of intact circulation and absence of compartment syndrome. Skin integrity is less important than these three indicators.

21. **The correct answer is (1).** Bronchodilators can produce the side effects listed in answer choice (1) for a short time after the client begins using them.

22. **The correct answer is (3).** Compartment syndrome refers to increased pressure in resulting from

edema in a closed area. It causes pain and reduced circulation and pressure on muscles that can result in permanent anesthesia and paralysis. Infection (2) would not cause these symptoms, venous stasis (4) would tend to cause a thrombosis, and a fat embolism (1), which is usually pulmonary, would cause shortness of breath, shock, and possibly death.

SUMMING IT UP

- A basic knowledge of growth—whether in physical or developmental terms or functional changes—is central to pediatric nursing

- Children are prone to a number of disorders that are fairly unique to this period of development, due, in part, to physiological differences and also to a less mature immune system.

- Remember that the NCLEX-PN exam will include questions about the four major Client Needs categories as they relate to children: Safe, Effective Care Environment; Health Promotion and Maintenance; Psychosocial Integrity; and Physiological Integrity.

answers exercises

Psychiatric Nursing

BASIC CONCEPTS

A. **Mental Health**—the ability to obtain satisfaction from life and function socially and at work
   1. **Awareness**—self-awareness and acceptance
   2. **Perception**—reality perception that can change with new information
   3. **Coping Mechanism**—constructive ways of coping with stress

B. **Mental Illness**—a continuum of problems in functioning
   1. **Mild**—occasional difficulty in occupational or social functioning
   2. **Severe**—inability to function in some or all of these areas:
     a. Relating to others
     b. Testing reality
     c. Coping with stress
     d. May be at risk of harming themselves or other people

C. **Holistic View of Mental Health**
   1. **Relationship**—mental and physical health are related
   2. **Factors**—illness is a combination of mental and physical factors
   3. **Determinants**—cultural determinants of mental health; attributes that are functional in one culture may be abnormal in another.

chapter 7

TIP

Know these stages of
development.

Theorists

A. Freud

1. **Psychoanalytic Theory:** Assumes that difficulties in adulthood are caused by unresolved conflicts from childhood
2. **Personality:** Is composed of the *ego* (consciousness), *id* (animal drives), and *superego* (moral standards)
3. **Psychosexual Development:** Progresses from the oral stage of the infant to anal (1–3 years), phallic (3–6 years), latency (6–12 years), and genital (12 years to adult)
4. **Mental Health:** A balance of love and work

B. Erikson

1. **Trust vs. Mistrust (infant):** Establishing trust by having needs met
2. **Autonomy vs. Shame (toddler):** Beginning independence, development of self control
3. **Initiative vs. Guilt (preschool):** Greater independence, planning, and trying out new things
4. **Industry vs. Inferiority (school-aged):** Winning recognition through accomplishments
5. **Identity vs. Role Confusion (adolescence):** Develop sense of "self"
6. **Intimacy vs. Isolation (young adulthood):** Establishing close and sharing relationships
7. **Generativity vs. Self Absorption (middle adulthood):** Guiding the next generation

C. Maslow—Hierarchy of Needs: Humans must satisfy needs at base of pyramid before focusing on those higher up

NOTE

Maslow's Hierarchy of Needs
helps set priorities for care—
i.e., *first* take care of
physiological needs—oxygen,
food, water).

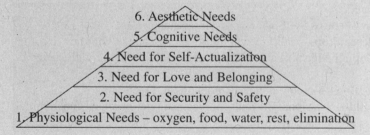

6. Aesthetic Needs
5. Cognitive Needs
4. Need for Self-Actualization
3. Need for Love and Belonging
2. Need for Security and Safety
1. Physiological Needs – oxygen, food, water, rest, elimination

D. Piaget's Theory of Cognitive Development

1. **Sensorimotor (newborn to 1 year):** Child learns about world through sensory and motor activities
2. **Preoperational (2 to 7 years):** Child can use symbols such as words to represent people and things
3. **Concrete Operations (7 to 11 years):** Able to use logic through patterns and reasoning, cause and effect
4. **Formal Operations (11 to 15 years and throughout life):** Abstract thought develops, scientific reasoning emerges

E. Behavioral Model: Views behavior as learned and changeable

1. **Conditioning Techniques:** Can alter behavior
2. **Reinforcement:** Giving privileges, other rewards
3. **Punishment:** Withdrawing privileges, depriving of rewards

F. Cognitive Framework: Emotions are a result of patterns of thinking, which can be changed
  1. Replace distortions with more accurate statements.
  2. Distract or divert away from thought patterns.
  3. Client monitors own thoughts.

G. Biomedical Model: Mental illness results from chemical imbalances; treatment may be focused on medications.

PERSONALITY AND SELF-CONCEPT

A. Components of a Healthy Personality
  1. **Realistic and Positive View of Self**
    a. Self-concept—person's belief's about himself or herself
    b. Self-esteem—person's judgment of his or her own worth
    c. Positive body image
  2. **Ability to Function in Role**
  3. **Clear Sense of Identity**

B. Nursing Interventions to Promote a Positive Self-Concept
  1. Include the client in decision-making whenever possible.
  2. Express faith that the client is able to change.
  3. Empathize with the client, but *do not offer sympathy.*
  4. Help the client to accept himself and his thoughts and feelings.
  5. Identify the client's strengths and help build on them.
  6. Never override the client's wishes because of "policy" or "routine."

C. Altered Body Image—A positive body image is an important aspect of self-esteem, and many clients will be coping with body-image disturbances. Helping the client to make a positive adjustment is the nurse's job. These changes may be in appearance, function, or caused by normal developmental stages.
  1. **Obesity**
    a. Encourage positive behaviors such as exercise, identifying times when overeating is likely, and strategies to deal with them.
    b. Help the client identify activities that don't involve eating.
    c. Decrease the client's guilt and anxiety about obesity.
  2. **Stroke**
    a. Assist client to maximize function as much as possible through physical or occupational therapy.
    b. Help client develop an altered body image that includes the affected side.
    c. Assist client in developing a means of communication.
    d. Include the family in planning care.
  3. **Pregnancy**
    a. Help both partners discuss feelings about body changes.
    b. Reassure client that changes are normal.

NOTE

Promoting a positive self-concept is a basic aspect of all therapeutic communication—answers that focus on this are usually correct.

4. **Aging**
   a. Encourage client to remain as independent as possible.
   b. Teach client about expected changes in sexual functioning and ways to cope with these changes.
   c. Assist client in maintaining social activities.
   d. Encourage exercise such as walking.

D. **Sexuality**
   1. Illness, injury, aging, depression, and certain medications all affect sexual desire and expression.
   2. Teach client expected changes and suggestions for management of them.
   3. Encourage verbalization of feelings and discussion between partners.

E. **Death and Bereavement**
   1. **Characteristic Stages of Grief**
      a. Denial
      b. Anger
      c. Bargaining
      d. Depression
      e. Acceptance
   2. **Nursing Interventions**
      a. Help the client acknowledge the pain of the loss.
      b. Provide support and empathy.
      c. Encourage client to allow time for healing, and provide information on what to expect during period of grief.
      d. Provide spiritual help from clergy member of the client's faith, if desired.
      e. Allow family time alone with deceased, if desired.

ANXIETY

Anxiety: A sense of apprehension caused by a poorly defined threat that may be external or caused by internal conflicts. Fear, in contrast, is a reaction to a specific threat.

A. **Assessment**—anxiety causes physiological symptoms such as tachycardia, increased blood pressure, dry mouth, muscle tension, and restlessness. These symptoms may be mild and occasional or constant and debilitating.
   1. **Mild**—increased alertness, attention, and motivation
   2. **Moderate**—narrowed awareness of environment, difficulty concentrating, uncomfortable physical symptoms of tension, and feelings of dread
   3. **Severe**—client becomes unable to focus on anything but relief; physical symptoms may include chest pains, hyperventilation, nausea
   4. **Panic**—feelings of terror, helplessness and loss of control; unable to function or solve problems, may lose touch with reality

B. **Nursing Interventions**—in order of severity of symptoms
   1. Establish a trusting relationship.
   2. Help client to identify and verbalize feelings.
   3. Assist client in developing coping mechanisms, such as progressive relaxation.
   4. Decrease environmental stimuli and provide structured environment.
   5. Provide physical outlets for nervous energy.
   6. Remain calm; speak clearly and simply.
   7. Medicate client with tranquilizers.

ANXIETY DISORDERS

A. **Dysfunctional Responses to Anxiety**
   1. **Panic disorder**—periodic episodes of intense anxiety apparently unrelated to stress
   2. **Phobia**—irrational fear of a specific object or situation
   3. **Obsessive Compulsive Disorder**—unconscious use of rituals or compulsions to control anxiety
   4. **Post-Traumatic Stress Disorder**—re-experiencing of a traumatic event and related feelings
   5. **Generalized Anxiety Disorder**—constant state of hyper-alertness
   6. **Hypochondria**—overly concerned with possible symptoms and fear of having a serious illness

Defense Mechanisms
(Unconscious ways of protecting the self from anxiety)

Compensation: A person makes up for a deficiency by strongly emphasizing another quality
   Example: A person who is physically handicapped becomes an outstanding scholar.

Denial: A person avoids anxiety by not acknowledging painful realities or feelings
   Example: A client with a serious medical problem doesn't seek treatment and dismisses symptoms or consequences of illness.

Displacement: The redirection of emotional feeling from one anxiety-producing object to a substitute
   Example: The boss yells at a woman, and she goes home and kicks the cat.

Identification: An attempt to assume the characteristics of a person one admires
   Example: A 5-year-old dresses like her mother.

Intellectualization: The use of excessive logic or reasoning to avoid experiencing disturbing feelings
   Example: A woman who fears social engagements explains that they are a frivolous waste of time.

Projection: The attribution of unacceptable feelings to another person or the environment
   Example: A child who is angry at a parent yells, "You hate me!"

Rationalization: The use of an acceptable reason for behavior rather than the real one
   Example: A student who fails a course says the professor was poorly organized.

Reaction Formation: The adoption of attitudes or beliefs that are the opposite of a person's real ones
   Example: A mother who is unaware that she is angry at her children becomes overly protective.

Regression: The retreat to an earlier form of behavior under stress
   Example: A 4-year-old begins wetting her pants after the birth of her baby sister.

Repression: The involuntary and unconscious forgetting of unbearable ideas or actions
   Example: A victim of rape does not recall the event.

Sublimation: The diversion of consciously intolerable feelings into socially acceptable ones
   Example: An aggressive person becomes a successful businessman.

Undoing: The performance of an action that is the opposite of a previous unacceptable one
   Example: A mother who has just punished her daughter gives her a cookie.

Behaviors Related to Anxiety

These are common ways in which people respond to anxiety; they are not considered mental illnesses but are not helpful.

B. **Withdrawal**—the person avoids social contact; includes physical isolation or refusal to communicate
   1. Encourage client to speak.
   2. Discourage use of silence or withdrawal as a defense. Stress importance of mutual responsibility for relationship.

C. **Regression**—the person uses earlier methods of comfort that once brought relief; acts dependent and childlike, uses food for comfort or sucks thumb, etc.
   1. Point out behavior to person.
   2. Reinforce the assumption of responsibility.

D. **Anger**—an attempt to regain control from sense of powerlessness caused by anxiety
   1. Assist client in recognizing feelings and exploring source of threat.
   2. Explore appropriate expression of feelings and encourage verbalization.

E. **Aggression**—like anger, an attempt to gain control
   1. The nurse can attempt to prevent aggression by noting an increase in anxiety and decreasing it (see above).
   2. Help client to understand behavior and identify alternative coping mechanisms.
   3. Distract or encourage harmless expression through hitting a soft object, etc.
   4. Setting limits and protecting self and others is the first priority, if acting on aggressive impulses seems likely.

F. **Manipulation/Acting Out**—an attempt to gain control over another person by indirect means (gifts, flattery, or intimidation)
   1. Encourage open communication about feelings and needs.
   2. Set limits.

ASSESSMENT AND TREATMENT

A. **Nursing Assessment of Mental Status**
   1. **General Description**—appearance, behavior
   2. **Mood and Affect**
   3. **Speech Characteristics**
   4. **Perceptual Disturbances**—seeing or hearing things that don't exist
   5. **Thought, Logic, and Concentration**
   6. **Impulse Control**
   7. **Reliability**

Disorders of Speech, Perception, and Thinking

Flight of Ideas: Continuous rapid speech with frequent, abrupt changes in topic

Hallucination: False sensory perception (hearing or seeing things that don't exist)

Delusion: Fixed false belief that can't be corrected by logic (I am God; people are out to hurt me)

Illusion: Misinterpretation of reality (seeing a friend turn into an evil monster)

Delirium: Disorientation, confusion, decreased consciousness (usually temporary, e.g., Sundowner Syndrome in elderly)

Dementia: Irreversible progressive loss of mental functioning (Alzheimer's)

B. Forms of Therapy
1. **Psychotherapy**—one-to-one relationship of a therapist and client
2. **Family Therapy**—designed to help change communication patterns among family members
3. **Group Therapy**—groups of people with similar problems help to change patterns of behavior through clear communication, peer pressure, common perceptions
4. **Electroconvulsive Therapy**—application of electric current that results in grand mal seizure; usually used for depression when other methods fail; preoperative care given prior to procedure
5. **Psychopharmacologic Therapy**—use of medications to treat problem symptoms; often favored by managed care because of lower cost

Therapeutic and Nontherapeutic Communication

Therapeutic communication involves building trust, listening, and communicating openly and honestly. It is an important aspect of *all* nursing care.

Therapeutic

Clarifying: Asking for more information: "What do you mean when you say you are depressed?"

Focusing: Encouraging the client to talk about a specific topic: "Let's talk more about your father."

Restating: Repeating what the client said: "You said you are afraid to see your mother?"

Sharing Perceptions: Asking the client to agree with the nurse's impressions: "You seem happier today."

Using Broad Openings: General statements designed to obtain information: "Tell me about your weekend."

Maintaining Silence: Saying nothing to allow the client time to think or sort through feelings.

Suggesting: Presenting alternative possibilities: "Would you consider saying no when she asks?"

ALERT!

NCLEX exam questions frequently ask for the correct nursing response to a client. Be alert for wrong answers that suggest nontherapeutic communication such as false reassurance.

Nontherapeutic

False Reassurance: Using cliches, pat answers, cheery advice: "You'll be feeling great in no time!"

Giving Advice: Not allowing the client to solve his or her own problems: "If I were you, I'd . . ."

Belittling: Minimizing the importance of the client's feelings: "You're not the only one who has ever lost a job."

Making Value Judgments: Showing a lack of acceptance of differences: "I can't believe you're thinking about divorce when you have 3 children."

DESTRUCTIVE COPING: DISORDERS OF ABUSE AND DEPENDENCE

A. **Alcohol Dependence**—alcoholism is a pattern of excessive alcohol use that impairs social or occupational functioning. Tolerance develops and withdrawal symptoms occur if use is discontinued.
   1. **Risk factors**—alcoholism in the family, smoking, cultural groups, low tolerance for frustration, low self-esteem
   2. **Alcohol Withdrawal**—four stages of withdrawal, which usually subside after five to seven days
      a. Diaphoresis, increased blood pressure, tremors, nausea, nervousness, tachycardia. Occurs within 8 hours of last drink. Monitor pt and obtain medication to relieve withdrawal, as ordered.
      b. Anorexia, delusions, hyperactivity, insomnia, visual hallucinations. Occurs shortly after stage one, 8 to 10 hours after last drink. Monitor and medicate prn.
      c. Above symptoms plus tonic-clonic seizures and hallucinations. Usually 12 to 48 hours after last drink. Seizure precautions, anticonvulsant medication, as ordered, monitor.
      d. Delirium tremens, hallucinations. Within three to five or more days after last drink. Monitor, offer fluids and light foods.
   3. **Wernicke's Encephalopathy**—occurs usually in chronic alcoholics, confusion, poor coordination (ataxia), eye movement abnormality (nystagmus). Treat with high doses of thiamine—vitamin B_1. This syndrome is usually *reversible*.
   4. **Korsakoff's Syndrome**—memory loss, learning deficit, confabulation (makes up stories to fill in memory gaps). This is an *irreversible* disorder.

B. **Drug Abuse and Dependence**—the chronic use of drugs other than alcohol that results in withdrawal symptoms when discontinued. Substitute medications are often used to decrease withdrawal, since abrupt discontinuation can often be dangerous.
   1. **Narcotic Dependence**—opium, heroin, morphine, codeine, meperidine (Demerol), methadone
      a. Withdrawal symptoms occur approximately 8 to 10 hours after last dose.
      b. Tears, sweating, yawning, tremor, dilated pupils, vomiting (usually lasts up to seven days). Treatment similar to that of alcohol withdrawal. Methadone may be used.
   2. **Sedative-Hypnotic Dependence**—barbiturates (Quaalude, Seconal), benzodiazepines (Librium, Valium)
      a. Withdrawal symptoms—sweating, anxiety, insomnia; seizures possible

    b. Treatment similar to that of alcohol withdrawal.

    c. Cocaine dependence—cocaine may be taken intranasally, by injection, or smoked. Crack, a concentrated form of cocaine that is smoked, has been called the most addictive drug there is.

  3. **Withdrawal Symptoms**—include intense craving, depression, extreme fatigue

C. Eating Disorders—extreme disturbances in eating behavior

  1. **Anorexia Nervosa**—intense fear of obesity, disturbed body image, weight loss of 15–25 percent

  2. **Bulimia**—episodes of binge eating, fear of being unable to stop; purging with induced vomiting, laxatives, or diuretics

  3. **Pica**—eating of nonnutritive substances on a regular basis; adults may eat chalk, starch, or paper

    a. **Treatment**

      (1) Physical—maintain adequate nutritional intake

      (2) Emotional—increase self-esteem

      (3) Behavioral—reinforce independent decision making

D. Abuse/Violence Within the Family

  1. **Types of Abuse**

    a. Physical—intentional injury inflicted on another person, often a child, wife, or elderly person

    b. Physical neglect—deprivation of essential physical needs such as food, medical care

    c. Emotional abuse—using insults or other verbal attacks to hurt the self-esteem of another person

    d. Emotional neglect—lack of a warm, caring relationship within the family

    e. Sexual abuse—exploiting others for sexual pleasure without their consent or understanding

  2. **Characteristics of Abusers**—history of suffering abuse themselves. May feel powerless and use abuse to assert superiority, exert control. Family is usually socially isolated, abuser is stronger than the abused. They tend to be impulsive, immature, and suspicious—frequently abuse alcohol or drugs.

  3. **Symptoms of Abuse in Elderly and Children**—bruises, patterned injuries (small burns from cigarettes, injuries often on parts of body usually hidden); broken bones in various stages of healing (accidental injuries tend to be distal to the body—wrists, knees, feet; intentional injuries are usually proximal—upper arm, thigh, etc.); victim tends to withdraw from contact with others; caretakers often have explanations that are not consistent with the injuries.

    a. Elderly victims tend to exhibit poor hygiene, neglect, pressure ulcers, and urine burns and are often ashamed to admit the problem.

    b. Child may protect parent for fear of further injury. Child does not seek parent out if hurt.

  4. **Nursing Interventions**—safety is the first priority in cases of abuse. Do not put client at risk.

    a. Reporting of elder and child abuse is mandatory in all fifty states.

    b. Document carefully, be specific in describing injuries, and include quotes from the client.

    c. Be knowledgeable about community resources such as crisis centers.

AFFECTIVE DISORDERS

Characterized by disturbances of mood.

A. **Bipolar Disorder**—alternating mania and depression, more common in women, onset before age 30.

1. **Manic Phase**—mood elevated, irritable; speech rapid; less need for sleep, possible weight loss; hyperactive, grandiose ideas; possible inappropriate sexual behavior; begins and ends more abruptly than depression

2. **Depressive Phase**—client may experience despair and lose interest in most usual activities; lack of appetite, withdrawal from others; potential for suicide

3. **Nursing Interventions**—during manic phase, make sure physiological needs are met. Set limits on behavior, prevent overt aggression—if client is easily provoked. Provide activities that channel excess energy. Administer and provide teaching about Lithium. When the client is depressed, assessing for suicide potential is a priority. Remove potentially harmful objects (belts, razors, etc.), observe on one-to-one basis, report any self-destructive behavior.

4. **Danger Signs of Potential Suicide**
   a. Presence of a plan
   b. Previous attempt
   c. Giving away personal items
   d. Abuse of alcohol or drugs
   e. Change in behavior—as depression lifts, may have more energy to act on suicidal impulses

B. **Major Depression**—may begin at any age, but affects twice as many women as men; most common in adults (both genders) ages 25–44, least common for those older than 65. Symptoms include a feeling of worthlessness, withdrawal, sleep disturbances, weight and appetite changes. Nurse should ensure that the client takes medication(s), eats proper meals, and gets sufficient sleep. Assess for suicide potential, as above.

THOUGHT DISTURBANCES

A. **Schizophrenia**—consists of disturbances in mood, affect, behavior, and thought. It is believed to have both genetic and environmental components.

1. **Symptoms**—include delusions, hallucinations, hostility and suspicion, social withdrawal as well as lack of attention to grooming or hygiene

2. **Nursing Interventions**
   a. Provide a safe, structured, and secure environment.
   b. Assist client to find ways of relating to others.
   c. Promote self-esteem by giving the client the opportunity to succeed at tasks.
   d. Encourage independent behavior.
   e. Assist in medical treatment—antipsychotics or possible electroconvulsive therapy (ECT).
   f. Establish trust and attempt to establish a relationship and promote social skills.
   g. Focus on reality and help the client recognize distorted perceptions.

B. **Paranoid Schizophrenia**—similar to above, but delusions are of persecution or grandeur, client is extremely suspicious and mistrustful of others

1. **Symptoms**—are similar to schizophrenia but include extreme anger, resentment, and possibly violence. May refuse food and medication because they are "poisoned."

2. **Nursing Interventions**—establish trust, encourage reality orientation, and promote as much involvement with others as tolerated—e.g., possibly games.

PHARMACOLOGICAL TREATMENT OF PSYCHIATRIC DISORDERS

A. **Antipsychotic Medications**
   1. **Phenothiazines/Thioxanthines (Thorazine, Stelazine, Trilafon, Prolixin)**—control hallucinations, and bizarre behavior; calming effect
      a. Side effects—extrapyramidal effects (30 percent), which affect voluntary movements and cause shuffling gait, tremors, restlessness, drooling, uncoordinated jerky movements, dry mouth, and blurred vision
   2. **Butyrophenone (Haldol)**—less sedative than phenothiazines; more effects on movement
   3. **Clozapine (Clozaril)**—newer drug for clients who don't respond to other medications; similar side effects; monitor liver function

B. **Antianxiety Drugs**—cause sedation, muscle relaxation; inhibit convulsions
   1. **Benzodiazepines**—Librium, Valium, Ativan
      a. Side effects—drowsiness, blurred vision, habituation
   2. **Nonbenzodiazepine Agents**—Buspar
      a. Side effects—drowsiness, headache, nausea, fatigue. Onset of effect takes one to four weeks. Does not increase CNS depression of alcohol and other drugs. Does not cause dependence.

C. **Antimanic Medications**—control mood disorders, especially the manic phase
   1. **Lithium Carbonate**—narrow therapeutic range, blood levels must be monitored. Adequate fluid and salt intake important.
      a. Side effects—gastrointestinal upset, hand tremors, hypothyroidism. When blood levels are too high, can cause nausea, vomiting, slurred speech, possible coma, convulsions, and death. *Treatment for toxicity*—gastric lavage, fluid balance correction, Mannitol to increase urine excretion.
   2. **Other Antimanic Drugs**—Carbamazepine (Tegretol), Valproic acid (Depakote)—mood stabilizers, originally used for seizure disorders
      a. Side effects—drowsiness, dry mouth, blurred vision (Tegretol). Monitor CBC with Tegretol, and liver function with Depakote.

D. **Antidepressant Medications**—Tricyclic antidepressants, which are sedating, are being used less frequently, as are MAO inhibitors, which have dangerous drug-food and drug-drug interactions
   1. **Selective Serotonin Reuptake Inhibitors (SSRIs)**—Prozac, Zoloft, Paxil. Onset of effect within seven to twenty-one days.
      a. Side effects—nausea, headache, insomnia, skin rash
   2. **Miscellaneous Antidepressants**—Trazodone (Desyrel) and Bupropion (Wellbutrin)
      a. Side effects—nausea, sedation (Desyrel); weight loss, dry mouth (Wellbutrin)

NOTE

Artane and Cogentin may be administered with antipsychotics to help control extrapyramidal symptoms.

EXERCISES: PSYCHIATRIC NURSING

1. Lucy J., a successful lawyer, is admitted in the morning for treatment of gastritis. Near the end of a 12-hour shift, the nurse notices which of the following symptom(s) that would suggest alcohol withdrawal?

   (1) Delirium tremens

   (2) Tremors, anorexia, and diaphoresis

   (3) Persistent hallucinations

   (4) Aggressive behavior and difficulty with balance

2. A 19-year-old client with a history of substance abuse begins to sweat profusely, develops a runny nose, and has dilated pupils. The nurse knows that these symptoms are characteristic of withdrawal from

   (1) amphetamines.

   (2) hallucinogens.

   (3) anxiolytics (such as Valium).

   (4) heroin.

3. A nurse is treating a 64-year-old man who has been abusing alcohol for the past ten years, since his wife died. Which of the following comments indicate that he is using the most common defense mechanism in substance abuse?

   (1) "I know I should quit drinking, but I am too lonely."

   (2) "Drinking is actually good for your heart."

   (3) "I will cut down my drinking to only weekends."

   (4) "I don't have a drinking problem. I am a successful businessman."

TIP

A superlative word—such as *best*—in an NCLEX-PN exam question usually signals that you will need to prioritize care decisions to answer correctly.

4. Nancy K. has an anxiety disorder for which she is being treated. The nurse enters her room and finds her in an agitated state, pacing around the room. Nancy states that she feels something awful is going to happen. The nurse knows that the *best* intervention at this time would be to

   (1) teach Nancy progressive relation.

   (2) distract Nancy by talking about a happy experience.

   (3) confront Nancy with her need to get herself in control.

   (4) take Nancy for a brisk walk outside.

5. A nurse is admitting a 15-year-old girl who, according to her parents, has been dieting excessively and now weighs 90 pounds—35 pounds below her previous weight. She is 5'5". On assessment, the nurse will expect which of the following findings that are characteristic of anorexia?

   (1) Temp. 96.6 degrees F; Pulse 62; BP 90/60

   (2) Temp. 99 degrees F; Pulse 88; BP 120/80

   (3) Temp. 101 degrees F; Pulse 92; BP 100/58

   (4) Temp. 98.6 degrees F; Pulse 74; BP 140/90

6. A 48-year-old accountant, Jerry, has been severely depressed and tells the nurse that he wishes he could "end it all." The *best* response for the nurse would be:

    (1) "Jerry, you have so much to live for. You should be grateful."
    (2) "Suicide is a permanent solution to a temporary problem."
    (3) "I'll talk to the RN or physician about changing your medication."
    (4) "Are you thinking of hurting yourself?"

7. The nurse is treating the alcoholic client who is in withdrawal with an antianxiety medication, increased fluid intake, a nutritious high-carbohydrate diet, and vitamin B_1 and other B vitamins. She realizes that thiamine prevents which of the following serious disorders associated with alcohol abuse?

    (1) Wernicke's encephalopathy
    (2) Pancreatitis
    (3) Gastritis
    (4) Cirrhosis of the liver

8. A nurse is caring for a 35-year-old woman who has been diagnosed with bipolar disorder. She is now in the manic phase and is sleeping little, dressing provocatively, and talking nonstop about whatever enters her mind. She is easily irritated and has no time for meals. The nurse's *first* priority in her care will be to

    (1) ensure that basic physiologic needs for food, rest, and hygiene are met.
    (2) monitor the side effects of mood-stabilizing medications.
    (3) help the client gain insight into the causes of her disorder.
    (4) prevent the client from suicidal impulses.

9. A nurse is caring for a depressed 42-year-old construction worker. He is withdrawn, does not volunteer to participate in any activities, and expresses feelings of worthlessness. One of the ways the nurse may help this client is to

    (1) provide structured activities that include some small group interactions.
    (2) allow the client time to be alone with his thoughts.
    (3) keep him constantly active so he won't have too much time to brood.
    (4) allow him to skip his usual daily shower and shave when he is not up to it.

10. The nurse was interviewing a frail, older woman who looked unkempt and dirty. Suspecting that she was a victim of abuse, the nurse asked the woman whether anyone was hurting her. The woman, looking at the floor, nodded yes. The woman's response to the question showed that she felt

    (1) humiliated and ashamed about the abuse.
    (2) angry and vengeful toward the abuser.
    (3) fearful of retaliation.
    (4) defensive and protective toward the abuser.

11. Side effects of antipsychotic drugs such as Thorazine include

    (1) nausea.
    (2) ototoxicity.
    (3) blurred vision.
    (4) Parkinsonian symptoms.

12. A nurse meets with a client who appears to be suffering from anxiety. Together, they review the physical signs and symptoms of a panic attack. Which signs and symptoms should the nurse be discussing with the client?
Select all that apply.

- ☐ **(1)** Dizziness
- ☐ **(2)** Tachycardia
- ☐ **(3)** Shortness of breath
- ☐ **(4)** Bradycardia

13. The nurse's *best* response to a client who is having auditory hallucinations that someone is commanding him to hurt someone would be to

(1) tell the client that the voices are not real.

(2) reassure the client since the voices are caused by anxiety.

(3) inform the RN and document the hallucinations.

(4) ask the client why he would want to hurt someone.

14. Robert M. is scheduled for electroconvulsive therapy. In preparation for the treatment, the nurse will give routine preoperative care, which, in addition to NPO status, includes:
Select all that apply.

- ☐ **(1)** a physical.
- ☐ **(2)** having the client sign a consent form.
- ☐ **(3)** reducing anxiety by explaining carefully what will happen.
- ☐ **(4)** providing IV hydration of 2 liters of D5W.

15. An 84-year-old nursing home client who was alert and oriented during the day was found wandering the halls and appeared disoriented at night. The nurse realized that this client was suffering from

(1) intermittent memory loss.

(2) low levels of medication at night.

(3) delirium.

(4) Sundowner's Syndrome.

ANSWER KEY AND EXPLANATIONS

1. 2	4. 4	7. 1	10. 1	13. 3
2. 4	5. 1	8. 1	11. 4	14. 1,2
3. 4	6. 4	9. 1	12. 1,2,3	15. 4

1. **The correct answer is (2).** The signs of alcohol withdrawal, which appear within the first 8–12 hours, are tremors, anorexia, and diaphoresis.

2. **The correct answer is (4).** Withdrawal from heroin has characteristic symptoms of a runny nose, diaphoresis, and dilated pupils.

3. **The correct answer is (4).** This comment is an example of denial, in which the client avoids anxiety by self-deception about serious problems. Denial is a very common defense mechanism used by substance abusers.

4. **The correct answer is (4).** The best way to help a highly anxious person is to engage them in large muscle activities which will help to drain off excess energy caused by the anxiety, eventually reducing it.

5. **The correct answer is (1).** An anorexic's temperature is typically decreased because of the lowering of the metabolism. Blood pressure and pulse are also lower.

6. **The correct answer is (4).** When a client expresses a suicidal wish, you should follow up on the client to see how intent he or she is about hurting himself or herself.

7. **The correct answer is (1).** Wernicke's encephalopathy is caused by a deficiency of vitamin B_1, or thiamine.

8. **The correct answer is (1).** The manic client may neglect to eat or sleep, due to excessive energy and flight of ideas.

9. **The correct answer is (1).** Structured activities will help keep the depressed client active, and small groups provide social contact without being overwhelming.

10. **The correct answer is (1).** It is typical for older people who have been abused to feel shamed and humiliated by the abuse.

11. **The correct answer is (4).** Side effects of antipsychotic drugs such as Thorazine, which affect dopamine levels, include Parkinsonian effects such as tremors.

12. **The correct answers are (1), (2), and (3).** Panic attacks may have physical and cognitive symptoms. These symptoms include tachycardia (rapid heartbeat), shortness of breath or rapid breathing, dizziness or lightheadedness, rapid speech, sweating, and abdominal pain or GI distress.

13. **The correct answer is (3).** Auditory hallucinations that are "commanding" a client to hurt someone can make the client a danger to himself or others. The RN or provider needs to know that this is occurring.

answers exercises

14. The correct answers are (1) and (2). In addition to NPO status, preoperative care for electroconvulsive therapy includes a physical and client consent.

15. The correct answer is (4). Sundowner's Syndrome is a type of delirium in which the client becomes confused only at night.

SUMMING IT UP

- Mental health is the ability to obtain satisfaction from life and function socially and at work.

- Psychiatric theorists—Freud, Erikson, Maslow, Piaget.

- Anxiety is a sense of apprehension caused by a poorly defined threat that may be external or caused by internal conflicts.

- Fear is a reaction to a specific threat.

- Exam questions frequently ask for the correct nursing response to a client.

- Be alert for wrong answers using nontherapeutic communication, such as false reassurance.

The Neurologic System

OVERVIEW

- Basic concepts
- Central nervous system
- Peripheral nervous system
- Autonomic nervous system
- Neurons
- Neurological assessment
- Neurologic system disorders
- Summing it up

BASIC CONCEPTS

The nervous system acts as the coordinating and communicating system of the body, bringing information to the brain and relaying instructions from it. It is divided into the *central nervous system*, the *peripheral nervous system*, and the *autonomic nervous system*. The *neuron* is its main functional unit.

CENTRAL NERVOUS SYSTEM

Protection: The central nervous system is protected by bone, the skull, vertebrae, the meninges (the protective membranes that are under the bony structures), and the cerebrospinal fluid, which serves as a buffer to the brain and spinal cord.

chapter 8

A. The Brain—the control center for thought and behavior; is subdivided into sections that have different functions. The location of an injury to the brain will determine what kind of deficits will occur.

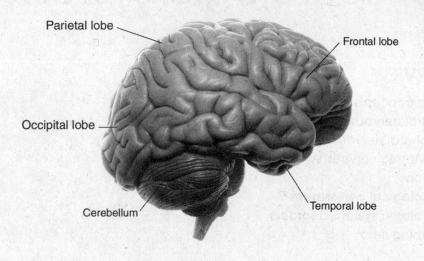

1. **Cerebrum**—the largest portion of the brain. Its outer layer (cortex) is divided into four areas:
    a. Frontal lobe—memory, abstract thought, personality, formation of words (Broca's area)
    b. Parietal lobe—sensory information (including pain), orientation in space, left and right
    c. Temporal lobe—speech interpretation, hearing, taste, smell, memory storage
    d. Occipital lobe—visual center, understanding of written material
2. **Cerebellum**—coordination of muscle movement
3. **Diencephalon**—located between the cerebrum and brain stem. It is divided into two sections:
    a. Thalamus—interpretation of sensation, including pain, temperature, and touch
    b. Hypothalamus—regulates the autonomic nervous system, sleep, appetite, temperature, controls hormonal secretion, water balance, and thirst
4. **Brain Stem**
    a. Midbrain—relay center for eye and ear reflexes
    b. Pons—respiratory reflexes and communication between cerebellum and nervous system
    c. Medulla—contains cardiac, respiratory, vomiting, and vasomotor centers

B. The Spinal Cord—continuation of the medulla, extends to the second lumbar vertebra
    1. **Structure**
        a. Vertebrae provide protection
        b. Intervertebral discs between vertebrae provide flexibility
        c. Nucleus pulposus is a gelatin-like substance in the discs
    2. **Function**
        a. Sensory tract conducts impulses to the brain (afferent nerve fibers)
        b. Motor tract conducts impulses from the brain (efferent nerve fibers)

PERIPHERAL NERVOUS SYSTEM

A. **Cranial Nerves**
   1. **Originate From the Surface of the Brain**
   2. **Twelve Pairs**

Number	Name	Function
I	Olfactory	smell
II	Optic	vision
III	Oculomotor	eye movement
IV	Trochlear	eye movement
V	Trigeminal	facial movement
VI	Abducens	eye movement
VII	Facial	facial movement
VIII	Vestibulocochlear	hearing, balance
IX	Glossopharyngeal	taste, swallowing
X	Vagus	vagal reflex
XI	Spinal Accessory	upper body movement
XII	Hypoglossal	tongue movement

B. **Spinal Nerves**
   1. **Thirty-One Pairs**—named for the corresponding part of the spinal column
   2. **Conduct Impulses**—necessary for sensation and voluntary movements

AUTONOMIC NERVOUS SYSTEM

The autonomic nervous system controls "automatic" body functions involving smooth muscle, cardiac muscle, and glands. It is divided into the sympathetic and parasympathetic systems.

A. **Sympathetic Nervous System**—prepares the body to meet an emergency—the "fight or flight" response with increased blood pressure, heart rate, sweating, cold hands, etc. (see below)

B. **Parasympathetic Nervous System**—maintains normal body functions (see below)

Body Part/System	Sympathetic	Parasympathetic
blood pressure	increases	normalizes
peripheral vasculature	constricts	no effect
respiration	increases rate	normalizes
pupils	dilate	constrict
gastrointestinal	inhibits peristalsis	stimulates peristalsis
bronchi	dilates	constricts

NEURONS

The basic units of the nervous system are the nerve cells, or neurons.

A. Structure
1. **Cell Body**—gray matter containing nucleus
2. **Dendrites**—conduct impulses *to* the cell body
3. **Axons**—conduct impulses *away from* the cell body

B. Types of Neurons
1. **Motor**—from CNS to muscles and glands
2. **Sensory**—impulses to the CNS
3. **Connecting**—connect motor and sensory neurons

C. Conduction
1. **Occurs Between Neurons over a *Synapse*** (chemical transmission—acetylcholine, serotonin, norepinephrine)
2. **Myelin Sheath**—increases the rate of conduction and protects the axon fibers

NEUROLOGICAL ASSESSMENT

Diagnostic Tests for Neurological Disorders:

Caloric testing
(oculovestibular reflex)

Cerebral angiography

Computed tomography (CT)

Electroencephalography (EEG)

Lumbar puncture

Magnetic resonance
imaging (MRI)

Myelography

Skull and spinal X-rays

A. Subjective
1. **History of Head Injury**—seizure
2. **Headache, Difficulty Concentrating, Memory Loss, Drowsiness**
3. **Paralysis, Dizziness, Weakness, Numbness**
4. **Visual or Speech Disturbances**
5. **Nausea, Vomiting**

B. Objective
1. **Vital Signs**—temperature, pulse, respirations, BP
2. **General Appearance**—symmetry of face
3. **Level of Consciousness**—most sensitive, reliable index of cerebral function. The Glasgow Coma Scale is a quick, standardized way of assessing consciousness in the critically ill (see page 159).
   a. Oriented to time, person, place
   b. Appropriate response to tactile and verbal stimuli
   c. Memory, problem-solving abilities
4. **Appropriate Behavior and Emotional Responses**
5. **Pupil Assessment**
   a. Light reflex—pupils constrict when light shone in eye
   b. Accommodation—pupils constrict to adapt to near vision
   c. Nystagmus—a jerking eye movement—note presence or absence
   d. PERRLA—an abbreviation commonly used in assessments. It means: Pupils are Equal, Round, and Reactive to Light. Accommodation is present.
   e. Pupil Abnormalities: dilation of one pupil, fixed in mid-position, or pinpoint and fixed
6. **Motor Function**—gait, balance, coordination, strength, posture
   a. Paralysis:
      (1) Hemiplegia—paralysis of one side of the body
      (2) Paraplegia—paralysis of lower limbs
      (3) Quadriplegia—paralysis of arms, legs, and trunk below level of spinal cord injury

b. Reflexes:
   (1) Babinski—abnormal in adults and children over one year—dorsiflexion of foot and fanning of toes
   (2) Corneal reflex—blink
7. **Speech**—presence of aphasia, ability to follow simple instructions
8. **Drainage from the Ears**
9. **Bladder and Bowel Control**

Glasgow Coma Scale

Eye Opening

Spontaneously	4
To sound	3
To pain	2
None	1

Motor Response

Obeys commands	6
Withdraws from pain	5
Moves due to pain	4
Decorticate pain response	3
Decerebrate pain response	2
No response to pain	1

Verbal Response

Oriented $\times$ 3	5
Confused conversation	4
Meaningless words	3
Meaningless sounds	2
None	1

15 is highest score
7 or less indicates coma

NEUROLOGIC SYSTEM DISORDERS

A. **Increased Intracranial Pressure (ICP)**—the skull has a limited amount of space, and an increase in fluid or a lesion causes pressure on the brain, which results in ischemia and loss of function. Causes include a tumor, hemorrhage, edema, inflammation, or an abscess. The area of the brain that is compressed determines which deficiencies are seen.
   1. **Assessment**
      a. Decreased level of consciousness—**(first and best indication of increased ICP)**
      b. Headache, restlessness, anxiety
      c. Changes in vital signs
         (1) Increased blood pressure with widened pulse pressure (difference between the systolic and diastolic pressures, usually 30–40 mmHg)
         (2) Increased pulse rate changing to bradycardia
         (3) Abnormal respiratory pattern—periods of apnea
         (4) Temperature increase
      d. Vomiting
      e. Unequal pupil size
      f. Paralysis

       g. Visual changes

       h. Severe headache—aggravated by movement

  2. **Diagnosis**

       a. Neurological exam findings

       b. CAT scan, MRI, EEG

       c. Radiology findings

  3. **Medical Treatment**

       a. Treat the underlying cause of ICP

       b. Maintain fluid balance

       c. Medications

          (1) Osmotic diuretics

          (2) Corticosteroids

          (3) Anticonvulsants

          (4) *DO NOT* give narcotics, sedatives, or barbiturates, which may mask signs of increased ICP

       d. Maintain adequate ventilation

       e. Surgical intervention

  4. **Nursing Interventions**

       a. Identify and treat problems of increased ICP

          (1) Perform frequent neurologic checks.

          (2) Elevate head of bed about 30 degrees to promote venous drainage.

          (3) Monitor I and O carefully.

          (4) Tell client to avoid coughing, sneezing, or valsalva maneuver (increases ICP) if possible.

       b. Maintain airway and respiratory function

          (1) Evaluate patency of airway frequently.

          (2) Administer oxygen if necessary.

       c. Prevent injury and avoid hazards of immobility

          (1) Monitor for leakage of CSF fluid from nose or ears.

          (2) Assess gag reflex, and protect from aspiration.

          (3) Care for eyes, skin, and mouth to prevent tissue damage.

          (4) Turn client or maintain on rotating bed to prevent skin breakdown.

          (5) Prevent constipation and use urinary catheter if incontinent.

       d. Maintain psychological well-being

          (1) Provide emotional support to client and family.

          (2) Provide means of communication such as a communication board if necessary.

B. Head Injury

  1. **Types**

       a. Concussion—violent jarring of brain against skull; period of unconsciousness

       b. Intracranial hemorrhage—subdural, subarachnoid or epidural hematoma, depending on the location of the bleeding

  2. **Assessment**—signs of trauma from injury, nausea and vomiting, lethargy, drainage of cerebrospinal fluid from ears, plus other symptoms of increased ICP

  3. **Diagnostic Tests**—same as for ICP

  4. **Nursing Interventions**

       a. If client is not admitted to a hospital, provide home-care head injury instructions (in writing)

          (1) Observe for increased sleepiness; if sleeping, wake q 2–3 hours to see if easily arousable

          (2) Return to hospital in case of decreased LOC, seizures, inability to arouse, bleeding or watery drainage from ears or nose, blurred vision, speech problems, or vomiting

b. Hospitalized client should be cared for as with increased ICP. Greater likelihood of cerebrospinal fluid leakage. *CSF will test positive for glucose on Dextrostix.*

C. **Cerebrovascular Accident (CVA)**—decreased blood supply to part of the brain from blockage due to thrombosis or embolism, or hemorrhage from rupture of blood vessel or aneurysm. Onset may be gradual (hemorrhage) or sudden (embolism). May be preceded by a TIA (transient ischemic attack), in which neurological problems are present for several minutes or hours, but resolve. A TIA is a warning sign of an impending CVA.

1. **Assessment**
   a. Symptoms will depend on location and size of brain area with reduced or absent blood supply. *A left CVA causes right-sided deficits often including speech problems*; a *CVA on the right side of the brain causes left-sided problems that are often associated with issues of safety and judgment. Hemiplegia* is the term for paralysis of one side of the body.
   b. An initial period of muscle flaccidity will be followed after weeks by spasticity. Visual and perceptual defects may be present.
2. **Diagnosis**
   a. CAT scan, EEG, angiography, MRI
3. **Medical Treatment**
   a. Remove cause, prevent complications, maintain function, and rehabilitate.
   b. Utilize anticoagulants, antihypertensives; corticosteroids and mannitol (if cerebral edema), anticonvulsants (if seizures).
4. **Nursing Interventions**
   a. Immediate priorities are to support life and prevent complications
      (1) Maintain patent airway and monitor for symptoms of hypoxia. Mechanical ventilation may be necessary.
      (2) Monitor neurological and cardiovascular status to prevent complications
   b. Maintain adequate nutrition and elimination
      (1) Provide tube feeding, IV, and soft foods when tolerated.
      (2) Prevent constipation.
   c. Promote musculoskeletal function and prevent contractures
      (1) ROM exercises, active or passive, depending on side.
      (2) Maintain legs and arms in neutral position with supports.
      (3) Support foot to prevent foot drop.
      (4) Reposition every 2 hours, but limit time on affected side.
   d. Provide emotional support to client and family and assist client in communication
   e. Rehabilitation and encouraging independence
      (1) Assist client to participate in ADLs.
      (2) Provide clothing that is easy to get in and out of.
      (3) Encourage social interaction.
      (4) Provide occupational and physical therapy if possible.

D. **Spinal Cord Injury**—injury in which the spinal cord is severed or compressed, causing partial or full loss of function below the level of the injury. Occurs most frequently in men between 20 and 40 years as a result of trauma—automobile accidents, diving, gunshot wounds, falls. Long-term rehabilitation potential depends on the extent of damage done to the cord, which may not be evident for several weeks.

1. **Assessment**—symptoms will depend on location of cord injury—cervical, thoracic, lumbar.
   a. Spinal shock occurs with complete cord transection—occurs within three days and lasts several weeks
      (1) Flaccid paralysis and sensory loss below the level of the injury

        (2) Decreased perspiration below injury

        (3) Bowel and bladder dysfunction

        (4) Cervical injury causes

           (a) Hypotension

           (b) Decreased body temperature

           (c) Bradycardia

           (d) Respiratory complications

        (5) After spinal shock, reflexes and autonomic activity return—spasticity

2. **Diagnosis**

    a. History of accident and clinical signs

    b. X-ray that indicates vertebral fracture

    c. CAT scan and MRI show spinal cord edema, fracture, and compression

3. **Medical Treatment**

    a. Immediate care—handle client with extreme care to stabilize head and neck before transfer. Use jaw lift for CPR.

    b. Next goals—supportive treatment to prevent shock and control hemorrhage.

    c. Client is put in traction using Crutchfield tongs or a halo ring and fixation pins to maintain vertebral alignment. Surgery for stabilization of upper spine, such as insertion of Herrington rods, may be performed. Rotation bed is used.

4. **Nursing Interventions**

    a. Assess for complications—infection, neurological changes, pressure ulcers, depression.

    b. Maintain respiratory function.

    c. Maintain cardiovascular stability by monitoring response to procedures, use of anti-embolism stockings.

    d. Ensure adequate nutrition and hydration by evaluating GI function to determine ability to tolerate po fluids, feedings.

    e. Bladder function is maintained by intermittent catheterization, initiating measures for bladder control such as using Crede maneuver to express urine. Monitor I and O.

    f. Initiate bowel retraining. Emphasize importance of regular, consistent routine.

    g. Proper bowel and bladder care prevent dysreflexia, an exaggerated reflex of the autonomic nervous system, which can be life threatening because of extreme hypertension.

    h. Emotional support to client and family

        (1) Young client may have great difficulty adjusting to paralysis. Suicide is possible.

        (2) Provide diversion, encouragement, support, and independence; do not give false reassurance.

        (3) Anticipate anger as part of grieving process.

        (4) Avoid sympathy, and emphasize client's potential.

    i. Encourage independence through physical therapy, rehabilitation, and exercise.

E. Brain Tumor—a benign or malignant growth that exerts pressure on the brain causing symptoms of increased ICP. Accounts for 2 percent of yearly cancer deaths.

    1. **Assessment**

        a. Headache, deficits in cerebral function

        b. Frontal lobe—aphasia, memory loss, personality changes

        c. Temporal lobe—aphasia, seizures

        d. Parietal lobe—motor seizures, sensory impairment

        e. Occipital lobe—homonymous hemianopsia (defective vision affecting right or left halfs of the visual field of the two eyes); visual hallucinations, visual impairment

        f. Cerebellum—impaired coordination, impaired equilibrium

2. **Diagnosis**
   a. CAT scan, MRI, EEG, angiogram
   b. Neurological exam
3. **Medical Treatment**
   a. Dexamethasone
   b. Anticonvulsants
   c. Radiation and chemotherapy if malignant
   d. Surgical excision—craniotomy
4. **Nursing Interventions**
   a. Check patent airway, assess vital signs, prevent neck flexion, and turn q 2 hours.
   b. Perform neuro checks and guard against aspiration.
   c. Prevent rises in ICP—discourage vigorous coughing, maintain seizure precautions, and administer seizure precautions as needed.
   d. Evaluate dressing—location and amount of drainage, evaluate CSF leak through incision, nose, ears. Reinforce dressing, do not change. Position in semi-Fowler's if there is a CSF leak from ears or nose.
   e. Provide appropriate pain relief, but *use narcotic analgesics with caution—they may mask signs of increased intracranial pressure.*
   f. Use eye patches to prevent corneal ulcerations if blink reflex absent.
   g. Prevent complications of immobility with range-of-motion, passive exercises.
   h. Teach client self care and involve family in treatment.

F. **Seizure Disorder—**may be a symptom of another disorder; epilepsy is a disease characterized by recurrent unprovoked seizure activity. Affects 1 to 2 percent of population.
   1. **Types of Seizures**
      a. *Grand mal*—may begin with an *aura*; the individual loses consciousness and enters a tonic phase (body rigid) and then a clonic phase with jerking muscle movements, cessation of respirations, and fecal and urinary incontinence. Lasts 1 to 2 minutes followed by a period of unresponsiveness.
      b. *Petit mal*—loss of consciousness that lasts less than a minute, normal activities may or may not cease. May be no memory of this period. May occur more than 100 times a day.
      c. *Motor seizures*—a seizure that may be limited to movements of one extremity—may precede a grand mal seizure.
      d. *Psychomotor seizure*—alters behavior and may produce automatic behaviors—lip smacking, repetitive hand movements.
      e. *Febrile seizure*—usually occurs in child six months to six years. Single episode in one day, lasts less than 15 minutes.
   2. **Diagnosis**
      a. Seizure characteristics
      b. EEG (differentiates epileptic from others), CT scan, MRI, brain mapping
   3. **Medical Management**
      a. Treat and remove cause, if possible.
      b. Anticonvulsant drugs to control seizures or reduce incidence as much as possible; most common drugs—Dilantin, phenobarbital, Tegretol, valium.
   4. **Nursing Interventions**
      a. Seizure treatment
         (1) Document accurately—activities prior to seizure, time of seizure (start and end), type of movements, presence of incontinence, periods of apnea and cyanosis, condition post seizure.
         (2) Protect client—loosen restrictive clothing, remove dangerous objects. **Do not** insert a tongue blade or anything else in the client's mouth. Protect head, allow free movement.

TIP

As you study these disorder descriptions, keep in mind the Data Collection phase of the Clinical Problem-Solving Process.

  b. Teaching
    (1) Avoid activities that precipitate seizure activity.
    (2) Avoid alcohol.
    (3) Take medication and wear medic-alert identification.
  c. Provide support and promote strategies that help maintain physical and emotional health.

G. **Multiple Sclerosis**—chronic disorder in which neurons in the brain and spinal cord become demyelinized. It is progressive, with remissions and exacerbations. It generally affects young adults between 20 and 40, more commonly women. The cause is unknown, possibly autoimmune or viral.
  1. **Assessment**
    a. Symptoms vary with the location of the demyelination—may include visual, motor, or sensory deficits as well as exaggerated mood changes, bowel and bladder problems
    b. Spasticity and paralysis as disease progresses
  2. **Diagnosis**
    a. No definitive diagnostic test—use symptoms and exclusion
    b. MRI, CT scan to exclude other diagnoses, and CSF fluid to analyze for possible alterations
  3. **Medical Treatment**—to reduce symptoms: urinary—cholinergic (Urecholine); inflammation and edema—glucocorticoids; immunosuppressants—interferon; muscle relaxants—Dantrium or Lioresal
  4. **Nursing Interventions**
    a. Encourage high-calorie, high-vitamin, high-protein diet, low in saturated fats.
    b. Help client establish a regular program of exercise and rest, as well as avoidance of stress, to avoid precipitating an exacerbation.
    c. Provide safety, encourage independence and participation in care, and allow time for expression of concerns.

H. **Meningitis**—an inflammation of the meningeal tissue of the brain and spinal cord, usually caused by a bacteria or virus. Cerebral edema results from the inflammation. Meningococcal meningitis is the only highly contagious form.
  1. **Assessment**
    a. Fever, stiff neck (nuchal rigidity), Kernig's sign (in supine position, extension of a bent leg causes resistance and pain), Brudzinki's sign (flexion of head causes flexion of both hips and knee)
    b. Severe headache, photophobia, fever
    c. Irritability, stupor, coma
  2. **Diagnosis**
    a. Lumbar puncture and fluid sample to obtain organism
    b. Culture and stain to ID organism
  3. **Medical Treatment**
    a. Isolation until organism is identified
    b. IV antibiotics
    c. Hydration, anticonvulsant meds, maintain oxygenation
  4. **Nursing Interventions**
    a. Assist with lumbar puncture by positioning the client on her side with her knees to her chest
      (1) Maintain isolation as indicated.
      (2) Begin antibiotics after samples are taken.
      (3) Maintain IV infusion.
      (4) Monitor for increased ICP.
      (5) Decrease environmental stimulus.

(6) Avoid positioning that causes discomfort.

(7) Practice seizure precautions.

(8) Take measures to decrease fever.

I. **Cerebral Aneurysm**—a dilation of the wall of a cerebral artery that is likely to rupture, causing an intracerebral hemorrhage. It is caused by congenital weakness, trauma, arteriosclerosis, or hypertension. It is usually asymptomatic until it ruptures.

1. **Assessment**
   a. Severe headache and eye pain
   b. Decreased LOC
   c. Neck stiffness
   d. Seizures and other symptoms of increased ICP

2. **Diagnosis**
   a. Cerebral angiogram
   b. CAT scan

3. **Medical Treatment**
   a. Corticosteroids—to reduce inflammation
   b. Antihypertensives—to decrease blood pressure
   c. Osmotic diuretics—to decrease fluid and ICP
   d. Surgery to ligate aneurysm

4. **Nursing Interventions**
   a. Bed rest with HOB elevated 30 degrees (to reduce ICP).
   b. Monitor for symptoms of increased ICP.
   c. Help client avoid coughing, sneezing, flexion of neck and Valsalva maneuver (increases ICP).
   d. Provide a quiet, dim, nonstimulating environment.

J. **Myasthenia Gravis**—a neuromuscular disorder characterized by weakness of the voluntary muscles due to a deficiency in acetylcholine or its receptor sites. The cause is unknown but thought to be an autoimmune reaction.

1. **Assessment**
   a. The first symptoms are frequently ptosis (drooping of the eyelids) and diplopia (double vision)
   b. Muscle fatigue that is better in the morning and gets worse later in the day and with activity
   c. Masklike expression due to weak facial muscles
   d. Difficulty with speech, eating, and chewing
   e. Eventual respiratory paralysis and failure

2. **Diagnosis**
   a. Electromyography (EMG)—shows a decreasing response of muscle to stimuli
   b. Tensilon test—IV injection of Edrophonium (Tensilon) will bring relief from symptoms for 5–10 minutes. This positive Tensilon test means the client has the disease.

3. **Medical Treatment**
   a. Anticholinesterase medications are used to increase the levels of acetylcholine at the neuromuscular junction.
   b. Corticosteroids are used to decrease the autoimmune response.

4. **Nursing Interventions**
   a. Administer medications and assess for side effects. Excessive doses of medication can lead to a cholinergic crisis—antidote is atropine (a cholinergic blocker).
   b. Monitor client for increased problems swallowing or breathing.
   c. Encourage optimal activity with rest periods.

d. Provide teaching about medications, need for a medical alert bracelet, support organizations.

K. Muscular Dystrophy—a hereditary disorder of progressive muscle wasting and weakness that usually starts when the child is between 1 and 5 years old. It is a sex-linked disorder that primarily affects males.

1. **Assessment**
   a. Muscle wasting and weakness
   b. Abnormal waddling gait
2. **Diagnosis**
   a. Electromyography—changes in neuromuscular electrical activity
   b. Muscle biopsy—muscle tissue replaced by fat
   c. Serum enzymes—increased CPK
3. **Medical Treatment**—none known except genetic counseling for subsequent pregnancies
4. **Nursing Interventions**
   a. Assist child in maintaining independence and contact with peers as long as possible.
   b. Assist and teach child and parents exercises to maintain function and use of assistive appliances, such as crutches and wheelchairs.
   c. Help family identify community agencies and support groups that can provide assistance.

L. Cerebral Palsy—a disorder caused by damage to part of the brain responsible for control of motor function that is caused by developmental brain defects, birth trauma, or anoxia to the brain

1. **Assessment**
   a. Spasticity and weakness of extremities
   b. Visual and speech problems
   c. Poor motor development
2. **Diagnosis**
   a. Neurological exam and history
   b. Diagnostic tests to rule out other causes of dysfunction
3. **Medical Treatment**
   a. Orthopedic surgery to correct contractures
   b. Neurosurgery to decrease spasticity, if appropriate
   c. Assistive appliances and braces
4. **Nursing Interventions**
   a. Assist with ADLs, communication, and education to maximize quality of life.
   b. Encourage normal growth and development.
   c. Help family to access community agencies for support.
   d. Assist in obtaining speech, physical, and other therapy as appropriate.

M. Parkinson's Disease—a progressive disorder that causes a decline in muscular function due to depletion of the neurotransmitter dopamine

1. **Assessment**
   a. Tremor at rest
   b. Rigidity—blank facial expression, shuffling steps
   c. Difficulty in initiating voluntary movement
   d. Gradual onset—clients usually over 60
2. **Diagnosis**—neurological assessment

3. **Medical Treatment**
    a. Anti-Parkinsonian agents—L-dopa, Sinemet: decrease rigidity and tremors
    b. Anti-cholinergic drugs—Cogentin
    c. Others include antispasmodics, dopamine agonists, antidepressants (Elavil)
4. **Nursing Interventions**
    a. Administer medications and monitor side effects.
    b. Encourage client's independence using assistive devices if needed.
    c. Maintain adequate nutrition.
    d. Encourage physical therapy and exercise as tolerated.
    e. Provide support to client and family and access to community resources.

N. **Bell's Palsy**—paralysis of one side of the face due to a lesion of the seventh cranial nerve—most clients recover in several weeks without any remaining problems
1. **Assessment**
    a. Mouth droop
    b. Inability to close eyelid on affected side
2. **Diagnosis**—no specific test
3. **Medical Treatment**
    a. Steroids (to reduce nerve edema and improve nerve conduction), analgesics
    b. Eye drops and ophthalmic ointment and patches at night
4. **Nursing Interventions**
    a. Help client chew on unaffected side.
    b. Promote passive and active facial exercises to prevent loss of muscle tone.
    c. Provide reassurance and support.

O. **Amyotrophic Lateral Sclerosis (Lou Gehrig's Disease)**—a rapidly fatal upper and lower muscular atrophy. Usually affects men, onset between the ages of 40 and 70.
1. **Assessment**
    a. Dysphagia
    b. Fatigue
    c. Muscle weakness of hands and feet
2. **Diagnosis**—ruling out other diseases by EMG and muscle biopsy
3. **Medical Treatment**—no cure or specific treatment. Death is usually by respiratory infection due to respiratory insufficiency.
4. **Nursing Interventions**
    a. Assistance with eating and physical therapy as indicated.
    b. Promote adequate respiratory function.
    c. Prevent complications of immobility.
    d. Improve quality of life through alternate means of communication, diversionary activities.
    e. Help to support client and family.

EXERCISES: THE NEUROLOGIC SYSTEM

1. The nurse answers a call bell and finds a frightened mother whose child, the client, is having a seizure. Which of these actions should the nurse take?

    (1) The nurse should insert a padded tongue blade in the client's mouth to prevent the child from swallowing or choking on his tongue.

    (2) The nurse should help the mother restrain the child to prevent him from injuring himself.

    (3) The nurse should call the operator to page for seizure assistance.

    (4) The nurse should clear the area and position the client safely.

2. A nurse admits a client who has a head injury and is at risk for increased intracranial pressure. Which of the following interventions will she perform to help this client?

    (1) Use the Glasgow Coma Scale to assess level of consciousness hourly.

    (2) Assess pupils for size, movement, and response to light.

    (3) Administer acetominophen q 3–4 hours for headache.

    (4) Elevate the head of the bed approximately 30 degrees.

3. A client with a head injury develops a clear nasal discharge. The nurse should

    (1) suction the nasal secretions to prevent coughing or sneezing.

    (2) discuss administering an antihistamine to promote client comfort.

    (3) test the discharge for glucose and inform the RN or physician.

    (4) encourage the client to blow his nose.

4. The nurse is assigned to report any sign of increased intracranial pressure on this client. What would most likely be the first sign of this?

    (1) A decorticate posture

    (2) A failure to respond to painful stimuli

    (3) A widening pulse pressure

    (4) An alteration in the level of consciousness

5. A 67-year-old man has been brought to the emergency department after suffering a stroke. When he regains consciousness, the nurse gives him an initial examination and notices that he is having great difficulty speaking in complete and comprehensible sentences. Upon further examination, the nurse also discovers that the client is having a difficult time writing simple sentences. Which area of the client's brain has been affected by the stroke? Identify with an "X" the appropriate area.

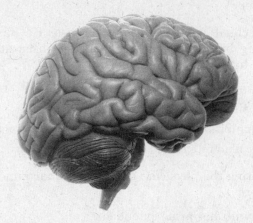

6. Reading the notes on her new client, a 48-year-old woman, the nurse sees that she is described as "alert and oriented x 3." This means that she

   (1) exhibited three types of alert and oriented behavior.

   (2) recognized three different items in her surroundings.

   (3) is alert and oriented to time, person, and place.

   (4) is aware of her surroundings and can describe where, when, and how she got there.

7. Sarah J. is admitted to the unit after a CVA that damaged the right side of her brain. The nurse knows to position her

   (1) on her right side with the head of the bed slightly elevated.

   (2) on her left side with the head of the bed slightly elevated.

   (3) in the prone position.

   (4) supine with the bed in trendelenberg.

8. The nurse working in a college health center admits a young woman who complains of a severe headache, fever, and neck stiffness. Her care is based on the knowledge that these symptoms are characteristic of

   (1) mononucleosis.

   (2) meningitis.

   (3) rheumatic fever.

   (4) Asian flu.

9. A nurse happens to be at the scene of an accident where an unconscious man who is not breathing is lying next to a ladder. Suspecting a possible neck injury, the nurse initiates rescue breathing using the following maneuver:

   (1) Jaw lift

   (2) Head tilt

   (3) Breathing through nose and mouth

   (4) Tongue sweep

10. An older male client has Parkinson's disease. He has been put on levodopa (L-Dopa) 500 mg bid. Which of the following observations would indicate the medication was having the desired effect?

    (1) The client is able to walk to the bathroom.

    (2) The client's sister states that he is more cheerful.

    (3) The client exhibits a decrease in rigidity of movement and tremors.

    (4) The client is able to eat soft food.

11. A nurse is assisting the physician during a lumbar puncture. The nurse helps to position the client

    (1) lying prone with her arms extended.

    (2) leaning over the side of the bed.

    (3) on her side with her knees curled up to her chest.

    (4) on her hands and knees.

12. Tom R., a newly admitted client, has a seizure disorder that is being treated with medication. Which of the following drugs would the nurse question if ordered for him?

    (1) Phenobarbitol, 150 mg hs

    (2) Amitriptylene (Elavil), 10 mg qid

    (3) Valproic acid (Depakote), 150 mg bid

    (4) Phenytoin (Dilantin), 100 mg, tid

TIP

A superlative word—such as *best*—in an NCLEX-PN exam question usually signals that you will need to prioritize care decisions to answer correctly.

13. The CVA client the nurse is caring for has expressive aphasia and becomes irritable and frustrated when he wants something. What would be the *best* intervention for this problem?

    (1) Try to anticipate his needs so that he does not become frustrated.

    (2) Speak in slow, simple language to help him understand.

    (3) Discuss the problem with his family while caring for him.

    (4) Offer a communication board so the client can point to what he wants.

14. A nurse arrives to check on a new trauma client who was in a serious automobile accident and is scheduled for surgery the following morning. The client, who appears to be unconscious, is lying flat on his back in the hospital bed. After checking his medical history, what must the nurse do first to assist in the patient's recovery? Read the exhibits below for additional information.

   (1) Check client's pulse rate.

   (2) Roll client on his side.

   (3) Elevate the client's head about 30°.

   (4) Have the client cough out any mucus or fluids.

Vital Signs

Blood pressure:	160/99 mmHg
Pulse rate:	80 mmHg
Breathing:	Abnormal: periods of apnea
Temperature:	99.8°F

Physical Symptoms

Vomiting. Left-side paralysis. Left pupil dilated compared to right pupil. Periods of loss of consciousness. Client complaining of severe headache. Sustained trauma to head during automobile accident.

Medication

1—manitol: 50 g every 23 hr
2—dexamethasone: 4 mg IV q6 hr

---

15. An adolescent client has symptoms of meningitis: nuchal rigidity, fever, vomiting, and lethargy. The nurse knows to prepare for the following test:

   (1) Blood culture

   (2) Throat and ear culture

   (3) CAT scan

   (4) Lumbar puncture

16. Frances R., a young woman who was in an automobile accident, received a head injury and is being treated for increased intracranial pressure. Which of the following medications ordered for her would the nurse question?

   (1) Dexamethasone (Decadron)

   (2) Mannitol (Osmitrol)

   (3) Phenytoin (Dilantin)

   (4) Secobarbital (Seconal)

exercises

ANSWER KEY AND EXPLANATIONS

1. 4	5. Broca's area	8. 2	11. 3	14. 3
2. 4	6. 3	9. 1	12. 2	15. 4
3. 3	7. 2	10. 3	13. 4	16. 4
4. 4				

1. **The correct answer is (4).** The primary role of the nurse when a client has a seizure is to protect the client from harming himself or herself. Forcing an object into the client's mouth (1) could cause injury, as could restraining the client (2). Calling the operator for seizure assistance (3) is unnecessary, since the primary intervention is to protect the client from self-injury.

2. **The correct answer is (4).** Choices (1) and (2) are assessments, not interventions. Acetominophen (3) would not help and could mask symptoms. Elevating the head of the bed (4) can help reduce intracranial pressure by promoting venous drainage.

3. **The correct answer is (3).** Cerebrospinal fluid will test positive for glucose, and this finding should be reported. Nasal suctioning (1) is contraindicated in a patient who has a head injury with nasal drainage. Antihistamines (2) increase intracranial pressure. Blowing the nose (4) will also increase intracranial pressure.

4. **The correct answer is (4).** The first sign of increased intracranial pressure is a change in the level of consiousness. Choices (1), (2), and (3) are later signs.

5. **The correct answer is Broca's area.** You should have placed an "X" on the diagram over the left frontal lobe.

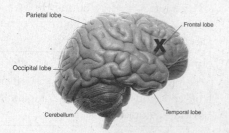

Broca's area is around the opercular and triangular sections of the inferior frontal gyrus. This area is responsible for speech, language processing, language comprehension, and controlling facial neurons. If Broca's area is damaged, a person is said to suffer from Broca's area aphasia, also called expressive aphasia, nonfluent aphasia, or motor aphasia. A person with this condition is unable to form grammatically complex sentences, and the sentences typically contain very few words related to content.

6. **The correct answer is (3).** "Alert and oriented x 3" is commonly used to describe an alert client who is oriented to time, person, and place.

7. **The correct answer is (2).** A client with a right-sided CVA would have left-sided paralysis, so having her lie on her left side leaves her functional side up. If she were lying on her right side, she would have no way to

move. The prone and supine trende-lenberg positions both increase intracranial pressure.

8. **The correct answer is (2).** A severe headache, fever, and neck stiffness are characteristics of meningitis.

9. **The correct answer is (1).** The jaw lift maneuver is used whenever there is a possibility of a neck injury.

10. **The correct answer is (3).** The characteristic problem in Parkinson's is rigidity of movement and tremors, and the medication for it is designed to reduce these.

11. **The correct answer is (3).** When the client is on her side with her knees curled up, her spine is extended and it is easier to insert a needle between the vertebrae.

12. **The correct answer is (2).** Elavil is an antidepressant that lowers the seizure threshold, so would not be appropriate for this client. The other medications are anti-seizure drugs.

13. **The correct answer is (4).** A communication board can help a client communicate his needs. Anticipating his needs will not help him learn to communicate, speaking as if to a child is demeaning, and discussing the client's problems in front of him as if he did not exist is rude.

14. **The correct answer is (3).** The client appears to be suffering from cerebral edema and increased intracranial pressure (ICP). Elevating his head about 30° may help promote venous drainage in the brain and may also decrease pressure and reduce brain swelling.

15. **The correct answer is (4).** Meningitis is an infection of the meninges, the outler layer of the brain. Since it is surrounded by cerebrospinal fluid, a lumbar puncture will help to identify the organism involved.

16. **The correct answer is (4).** Mannitol (2) is an osmotic diuretic to promote diuresis that can decrease intracranial pressure. Dexamethasone (1) is a glucocorticoid and anti-inflammatory drug that can decrease swelling. Phenytoin (3) is an anticonvulsant to prevent seizures. Secobarbital (4) is a sedative agent and sleep medication. Sedatives and narcotics can mask symptoms of increased ICP and cause respiratory depression.

answers exercises

SUMMING IT UP

- The nervous system acts as the coordinating and communicating system of the body. It brings information to the brain and relays instructions from it.
- The nervous system is divided into the central nervous system, the peripheral nervous system, and the autonomic nervous system.
- Neurons, or nerve cells, are the basic units of the nervous system.

The Sensory System

OVERVIEW

- Basic concepts
- The eye
- Eye disorders
- The ear
- Ear disorders
- Summing it up

BASIC CONCEPTS

Hearing and vision are the primary senses with which we take in information about the outside world. An impairment of either can make it difficult for an individual to take in information and communicate with others. This has a profound impact on every aspect of the client's life, from the client's ability to perform the activities of daily living to his or her feelings of self-esteem and emotional well-being.

Sensory function is influenced by many factors, including the normal process of aging, illness, and environmental exposure to excessive noise or toxins. Health behaviors such as smoking and the use of certain medications can also have an effect.

THE EYE

A. The Eye
  1. **External Structures**—primarily for protection
      a. Eyebrow, eyelids, eyelashes
      b. Lacrimal gland and associated structures—lubricate, clean, and protect eye
      c. Conjuctiva—tissue that covers the inside of the eyelids and the white anterior sclera.
  2. **Internal Structures**
      a. Eyeball
          (1) Sclera—white part of the eye—tough, connective tissue
          (2) Cornea—transparent tissue over the pupils that permits light rays to enter
          (3) Ciliary muscle—allows iris of eye to contract and dilate
          (4) Retina—receptors of the optic nerve, contains rods and cones
          (5) Lens—transparent structure behind the lens that focuses light rays on the retina

(6) Aqueous and vitreous humor—fill the anterior and posterior parts of eye—maintain form and transparency of eye as well as contributing to maintenance of eye pressure

(7) Optic nerve—leaves the eye through retina at the optic disc

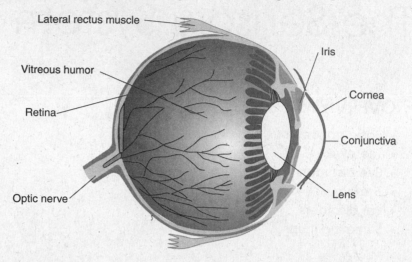

Diagnostic Tests for the Eye

Ophthalmoscope: A device for visualizing the internal structures of the eye.

Tonometer: An instrument used for measuring intraocular pressure. Normal intraocular pressure is 12-22 mmHg.

Snellen Chart: A test of visual acuity using the client's performance compared to a person with normal vision. Thus, a person who has 20/30 vision can read at 20 feet what a normal person can read at 30 feet.

Biomicroscopy (Slit Lamp Exam): A binocular microscope used to assess the anterior eye for abnormalities of the cornea, iris, lens, and depth of anterior chamber angle

EYE DISORDERS

A. **Conjunctivitis**—inflammation of the conjunctiva due to viral or bacterial infection, allergies, or chemical irritants
1. **Assessment**
   a. Burning, tearing, and *redness of the conjunctiva* of the eye. Bacterial conjunctivitis is characterized by a purulent discharge that may stick the eyelids together.
   b. Usually begins in one eye and spreads to the other—very contagious.
2. **Treatment**
   a. Opthalmic antibiotic eye ointment if bacterial
3. **Nursing Interventions**
   a. Prevent transmission
   (1) Teach not to rub eyes.
   (2) Emphasize handwashing.
   b. Medication administration
   (1) Warm compresses if needed to remove crusts.
   (2) Demonstrate instillation of prescribed ointment or drops.

B. Cataract—normally transparent lens becomes clouded and opaque. Cataracts are associated with aging, diabetes, steroids, and longtime sun exposure. They may also be hereditary or related to infections.

1. **Assessment**
   a. Progressive *blurring* and gradual loss of vision
   b. Poor night vision with a glare in bright light

2. **Diagnosis**
   a. Opaque or cloudy white pupil
   b. Absence of red reflex on ophthalmoscope exam
   c. Slit lamp exam

3. **Medical Treatment**
   a. Surgical removal of opaque lens
   b. Replace with glasses, contact lenses, or artificial lens

4. **Nursing Interventions**
   a. Preoperative care with administration of preoperative medications—often mydriatics to dilate pupils.
   b. Administration of pain medication, steroids to decrease inflammation, and antibiotics to prevent infection.
   c. Teach client to avoid increasing intraocular pressure—coughing, bending, or rapid head movements and to avoid vomiting or constipation.
   d. Position client on unoperated side in low Fowler's position.
   e. Use eyepads as ordered.
   f. Monitor for intraocular hemorrhage that causes sudden, severe pain.

C. Glaucoma—increased intraocular pressure due to an imbalance in the production and drainage of aqueous humor as the angle of drainage closes. *Acute* (closed angle) involves a sudden onset of symptoms and requires immediate treatment. *Chronic* (open-angle) has a slow progression of symptoms that may be ignored. If not diagnosed early, glaucoma can lead to permanent loss of vision.

1. **Assessment**
   a. Usually over 40 years of age, often with family history of the disease
   b. Painless loss of peripheral vision—*tunnel vision*
   c. Halos around lights
   d. Pain, malaise, nausea, and vomiting (late symptoms)
   e. Permanent loss of vision

2. **Diagnosis**
   a. Tonometry indicates increased intraocular pressure (> 22mm Hg)
   b. Measurement of visual fields
   c. History of symptoms

3. **Medical Treatment**
   a. Miotics decrease intraocular pressure by constricting pupil and increasing outflow of humor
   b. Iridectomy—surgical incision to remove part of iris to allow for drainage of humor
   c. Medications that decrease the production of aqueous humor
      (1) Beta blockers (Timoptic)
      (2) Osmotic diuretics (Osmitrol)
      (3) Carbonic anhydrase inhibitors (Diamox)

4. **Nursing Interventions**
   a. Teach client to administer eye medications that must be continued to control disease.
   b. Inform client to avoid drugs containing atropine.
   c. Stress the importance of regular medical follow-up.

      d. Teach need to wear a medic-alert bracelet.

      e. Instruct client to avoid salt in diet.

D. Detached retina—detachment of the part of the eye that sends visual stimuli to the optic nerve. Blindness results if the detachment is complete. It is often described as a veil or curtain over the eye.

1. **Assessment**
   a. Spots and *flashes of lights, floating spots, and loss of vision in affected area*
   b. Sudden onset, no pain; may be related to trauma; cause often unknown
2. **Diagnosis**
   a. Ophthalmoscope exam of retina
   b. Visual acuity assessment
3. **Medical Treatment**
   a. Goal of treatment is to seal the hole by causing an inflammation that will lead to scar adhesion
      (1) Laser—photocoagulation
      (2) Cryosurgery
      (3) Electrodiathermy
4. **Nursing Interventions**
   a. Complete bed rest pre- and postoperatively as ordered.
   b. Sedate as needed to keep client comfortable and quiet.
   c. Position so area of detachment is dependent.
   d. Patch eye to limit eye movement.
   e. Provide support and a safe environment.

Assisting the Client Who Has Visual Deficits

GOAL: To provide independence, safety, and increased access to social and diversional activities

SAFETY

Keep area free of clutter—no throw rugs, electrical cords in walkways.
Use hand grips in bathrooms, nonskid stripping in tub.
Use medications that are easily identified by shape or in containers with raised markings for each day.
Keep the environment stable. Do not rearrange objects or furniture unless necessary.

DIVERSION

Provide radios and books on tape or large-print books.
Supply telephones with programmed automatic dialing—include numbers of friends as well as emergency phone numbers.

SELF CARE

Assist client in locating meals on wheels or shop-by-phone grocery.
Encourage microwave for cooking, using nonbreakable utensils.
Have a "talking clock" that announces the time.

THE EAR

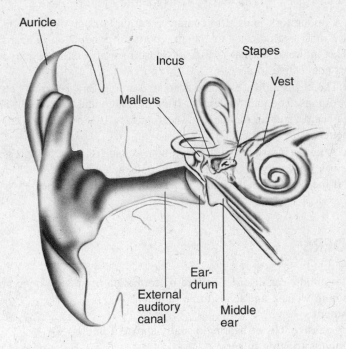

A. The Ear

1. **Outer Ear**
   a. Pinna or auricle—outer part of ear made of cartilage, collects sound
   b. External (auditory canal)—transmits sound to tympanic membrane; outer part secretes cerumen (wax), which provides protection
   c. Tympanic membrane (eardrum)—conducts sound vibrations to middle ear

2. **Middle Ear**
   a. Contains three small bones (malleus, incus, stapes)—which conduct sound waves to oval window and inner ear
   b. Eustachian tube—connects nasopharynx and middle ear, bringing air in and equalizing pressure on both sides of tympanic membrane
   c. Conductive hearing loss—is due to problems in the external or middle ear that interfere with transmission of sound waves

3. **Inner Ear**
   a. Cochlea—contains organ of Corti, which receives sound waves and transmits them to the hearing center of the brain through the auditory nerve (cranial nerve VIII)
   b. Bony labyrinth—contains the vestibule and semicircular canals, which maintain balance
   c. Sensorineural hearing loss—is due to malfunction of the inner ear, auditory nerve, or the auditory center in the brain

> **Diagnostic Tests for the Ear**
>
> **Rinne Test:** A tuning fork is used to compare hearing through air and bone. A positive Rinne test indicates the client reports air conduction is heard longer than bone. This indicates normal hearing or sensorineural loss. A negative test indicates conductive loss.
>
> **Weber Test:** The client indicates where a midline tuning fork is heard better. The normal response is equal bilaterally. If there is a conductive loss in one ear, sound is heard better in the ear with hearing loss. If sensorineural, it will be heard better in the good ear.
>
> **Audiometry:** A test of hearing that assesses both sound frequency (high or low pitch) and decibels (intensity of sound). Hearing aids magnify sound and are not as helpful if the problem is difficulty hearing different frequencies.

EAR DISORDERS

A. **Otosclerosis**—middle ear disorder caused by formation of spongy bone around the stapes. More common in women and tends to be familial.
1. **Assessment**
    a. Progressive loss of hearing, usually apparent in 20s–30s
    b. Tinnitus (ringing in ears)
2. **Diagnosis**
    a. Hearing test—conductive hearing loss
3. **Medical Treatment**
    a. Stapedectomy—replacement of stapes with a prosthesis
4. **Nursing Interventions**
    a. Postoperative Care
       (1) Client must maintain bed rest for 24 hours.
       (2) Avoid increasing pressure in ear with coughing, sneezing—may dislodge prosthesis.
       (3) Prevent infection by instructing client to take antibiotics and avoid people with colds.

B. **Acute Otitis Media**—infection of middle ear common in infants and young children due to characteristics of their Eustacian tubes
1. **Assessment**
    a. History of upper-respiratory infection
    b. Ear pain, irritability in infants
    c. May be accompanied by fever
2. **Diagnosis**
    a. Exam of tympanic membrane with otoscope—red and bulging
    b. Pus may be present if membrane ruptured
3. **Medical Treatment**
    a. Antibiotics
    b. Antipyretics and analgesics if needed
4. **Nursing Interventions**
    a. Review medication instructions and emphasize completing all antibiotics.
    b. Arrange for follow-up care.
    c. Instruct the client on signs and symptoms to report.

C. Meniere's Disease—chronic disease of the inner ear that causes vertigo (dizziness), tinnitus, and sensorineural hearing loss

1. **Assessment**
   a. Vertigo, tinnitus, hearing loss during attacks
   b. Attacks may last 10 minutes to several hours—may function normally between attacks
   c. Disease usually gets progressively worse, with more frequent and longer attacks and progressive hearing loss

2. **Diagnosis**
   a. Tests to rule out other possible problems.
   b. Hearing test indicates sensorineural hearing loss.

3. **Medical Treatment**
   a. Diuretics, low-sodium diet, antihistamines, antiemetics, mild sedatives
   b. Surgical destruction of labyrinth (causes irreversible hearing loss)

4. **Nursing Interventions**
   a. Teach methods to combat dizziness—rising slowly from sitting position.
   b. Tell client that reading and exposure to bright lights may trigger vertigo.
   c. Preoperative and postoperative care as needed.
   d. Instruct client to expect vertigo and nausea for one to two days after surgery.

Assisting the Client Who Has Impaired Hearing

GOAL: To promote better communication, increase safety, and self-confidence

COMMUNICATION

Speak face-to-face, articulating clearly but without exaggeration or shouting.
Avoid covering your mouth while talking.
Assist client in hearing-aid care—keep it dry, clean, and have extra batteries.
Avoid noisy environments that make hearing more difficult; hearing aids exaggerate background noise.
Provide alternate methods of communication—ask about sign language and lip-reading skills, and obtain magic slate and pencil.

SAFETY

Have client obtain light-activated devices for the home—smoke alarms, doorbell, security alarms.
Suggest possibility of a TDD (telephone device for the deaf) or videophone for communicating.

EXERCISES: THE SENSORY SYSTEM

1. The nurse is assessing a client with cataracts. She could expect the client to have which of the following symptoms?
   Select all that apply.

   ☐ **(1)** Blurred vision that has been getting progressively worse.

   ☐ **(2)** Difficulty with glare and with seeing in bright light.

   ☐ **(3)** A persistent, dull eye pain.

   ☐ **(4)** Intact peripheral vision.

2. After cataract surgery, the nurse will give the client discharge instructions that will include the following:

   (1) No restrictions on activity.

   (2) Advise using dark glasses for the first few days.

   (3) Prevent an increase in intraocular pressure by refraining from bending, straining, coughing, etc.

   (4) Place cool witch hazel compresses on eye qid.

3. The nurse is providing preventive health instruction to an adult group and explains that glaucoma is the most preventable cause of blindness. He describes the symptoms, one of which is:

   (1) watery eyes.

   (2) intact peripheral vision.

   (3) decreased accommodation to near objects.

   (4) seeing halos around lights.

4. A client receiving treatment for glaucoma with the miotic agent pilocarpine is getting instructions from the nurse. Which comment by the client indicates the need for further teaching?

   (1) "It will be great to be able to see more clearly now."

   (2) "I will need these eyedrops for the rest of my life."

   (3) "These drops will lower the pressure inside my eye."

   (4) "I will take an antiemetic to prevent vomiting, which increases intraocular pressure."

5. Mrs. Bloom, a 78-year-old client, is experiencing vision disturbances and is diagnosed with cataracts in both eyes. Identify with an "X" the area of Mrs. Bloom's eyes that are affected.

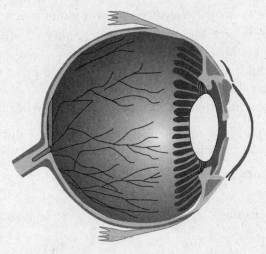

6. In the clinic, a client tells the nurse that he suddenly lost his vision and can only see spots and flashes of light in his right eye. The client needs to be transferred quickly with his head lower than his body and is sedated to keep him comfortable and quiet. The nurse explains to his wife that her husband has

   (1) macular degeneration.

   (2) glaucoma.

   (3) retinal detachment.

   (4) cataracts.

7. An 80-year-old man is receiving instructions from the nurse about hearing-aid care. Which comment indicates the need for further teaching?

   (1) "It will be nice to be able to hear my grandchildren when we go swimming."

   (2) "When I'm not using it, I'll take the battery out and turn it off."

   (3) "I'll clean the middle hole with a toothpick or pipe cleaner."

   (4) "I need to keep extra batteries on hand."

8. The nurse is assessing a client who has just been tested for visual acuity and was told his vision was 20/50. The client asks what this means, and the nurse answers,

   (1) "You can see approximately 2/5 as well as the normal person."

   (2) "You can see at 20 feet what a person with normal vision can see at 50 feet."

   (3) "Your vision is the same as that of a 20-year-old man, even though you are 50."

   (4) "You can see at 50 feet what a person with normal vision can see at 20 feet."

9. The nurse is explaining acute otitis media to the mother of the 4-month-old boy who has just been given medication for his earache. Which statement by the mother indicates there is no need for further teaching?

    (1) "I will have to keep Johnny's ears covered more now that it is cold outside."

    (2) "I don't like to give him too many drugs. May we stop the antibiotic as soon as he feels better?"

    (3) "I see, so children are more likely to get these infections after colds because of the shape of their Eustacian tubes."

    (4) "How did the infection get into his inner ear? Will it go to his brain?"

10. When a client presents with hearing loss, the nurse differentiates between conductive and sensorineural loss by using the following test(s):

    (1) Tympanogram

    (2) Otoscope

    (3) Weber and Rinne

    (4) Snellen

ANSWER KEY AND EXPLANATIONS

1. 1,2,4	3. 4	5. lens of the eye	7. 1	9. 3
2. 3	4. 1	6. 3	8. 2	10. 3

1. **The correct answers are (1), (2), and (4).** Cataracts are a painless clouding of the lens; the condition is common in older people.

2. **The correct answer is (3).** One of the important aspects of client teaching after cataract surgery is the avoidance of increased intraocular pressure, which can be caused by the Valsalva maneuver, bending, coughing, and the like.

3. **The correct answer is (4).** The most common type of glaucoma, chronic open-angle glaucoma, does not affect near vision. It is characterized by loss of peripheral vision, a dull ache in the eyes, and halos around lights. Acute closed-angle glaucoma causes pain, sensations of pressure, pupil dilation, blurred vision, photophobia, nausea, and vomiting. It is a medical emergency.

4. **The correct answer is (1).** Pilocarpine reduces intraocular pressure but does not improve vision.

5. **The correct answer is the lens of the eye.** In a client suffering from cataracts, the normally transparent lens becomes cloudy and opaque.

6. **The correct answer is (3).** This client's symptoms are characteristic of retinal detachment, an emergent condition that may be related to trauma, but the cause is often unknown.

7. **The correct answer is (1).** Hearing aids are not to be used in or around water.

8. **The correct answer is (2).** Using the Snellen chart for visual acuity, the client sits at 20 feet and reads the smallest line he or she can. The numerator is 20, and the denominator is the distance at which the normal person could see the line.

9. **The correct answer is (3).** Otitis media is an infection of the middle ear. It is common in infants and children due to the characteristics of their Eustacian tubes.

10. **The correct answer is (3).** The Weber and Rinne tests distinguish between conductive and sensorineural hearing loss. A Snellen chart is used to test vision, an otoscope is used for inspection of the ear, and a tympanogram measures the compliance of the tympanic membrane.

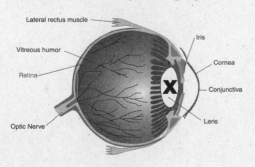

SUMMING IT UP

- Hearing and vision are the primary senses with which we gather information about the outside world.
- Sensory function is influenced by many factors, including the normal process of aging, illness, and environmental exposure to excessive noise or toxins.
- Health behaviors such as smoking and the use of certain medications can also have an effect on hearing and vision.

The Endocrine System

chapter 10

OVERVIEW

- Basic concepts
- Endocrine glands
- Endocrine disorders
- Pancreas
- Summing it up

BASIC CONCEPTS

The endocrine system is composed of glands that secrete hormones that regulate body activities. Hormones are carried by the bloodstream to their target organs. They are regulated by the central nervous system with releasing and inhibiting factors, by negative feedback mechanisms, and by changing levels of substances in the blood, such as glucose. Some hormones follow cyclic patterns, such as cortisol and reproductive hormones.

ENDOCRINE GLANDS

A. **Pituitary Gland**—composed of anterior and posterior lobes
  1. **Anterior Lobe**
    a. Follicle-stimulating hormone—stimulates ovarian follicle growth and estrogen production in women
    b. Luteinizing hormone—induces ovulation and development of corpus luteum, which produces progesterone in women; stimulates testosterone secretion in men
    c. Adrenocorticotropic hormone (ACTH)—stimulates the adrenal cortex to produce and secrete glucocorticoid hormones
    d. Thyroid-stimulating hormone—regulates the activity of the thyroid gland
    e. Growth hormone—stimulates growth of body cells
    f. Prolactin—stimulates milk production during lactation
  2. **Posterior Lobe** (stores and releases hormones produced by the hypothalamus)
    a. Antidiuretic hormone—promotes sodium and water retention, raises blood pressure
    b. Oxytocin—stimulates uterine contractions during and after labor and milk secretion during lactation

B. **Thyroid Gland** (controlled by the pituitary's release of TSH)
  1. **Thyroxine**—regulates the metabolic rate of the body's cells

C. **Adrenal Glands**
   1. **Glucocorticoids (includes cortisol and cortisone)**—mediate the body's response to stress, promote the retention of sodium and water, and the excretion of potassium
   2. **Mineralocorticoids (includes aldosterone)**—sodium and water retention, potassium excretion
   3. **Sex hormones (androgens, estrogen, and progesterone)**—affect development of secondary sex characteristics
   4. **Epinephrine and norepinephrine**—cause "fight or flight" stress response (vasoconstriction, increase cardiac output, increase metabolism, increase blood glucose levels)

D. **Pancreas**
   1. **Insulin**—causes cells to take in glucose and lowers glucose level of the blood
   2. **Glucagon**—increases blood sugar levels by causing the liver to break down glycogen to glucose

E. **Parathyroid Gland**
   1. **Parathyroid hormone**—regulates calcium and phosphorus levels in the blood

ENDOCRINE DISORDERS

Diagnostic Tests for Endocrine Disorders

Stimulation testing
Suppression testing

Radioactive iodine uptake
T3 and T4 resin uptake
Thyroid stimulating hormone (TSH)
Thyroid scan
Needle aspiration of thyroid tissue

Glucose tolerance test (GTT)
Glycosylated hemoglobin

Adrenal Glands

A. **Addison's Disease**—caused by a deficiency of the hormones produced by the adrenal gland, decreased cortisol, and mineralocorticoids
   1. **Assessment**
      a. Fatigue, anorexia, nausea, vomiting, diarrhea, and abdominal pain
      b. Weight loss, frequent hypoglycemia, dehydration
      c. Decreased cardiac output, lethargy, depression
      d. Bronze skin tone of nipples, buccal mucosa, decreased pubic and axillary hair
   2. **Diagnosis**
      a. Blood chemistry: decreased Hgb, decreased Hct, decreased cortisol, decreased glucose, decreased sodium, decreased chloride, decreased aldosterone levels, increased BUN, increased potassium
      b. Decreased basal metabolic rate
      c. EKG indicates prolonged PR and QT intervals
   3. **Medical Treatment**
      a. Glucocorticoids—cortisone (Cortone) and hydrocortisone (Solu-Cortef)
      b. Mineralocorticoids—flurocortisone (Florinef)

   c. Treatment of Addisonian crisis—a medical emergency caused by stress such as surgery or rapid withdrawal of medication from a person on long-term steroid therapy—IV hydrocortisone with 3 to 5 liters of normal saline

  4. **Nursing Interventions**

    a. Teach client about need for lifelong corticosteroid replacement treatment, as well as side effects of medication, such as mood changes.

    b. Teach the need to avoid stress, trauma, and infections, and to notify provider if these occur, since medication may need to be modified.

    c. Modify diet to one high in protein, carbohydrates, and sodium.

    d. Explain disease process and signs of adrenal insufficiency.

B. Cushing's Syndrome—caused by excessive secretion of corticosteroids, especially cortisol, due to either problems with the adrenal or pituitary gland or prolonged administration of corticosteroids

  1. **Assessment**

    a. Abnormal fat distribution—moon face, buffalo hump, obese trunk with thin arms and legs

    b. Fragile, easily bruised skin, osteoporosis, high blood sugar, masculine characteristics in females, such as excess hair, hypertension

    c. Mood swings, increased susceptibility to infections, fatigue, and muscle weakness

  2. **Diagnosis**

    a. History and physical exam

    b. Plasma and urinary cortisol levels

    c. Dexamethasone suppression test

  3. **Medical Treatment** (eliminating the cause)

    a. Surgical removal of adrenal glands followed by lifelong corticosteroid replacement

    b. Tapering steroid therapy

  4. **Nursing Interventions**

    a. Prevent injury related to osteoporosis.

    b. Promote stress-free environment.

    c. Encourage diet low in calories and sugar, high in protein and potassium.

    d. Explain the need for lifelong hormone replacement therapy (if adrenal glands removed) and discuss side effects.

    e. Assist client in coping with body image changes related to disease.

Thyroid Gland

C. Hypothyroidism (myxedema or, if present at birth, cretinism)

  1. **Assessment**

    a. Dry skin and hair, sensitivity to cold, fatigue, low metabolic rate

    b. Constipation, weight gain, depression

    c. Possible *goiter*—an enlarged thyroid gland

  2. **Diagnosis**

    a. Decreased TSH, decreased T4, decreased T3, increased TRH

  3. **Medical Treatment**

    a. Thyroid hormone replacement—lovothyroxine (Synthroid), dessicated thyroid, or liothyronine (Cytomel); dosage gradually increased to optimal

    b. Emergency treatment of myxedema coma—IV thyroid hormones, correction of hypothermia, hypoventilation

  4. **Nursing Interventions**

    a. Conduct thyroid hormone replacement teaching—take dose in a.m. to prevent insomnia; know signs and symptoms of thyrotoxicosis.

b. Discuss measures for weight control, management of constipation, and cold intolerance.

D. **Hyperthyroid (Grave's Disease)**—more common in women, usually occurs between ages 20–40
   1. **Assessment**
      a. Increased metabolic rate—acceleration of all body processes
      b. Nervousness, irritability, tachycardia, diarrhea, weight loss
      c. Intolerance to heat
      d. Enlargement of thyroid gland (goiter)
      e. Exophthalmos—fluid collects in eye sockets, causing eyeballs to protrude, usually does not improve with treatment
   2. **Diagnosis**
      a. Increase iodine uptake; increase T3; increase T4
   3. **Medical Treatment**
      a. Drug therapy—antithyroid drugs such as propylthioruacil to block synthesis of thyroid hormone; beta blockers to decrease sympathetic activity and alleviate symptoms
      b. Radioactive iodine therapy—isotope of iodine given to destroy thyroid gland
      c. Surgery—thyroidectomy to remove thyroid
      d. Thyroid storm—uncontrolled hyperthyroidism; ventilation, IV therapy, medications such as antithyroid drugs, corticosteroids, sedatives, and cardiac drugs
   4. **Nursing Interventions**
      a. Encourage high-calorie, high-nutrient diet.
      b. If exophthalmos, protect eyes with eyedrops, dark glasses.
      c. Teach side effects of medications, symptoms of hypo-hyperthyroidism.

Parathyroid

E. **Hyperparathyroidism**—increased production of hormone; primarily due to parathyroid tumor; secondary caused by kidney disease, osteomalacia
   1. **Assessment**
      a. Excessive removal of calcium from bones leading to high blood level of calcium and weak bone structure, causing pathologic fractures; low blood phosphate levels
      b. GI symptoms—constipation, nausea and vomiting, epigastric discomfort
      c. Renal colic, kidney stones, polyuria, polydipsia
      d. Hypertension
      e. Depression, slowed mental processes, personality changes
   2. **Diagnosis**
      a. Elevated serum calcium levels
      b. Decreased serum phosphate levels
      c. X-rays reveal bone demineralization
   3. **Medical Treatment**
      a. Surgical removal of the parathyroid gland
      b. Decrease level of circulating calcium—loop diuretic or increase volume in circulation to dilute
   4. **Nursing Interventions**
      a. Limit high-calcium foods and encourage increase in fluid intake to reduce calcium concentration. Provide diet high in phosphorus.
      b. Encourage mobility to decrease bone demineralization that occurs with bed rest.
      c. Institute safety measures to decrease incidence of falls.
      d. If surgical removal of parathyroid gland, perform routine preoperative and postoperative care.

e. Secondary parathyroidism due to renal failure requires calcium supplementation, because malabsorption and low levels of calcium lead to excessive parathyroid hormone production.

F. Hypoparathyroidism—deficient parathyroid hormone production
1. **Assessment**
   a. Numbness, tingling, muscle cramping of extremities
   b. *Acute*—possible seizures, laryngospasm, cardiac arrhythmias
   c. *Acute*—positive *Chvostek's sign:* taps on facial nerve cause muscle spasm of face, a sign of tetany
   d. *Chronic* hypocalcemia leads to poor tooth enamel; mental retardation; loss of hair; coarse, dry skin; cataracts; and renal stones
2. **Diagnosis**
   a. Decreased serum calcium, increased serum phosphorus
   b. Decreased urinary calcium output, decreased urinary phosphorus output
   c. X-rays reveal increased bone density
3. **Medical Treatment**
   a. *Acute care:* IV calcium gluconate, anticonvulsives, and sedatives. Tracheostomy if laryngospasm has caused obstruction. Parathyroid hormone IM.
   b. *Chronic care:* Oral calcium salts (OS CAL) and vitamin D; high-calcium, low-phosphorus diet
4. **Nursing Interventions**
   a. Help client increase calcium levels by administering calcium supplements, evaluating status.
   b. Decrease problems with neuromuscular irritability by keeping a quiet environment, low lights, and maintaining seizure precautions.
   c. Prevent respiratory distress by frequent assessments, tracheostomy set availability, bronchodilators.

PANCREAS

Diabetes Mellitus—a group of chronic disorders that involves an increase in blood glucose—hyperglycemia. It is the most common endocrine problem, and today the number of diabetics—especially type 2—is rapidly increasing. Insulin is secreted by the beta cells in the Islets of Langerhans in the pancreas.

Cause: Lack of insulin, insulin deficiency, or the body's insensitivity to insulin

Result: Insulin is needed for the cells to utilize carbohydrates for energy. If there is not enough insulin, the cell will break down fats and proteins, resulting in protein wasting and ketone production. In addition, the level of glucose in the blood will stay high.

Treatments: Increasing insulin sensitivity, providing insulin, lowering blood glucose

Types of Diabetes

A. **Type 1 Diabetes**—(previously called juvenile diabetes—10–15 percent of diabetic cases)
1. **Assessment**
   a. Onset usually before age 40; involves total destruction of beta cells; insulin injections required for rest of client's life
   b. Individual usually thin, onset abrupt; client experiences weight loss, fatigue
   c. Polyphagia (increased hunger); polydipsia (increased thirst); polyuria (increased urination)

Insulin Preparations

Drug	Appearance	Onset	Peak	Duration	Compatible Mixed With
Regular Insulin	Clear	½–1 hr	2–4 hrs	6–8 hrs	All insulin preparations
Semilente Insulin	Cloudy	½–1 hr	4–6 hrs	12–16 hrs	Lente preparations
NPH Insulin	Cloudy	1–1½ hrs	8–12 hrs	18–24 hrs	Regular insulin injection
Lente Insulin	Cloudy	1–1½ hrs	8–12 hrs	18–24 hrs	Regular and semilente insulins
Ultralente Insulin	Cloudy	4–8 hrs	16–20 hrs	30–36 hrs	Regular and semilente insulins

Oral Hypoglycemic Agents

Drug	Dosage	Onset	Duration
First-generation sulfonylureas			
Acetohexamide (Dymelor)	250–1500 mg/day	½ hr	12–24 hrs
Chlorpropramide (Diabinese)	100–500 mg/day	1 hr	24–72 hrs
Tolazamide (Tolinase)	100–1000 mg/day	4–6 hrs	14–24 hrs
Tolbutamide (Orinase)	250–2000 mg/day	½ hr	6–12 hrs
Second-generation sulfonylureas			
Glipzide (Glucotrol)	2.5–40 mg/day	1–1½ hrs	16–24 hrs
Glyburide (DiaBeta, Micronase)	1.25–20 mg/day	2–4 hrs	24 hrs

Diabetic Complications

Diabetic Hypoglycemia	Ketoacidosis (DKA)	Nonketotic Coma (HHNK)
Type 1 DM	Type 1 DM	Type 2 DM
↑ insulin ↓ food	Insufficient insulin	Uncontrolled diabetes
Rapid onset	Slow onset (8 hrs)	Slow onset (days)
Normal respirations	Kussmaul's breathing	Normal respirations
Normal breath odor	Sweet "acetone" breath	Normal breath odor
Tachycardia	Tachycardia	Tachycardia
Blood pressure nml	↓ blood pressure	↓ blood pressure
Hunger	↓ appetite	Hunger
No thirst	↑ thirst	↑ thirst
Nausea	N & V	N & V
Pale, clammy skin	Hot, dry skin	Hot, dry skin
Confused	Drowsy, confused ⇒ coma	Confused, dull ⇒ coma
Glucose: < 50–70 mg/dL	Glucose > 350–900 mg/dL	Glucose ↑↑ 800–2400 mg/dL
Ø ketones	High ketones	Ø ketones
Treatment: oral or IV glucose, IM glucagon	**Treatment:** IV normal saline, then add potassium, glucose, and insulin	**Treatment:** IV hydration, then glucose and insulin

d. Cause may be genetics, viruses, possibly autoimmune response

e. Prone to ketosis, possible ketoacidosis

f. Oral hypoglycemics not used

B. Type 2 Diabetes—(adult onset—85–90 percent of diabetics)

1. **Assessment**

   a. Due to partial deficiency of insulin production as well as insensitivity of the cells to insulin

   b. Primarily occurs in obese adults over 40; onset gradual

   c. Fatigue, drowsiness, blurred vision

   d. No ketoacidosis, no ketosis

   e. Diet very important—approximately 25 percent need insulin; 40 percent use oral hypoglycemic agents; weight loss encouraged

   f. Complications of both—neuropathy, retinopathy, nephropathy, vascular disease, coronary heart disease, atherosclerosis

   g. Ketoacidosis and ketosis more common in type 1

2. **Diagnosis**

   a. Fasting blood glucose > 126 on two occasions (normal fasting: < 110 mg/dL; 2-hour post prandial is < 140 mg/dL)

   b. Random blood glucose of 200 mg/dL on at least two occasions

   c. Oral glucose tolerance test (most sensitive) is > 200 mg/dL at 2 hours

   d. Urine positive for glucose and ketones

   e. Increased glycosylated hemoglobin assay (HbA1c)—normal: 3.5–6.2 percent

   f. History and presenting signs and symptoms

3. **Medical Treatment**

   a. Insulin—beef, pork, or human. Human is the purest and least likely to cause allergy. Delivery by injection or by pump. Amount given is determined by client's blood glucose, response to treatment.

   b. Oral hypoglycemic agents—if diet and exercise cannot control blood sugar

   c. Regularly scheduled exercise—exercise reduces insulin needs, increases utilization of glucose, causes a less drastic fluctuation of blood sugar levels

   d. Diabetic diet

      (1) Low calorie if weight loss desired

      (2) Designed to maintain stable blood glucose level

4. **Nursing Interventions**

   a. Client care

      (1) Administer insulin or oral hypoglycemic agents. Monitor for hypoglycemia during drug's time of peak action.

      (2) Provide prescribed diet and monitor intake.

      (3) Monitor blood glucose with fingersticks or urine tests, if ordered..

      (4) Provide excellent skin care; monitor I & O and weight.

      (5) Support client with lifestyle changes.

      (6) Monitor for presence of diabetic complications

         (a) Atherosclerosis, coronary artery disease, peripheral vascular disease

         (b) Kidney—pyelonephritis and diabetic nephropathy

         (c) Ocular disorders—cataracts, diabetic retinopathy

         (d) Peripheral neuropathy—diarrhea, constipation, neurogenci bladder, impotence, decreased sweating

   b. Client teaching

      (1) Planning meals—using exchange lists; importance of regularity

      (2) Insulin administration—room temperature, roll in hands to distribute; when mixing draw up clear insulin first. Only regular (clear) insulin can be mixed with other insulins. *Injection:* rotate injection sites to prevent lipodystrophy; within 1 anatomical area about one inch apart is preferred.

NOTE

Only regular insulin may be given IV. Client must eat immediately after fast-acting insulin is given (humalog—onset < 15 minutes, peak 1 hour).

NOTE

If you are uncertain what is wrong with an unconscious diabetic, give glucose, since untreated hypoglycemia can cause brain damage.

Most rapid absorption is from abdomen. **Lipodystrophy** is associated with injecting cold insulin and poor site rotation.

(3) Oral hypoglycemics—importance of taking medication regularly and avoiding alcohol; may cause antabuse-like reaction. Metformin increases sensitivity to insulin.

(4) During illness, blood glucose goes up—need to notify physician.

(5) Careful foot care, monitoring for infections is necessary.

(6) Recognizing and treating hypo-hyperglycemia; medical alert bracelet. Remember: "Hot and dry, sugar's high; cold and clammy, need some candy."

EXERCISES: THE ENDOCRINE SYSTEM

1. In teaching a newly diagnosed client with diabetes about the exchange system, the nurse explains that potatoes would be considered a

    (1) vegetable exchange.

    (2) meat exchange.

    (3) starch-bread exchange.

    (4) fruit exchange.

2. The nurse is caring for a client who has been newly diagnosed with diabetes. The care plan includes careful monitoring of intake and output. The nurse will expect to find the following, which is a typical presentation of diabetes:

    (1) Anuria

    (2) Polyuria

    (3) Hematuria

    (4) Oliguria

3. The clinic nurse is evaluating a man wearing a diabetic MedicAlert® band, who appears confused, with hot, dry, flushed skin. His respirations are deep and fast, and he says he is nauseated. His breath smells fruity. The nurse recognizes that he needs immediate care because he has the following diabetes-related condition:

    (1) Ketoacidosis

    (2) Hypoglycemia

    (3) Neuropathy

    (4) Retinopathy

4. The breakfast trays are delayed, and the client with diabetes, who received her insulin an hour ago, tells the nurse that she is feeling sweaty and shaky and that she feels a tingling sensation on her fingers and around her mouth. The nurse quickly brings her

    (1) a glass of orange juice.

    (2) a supplemental dose of insulin.

    (3) coffee.

    (4) peanut butter.

5. A nurse is doing a community blood glucose screening and gets a reading of 206 when testing an overweight woman. Upon questioning, the woman has a history of two macrosomic infants and complains of fatigue, constant hunger and thirst, and frequent urination. The nurse refers her for further screening and treatment, since it is likely she suffers from

    (1) type I diabetes.

    (2) type II diabetes.

    (3) hypoparathyroidism.

    (4) Graves' disease.

TIP

Question 1 is an example of how NCLEX-PN questions assess both Client Needs (Physiological Integrity: Basic Care and Comfort) and the Nursing Process (Teaching and Learning).

6. The client with diabetes is demonstrating her knowledge of self-care by discussing the diet that has been prescribed for her, the symptoms of hyper- and hypoglycemia, as well as the role of exercise in her treatment. Which comment would indicate the need for further teaching?

   (1) "If I decide not to eat bread at a meal, I can exchange it for a cup of rice."

   (2) "I am likely to get hyperglycemic if I eat too many simple carbohydrates at one time."

   (3) "I have always exercised—my husband and I bowl together at least once a week."

   (4) "I need to be especially careful about infections and will let my health provider know if I get one."

7. A nurse on the medical floor walks in the room of the client with diabetes to find him unconscious. She is not sure when he ate last or when or whether he took his insulin. The nurse's *best* response would be to

   (1) inform the RN and prepare to give glucagon.

   (2) obtain the glucometer and determine the client's blood sugar.

   (3) call the lab to get a stat glucose on the client.

   (4) check his vitals as well as his level of consciousness using the Glasgow coma scale.

8. The nurse is reinforcing the importance of proper foot care to the older client with diabetes. The woman states that they surely must have something more important to discuss. The nurse correctly replies,

   (1) "Foot care as well as any other type of hygiene is always important."

   (2) "We can skip this if you prefer."

   (3) "All right, just remember that you will be more prone to foot odor."

   (4) "Diabetics can easily develop severe foot injury or infection without knowing it."

9. A nurse is drawing blood from the client with diabetes for a glycosolated hemoglobin test. She explains to the woman that the test is used to determine

   (1) the highest glucose level in the past week.

   (2) her insulin level.

   (3) glucose levels over the past four months.

   (4) her usual fasting glucose level.

10. A client who has an overactive thyroid gland has been scheduled for an outpatient thyroid scan. Before the scan, the nurse must educate the client about how to prepare himself for the test, what will happen to him during the test, and what he will need to do after the test. List these instructions in chronological order.

    (1) Avoid contact with urine.   _____

    (2) Administer the radioisotope.   _____

    (3) Stop using iodized salt and stop eating seafood.   _____

    (4) Stop taking thyroid medication.

11. The client, who is 62 years old, overweight, and has a family history of diabetes, presents to the nurse for her first follow-up visit after his diet and exercise plan has been put in place. Without checking the chart, the nurse knows that this client most likely has

    (1) type 1 diabetes.

    (2) type 2 diabetes.

    (3) gestational diabetes.

    (4) impaired glucose tolerance.

12. The client is receiving instruction from the nurse about glucose monitoring. She asks how she will know if she is hypoglycemic. The nurse replies,

    (1) "You will most likely have symptoms of low blood sugar, and your blood sugar reading will be < 60."

    (2) "Your blood sugar reading will be between 65 and 75, and you will most likely have blurred vision."

    (3) "Your glucometer reading will be your 2-hour postprandial reading minus 40, and you will feel sleepy."

    (4) "Your blood sugar will not register on the machine, and you will feel extremely lightheaded."

13. When gathering data for a client who is hyperthyroid, the nurse is careful to include which of the following data?

    (1) Weight, temperature, mental status, pulse rate

    (2) Height, vision, deep tendon reflexes, balance

    (3) Oxygen saturation, blood sugar, peripheral pulses, capillary refill time

    (4) Waist to hip ratio, skin tone, hearing, CBC

14. For an average adult, the full replacement dose of levothyroxine sodium for the treatment of hyperthyroidism is 1.7 mcg/kg/day. About how many mcg of levothyroxine sodium should be prescribed daily to an adult male weighing 154 pounds? (Round your answer to the nearest ten.)

    Answer: _____ mcg/day

15. You are teaching Mrs. Lewis to administer her own insulin injections. She has a combination of NPH and Regular insulin ordered. Your instructions would include

    (1) using two separate syringes when administering these two forms of insulin.

    (2) always drawing from the Regular insulin bottle first.

    (3) always drawing from the NPH bottle first.

    (4) It would not make any difference which insulin goes into the syringe first.

ANSWER KEY AND EXPLANATIONS

1. 3	4. 1	7. 1	10. 3,4,2,1	13. 1
2. 2	5. 2	8. 4	11. 2	14. 120
3. 1	6. 3	9. 3	12. 1	15. 2

1. **The correct answer is (3).** Potatoes are considered a starch exchange on the diabetic exchange system diet.

2. **The correct answer is (2).** Polyuria is one of the "three Ps" of diabetes: polyuria, polyphagia, and polydipsia.

3. **The correct answer is (1).** The symptoms of ketoacidosis are Kussmaul respirations (which are rapid and deep), nausea and vomiting, as well as hot, dry flushed skin. Hypoglycemia initially presents with sweating, palpitations, anxiety, and tremulousness. Neuropathy, which usually affects the legs and feet in diabetics and involves sensory changes, as well as retinopathy, an eye condition that frequently affects diabetics, are not acute conditions.

4. **The correct answer is (1).** Orange juice is a source of quickly absorbed glucose, which this client needs. The client is experiencing hypoglycemia since she has not eaten since her insulin shot. More insulin would be harmful. Coffee is not a source of glucose, and peanut butter would eventually provide glucose, but not as quickly as orange juice.

5. **The correct answer is (2).** The woman's blood sugar reading, weight, history of large babies, and symptoms of fatigue, hunger, thirst, and frequent urination are all highly suggestive of diabetes. Type 1 diabetes usually presents earlier in life, and its symptoms are not as subtle. They are not usually overweight when diagnosed, nor do they have large babies. Hypoparathyroidism involves the body's calcium/phosphorus balace, and Graves' disease is a hyperthyroid condition.

6. **The correct answer is (3).** Choices (1), (2), and (3) are correct statements about diabetic care. However, bowling once a week is exercise that is not of sufficient intensity nor is it frequent enough to help in diabetes management.

7. **The correct answer is (1).** If a client with diabetes is unconscious, it is best to give a source of quick glucose, such as glucagon, since hypoglycemia can cause permanent brain damage. Glucose will not cause any permanent harm to the client suffering from coma due to diabetic ketoacidosis.

8. **The correct answer is (4).** Proper foot care is one of the most important things to teach clients with diabetes, because they often cannot feel injuries to their feet, and neglected infections can—and frequently do—cause loss of a leg or death.

9. **The correct answer is (3).** Glycosylated hemoglobin levels reflect the average blood glucose level during the preceding four to six weeks, and therefore can be used for evaluating

long-term effectiveness of diabetes therapy.

10. **The correct order of answers is (3), (4), (2), (1).** A thyroid scan visualizes radioactive iodine distributed in the thyroid gland. About one week before the scan, the client should stop ingesting iodized salt and seafood that contains iodine: This excess iodine could interfere with the scan. The client should also be instructed to stop taking thyroid medication the day before the scan; this also could interfere with the scan. Radioactive iodine in the form of a dye is administered to the client on the day of the scan. Following the test, the client should avoid contact with his own urine, because it will contain traces of radioactivity for some time.

11. **The correct answer is (2).** Older, overweight clients typically develop type 2 diabetes, which tends to be familial, whereas type 1 diabetes is not.

12. **The correct answer is (1).** A blood sugar reading of < 60 is hypoglycemic, and the symptoms of hypoglycemia (tremors, sweating, and tachyardia) typically accompany this finding.

13. **The correct answer is (1).** Weight loss, increased temperature, nervousness and irritability, as well as tachycardia, are signs of hyperthyroidism.

14. **The correct answer is 120.** The complete answer is 120 mcg/day.

    1 kg = 2.2 lbs, so 154 lbs = 7 kg

    1.7 mcg/kg × 70 kg = 119 mcg

    When you round the answer to the nearest ten, you have 120. The client should receive approximately 120 mcg of medicine per day.

15. **The correct answer is (2).** NPH insulin contains a protein that slows its absorption. You do not want to contaminate the pure form of Regular insulin, which could affect its absorption time.

answers exercises

SUMMING IT UP

- The endocrine system is made up of glands that secrete hormones that regulate body activities.

- Hormones are carried by the bloodstream to their target organs and are regulated by the central nervous system.

The Gastrointestinal System

OVERVIEW

- Basic concepts
- Digestive system
- Assessment of the GI System
- GI system disorders
- Liver
- Gallbladder
- Pancreas
- Summing it up

BASIC CONCEPTS

The gastrointestinal (GI) system's primary functions are to break down nutrients, and supply the body with sufficient nutrients, fluids, and electrolytes to maintain body functions. This process requires enzymes and hormones are supplied by the GI system and the accessory organs: the liver, gallbladder, and pancreas.

DIGESTIVE SYSTEM

A. **Anatomy and Physiology**
   1. **Mouth, Tongue, and Teeth**
      a. Begins digestive process by chewing, lubricating, and breaking down food with ptyalin from the salivary glands
      b. Functions to chew, swallow, and taste foods; enables speech
   2. **Salivary Glands**—secretions form saliva
      a. Parotid—below the ear
      b. Submaxillary—floor of mouth
      c. Sublingual—floor of mouth
   3. **Pharynx**—transports food to esophagus (also air to larynx)
      a. Nasopharynx
      b. Oropharynx
      c. Laryngopharynx
   4. **Esophagus**—muscular tube that conducts food to the stomach
   5. **Stomach**
      a. A pouch between the esophagus and the duodenum; changes size depending on contents; it stores ingested food and changes it into chyme

(1) Liquifies food with hydrochloric acid

(2) Begins to digest protein with pepsin

b. Divided into the upper portion (fundus), the body, and the lower portion, the pylorus

(1) Cardiac sphincter of the fundus controls entrance of food to the stomach

(2) Pyloric sphincter controls the passage of food into the duodenum

6. **Small Intestine**—approximately 20 feet long and 1 inch in diameter

a. Primary site of digestion and absorption of food

(1) Duodenum

(2) Jejenum

(3) Ileum

(4) Ileocecal valve (between the small and large intestines)

b. Functions

(1) Further liquefies and breaks down food

(2) Peristaltic movement pushes food toward large intestine

(3) Numerous villi on mucosal layer promote food absorption

(4) Primary area for the absorption of nutrients

7. **Large Intestine**—extends from ileocecal valve to the anus, approximately 5 to 6 feet long

a. Divisions

(1) Cecum—attaches to the ileum at the ileocecal valve to the the distal end

(2) Ascending colon—goes up right side of abdomen to the liver, then turns

(3) Transverse colon—from the liver border across the abdomen to the lower border of the spleen

(4) Descending colon—down the left side of the abdomen to the brim of the pelvis

(5) Sigmoid colon—S-shaped part, ends at the rectum

(6) Rectum—approximately 6 to 8 inches long, ends at the anus

b. Functions

(1) Reabsorption of flujds, electrolytes, glucose, and urea

(2) Peristaltic movement propels contents to rectum

(3) Bacteria

(a) Produce and release vitamin K and vitamin B complex

(b) Break down undigested residue for absorption or excretion

(4) Rectum and anus initiate desire for defecation as fecal material enters.

(a) Valsalva maneuver is used to expel feces as rectum and colon contract. This maneuver increases intrathoracic pressure and decreases venous return to the heart.

(b) As Valsalva maneuver ends, the venous return to the heart increases, which may cause problems in cardiac clients.

8. **Liver**

a. Located in upper right quadrant of abdomen and protected by the rib cage

b. Blood supply

(1) Nutrient-rich blood from the stomach, intestines, pancreas, and spleen travels through the portal vein into the liver.

(2) Oxygen is supplied by the hepatic artery.

c. The liver produces 600–800 cc of bile that drains from the liver via the common bile duct. Bile is stored in the gallbladder.

d. The liver can still function with up to 90 percent damage.

e. Functions

(1) Synthesis of carbohydrates, fats, and proteins

(2) Metabolizes drugs and toxic substances that have been ingested

(3) Stores glycogen and vitamins A, B_{12}, D, and K

(4) Synthesizes prothrombin for normal clotting

      (5) Breaks down old blood cells

      (6) Helps regulate blood glucose levels

  9. **Gallbladder**

    a. Small sac of smooth muscle at the edge of the inner surface of the liver

    b. Bile goes from hepatic duct to the cystic duct, entering the gallbladder for storage; it then leaves through the cystic duct through the common bile duct to the duodenum

    c. Functions

      (1) It is a reservoir for bile and can store 20–50 cc.

      (2) Bile is important to the process of digestion of fats in the intestine.

 10. **Pancreas**

    a. Small organ that adheres to the duodenum; composed of exocrine and endocrine tissue

    b. Functions

      (1) Exocrine cells secrete digestive enzymes.

      (2) Endocrine function is related to the islets of Langerhans, whose beta cells secrete insulin and alpha cells secrete glucagon.

ASSESSMENT OF THE GI SYSTEM

A. Evaluate Client History

  1. **Changes in Bowel Habits**

  2. **Changes in Dietary Habits**

  3. **Weight Loss or Gain**

  4. **Pain Characteristics and Location**

  5. **Nausea and Vomiting**

    a. Precipitating factors

    b. Associated symptoms

  6. **Flatulence**

B. Assess Vital Signs

C. Physical Assessment

  1. **Mouth**

    a. Condition of teeth, tongue

    b. Presence of gag reflex

    c. Mucous membranes—color, texture, lesions

  2. **Abdomen**

    a. Divide abdomen into four quadrants (center is umbilicus), and describe findings in terms of quadrants.

    b. Evaluate contour and presence of scars, ostomies.

    c. Assess bowel sounds (5 minutes auscultation before bowel sounds are considered absent).

    d. Percuss for distention or air.

    e. Palpate

      (1) Presence of masses

      (2) Tenderness

    f. Assess rectal area for lesions, hemorrhoids, skin condition.

Assessment of the Digestive System

GI Blood and Laboratory Tests

ALT or SGPT (alanine aminotransferase): An enzyme that can build up in the bloodstream when liver cells are injured, so it is an indicator of hepatic disease, especially hepatitis and cirrhosis without jaundice.

AST or SGOT (aspartate aminotransferase): A hepatic enzyme that serves as an indicator of hepatic and cardiac diseases.

LDH (lactic dehydrogenase): Another liver enzyme used to assess hepatic function.

Alkaline Phosphatase: Indicator of biliary obstruction such as by a tumor or abscesses. It also influences bone calcification and lipid and metabolite transport.

Plasma Ammonia: An indication of liver disease, since the liver normally breaks down ammonia to urea.

Serum Amylase: Amylase is an enzyme synthesized by the pancreas and salivary glands that helps digest starch and glycogen. The test is used to diagnose acute pancreatitis and assess pancreatic injury.

Serum Lipase: An enzyme synthesized by the pancreas that remains elevated longer than amylase.

Serum Bilirubin: Used to help evaluate liver function or diagnose biliary obstruction and hemolytic disease. Bilirubin is the major by-product of red blood cell breakdown.

Serum Chloride: Indicates acid-base imbalances and fluid status. Prolonged vomiting can cause low chloride levels.

Hepatitis B Surface Antigen (HBsAg): Earliest marker of infection with Hepatitis B.

Fecal Occult Blood: Detects gastrointestinal bleeding and aids in early detection of colorectal cancer.

Serum Protein Electrophoresis: Measures levels of albumin and globulins, the major blood proteins. It helps diagnose liver disease as well as protein deficiency, renal disorders, and GI and neoplastic diseases.

Prothrombin Time: Measures the time it takes for a fibrin clot to form. It is an indicator of the extrinsic coagulation system function and is used to monitor the effects of oral anticoagulant therapy. It is also used to monitor the effects of liver (and other) diseases on clotting.

Percutaneous Liver Biopsy: Needle aspiration of liver tissue for cell analysis to identify liver disorders. Tests for clotting disorders should precede this test, and it should not be done if the platelets are less than 100,000 or the prothrombin time less than 15 seconds.

GI Diagnostic Procedures

Barium Enema: An X-ray study of the large intestine after a barium enema. It is used to help diagnose inflammatory bowel disease as well as lesions, polyps, diverticula, and structural changes of the large intestine.

Cholangiography: A contrast medium is introduced into the common bile duct to help detect calculi as well as the size and patency of the ducts. X-ray and fluoroscopic examination is done after the medium is instilled.

Cholecystography: An X-ray of the gallbladder, 12–14 hours after the ingestion of contrast medium, to evaluate gallbladder function.

Upper GI and Small Bowel Series: Flouroscopic examination of the esophagus, stomach, and small intestine after ingestion of barium.

Gallbladder Scan: A series of images is taken after IV injection of a radioactive tracer. It also scans the liver, bile ducts, and duodenum. It helps diagnose cholecystitis, cholethiasis, biliary obstruction, biliary anomalies, liver disease, and cancer of the hepatobiliary system.

Liver-Spleen Scan: A nuclear scan of the liver and spleen, which is used to screen for hepatic metastases as well as cirrhosis and hepatitis.

Gallbladder and Biliary System Ultrasonogrophy: Ultrasound images, which do not depend on hepatic and gallbladder function, are used to confirm a diagnosis of cholelithiasis, to diagnose acute cholecystitis, and to distinguish between obstructive and nonobstructive jaundice.

Liver Ultrasonography: Cross-sectional images of the liver, which are used to distinguish between obstructive and nonobstructive jaundice, and screen for liver disease and cancer.

Pancreatic Ultrasonography: Cross-sectional images of the pancreas, used to diagnose pancreatitis, pancreatic cancer, and aid in needle biopsy insertion.

Colonoscopy: Visual examination of the large intestine that is used to aid in diagnostic and therapeutic procedures, such as biopsy, cultures, evaluation of inflammatory disease, locate the origin of lower GI bleeding; and aid in diagnosing strictures and malignant lesions.

Endoscopy: Visualization of the esophagus, stomach, and upper duodenum. Used for clients with hematemesis, melena, or substernal or epigastric pain. It is used to obtain biopsies, to determine the site of upper GI bleeding, and to diagnose structural abnormalities and upper GI disease.

Proctosigmoidoscopy: Endoscopic visualization of the sigmoid and descending colon to aid in diagnosing disorders of the lower GI tract.

NOTE

Nursing interventions for these tests include explaining the procedures to the client, instructing the client to remain NPO, administering cathartics and enemas as ordered, and administering contrast dye as prescribed.

GI SYSTEM DISORDERS

A. **Nausea and Vomiting**
   1. **Nausea**—an uncomfortable feeling that precedes and is associated with vomiting. Vomiting is the involuntary reflex in which the stomach contents are expelled.
      a. Fluid and electrolyte loss is the main consequence of repeated vomiting.
      b. Infants and the elderly are most at risk of dehydration.
      c. Severe vomiting can result in metabolic alkalosis due to loss of stomach acids. Loss of the contents of the small intestine can, less commonly, result in metabolic acidosis.
   2. **Medical Treatment**—goal is to eliminate the cause and treat the symptoms
      a. Causes of nausea and vomiting are multiple, and a careful history and physical assessment are needed to make a determination.

(1) Hematemesis—the presence of blood in the vomitus. It may be bright red or look like coffee grounds if it has been broken down by the digestive process.

(2) Fecal odor in vomitus indicates the presence of intestinal contents in the stomach—an indication of intestinal obstruction.

b. Antiemetics and IV fluid replacement are used to treat the symptoms.

Medications for Nausea and Vomiting

Class	Trade Name	Generic Name
Antihistamines	Dramamine	Dimenhydrinate
	Benadryl	Diphenhydramine
	Atarax	Hydroxyzine
	Vistaril	Hydroxyzine pamoate
	Antevert	Meclezine HCL
	Phenergan	Promethazine HCL
Phenothiazines	Thorazine	Chlorpromazine
	Compazine	Prochlorperazine
Anticholinergic	Tigan	Trimethobenzamide

3. **Nursing Interventions**
   a. Maintain NPO until able to tolerate fluids.
   b. Administer IV fluids as ordered, maintain accurate I & O.
   c. Monitor laboratory electrolytes.
   d. Give frequent mouth care.
   e. Avoid sudden changes in position.
   f. Eliminate noxious stimuli from environment.
   g. Begin oral intake slowly with clear liquids.
   h. Assess for weight loss, change in vital signs.
   i. Administer antiemetics as ordered.

B. **Constipation**—interval between bowel movements is longer than usual for the client and the stool is hard and dry
   1. **Assessment**
      a. History
         (1) Client's diet lacks sufficient fiber, and fluid intake is inadequate.
         (2) Client immobility.
         (3) Disease of the colon or rectum is present.
         (4) Medication is taken with side effect of constipation.
      b. Clinical findings
         (1) Abdominal distention
         (2) Decreased amount of stool
         (3) Dry, hard stool
   2. **Medical Treatment**
      a. Cathartics—milk of magnesia, senna, cascara, biscadoyl
      b. Stool softeners—docusate calcium, docusate sodium
   3. **Nursing Interventions**
      a. Increase fluid intake to 3,000 cc/day. Include high-fiber foods in diet.
      b. Administer medications as ordered.
      c. Prevent accumulation of stool in the colon—ask client not to ignore urge to defecate. Massage abdomen to stimulate peristalsis.

    d. Teach client about proper diet, increasing fluid intake, medication regimen (bulk-forming laxatives are best), increasing activity, and establishing a regular bowel routine.

C. Diarrhea—significant increase in number of stools and stools are watery or loosely formed

  1. **Assessment**
    a. Evaluate possible causes including intestinal infections, food poisoning, malabsorption problems, psychological factors.
    b. Stools are frequent and loose and may contain undigested food, mucus, pus, or blood.
    c. Stools are often foul-smelling.
    d. Abdominal cramping, distention, and vomiting may be present.
    e. Hyperactive bowel sounds.
    f. Dehydration, hypovolemia, hypokalemia, and shock possible—especially in infants and the elderly.

  2. **Medical Diagnosis**
    a. Stool culture
    b. X-ray of GI tract

  3. **Medical Treatment**
    a. Identify and treat the underlying problem.
    b. Order anti-diarrheal medications.
    c. Initiate IV fluid replacement therapy as needed.

  4. **Nursing Interventions**
    a. Decrease food intake, soft diet, increase fluids.
    b. Maintain good skin care to prevent rectal skin excoriation.
    c. Decrease activity.
    d. Assess for changes in hydration, weight, abdominal distention, and vital signs.
    e. Use good hand-washing technique to prevent spread.
    f. Enteric precautions if the diarrhea is of infectious origin.

D. Oral Cancer—may occur anywhere in the mouth (lips, tongue, salivary glands, pharynx, tonsils), often curable if discovered early. Risk factors are smoking, chewing tobacco, and poor oral hygiene.

  1. **Assessment**
    a. Leukoplakia—whitish patch on oral mucosa or tongue
    b. Pain and dysphagia

  2. **Medical Diagnosis**
    a. Biopsy of lesion

  3. **Medical Treatment**
    a. Surgical excision of area affected and reconstruction if possible
    b. Radiation
    c. Chemotherapy

  4. **Nursing Interventions**
    a. Preoperative care, good oral hygiene, client education about surgery.
    b. Postoperative priorities include maintaining patent airway, promoting drainage, evaluating ability of client to handle secretions, and positioning appropriately.
    c. Notify RN immediately if incision site swelling occurs.
    d. Assess for respiratory distress or hypoxia.
    e. Maintain optimal oral hygiene.
    f. Maintain nutrient intake by tube or parental feedings if necessary, or with bland and soft foods.
    g. Provide discharge planning by helping identify rehabilitation needs such as speech therapy.

h. Teach client symptoms of complications and to notify provider of infection, increased pain, difficulty swallowing, or suture line bleeding.

E. **Gastroesophageal Reflux Disease (GERD)**—backflow of gastric acid into the esophagus, often associated with a hiatal hernia
   1. **Assessment**
      a. Heartburn, pain often occurring after meals and relieved by antacids
      b. Regurgitation of stomach contents into the mouth
      c. Discomfort with increased abdominal pressure such as lifting
   2. **Medical Diagnosis**
      a. Barium swallow
      b. Esophagoscopy
   3. **Medical Treatment**
      a. Medications: antacids and GI stimulants such as metoclopramide (Reglan)
      b. Surgical correction of hiatal hernia if present
   4. **Nursing Interventions**
      a. Administer medications as ordered.
      b. Assist client to modify diet to decrease highly seasoned foods, fatty foods and caffeine, all of which can cause discomfort, and to have small frequent meals.
      c. Instruct client to avoid carbonated beverages and decrease or stop smoking.
      d. Teach client to avoid eating before bedtime.
      e. Have client elevate the head of the bed on blocks (4 to 6 inches).

F. **Peptic Ulcer Disease**—ulceration of the gastric mucosa from hydrochloric acid. Most common site is the duodenum. Contributing factors include *H. pylori* bacteria, acid production, stress, smoking and alcohol, and use of NSAIDs or steroids.
   1. **Assessment**
      a. Gnawing or burning epigastric pain
      b. Gastric ulcers—food may cause the pain, vomiting may relieve it; duodenal ulcers, pain with an empty stomach, relieved by eating
      c. May be nausea and vomiting with gastric ulcers
      d. If gastric bleeding present, may be melena and/or hematemesis; possible hypovolemic shock
   2. **Medical Diagnosis**
      a. Clinical findings
      b. Endoscopy
      c. Upper GI series (barium swallow)
      d. Gastroscopy with test for *H. pylori*
      e. Signs of perforation: hypotension (blood pressure decrease of 10 mmHg or more), sudden severe upper abdominal pain, rigid abdomen, absent bowel sounds, shallow, rapid respirations
   3. **Medical Treatment**
      a. Antibiotics to eliminate *H. pylori*
      b. Dietary modification—often highly individual, foods that cause pain are avoided
      c. Medications—antacids, H2 receptor antagonists, acid pump inhibitors, prokinetics, anticholinergics
   4. **Nursing Interventions**
      a. Help client identify diet modifications to relieve pain.
      b. Instruct client to use acetominophen instead of aspirin.
      c. Assess for symptoms of hemorrhage or perforation—notify RN.
      d. If perforation, client should be npo and prepared for surgery. Monitor.

G. Dumping Syndrome—a condition following gastric surgery in which the intestine is unable to handle a large amount of food that has been adequately mixed with gastric secretions

   1. **Assessment**
     a. Post–gastric surgery client
     b. Weakness, dizziness, tachycardia, diaphoresis after meal; followed by epigastric fullness, abdominal cramping, and diarrhea

   2. **Medical Treatment**
     a. Self-limiting

   3. **Nursing Interventions**
     a. Encourage small, frequent meals (five to six per day).
     b. Decrease carbohydrates, salt intake; increase proteins and fats. Low roughage.
     c. Liquids between meals only.
     d. Have client lie down for 20–30 minutes after meals to delay gastric emptying.

Drug Treatment for Peptic Ulcer

Drug Classification	Generic and Trade Names	Nursing Considerations
Antacids	Magnesium and aluminum hydroxide (Maalox)	Administer after meals.
	Aluminum hydroxide gel (AlternaGEL)	Monitor for constipation.
Anticholinergics	Propantheline (Pro-Banthine)	Take 30 minutes before meals.
	Dicyclomine (Bentyl)	Monitor for drowsiness, urinary retention, constipation.
Histamine 2 Receptor Antagonists	Cimetidine (Tagamet) Ranitidine (Zantac) Famotidine (Pepcid)	Take 1 hour before meals. Monitor blood count and kidney and liver function.
Prostaglandin	Misoprostol (Cytotec)	Do not give during pregnancy. For NSAID-induced ulcers. Monitor for headache, GI problems.
Proton Pump Inhibitors	Omeprazole (Prilosec) Lansoprazole (Prevacid)	Administer before meals. May cause headache, nausea, dizziness.

H. Gastric Cancer—Symptoms are often not apparent until the disease has metastasized into adjacent organs. More common in men, Asians; associated with highly salted or smoked foods, peptic ulcer, low intake of vegetables and fruits, chronic gastritis.

   1. **Assessment**
     a. Weight loss, anorexia
     b. Feeling of fullness, pain after eating that cannot be relieved by antacids
     c. Fatigue and anemia from blood loss
     d. Regurgitaion, indigestion

   2. **Medical Diagnosis**
     a. Increased serum AST, LD, amylase

b. Positive fecal occult blood test
c. Gastroscopy biopsy positive for cancer cells
d. Upper GI series shows gastric mass
3. **Medical Treatment**
   (1) Surgery—gastrectomy, subtotal gastrectomy (Billroth I or II)
   (2) Type depends on location and extent of lesion
   (3) Dumping syndrome (see page 209) may result
   a. Chemotherapy
   b. Radiation
   c. TPN (total parental nutrition)
4. **Nursing Interventions**
   a. Postsurgical care and teaching.
   b. Monitor nutritional status and weight.
   c. Support and advocacy during chemotherapy and radiation.
   d. Teach and provide comfort measures.

I. **Appendicitis**—inflammation of the appendix caused by bacterial infection. The most common reason for abdominal surgery in childhood after the age of 2.
1. **Assessment**
   a. Severe upper abdominal pain that localizes to the right lower quadrant
   b. Rebound tenderness
   c. Anorexia and vomiting
   d. Rigid abdomen
   e. Fever
2. **Medical Diagnosis**
   a. History and physical exam
   b. Elevated WBC
3. **Medical Treatment**
   a. Immediate surgical removal of appendix
   b. If appendix is ruptured, peritonitis results
      (1) Client needs antibiotics, IV therapy, possible surgery, NG tube for intestinal decompression
      (2) Maintain bed rest in semi-Fowler's position
      (3) Client must be NPO, I & O maintained
4. **Nursing Interventions**
   a. Notify RN immediately of any change in status or sudden decrease in pain.
   b. Provide preoperative care.
   c. Provide postoperative care, including NG tube and antibiotic therapy if appendix ruptured.
   d. Assess drainage, monitor abdomen for distention and assess peristaltic activity.
   e. Advance diet starting with clear fluid once peristalsis returns.

J. **Intestinal Obstruction**—complete or partial blockage of the small or large intestine; can be due to mechanical problems such as tumors, neurological difficulties such as paralytic ileus; increased pressure above blockage and decreased peristalsis below; the higher the obstruction, the more severe the symptoms
1. **Assessment**
   a. Small intestine obstruction
      (1) Vomiting—possibly fecal
      (2) Abdominal distention
      (3) Absence of stools
      (4) Dehydration

ALERT!

As with all undiagnosed abdominal pain, initially maintain client NPO; *do not* use heat on abdomen, give enema, or give strong narcotics. *Do* place in position of comfort on bed rest, assess hydration, abdominal distention, bowel sounds, pain, passage of flatus or stool.

Chapter 11: The Gastrointestinal System

211

    b. Large bowel obstruction—slower progression of symptoms
      (1) Constipation
      (2) Abdominal distention
      (3) Cramp-like pain in lower abdomen

2. **Medical Diagnosis**
    a. Client history and physical exam
    b. Flat plate X-ray of abdomen
    c. Laboratory studies

3. **Medical Treatment**
    a. Surgery
    b. Miller-Abbott or Cantor tube for intestinal decompression
    c. IV hydration
    d. Prophylactic antibiotics
    e. I & O monitoring

4. **Nursing Interventions**
    a. Assess and document client's symptoms.
    b. Record intake and output, including amount and character of drainage from decompression tube.
    c. Maintain NPO.
    d. Monitor hydration.
    e. Perform routine postoperative care (if surgery).

K. Diverticular Disease (Diverticulosis/Diverticulitis)—diverticulosis is an outpouching of the mucosa of the colon; diverticulitis is an inflammation of the outpouching (diverticulum)

1. **Assessment**
    a. Abdominal cramps
    b. Lower-quadrant tenderness
    c. Constipation or constipation and diarrhea
    d. Elevated WBC
    e. Fever
    f. Occult bleeding

2. **Medical Diagnosis**
    a. Client history and physical exam
    b. Laboratory studies
    c. Stool examination for occult blood
    d. Sigmoidoscopy, colonoscopy
    e. Barium studies

3. **Medical Treatment**
    a. High-residue diet
    b. Drug treatment—bulk laxatives, antibiotics, stool softeners, and anticholinergics
    c. Surgery may be needed for obstruction/hemorrhage

4. **Nursing Interventions**
    a. Provide increased dietary fiber.
    b. Increase intake of fluids.
    c. Administer prescribed medication and monitor for side effects.
    d. Teach client about dietary restrictions, avoidance of constipation, and activity that increases intra-abdominal pressure.

L. Hernia—protrusion of an organ (usually refers to the intestines) through an abnormal opening

1. **Assessment**
    a. Types—categories
      (1) Reducible—may be manually replaced into its normal position

      (2) Irreducible—may not be manually replaced into position

      (3) Incarcerated—obstruction of intestinal flow

      (4) Strangulated—blood supply is cut off (surgical emergency)

    b. Types—location

      (1) Inguinal—a weakness in the groin area where the spermatic cord (men) or round ligament (women) passes through the abdominal wall; more common in men

      (2) Femoral—the intestine protrudes through the femoral ring; more common in women

      (3) Umbilical—common in babies where the umbilical opening doesn't close adequately, or in adults with weak abdominal muscles

      (4) Incisional—weakness in the abdominal wall due to a previous incision

2. **Medical Diagnosis**

    a. History

    b. Clinical findings

3. **Medical Treatment**

    a. Surgical repair

      (1) Herniorrhaphy—surgical repair of the hernia

      (2) Hernioplasty—surgical reinforcement of the weakened area

    b. Truss—a support worn to keep the hernia in place

4. **Nursing Interventions**

    a. Preoperative and postoperative care.

    b. Instruct client to avoid activities that increase intra-abdominal pressure such as heavy lifting.

    c. Take measures to avoid urinary retention.

M. Inflammatory Bowel Disease—Crohn's Disease (primarily affects the small bowel) and Ulcerative Colitis (primarily affects the large bowel)

1. **Assessment**

    a. Abdominal pain, diarrhea, nausea, and vomiting

    b. Stool may contain occult blood

2. **Medical Diagnosis**

    a. Stool analysis to rule out infection

    b. Barium enema

    c. Proctosigmoidoscopy and colonoscopy

3. **Medical Treatment**

    a. Corticosteroids to reduce inflammation

    b. Antibiotics

    c. Immunosuppressants

    d. Antidiarrheals

    e. May need surgery if fistula, obstruction, perforation occur

4. **Nursing Interventions**

    a. Diet modifications—low-fiber, high-calorie, high-nutrient diet. Limit milk intake.

    b. Evaluate fluid status, I & O monitoring.

    c. Perianal skin hygiene to prevent excoriation.

    d. Monitor lab values for anemia or electrolyte imbalance.

N. Gastroenteritis—inflammation of the intestinal tract, with diarrhea, vomiting, and abdominal cramping. Caused by amoebae, bacteria, ingestion of toxins, or viruses. Also called intestinal flu, viral enteritis, food poisoning.

1. **Assessment**

    a. Abdominal discomfort

    b. Nausea and diarrhea

2. **Medical Diagnosis**
   a. Stool culture
   b. Blood culture
3. **Medical Treatment**
   a. Antibiotic therapy
   b. Antidiarrheals
   c. Antiemetics (should not be given to clients with viral or bacterial enteritis)
4. **Nursing Interventions**
   a. Administer medications.
   b. Replace lost fluid with clear liquids or sports drinks.
   c. Monitor intake and output.
   d. Wash hands thoroughly after giving care to avoid spreading infections.
   e. Teach client about avoiding infection—washing hands, eating only thoroughly cooked foods, avoiding drinking water or eating raw fruits or vegetables in a foreign country.

O. Colorectal Cancer
1. **Assessment**
   a. Change in bowel habits
   b. Change in shape of stool
   c. Weakness and fatigue, weight loss
   d. Rectal bleeding
   e. Diarrhea and constipation
2. **Medical Diagnosis**
   a. Sigmoidoscopy, colonoscopy
   b. Hemoccult stool test
   c. Rectal exam
3. **Medical Treatment**
   a. Surgical removal of the tumor—may involve a permanent colostomy
   b. Radiation
   c. Chemotherapy
4. **Nursing Interventions**
   a. Provide postoperative care, including NG tube, dressing for drainage, Penrose drain if present.
   b. Assist client and family in performing colostomy care.
   c. Have client return for frequent medical checkups.
   d. Teach client symptoms to report to physician.
      (1) Pain
      (2) Change in stool or bleeding
      (3) Weight loss
      (4) Sustained vomiting or diarrhea

P. Hemorrhoids—varicose veins of the anus or rectum; may occur internally, externally, or both; can be caused by straining due to constipation, diarrhea, increased venous pressure from heart failure, increased abdominal pressure (as in pregnancy), or prolonged sitting
1. **Assessment**
   a. Pain with bowel evacuation
   b. Rectal bleeding
   c. Anal itching
2. **Medical Treatment**
   a. Surgery—hemorrhoidectomy
   b. Ligation of internal hemorrhoids
   c. Treatment with analgesics and stool softeners

3. **Nursing Interventions**
   a. Postoperative care—give sitz baths, other comfort measures, maintain position of comfort on side, increase liquids, bulk, and stool softeners.
   b. Assist with treatment of constipation and other causes of hemorrhoids.

LIVER

A. **Hepatitis**—inflammation of the liver; caused by one of five viruses: hepatitis A, B, C, D, or E
   1. **Causes**
      a. Hepatitis A—contaminated food, water, feces
      b. Hepatitis B—blood and body secretions
      c. Hepatitis C—blood and body secretions
      d. Hepatitis D—blood and body secretions
      e. Hepatitis E—fecal/oral
   2. **Assessment**
      a. Preicteric (before the appearance of jaundice)
         (1) Anorexia, constipation, and diarrhea
         (2) Fatigue, fever, headache
         (3) Hepatomegaly, splenomegaly
         (4) Nausea and vomiting
         (5) Pruritis
         (6) Right upper quadrant abdominal pain
      b. Icteric
         (1) Clay-colored stools
         (2) Dark urine
         (3) Fatigue
         (4) Jaundice
         (5) Symptoms of preicteric phase: weight loss, hepatosplenomegaly, pruritis, fatigue
      c. Posticteric
         (1) Decreased hepatomegaly
         (2) Decreased jaundice
         (3) Fatigue
         (4) Improved appetite
   3. **Medical Diagnosis**
      a. Blood chemistry: increased ALT, AST, alkaline phosphatase, LD, bilirubin, ESR
      b. Positive Hepatitis A antibody, positive Hepatitis B surface antigen, positive immunoglobulin (Ig) antidelta antigens (type D), positive Hepatitis E antigen
      c. Urine chemistry indicates increased urobilinogen
   4. **Medical Treatment**
      a. Antiemetic (Compazine)
      b. Vitamins and minerals
   5. **Nursing Interventions**
      a. Provide high-calorie, low-fat diet in small, frequent meals.
      b. Monitor fluid status with I & O, as well as vital signs.
      c. Provide rest periods.
      d. Change position q 2 hours to prevent skin breakdown.
      e. Monitor for signs of bleeding.
      f. Teach client how to avoid infecting others.

B. Cirrhosis—cell degeneration of the liver in which scar tissue replaces functioning tissue; a complication of alcoholism, hepatitis, certain metabolic disorders

  1. **Assessment**

    a. Early signs include GI disturbances, anorexia, indigestion, change in bowel habits, and right upper quadrant discomfort due to enlarging liver

    b. Jaundice

    c. Spider angiomas on the face, neck, and shoulders

    d. Palmar erythema—reddened areas on palms

    e. Coagulation disorders

    f. Impotence in males, vaginal bleeding in females

    g. Peripheral neuropathy

    h. Hepatosplenomegaly

    i. Portal hypertension

      (1) Esophageal varices—bleed easily

      (2) Hemorrhoids

      (3) Visible veins on abdominal wall

      (4) Development of edema and ascites

    j. Hepatic encephalopathy (coma) because of high levels of ammonia in the blood

  2. **Medical Treatment**

    a. Rest; high-nutrient, low-fat, and low-protein diet; vitamin supplementation

    b. Abstinence from alcohol

    c. Corticosteroids

    d. Shunt to decrease portal hypertension

    e. Diuretics and paracentesis for anscites

    f. Esophageal varices—treat bleeding if it occurs

    g. Prevent encephalopathy by decreasing ammonia formation: decreasing dietary protein, neomycin to sterilize intestine to reduce protein breakdown

  3. **Nursing Interventions**

    a. Help client get proper diet with adequate nutrients and low protein; encourage. rest.

    b. Have client abstain from alcohol, hepatotoxic drugs, aspirin.

    c. Decrease discomfort due to pruritis—skin care.

    d. Assess for bleeding.

    e. Measure abdominal girth daily.

GALLBLADDER

A. Cholelithiasis (gallstones) and Cholecystitis (gallbladder inflammation usually associated with gallstones)

  1. **Assessment**

    a. Indigestion after a high-fat meal

    b. Flatulence, belching

    c. Nausea and vomiting

    d. Right upper-quadrant pain radiating to back or shoulder

    e. Fever

    f. Jaundice and clay-colored stools

    g. Dark urine

  2. **Medical Diagnosis**

    a. History and physical

    b. Lab findings—increased WBC, serum amylase

    c. Oral cholecystography

    d. IV cholangiography

    e. Ultrasound of gallbladder

3. **Medical Treatment**
   a. IV hydration
   b. Analgesics, antibiotics, antispasmodics
   c. Low-fat diet
   d. Lithotripsy (use of shock waves to disintegrate stones)—useful if only a few stones
   e. Surgical removal of gallbladder (cholecystectomy) or gallstones (cholecystostomy)
4. **Nursing Interventions**
   a. Administer medications.
   b. Monitor IV therapy and hydration.
   c. Assess vital signs at least every 4 hours.
   d. Provide postoperative care: monitor dressing and T-tube (may be inserted into the common bile duct).
   e. Advise client to remain on low-fat diet and avoid alcohol and gas-forming. foods.

PANCREAS

A. **Pancreatitis**—acute or chronic inflammation of the pancreas, often associated with alcoholism
   1. **Assessment**
      a. Severe abdominal pain made worse by eating
      b. Vomiting
      c. Abdominal distention, bluish discoloration of flank and around umbilicus
      d. Tachycardia
   2. **Medical Diagnosis**
      a. High blood sugar
      b. Jaundice, fever, steatorrhea (fat in the stool)
      c. Increase in serum amylase and lipase
      d. History and clinical signs
      e. Pancreatic scan
      f. X-ray
      g. Endoscopy
   3. **Medical Treatment**
      a. Medications: analgesics (Demerol, no opiates because they may cause spasms), smooth muscle relaxants, anticholinergics, antacids, antibiotics
      b. NPO, IV fluids
      c. Bed rest
      d. Bland diet—carbohydrate, low fat, low protein; no spices, alcohol, tea, coffee
      e. Pancreatic enzyme replacements if needed
   4. **Nursing Interventions**
      a. Administer medications.
      b. Position client on side or semi-Fowler's.
      c. Maintain NG tube.
      d. Small frequent feedings when food started.
      e. Monitor blood glucose.
      f. Assess bowel function.
      g. Monitor for electrolyte imbalances and report to RN—especially hypocalcemia and dehydration.

B. Pancreatic Cancer—poor prognosis, five-year survival rate is low

1. **Assessment**
   a. Abdominal pain aggravated by eating
   b. Nausea, vomiting, anorexia
   c. Weight loss
   d. Jaundice
   e. Hyperglycemia
2. **Medical Diagnosis**
   a. History and physical exam
   b. Pancreatic scan and ultrasound
   c. X-ray studies
   d. Lab tests—elevated bilirubin, amylase, lipase
3. **Medical Treatment**
   a. Surgery is Whipple's procedure: removing the upper pancreas, duodenum, distal portion of the stomach and common bile duct
   b. Radiation and possibly chemotherapy
4. **Nursing Interventions**
   a. Maintain adequate hydration and nutrition.
   b. Evaluate for bleeding.
   c. Control hyperglycemia.
   d. Maintain NPO and nasogastric suction after surgery until peristalsis returns.
   e. Provide emotional support.

EXERCISES: THE GASTROINTESTINAL SYSTEM

1. The newly admitted client has just had colon surgery. A nursing action important to this client's care is

   (1) obtaining a stool specimen.

   (2) maintaining the suction on the NG tube, which provides gastric decompression.

   (3) taking the client's VS 30 minutes after he returns to his room.

   (4) offering a bedpan immediately after the client is in bed.

2. Tamika C., a 23-year-old one-day postoperative cholecystectomy client, is to be kept NPO until she

   (1) voids a minimum of 200 cc.

   (2) has a gag reflex.

   (3) has active bowel sounds and is passing flatus.

   (4) is alert and oriented and has been out of bed to the chair.

3. Elizabeth C. has been experiencing constipation after a hip fracture. The nurse knows that the client's problem is the result of immobility, decrease in fluid intake, and a lack of interest in food. Which of the following nursing measures would help to relieve the client's constipation?
   Select all that apply.

   ☐ **(1)** Increase the attractiveness of high-fiber foods and offer drinks that are appealing to her.

   ☐ **(2)** Provide mild stool softeners that have been ordered for her.

   ☐ **(3)** Make sure that she has sufficient high-quality protein in her diet.

   ☐ **(4)** Offer her the bedpan each day at the same time to establish a pattern.

4. A client diagnosed with pancreatitis is admitted to your unit. His wife states that he likes to drink beer at night when he watches TV. An astute nurse would include which of the following in her plan of care for this client?

   (1) Ask his physician if he can approve an order for his wife to bring beer for the client.

   (2) Check his urinary output.

   (3) Hold all pain medication.

   (4) Monitor him for symptoms of alcohol withdrawal.

5. Which foods listed below should be excluded from the diet of a client with ulcerative colitis?

   (1) Cream of wheat, apple juice

   (2) Scrambled eggs, muffin, lemon tea

   (3) Toast and jelly with tea

   (4) Oatmeal with milk and orange juice

6. The nurse was instructing a woman who has Crohn's disease about a high-calorie, high-protein, low-residue diet. The woman seemed to understand the teaching, and she began to list foods that she should avoid. The nurse soon realized that the woman did not fully understand when the client listed which of the following foods?
Select all that apply.

☐ **(1)** Raw vegetables
☐ **(2)** Popcorn
☐ **(3)** Red meat
☐ **(4)** Sponge cake

7. A client with acute pancreatitis is admitted to the med surg unit where the nurse is working. When caring for him, the nurse is aware that an important goal of nursing care for this client is

(1) monitoring respiratory function and providing supplemental O_2 if needed.
(2) daily weighing to monitor fluid status.
(3) controlling nausea and vomiting.
(4) monitoring urine for albumin and ketones.

8. Mr. Anderson has been suffering from multiple symptoms and goes to the emergency department of his local hospital. The nurse on duty performs an initial evaluation of the client. Based on the nurse's examination of Mr. Anderson, which test would you expect to be recommended?

7/16/09 14:15	Skin showing spider telangiectasias on chest and back. Multiple unexplained bruises. BP 156/84. HR 70/min. Patient shows signs of edema in legs and ascites in abdominal region. Complaining of shortness of breath and feelings of fullness. Abdominal discomfort in upper right quadrant. Patient rates pain at 7 on a scale of 1-10.

(1) EKG
(2) X-ray studies
(3) Liver biopsy
(4) Ultrasound of abdomen

9. A nurse is admitting a client with acute abdominal pain of unknown etiology. In caring for this client, she must *never*

(1) give the client something to eat or drink.
(2) change the client's position.
(3) apply cold packs.
(4) assess bowel sounds.

10. The nurse is treating a client with a nasogastric tube due to a bowel obstruction. The tube is put in place to

(1) suction the airway if necessary.
(2) provide a method of feeding.
(3) decrease gastric distention.
(4) allow aspiration of fluid for diagnostic purposes.

TIP
Test items can be confusing—and may lead to wrong answer choices—if you do not read them carefully. In Question 6, did you notice the phrase *did not fully understand*?

11. A nurse works with older long-term care clients who are at risk for constipation. Which of the following interventions would be *least effective* in the prevention and treatment of this problem?

    (1) Increasing fluid intake

    (2) Increasing dietary fiber

    (3) Use of stimulant laxatives

    (4) Use of bulk-forming laxatives

12. The nurse is caring for an older client experiencing diarrhea. When caring for the client, which assessment should receive priority in his care?

    (1) Auscultation of bowel sounds

    (2) Dietary history

    (3) Urinary output

    (4) Stool guiac

13. A nurse is examining a school-aged child who has presented to the emergency room with acute abdominal pain. The boy has a rigid abdomen, lower right quadrant pain, rebound tenderness, a fever, and nausea and vomiting. The nurse knows that these symptoms are characteristic of

    (1) ulcerative colitis.

    (2) gastroenteritis.

    (3) pancreatitis.

    (4) appendicitis.

14. The nurse is teaching a client with a duodenal ulcer self-help measures to relieve the pain. Which comment by the client would indicate the need for further teaching?

    (1) "I will try to avoid the foods that precipitate stomach pain."

    (2) "I will make lifestyle changes to decrease stress."

    (3) "I will eliminate or at least cut down on my alcohol consumption."

    (4) "If my stomach is hurting, I will take aspirin or ibuprofen."

15. In caring for a client with a peptic ulcer who is at risk for hemorrhage, the nurse must be alert for early signs of hypovolemic shock, which include

    (1) pale, clammy skin and decreased blood pressure.

    (2) bradycardia and irregular respirations.

    (3) tachycardia and increased blood pressure.

    (4) increased pulse rate and decreased urine output.

ANSWER KEY AND EXPLANATIONS

1. 2	4. 4	7. 3	10. 3	13. 4
2. 3	5. 4	8. 3	11. 3	14. 4
3. 1,2,4	6. 1,2	9. 1	12. 3	15. 4

1. **The correct answer is (2).** Removing excess fluid and undigested food particles gives the digestive system time to heal.

2. **The correct answer is (3).** The bowel is manipulated during abdominal surgery, which can disturb elimination, and anesthesia decreases bowel mobility.

3. **The correct answers are (1), (2), and (4).** Although protein is an important nutrient, protein intake is the only one of the foods mentioned in the answer choices that will not help relieve constipation. Increasing intake of fluids and high-fiber foods are the diet indications for this purpose.

4. **The correct answer is (4).** Since pancreatitis is often related to excessive alcohol intake, and his wife mentions that he likes to drink beer, this client may have an alcohol addiction and be at risk for neurological changes or seizures.

5. **The correct answer is (4).** High-fiber foods and dairy products are likely to exacerbate the symptoms of ulcerative colitis.

6. **The correct answers are (1) and (2).** Sponge cake and red meat are low-residue foods, whereas raw vegetables, popcorn, and whole-grain products such as breads and cereals are all high in fiber and residue. Sponge cake and red meat are also higher in caloric intake than the foods mentioned in the other answer choices.

7. **The correct answer is (3).** Nausea and vomiting as well as pain are characteristic of pancreatitis, which is frequently associated with excessive alcohol intake. Altered respiratory function, changes in fluid status, or urinary excretion of protein or ketones are not associated with pancreatitis.

8. **The correct answer is (3).** Based on the signs and symptoms observed by the nurse, the client is most likely suffering from cirrhosis. The best test to detect cirrhosis is a liver biopsy.

9. **The correct answer is (1).** In case the client has an emergent condition requiring immediate surgery, they should be kept npo.

10. **The correct answer is (3).** In the case of a bowel obstruction, a nasogastric tube is used to decrease gastric distention. The airway cannot be suctioned with this tube in place, feeding would not be appropriate with gastric distention, and since the diagnosis has been made, it is unlikely that aspiration of fluid would be used for any diagnostic purposes.

11. **The correct answer is (3).** The use of stimulant laxatives tends to make the person unable to have normal bowel function without them. The other interventions would be effective.

12. **The correct answer is (3).** An older client with diarrhea is at risk for dehydration, and urinary output is a sensitive indicator of hydration

status. The other assessments would not be as useful.

13. **The correct answer is (4).** The symptoms of pain, a rigid abdomen, fever, nausea, and vomiting are indicative of an inflammatory process in the abdomen. The localization of the pain to the right lower quadrant and the presence of rebound tenderness suggest appendicitis.

14. **The correct answser is (4).** Aspirin and ibuprofen are irritating to the stomach and would be contraindicated for a person with a duodenal ulcer.

15. **The correct answer is (4).** The early signs of hypovolemic shock are tachycardia, which is an attempt by the body to compensate for lowered blood volume, and decreased urine output, because there is less fluid available and the kidney is compensating by decreasing the amount of urine.

SUMMING IT UP

- The gastrointestinal system's primary function is the breakdown of food, as well as supplying the body with sufficient nutrients, fluids, and electrolytes to maintain body functions.

- Enzymes and hormones are involved in the breakdown and absorption of food and are supplied by the gastrointestinal system as well as the accessory organs: liver, gallbladder, and pancreas.

The Urinary and Renal Systems

OVERVIEW

- Basic concepts
- Anatomy and physiology
- Urinary and renal assessment
- Urinary and renal disorders
- Summing it up

BASIC CONCEPTS

The urinary and renal systems not only remove waste products from the body, but they also maintain electrolyte, fluid, and acid-base balance.

ANATOMY AND PHYSIOLOGY

A. **Kidneys**—two bean-shaped organs that are on each side of the posterior part of the diaphragm, just below the twelfth rib. The right kidney is slightly lower than the left and is below the liver.
   1. **Structure**
      a. Cortex—outer layer, contains blood vessels and nephrons
      b. Medulla—inner layer, contains the collecting tubules
      c. Renal pelvis—a collecting funnel that leads into the ureter
      d. The fibrous capsule is the outer layer, and the hilus is the entry site for the renal artery and nerves and the exit point for the ureter and renal vein
   2. **Functions**
      a. Excretes waste products of metabolism
      b. Regulates fluid volume, excreting approximately 60 cc per hour of urine (filters 125 cc of body fluid per minute, the glomerular filtration rate)
      c. Maintains balance of acid-base and regulates electrolytes
      d. Regulates blood pressure
      e. Regulates red blood cell production through the production of erythropoietin
      f. Activates vitamin D, which helps the body use calcium

B. **Nephron**—the part of the kidney that produces urine; the kidney contains over a million nephrons

chapter 12

1. **Structure**
    a. Glomerulus—the branches of the renal artery form capillary networks called glomeruli, which are enclosed in Bowman's capsule, a thin-walled sac. This is a filtering unit where the process of urine formation begins.
    b. Renal tubules—the proximal convoluted tubules are responsible for starting the reabsorption of the fluid from Bowman's capsule. It then goes through the Loop of Henle and the distal convoluted tubules, where the collecting tubules pass the finished urine into the pelvis.

C. **The Urinary Tract**
    1. **The Ureters**—two long, narrow tubes that transport urine from the kidney to the bladder by peristalsis
    2. **Bladder**—an elastic, muscular organ that stores urine; it is capable of expansion and assists with voiding
    3. **Urethra**—a short, narrow tube that goes from the bladder to the external opening called the urinary meatus
        a. The female urethra is approximately 1¼ to 2 inches long.
        b. The male urethra is approximately 8 inches long and transports both urine and sperm.

D. **Functions of the Urinary Tract**
    1. **Excretion of Urine**
        a. The ureters conduct the urine from the kidney to the bladder.
        b. The bladder holds the urine.
            (1) Stretch receptors in the bladder are stimulated when it is filled with urine, and the first urge to void (in adults) will be at about 200 cc. A feeling of bladder fullness usually occurs at about 400 cc of urine. A typical daily output is between 1,200 and 1,500 cc/day, varying with fluid intake and exercise, as well as other factors.
            (2) The capacity of the bladder ranges from 1,000 to 1,800 cc of urine.
        c. The urethra carries urine to the exterior of the body.
        d. Urinary output is a sensitive indicator of kidney perfusion and blood pressure. When it falls below 30 cc per hour, the client must be carefully assessed and steps taken to maintain adequate renal circulation.

URINARY AND RENAL ASSESSMENT

A. **Health History**
    1. **Presenting Problem**
        a. Pain in flank, groin, dysuria
        b. Changes in patterns of urination—frequency, nocturia, urgency, incontinence
        c. Changes in amount of output—polyuria, anuria, oliguria
        d. Change in color, consistency, odor of urine
    2. **Lifestyle**
        a. Health habits such as exercise, employment, and possible exposure to chemicals
        b. Nutrition, alcohol, smoking, medications, and recreational drug use
    3. **Past Medical History**
        a. Hypertension, diabetes, gout, cystitis, kidney infections
        b. Hospitalizations, surgery for urinary or renal problems
        c. Family history—questions about the above disorders in immediate family, parents

> **Urinary Terminology**
> **Anuria:** No urinary output
> **Bacteruria:** Bacteria in the urine
> **Dysuria:** Painful urination
> **Hematuria:** Blood in the urine
> **Nocturia:** Awakening at night to urinate
> **Oliguria:** Diminished amount of urine
> **Polyuria:** Excessive amount of urine
> **Pyuria:** Pus in the urine

B. Physical Examination
1. Inspect the skin, mouth, face, eyes, abdomen, and extremities for changes related to the urinary/renal system—edema, dehydration, bleeding tendencies.
2. Palpate and percuss bladder for distention.
3. Palpate kidneys for tenderness; percuss costovertebral angle for tenderness.
4. Palpate flank area for pain.
5. Auscultate aorta and renal arteries for bruits.

C. Diagnostic Tests
1. **Blood Tests**
   a. IBUN (blood urea nitrogen)—indicates the ability of the kidney to filter waste (urea). Normal: 10 to 20 mg/dL. Elevated if kidney function is decreased.
   b. Creatinine—indicates the kidney's ability to handle the breakdown of creatine. Normal: 0.5 to 1.3 mg/dL. Elevated if kidney function is decreased.
   c. Hematocrit levels are decreased in renal failure due to low erythropoietin secretion. Normal: 37–54 percent (lower values are for women).
   d. Electrolyte levels (sodium, potassium, chloride and bicarbonate): Abnormal values may indicate impairment of kidney's ability to filter, reabsorb, or excrete these substances.
2. **Urine Tests**
   a. Specific gravity—indicates urine concentration, changes in dehydration or kidney problems. Normal: 1.003 to 1.030.
   b. Creatinine clearance—urinary output is measured for 24 hours. Decreased in kidney dysfunction.
   c. Protein is normally not present in urine. Proteinuria may indicate kidney disease.
   d. Blood is also normally not in the urine. Hematuria may indicate a disease of the kidney or urinary tract.
3. **Intravenous Pyelogram**—injection of contrast dye for X-ray visualization of kidney and ureters
4. **Cystoscopy**—direct visualization of urethra and bladder by cystoscope

URINARY AND RENAL DISORDERS

A. Urinary Tract Infections
1. **Types** (the infections ascend up the urinary/renal system)
   a. Pyelonephritis—inflammation of the renal pelvis (upper UTI)
   b. Cystitis—inflammation of the bladder (lower UTI)
   c. Urethritis—inflammation of the urethra (lower UTI)

NOTE

Renal disorders can stem from
a variety of factors, such as a
family history of renal disorders,
other medical conditions,
medications, trauma and
injury, frequent urinary tract
infections, hypertension, or a
diet high in sodium.

2. **Causes**
   a. Urinary stasis and reflux of urine back into kidney are the main causes of UTIs.
   b. Organism is primarily *E. coli* (80–90 percent of the time).
3. **Contributing factors**
   a. Female urethra is close to the rectum and vagina
   b. Urine reflux into the bladder
   c. Urinary stasis in the bladder
   d. Obstruction to the flow of urine
   e. Diabetes (bacteria like sugar)
   f. Sexual intercourse
   g. Catheterization or examination by cystoscope
4. **Assessment**
   a. Cystitis
      (1) Frequency and urgency
      (2) Voiding small amounts each time
      (3) Hematuria
      (4) Fever
      (5) Incomplete bladder emptying
   b. Pyelonephritis
      (1) Flank pain, dysuria
      (2) Fever and chills
      (3) Costovertebral angle tenderness
      (4) Same symptoms as cystitis, above
   c. Urinalysis indicates pus, bacteria, and red blood cells. Urine culture and sensitivity indicates causative bacteria and the antibiotic that will be effective.
5. **Medical Treatment**
   a. Sulfonamides, urinary antiseptics, urinary analgesics
   b. Encourage increased fluid intake—washes the bacteria down
   c. Carbonated beverages and foods containing baking powder or baking soda should be discouraged
   d. Urine acidity is promoted by a diet including cranberries, prunes, plums, meats, and eggs
6. **Nursing Interventions**
   a. Teach the need to complete the course of antibiotics.
   b. Encourage fluid intake (eight to ten glasses a day) and dietary changes to promote urine acidity.
   c. Discuss the use of a sitz bath to decrease pain.
   d. Teach (and practice) preventive measures, such as showering as preferable to bathing. If bathing, avoid bubble bath.
   e. Voiding immediately after intercourse.
   f. Wiping perineal area from front to back.
   g. Using strict aseptic technique when catheterizing clients.

B. **Urinary Incontinence**
   1. **Types**
      a. Stress incontinence—release of urine when intra-abdominal pressure is increased, such as when coughing, laughing, or sneezing
      b. Urge incontinence—inability to control leakage before reaching the toilet
      c. Overflow incontinence—voiding small amounts frequently, but not emptying bladder
   2. **Causes** (often several)
      a. Decreased bladder sensation and tone
      b. Relaxation of pelvic muscles
      c. Urinary tract infection

3. **Assessment**
   a. Determine pattern of problem—client report, bladder diary
   b. Urodynamic analysis if needed
   c. Assess for infection or other contributing medical problems
4. **Medical Treatment**
   a. Surgery for uterine, bladder prolapse, extreme loss of muscle tone
   b. Medications to help maintain client decrease urgency and frequency—antispasmodics and anticholinergics
   c. Treatment of urinary tract infection
5. **Nursing Interventions**
   a. Teach client Kegel exercises (which involve contraction of the pelvic floor muscles) to increase pelvic muscle tone.
   b. Establish toileting schedule to help retrain bladder.
   c. Decrease barriers to continence—access to toilet, mobility problems.

C. **Renal Calculi**
   1. **Assessment**
      a. Sudden, severe pain—may be intermittent or constant
      b. History of urinary stasis, infection, previous stones
      c. Nausea, diaphoresis, pallor
      d. Possible hematuria
      e. Tests: intravenous pyelogram, retrograde pyelogram, or X-ray of kidney, bladder, and ureters
   2. **Medical Treatment**
      a. Nephrolithotomy—incision into the kidney to remove the stone
      b. Ureterolithotomy—incision into the ureter to remove the stone
      c. Increased fluid intake
      d. Cystoscopy to move stone
      e. Insertion of urethral catheter to allow continued flow
   3. **Nursing Interventions**
      a. Administer analgesics.
      b. Encourage increased fluid intake and decreased calcium intake, if appropriate.
      c. Strain all urine and check for presence of stone or blood clots.
      d. Preoperative and postoperative care if surgery performed.

D. **Glomerulonephritis**—an inflammation of the glomeruli in both kidneys due to an antigen-antibody response. It causes increased permeability, cell hyperplasia, and scarring, which leads to loss of renal function. Bacteria that can cause this are *Staphylococcus aureus* and group A beta-hemolytic strep.
   1. **Assessment**
      a. Headache, fever, chills
      b. Nausea and vomiting
      c. Edema, lower extremity, facial, may progress to generalized edema (anasarca)
      d. Oliguria
      e. Hypertension
   2. **Medical Treatment**
      a. Antihypertensives
      b. Antibiotics
      c. Decrease intake of sodium and potassium
   3. **Nursing Interventions**
      a. Monitor intake and output as well as fluid and dietary restrictions.
      b. Weigh daily. Be sure to weigh the client at the same time and with the same scale.
      c. Check blood pressure every 2–4 hours.

d. Administer antihypertensives and antibiotics as ordered.

e. Assess for complications of hypertension such as congestive heart failure and chronic renal failure—report to RN.

f. Provide support and teach symptoms to report to provider.

g. Discuss self-care measures, including need for rest and measures to prevent urinary tract infections.

E. **Acute Renal Failure**—Three types: *Prerenal*—usually caused by decreased blood flow through the kidneys from either hypotension, hemorrhage, burns, or cardiogenic shock. *Intrarenal*—conditions that cause damage to the nephrons: diabetes, blood transfusion reactions, nephrotoxic, or antibiotics. *Postrenal*—mechanical obstruction between the tubules and the urethra. May be calculi, tumors, protate enlargement, trauma, etc. Failure may occur over several days or hours.

  1. **Assessment**

    a. Low urine output (< 500 mL/ 24 hours)

    b. Specific gravity may be fixed at 1.010 (an indication of severe renal damage)

    c. Hypertension

    d. Nausea, vomiting, diarrhea, and eventually coma

  2. **Medical Treatment**

    a. First, treat the cause of the failure.

    b. Monitor electrolytes, hourly urine output.

    c. Weigh daily.

    d. Diet modifications: Limit protein, decrease nitrogen, decrease potassium, decrease phosphate, decrease sulfate, decrease sodium, and provide vitamin supplementation.

    e. Monitor for symptoms of CHF, fluid overload, or electrolyte imbalances.

  3. **Nursing Interventions**

    a. Monitor fluid balance with I & O, IV fluids, daily weights, monitoring lab values.

    b. Check for hypervolemia or hypovolemia hourly. Decrease fluid intake as ordered, administer diuretics, cardiac glycosides, and antihypertensives as ordered. Monitor effects of medication administration.

    c. Check urine-specific gravity and osmolality/osmolarity as ordered.

    d. Administer TPN as ordered.

    e. Restrict protein intake.

    f. Support and help reduce anxiety of client and family.

    g. Provide teaching and discharge planning concerning diet to be maintained, medications, signs and symptoms of UTI or recurrent renal disease to report to provider.

F. **Chronic Renal Failure**—gradual loss of renal function through progressive, irreversible destruction of kidneys until the nephrons are replaced by scar tissue. Caused by recurrent infections, urinary tract obstruction, diabetes, hypertension.

  1. **Assessment**

    a. Weakness, fatigue, and headaches

    b. Nausea and vomiting, diarrhea, or constipation

    c. Decreased urinary output, dyspnea

    d. Anemia

    e. Central nervous system irritability—possible convulsions

  2. **Medical Treatment**

    a. Low-salt diet, decreased protein intake.

    b. Mannitol is tried to determine if failure is reversible—12.5 gm of 25 percent solution given in 3 minutes. If flow rate can be increased to 40 cc/hour, renal failure is reversible. Keep urine flow at 100 cc/hour with mannitol.

c. Hemodialysis—blood from the client flows through the dialysis machine where it is removed by contact with the dialysate.

d. Peritoneal dialysis—usually temporary and used for a client in reversible renal failure. The peritoneum is used as a dialyzing membrane and substitutes for kidney function. Removes urea and creatinine, the end products of protein metabolism.

3. **Nursing Interventions**

a. Assess hourly for signs of uremia (fatigue, loss of appetite, apathy, confusion), which causes changes in mental function. Orient to time, place, and date.

b. Monitor and prevent changes in fluid and electrolyte balance.

c. Promote maintenance of skin integrity—provide care for pruritis.

d. Prevent client injury from bleeding complications.

e. Help maintain or regain optimal cardiovascular function.

f. Since digitalis is excreted by the kidneys, modify dose as ordered.

g. Provide care for a client receiving dialysis.

EXERCISES: THE URINARY AND RENAL SYSTEMS

1. The nurse is treating several incontinent clients who have been catheterized on the geriatric ward of the hospital. She is aware that one of the most common sites of a nosocomial infection is the urinary tract. To minimize the possibility of her clients acquiring urinary tract infections, the nurse is careful to

   (1) wear gloves when handling the catheters.

   (2) irrigate the catheters daily.

   (3) empty the collection bags several times during a shift.

   (4) use strict aseptic technique when inserting Foley catheters.

2. A 56-year-old woman states that she is having problems holding her urine. The nurse's assessment will take into consideration the possible causes of incontinence, which include which of the following?
   Select all that apply.

   ☐ (1) Excessive fluid intake

   ☐ (2) Neurogenic bladder resulting from diabetes

   ☐ (3) Relaxation of the pelvic musculature

   ☐ (4) Urinary tract infection (UTI)

3. In a report, you learn that Mrs. Watson has been incontinent. After determining that no physiological problem exists, the best way to prevent her incontinence would be

   (1) to tell her to push the call bell for the clinical assistant whenever she feels the need to void.

   (2) put a brief on her to prevent "accidents" that might cause her embarrassment.

   (3) insert a Foley catheter.

   (4) offer her the bed pan or assist her to the commode every 2 hours.

4. There is concern that Ms. Thompson is retaining fluid. If the adult kidney filters approximately 50 cc of fluid per hour, how much urine output must the client have per day to be considered within normal limits?

   (1) 300–750 cc

   (2) 1,200–1,00 cc

   (3) 1,750–2,250 cc

   (4) 5,000–10,000 cc

5. The results of the urine C&S on a client who has an indwelling Foley are positive for UTI. You realize that this is a nosocomial infection. What is the most likely reason for this infection?

   (1) Transmission from another client because of a nurse failing to wash her hands

   (2) Using the wrong size Foley catheter and injuring the urethral tissue

   (3) Reflux of urine into the bladder because the collecting bag has been raised above the level of the bladder

   (4) The client caught a cold while being transported to X-ray

6. A client you discharged from your unit three days ago calls and tells you he has gained 8 pounds. You know he has been prescribed Lasix, which he states he is taking as ordered. You tell him to

   (1) weigh himself at the same time each morning wearing similar or no clothes to determine the accuracy of the weights he is reporting.

   (2) make an appointment with his physician to evaluate the situation.

   (3) start exercising more frequently.

   (4) have him call 911 for transport to the emergency room.

7. Mr. Pope has glomerulonephritis and is concerned about his diet. You explain that he is at risk for

   (1) fluid overload.

   (2) hypokalemia.

   (3) blood urea nitrogen decrease.

   (4) hyponatremia.

8. The nurse is teaching Ms. Cowan, who has had several recent urinary tract infections (UTIs), how to prevent their recurrence. Which of the following suggestions would be more likely to cause UTIs rather than help prevent them?

   (1) Taking showers instead of baths

   (2) Drinking 8−10 glasses of water a day

   (3) Using bubble bath

   (4) Wiping the perineum from front to back

9. A nurse is counseling a woman who is seven months' pregnant about the discomforts of late pregnancy. The woman says that she has recently been leaking urine when she laughs, coughs, or sneezes. The nurse replies, "That is a common problem. It is called _____."

   (1) stress incontinence.

   (2) overflow incontinence.

   (3) urge incontinence.

   (4) mixed incontinence.

10. The nurse is copying orders for the client with renal calculi. The orders include "Intake and output, strain urine, regular diet, restrict fluid to less than 1 liter over replacement." Which one would the nurse question?

    (1) Intake and output
    (2) Strain urine
    (3) Regular diet
    (4) Restrict fluid to less than 1 liter over replacement

ANSWER KEY AND EXPLANATIONS

1. 4	3. 4	5. 3	7. 1	9. 1
2. 2,3,4	4. 2	6. 1	8. 3	10. 4

1. **The correct answer is (4).** Wearing gloves while handling the catheter (1) primarily protects the caregiver. Frequent irrigation (2) is likely to introduce infection, as is frequently emptying of the collection bag (3), since the closed system is opened at this time. Aseptic technique when inserting the catheter is a primary way to prevent the introduction of infection.

2. **The correct answers are (2), (3), and (4).** A neurogenic bladder, relaxation of the pelvic musculature, and UTIs can all contribute to incontinence. Although many people with incontinence may restrict fluid intake in an attempt to reduce the symptoms, fluid intake is generally beneficial to the functioning of the genitourinary system.

3. **The correct answer is (4).** Muscle control decreases with age, and clients frequently lose control. By emptying the bladder q2h, you decrease the leakage and help retrain the musculature.

4. **The correct answer is (2).** Multiplying 50 cc by 24 hours (one day) equals 1200. Although an adult kidney filters approximately 50 cc of fluid per hour, this amount varies with many factors, including rate of perspiration, fluid intake, and the client's cardiac and renal status.

5. **The correct answer is (3).** While urine is sitting in the drainage collection bag, it changes consistency and can be contaminated. This is the biggest source of nosocomial source of infections.

6. **The correct answer is (1).** Consistency in daily weight is important to accurately assess whether a client has truly gained weight.

7. **The correct answer is (1).** Because the kidneys are impaired, the client is at risk for fluid overload. His protein and sodium intake will be restricted in addition to fluids.

8. **The correct answer is (3).** A bubble bath can irritate the urethra and promote infections. The suggestions in the other answer choices will help prevent UTIs.

9. **The correct answer is (1).** Leakage of urine while coughing, sneezing, or otherwise increasing intra-abdominal pressure is called stress incontinence.

10. **The correct answer is (4).** Fluid intake should be increased in a client with renal calculi to ensure dilute urine and to help wash out the stone.

answers **exercises**

SUMMING IT UP

- The urinary and renal systems not only remove waste products from the body, but they also maintain electrolyte, fluid, and acid-base balance.

The Hematologic and Immune Systems

chapter 13

OVERVIEW

- Basic concepts
- Physiology of the blood
- Physiology of the immune system
- Hematological system disorders
- Immune system disorders
- Summing it up

BASIC CONCEPTS

Blood is essential for delivering oxygen and nutrients to the cells of the body and for removing wastes. The immune system protects the body against foreign substances. They work together to protect and maintain physiological integrity.

PHYSIOLOGY OF THE BLOOD

A. Blood Functions
1. **Transports Oxygen from the Lungs to the Tissues**
2. **Transports Carbon Dioxide and Waste Products from Cells for Excretion**
3. **Transports Hormones and Nutrients to Body Cells**
4. **Helps Maintain Homeostasis**—balance of acid-base, electrolytes, fluids

B. Blood Components
1. **Plasma**—about half of the blood volume, is 90 percent water
   a. Contains blood proteins—fibrinogen (clot formation), prothrombin (coagulation), albumin, (blood protein), gamma globulin (prevention of infection)
   b. Contains hormones, electrolytes, nutrients, oxygen, CO_2, waste products, urea, lactic acid, and uric acid
2. **Erythrocytes (red blood cells—RBCs)**
3. **Formed in the Red Bone Marrow**—erythropoiesis is the word for RBC production
4. **Vitamin B_{12} and Folic Acid**—needed for normal RBC production
5. **Hemoglobin**—the primary component of the RBC
   a. Main function is to carry oxygen and carbon dioxide
   b. Life span of a RBC is approximately 120 days
   c. Percentage of the blood made up of erythrocytes is called the hematocrit (hct.)

237

6. **Leukocytes (white blood cells—WBCs)**
   a. Primary function is to fight infection.
   b. Leukocytosis is an increase in leukocytes; leukopenia is a decrease in the number of WBCs.
   c. Classification of leukocytes
      (1) Granulocytes (have visible granules in cytoplasm): neutrophils, eosinophils, basophils
      (2) Agranulocytes (lack cytoplasmic granules): lymphocytes and monocytes
   d. Formed in the red bone marrow and by lymphatic tissue in lymph nodes, thymus, and spleen.
   e. Normal range of WBCs is 5,000 to 10,000 per cubic millimeter.
7. **Thrombocytes (platelets)**
   a. Aid in the clotting process
   b. Normal range—200,000 to 400,000 per cubic millimeter
8. **Blood Group Classification**
   a. A, B, AB, and O are the major groups
      (1) AB has no anti-A or anti-B antibodies—the universal recipient
      (2) Type O has no type A or type B antigens—the universal donor
      (3) Type B has B antigens and anti-A antibodies
      (4) Type A has A antigens and anti-B antibodies
   b. Rh factor is on the red cell—blood is classified by the presence or absence of the Rh antigen
      (1) 85–95 percent of the population is Rh positive (have Rh antigen)
      (2) Rh-negative persons can form antibodies against Rh-positive red blood cells

C. Client Assessment
1. **History of Present Illness**
   a. Evaluate disorder's affect on client's ability to perform ADLs (activities of daily living)
   b. Time of onset of symptoms, duration of illness
   c. Presence of bleeding episodes at this time
   d. Pain control
2. **Medical History**
   a. History of a disease affecting bone marrow, organs that produce blood
   b. History of therapy—chemotherapy and/or radiation—which depress bone marrow activity
   c. If client is female, history of bleeding problems perinatally in mother and/or baby
   d. Presence of disease process or aging that may affect bleeding tendencies
3. **Family History of Hematologic Problems**
   a. Does any family member have a history of hematologic problems?
4. **Objective Data**
   a. Nutritional status, anemia
   b. Lab values including CBC, coagulation studies, blood chemistry
   c. Respiratory assessment
   d. Cardiovascular assessment
   e. Presence or absence of enlarged lymph nodes

D. Assessment of the Elderly
1. Nail beds—capillary refill is often difficult to assess due to yellowing and thickening of nails
2. Hair distribution—thin or absent hair on trunk and extremities may indicate poor oxygenation

3. Skin moisture and color—dry skin is normal in the elderly, as well as some yellowing of the skin. Pallor may be associated with not going out as much as younger people.

PHYSIOLOGY OF THE IMMUNE SYSTEM

A. **Immune System Functions**—purpose is to recognize and neutralize foreign substances so the body can protect itself; forms antibodies against foreign proteins
   1. **Defense Against Infection from Outside Microorganisms**
   2. **Maintaining Homeostasis by Removing Old Cells (primarily through the spleen)**
   3. **Surveillance of Circulating Cells and Destroying Abnormal or Outside Cells**

B. **Types of Immune Responses**
   1. **Natural**
      a. No prior contact with an antigen. It may be related to a genetic tendency or species-specific immunity.
   2. **Acquired**
      a. Active—the body produces antibodies in response to antigen
         (1) Natural—antigen is contacted through exposure (recovery from chicken pox)
         (2) Artificial—immunization with an antigen (a live or attenuated vaccine, e.g., Sabin polio, measles, tetanus, diphteria); may need to get boosters
      b. Passive—antibodies produced by one person and transferred to another
         (1) Natural—maternal immunoglobulin in the newborn from breast milk and placenta
         (2) Artificial—injection of serum from human or animal; short-lived but immediate, e.g., gammaglobulin injection after exposure, as when hepatitis immune globulin is given to a nurse who has had a blood exposure to Hepatitis B

C. **Characteristics of Immune Responses**
   1. **Specificity**—antibodies to one antigen will not protect from another type. Example: Chicken pox antibodies will not protect against measles.
   2. **Memory**—ability to remember one antigen and produce the specific antibody for it. Memory cells are produced after the first exposure to an antigen, which produce a stronger immune response on the second exposure. Example: Continued resistance to chicken pox over time.
   3. **Self-Recognition**—the body can recognize its own proteins as different from foreign proteins, so foreign proteins can be attacked without injury to the body. Not recognizing its own cells results in an autoimmune disorder such as lupus.

D. **Components of Immune Response**
   1. **Organs**—include thymus, bone marrow, lymph nodes, spleen, tonsils, appendix, Peyer's patches of small intestine
   2. **Main Cell Types (WBCs)**—primarily lymphocytes, plasma cells, and macrophages. They all originate in the stem cell in the bone marrow.
      a. Granulocytes
         (1) Eosinophils—increase with allergies and parasites
         (2) Basophils—contain histamine and increase with allergy and anaphylaxis
         (3) Neutrophils—involved in phagocytosis

       b. Agranulocytes
          (1) Monocytes—macrophages, perform phagocytosis
          (2) Lymphocytes—B and T cells, involved in cellular and humoral immunity

E. Immune Response Classification
     1. **Cellular Immunity**
        a. Involves T cells: persist in tissues over time (may be years)
        b. Functions in transplant rejection, delayed hypersensitivity, tumor surveillance
     2. **Humoral Immunity**
        a. B cells
          (1) Produce circulating antibodies (gamma globulin)
          (2) Only survive for days
        b. Functions: bacterial phagocytosis, bacterial lysis, virus and toxin neutralization

F. Factors That Affect Immune Function
     1. **Age**—newborn and elderly have less immunity
     2. **Metabolism**—thyroid and adrenal hormone deficiencies lower the immune response; steroids inhibit the inflammatory response
     3. **Emotional Stress**—may cause a decrease in production of immune cells
     4. **Hormones**—women have more autoimmune diseases than men
     5. **Environment**—unsanitary living conditions and exposure to pathogens
     6. **Nutrition**—poor nutrition can decrease immune responses

HEMATOLOGICAL SYSTEM DISORDERS

A. Anemias—decreased numbers of red blood cells and/or lower hematocrit and hemoglobin
     1. **Iron Deficiency Anemia**—caused by inadequate intake, absorption of iron, or excessive iron loss
     2. **Assessment**
        a. Decreased hgb. and hct.
        b. Small and pale (microcytic and hypochromic) red blood cells
        c. Fatigue and lethargy
        d. Pale mucous membranes
     3. **Medical Treatment**
        a. Iron replacement in the diet
        b. Increased folic acid intake
     4. **Nursing Interventions**
        a. Help client arrange periods of rest
        b. Administer iron preparations
          (1) Give after meals.
          (2) Give IM by z-track method; use separate needles to withdraw medication and to inject (irritation and tissue staining are a problem). Do not massage area.
          (3) Provide dietary teaching about iron sources.
          (4) Suggest increased fluid and roughage to prevent constipation.
     5. **Pernicious Anemia**—caused by a lack of intrinsic factors needed to absorb vitamin B_{12}; may be caused by gastrectomy or gastric mucosa atrophy; macrocytic anemia.
        a. Assessment
          (1) Smooth, sore, red tongue
          (2) Weakness and lethargy
          (3) Pale skin
          (4) Paresthesia in the extremities
          (5) Loss of balance

NOTE

Liquid preparations should be diluted and given through a straw to prevent staining teeth

6. **Medical Treatment**
   a. Lifelong vitamin B_{12} injections
7. **Nursing Interventions**
   a. Provide nutritious diet high in iron, protein, and vitamins.
   b. Encourage rest as needed.
   c. Avoid spicy foods that may irritate tongue.
   d. Provide assistance when ambulating.
   e. Provide education about need for continued supplementation.
8. **Aplastic Anemia**—caused by depression of the red bone marrow in producing red blood cells
9. **Assessment**
   a. Weakness and pallor
   b. Dyspnea
   c. Fever and infections
   d. Thrombocytopenia leading to bleeding problems
10. **Medical Treatment**
    a. Blood transfusions
    b. Bone marrow transplant
11. **Nursing Interventions**
    a. Administer medications and assist in blood transfusions.
    b. Monitor for infection and minimize risk
       (1) Neutropenic precautions
       (2) Nutritious diet
    c. Monitor for signs of bleeding and minimize risk
       (1) Soft toothbrush
       (2) Avoid IM injections
       (3) Hematest stool and urine
    d. Appropriate discharge teaching.

B. **Sickle Cell Anemia** (see Chapter 6, Pediatric Nursing)

C. **Leukemia**—involves an abnormal proliferation of white blood cells. It causes anemia from destruction of red blood cells, infection from decreased production of healthy white blood cells, bleeding tendencies due to decreased number of platelets.
   1. **Types of Leukemias**
      a. Acute lymphocytic leukemia (ALL)
         (1) Primarily in children—peak age 4 years old.
         (2) Prognosis is good with chemotherapy.
         (3) Leukemia cells may invade the meninges and cause increased intracranial pressure.
      b. Acute myelogenous leukemia (AML)
         (1) Affects all ages, greater incidence with increased age.
         (2) Poor prognosis.
      c. Chronic lymphocytic leukemia (CLL) and Chronic myelogenous leukemia (CML)
   2. **Assessment**
      a. Anemia, infection, and bleeding tendencies
      b. Fatigue and lethargy
      c. CNS irritability
      d. Bruises easily
      e. Bone and joint pain
      f. Enlarged liver and spleen

3. **Medical Treatment**
   a. Medications—steroids and chemotherapy
   b. Bone marrow transplant
   c. Red blood cell and platelet transfusions
4. **Nursing Interventions**
   a. Monitor for infections—signs are fever, inflammation, and pain.
   b. Protect client from exposure to infection.
   c. Instruct client to avoid live virus immunizations.
   d. Maintain hydration.
   e. Use acetaminophen instead of aspirin for pain relief (aspirin decreases platelet function).

D. **Hemophilia** (see Chapter 6, Pediatric Nursing)

IMMUNE SYSTEM DISORDERS

A. **Autoimmune Diseases**
   1. **Autoantibodies**—during normal breakdown of body tissue, the injury may cause cells that do not usually appear in the system to circulate, and the immune system can detect them as foreign. Autoantibodies are then formed that attack the person's own antigens.
   2. **Autoimmune Responses**—may be systemic- or organ-specific
   3. **Systemic**
      a. Systemic lupus erythematosus (SLE)
      b. Rheumatoid arthritis
   4. **Local**
      a. Myasthenia Gravis
      b. Graves' Disease
      c. Addison's Disease
      d. Insulin Dependent Diabetes

B. **Anaphylactic Reaction**—an antigen/antibody response, which causes a life-threatening release of histamine, vasodilation, and capillary permeability
   1. **Assessment**
      a. Hypotension
      b. Urticaria, erythema, generalized burning and itching
      c. Bronchospasm, wheezing
      d. Sense of impending doom
   2. **Medical Treatment**
      a. Epinephrine
      b. Benadryl
      c. Oxygen and IV fluids
      d. Corticosteroids
   3. **Nursing Interventions**
      a. Obtain client history to screen for possible drug reactions.
      b. Monitor oxygen, IV fluids, vital signs.
      c. Instruct client to avoid causative agent.

C. **Systemic Lupus Erythematosus**—an autoimmune disorder that affects multiple body systems and is characterized by exacerbations and remissions
   1. **Assessment**
      a. Skin rash in response to sun; may be "butterfly rash" on face
      b. Arthritis

ALERT!
Know that fever, inflammation, and pain are universal signs of any infection.

ALERT!
Do not administer live vaccines to *any* immune-suppressed person.

  c. Kidney problems including proteinuria, hypertension

  d. Neurological difficulties, psychiatric symptoms, or seizures

  e. Blood disorders such as anemia, low white blood cell count

 2. **Medical Treatment**—does not cure, only relieves symptoms

  a. Corticosteroids

  b. Immunosuppressants

 3. **Nursing Interventions**

  a. Teach proper medication regimen, including not to stop prednisone abruptly.

  b. Help client avoid sunlight.

  c. Review signs to report to physician—infection or exacerbation of disease.

  d. Monitor kidney function—edema, hypertension, hematuria, decreased urinary output, report to the physician.

D. Acquired Immunodeficiency Syndrome (AIDS)—a retrovirus, which primarily affects the helper T cells, causing the immune system to be suppressed

 1. **Background**

  a. Transmission through blood and body fluids. Ways include transfusion of infected blood products (in the United States, screening began in 1985), sharing contaminated needles or accidental needle sticks, perinatal transmission to newborns of infected mothers, and sexual transmission. It is not transmitted by hugging, kissing, holding hands or other nonsexual contact or by touching inanimate objects—glasses, table, or animals/insects. Household bleach (sodium hypochlorite in a 1:10 concentration with water) is effective in killing the virus.

  b. Clients may be carriers without symptoms of the disease. The incubation period may be several months to a number of years.

  c. Standard (Universal) precautions will protect the health-care worker from exposure.

 2. **Assessment**

  a. Early nonspecific changes

   (1) Chronic fatigue

   (2) Persistent diarrhea

   (3) Weight loss

   (4) Lymphadenopathy (enlarged lymph nodes)

  b. HIV encephalopathy—AIDS dementia

  c. Kaposi's sarcoma—red or purple raised lesions on the body

  d. Pneumocystis carinii pneumonia (most common opportunistic infection)

 3. **Medical Diagnosis**

  a. HIV-1 antibody test—ELISA (has false positives), confirmed by the Western Blot Test (usually become positive within one month of exposure)

  b. Antigen test—can detect infection as early as two weeks after it occurs

 4. **Medical Treatment**

  a. Antivirals

  b. Medications to treat the opportunistic infections

 5. **Nursing Interventions**

  a. Client and public teaching about preventing transmission

   (1) Safe sex condom use

   (2) Perinatal transmission if pregnancy occurs

   (3) No recapping needles

   (4) No donation of blood, plasma, body organs, semen

   (5) HIV-positive women should not breastfeed

  b. Supportive care for presenting symptoms.

  c. Assist client to access services.

  d. Encourage verbalization of concerns.

EXERCISES: THE HEMATOLOGIC AND IMMUNE SYSTEMS

1. After entering a client's room, the nurse notes a small spill of blood in the bathroom. To clean it up, she uses

    (1) the hospital disinfectant.
    (2) solution of 1:10 sodium hypochlorite (bleach) and water.
    (3) hydrogen peroxide and alcohol wipes.
    (4) absorbent gel granules.

2. A postsurgical client has a platelet count of 5,000. The nurse should carefully monitor the client for symptoms of

    (1) phlebitis.
    (2) bleeding.
    (3) infection.
    (4) neuropathy.

3. Christopher, a 7-year-old boy, is experiencing an anaphylactic reaction from ingesting peanuts. In the emergency department a code team is present, and the physician orders the delivery of 0.01 mg/kg (weight of the child) epinephrine in a 1:1000 aqueous solution subcutaneously stat. Christopher's mother reports that he weighs 66 pounds. The nurse has a pre-filled syringe of 1:1000 (1 mg/mL) epinephrine. How many milliliters of epinephrine should be administered to the client?

    Answer: _____ mL

4. The nurse has just finished giving an intramuscular injection to a client. To prevent an accidental puncture from a contaminated needle, the *best* action for the nurse would be to

    (1) recap the needle and dispose of it in the sharps container.
    (2) do not recap the needle and dispose of it in the sharps container.
    (3) break the needle and deposit it in the hazardous waste container.
    (4) do not break the needle and deposit it in the hazardous waste container.

5. The nurse puts on a gown, glove, and mask to treat a client on chemotherapy. The *primary* purpose of these reverse precautions is to

    (1) protect the nurse from contact with the substances used for chemotherapy.
    (2) prevent the nurse from transmitting an infection from the client to another client.
    (3) protect the immune-compromised client from infection by the nurse.
    (4) protect the nurse from contact with body fluids.

TIP

Be sure to read each question carefully and note every important word. In Question 5, it is important to pay attention to the word *primary* to determine the correct answer.

6. A nurse is checking a client's lab results to see whether they indicate any possibility of infection. Which of the following would indicate that no infection is present?

    (1) Increased white blood count

    (2) Increased erythrocyte sedimentation rate

    (3) Increased number of neutrophils

    (4) Decreased hemoglobin

7. A nurse received her hepatitis B vaccination. She is aware that the vaccination works on the following part of the chain of infection:

    (1) Reservoir

    (2) Portal of exit

    (3) Mode of transmission

    (4) Susceptible host

8. When evaluating the older client's hematologic system, the nurse doesn't check for capillary refill because

    (1) pressing on the nail is painful for older people.

    (2) cyanotic nail beds are a normal finding in older clients.

    (3) nails of older clients are typically thickened and discolored.

    (4) blood is thicker in older clients, thus delaying capillary refill.

9. The nurse is helping Sally G., a young woman with systemic lupus erythematosus, to prepare for discharge and is giving her instructions for self-care. Which of the following statements indicate that no further teaching is needed? **Select all that apply.**

    ☐ **(1)** "I should stay out of the sun as much as possible."

    ☐ **(2)** "I need to call the doctor if I have any symptoms of decreased urine output or edema."

    ☐ **(3)** "It is important that I don't stop taking my prednisone."

    ☐ **(4)** "I must be careful to use my own toilet articles so that I don't infect anyone else."

10. Which comment by the AIDs client indicates the need for further teaching?

    (1) "I must have gotten infected when I used IV drugs and would share needles."

    (2) "I'm afraid to touch my granddaughter for fear I might give it to her."

    (3) "It is important to remember that HIV may be transmitted through sexual contact."

    (4) "I will not be able to donate blood or body organs in the future."

ANSWER KEY AND EXPLANATIONS

1. 2	3. 0.3	5. 3	7. 4	9. 1,2,3
2. 2	4. 2	6. 4	8. 3	10. 2

1. **The correct answer is (2).** A 1:10 solution of sodium hypochlorite (bleach) and water is recommended by infection control experts for blood spills. Regular disinfectants, hydrogen peroxide, and alcohol are not used for this purpose. Absorbent products do not have any antimicrobial action.

2. **The correct answer is (2).** Platelet aggregation is an important part of the clotting process. Normal platelet counts are over 150,000, so this client would be at risk for bleeding. Phlebitis is inflammation related to a clot, and infection as well as neuropathy are unrelated to clotting.

3. **The correct answer is 0.3.** Use the following equations to solve:

   1 kg = 2.2 lbs.,
   therefore 66 lbs = 30 kg

   30 kg × 0.01 mg/kg =
   0.3 mg epinephrine solution

   $$\frac{1 \text{ mg}}{1 \text{ mL}} = \frac{0.3 \text{ mg}}{x}$$

   $x = 0.3$ mL

4. **The correct answer is (2).** Recapping or breaking a needle are dangerous practices that are likely to increase the possibility of a needle-stick injury. The appropriate place for disposing of a needle is in the sharps container.

5. **The correct answer is (3).** These are known as reverse precautions to protect the immune-compromised client. They also have the effect of protecting the nurse if contact with body fluids is anticipated (4) and could prevent transmission of infection if present (2). However, these are not the primary intent, since neither of these situations would call for a gown, glove, and mask. Presumably the nurse will not have contact with chemotherapy drugs (1).

6. **The correct answer is (4).** The white blood cell count (1) and erythrocyte sedimentation rate (2) are increased in the presence of infection. In addition, neutrophils (3), a type of white blood cell, are also increased. The hemoglobin is not usually affected by infection.

7. **The correct answer is (4).** The hepatitis B vaccination interrupts the chain of infection by making the host resistant to infection. It does not affect any reservoir (1), portal of exit (2), or mode of transmission (3).

8. **The correct answer is (3).** The nails of older clients are often thick and hypertrophied, making it difficult to assess capillary refill. Pressing on the nail bed is no more painful for an older client (1) than anyone else. Cyanotic nail beds are not normal (2), and blood is not thicker (4).

9. **The correct answers are (1), (2), and (3).** Staying out of the sun, tapering steroid medication, and monitoring for kidney problems are important for an SLE client's self-care. It is not an infectious disorder.

10. **The correct answer is (2).** The HIV virus cannot be transmitted by touch, only through contact with blood or body fluids.

SUMMING IT UP

- Blood is essential for delivering oxygen and nutrients to the cells of the body and for removing wastes.

- The immune system protects the body against foreign substances. It works to protect and maintain physiological integrity.

Oncology

BASIC CONCEPTS

Cancer is the second leading cause of death in the United States (heart disease is the first). One in three Americans will develop some kind of cancer, with lung cancer having the highest mortality rate. The most common type of cancer overall is skin cancer; the two most common cancers in men are cancer of the prostate and the lungs; in women they are cancer of the breast and the lungs.

Cancer Cells

Normal cells are governed by regulatory mechanisms that control their growth and reproduction. Cancer cells have lost these control mechanisms and grow uncontrollably. Cancer cells are also not differentiated as well as normal tissue and thus cannot perform the same functions. These cells are not as easily attached or encapsulated as normal cell groups and can metastasize to distant areas of the body.

Cancer Risk Factors

Risk factors for developing cancer are multiple, although environmental factors are thought to be responsible for 60–90 percent of cancers. Known carcinogens include radiation; chemicals, such as nitrites, asbestos, vinyl chloride, and DES; cigarette smoke; and hormones. Certain viruses have been linked to some types of cancer. Individuals who are immunosuppressed are more likely to develop cancer. However, none of these completely rule out genetic links as well as dietary and psychological factors.

chapter 14

Preventive Measures

A. **Dietary**—avoid obesity; decrease fat intake; increase fiber; increase consumption of vitamins A, C, and E, preferably from natural sources such as fruits and vegetables

B. **Carcinogen Exposure**—avoid smoking and exposure to asbestos, chemicals, and radiation; obtain adequate rest and exercise to decrease stress

CANCER DIAGNOSIS

NOTE

Common Metastasis of Cancers

Brain: Central nervous system

Breast: Bones and lung

Colorectal: Liver

Lung: Brain

Prostate: Bones and legs

A. **Early Detection**
   1. **Screening/Self-Monitoring**
      a. Pap smear—cervical cancer
      b. Breast self-exam, mammogram—breast cancer
      c. Colonoscopy—colon cancer
      d. PSA level—prostate cancer
      e. Skin inspection—skin cancer
   2. **Seven Warning Signs of Cancer (CAUTION)**
      a. C—Change in bowel or bladder habits
      b. A—Any sore that does not heal
      c. U—Unusual discharge or bleeding
      d. T—Thickening or lump in breast or elsewhere
      e. I—Indigestion or difficulty swallowing
      f. O—Obvious change in wart or mole
      g. N—Nagging cough or hoarseness

B. **Identification, Diagnosis, and Staging**
   1. **Characteristics of Types of Neoplasms**
      a. Benign—usually encapsulated, localized, and grow slowly
      b. Malignant—undifferentiated margins, will grow and metastasize
   2. **Types of Malignant Neoplasms**
      a. Carcinoma—arise from epithelial cells (those covering the internal and external surfaces of the body) and are usually solid tumors. Examples: skin, stomach, colon, breast, rectal
         (1) Squamous cell carcinoma—surface epithelium
         (2) Adenocarcinoma—glandular or parenchymal tissue
      b. Sarcoma—arise from connective tissue such as bone or muscle
      c. Lymphoma—arise from lymphoid tissue (infection-fighting cells)
      d. Leukemias and myelomas—arise from blood-forming organs
   3. **Diagnosis**
      a. Laboratory and imaging tests usually first identification of a problem.
      b. Tissue biopsy is the definitive means of diagnosis.
   4. **Cancer Staging**—identifies the severity of the disease by describing the extent of metastasis
      a. TNM system
         (1) T = primary growth
         (2) N = lymph node involvement
         (3) M = metastasis
            (a) T–1 to T–4: T–1 is the smallest tumor; T–4 is the largest
            (b) N–0 to N–4: N–0 is no node involvement; N–4 is increasing number of nodes involved

(c) M–0 or M–1: M–0 is no metastasis; M–1–3 indicates increasing degrees of metastasis

(d) Stages 0–IV: severity of cancer; increasing numbers indicate increased size, nodal involvement, metastases.

CANCER TREATMENT

A. **Types**—depend on protocols for different types and stages of cancer, as well as the goals of treatment

1. **Surgery**—used either to reduce the size of a tumor (palliative surgery) or to completely remove a primary localized tumor. For localized disease, it has the highest probability of cure. However, the surgery may cause functional or cosmetic problems.

   a. Preoperative care

      (1) Help the client attain optimum health status prior to the surgery.

      (2) Provide emotional support to client and family.

   b. Postoperative care

      (1) Provide traditional care for postoperative client.

      (2) Offer emotional support and accurate information.

   c. Help client recover and continue with follow-up treatment if needed

      (1) Make appropriate referrals for post-discharge follow-up.

      (2) Encourage family involvement.

2. **Radiation**—may be internal or external, uses ionizing radiation to destroy cancer cells. Effects are not limited to cancer cells; all exposed cells are affected, and rapidly dividing cells are most susceptible. Systemic effects are related to cellular breakdown products.

   a. External radiation—high-energy beams directed to the affected area. Irradiated cells lose the ability to reproduce. Side effects include fatigue, nausea and vomiting, skin irritation, scaling, erythema, and dryness.

   b. Nursing Interventions

      (1) Explain procedure and expected side effects.

      (2) Promote high-protein, carbohydrate, and fat-free, low-residue diet; increase fluids.

      (3) Administer medications: Compazine (anti-emetic) and Lomitil (for diarrhea).

      (4) Provide skin care, avoiding lotions and soap. Do not expose skin to sunlight.

   c. Minimizing risk to health-care workers

      (1) Internal radiation is more dangerous than external.

      (2) The more time spent exposed to the radiation source and the closer to the source, the greater the exposure.

      (3) Pregnant women and persons under 18 should not visit or care for a client with a radioactive implant.

      (4) Mark the client's room with radiation safety precautions.

   d. Internal—radioactive material is injected or implanted into the client's body for a period of time

      (1) Sealed—radioisotope is enclosed in a container; body fluids should not become contaminated.

         (a) Precautions still needed, even though implant is sealed.

      (2) Unsealed—radioisotope is not enclosed. It circulates in the body and contaminates body fluids.

         (a) Administered orally (liquid). High-risk period is during first four days.

       (3) Side effects—acute are right after; chronic are months or years after treatment

         (a) Alopecia (hair loss), mouth dryness, mucositis, esophagitis (mouth and throat inflammation), nausea and vomiting, erythema, dry and wet desquamation

         (b) Extent of side effects are influenced by the body site irradiated, the radiation dose, the size of the site irradiated, and the method of radiation therapy

3. **Chemotherapy**—drugs kill the cancer cells but also harm rapidly dividing cells. Different drugs attack cancer cells at different stages of their life cycle, thus combinations may be more effective than one type alone. It is usually used when cancer cells have metastasized, when the risk of recurrence is high, or as a palliative measure to slow the growth of a tumor.

  a. Types of chemotherapy

    (1) Cell cycle specific (act on a specific stage of the cell reproductive cycle)

      (a) Antimetabolites—methotrexate, 5-fluorouracil

      (b) Plant alkaloids—vincristine, vinblastine

    (2) Cell cycle nonspecific (act during any phase of reproductive cycle, some will work in the resting phase). These agents are dose dependent and are more toxic to normal tissue than others.

      (a) Alkylating agents—cytoxan, cisplatin

      (b) Antitumor antibiotics—adriamycin, bleomycin

      (c) Nitrosoureas—streptozocin, methyl CCNU, BCNU

    (3) Hormones—affect the growth hormonal environment

      (a) Alter the growth of hormone-dependent tumors

      (b) Antihormones—(Tamoxifen) block tumor growth by depriving the tumor of hormones it needs to grow

4. **Side Effects of Chemotherapy**

  a. Alopecia—nursing interventions include applying an ice cap and scalp tourniquet to reduce the amount delivered to hair follicles.

  b. Nausea, vomiting, and anorexia—the nurse can adjust to altered food preferences, administer antiemetic drugs (Reglan), offer high-calorie and protein supplements.

  c. Leukopenia—decreased white blood cells, suppresses the client's immune function.

  d. Platelet suppression—if below 50,000, the client is prone to bleeding gums and nose and easy bruising. The nurse should suggest the client use a soft toothbrush and take care with trimming nails and any other activity that might lead to abrading the skin.

5. **Safe Administration of Chemotherapy**

  a. Special training is necessary before administering chemotherapy.

  b. Surgical latex gloves and a long-sleeved gown should be worn.

  c. Label all prepared drugs, and double bag them before transport.

  d. Dispose of all materials in hazardous waste containers.

  e. Have materials ready to clean up an accidental spill.

6. **Bone Marrow Transplants**—Used in clients being treated for leukemia. The high doses of chemotherapy and whole-body radiation used to treat leukemia kill bone marrow. If it is not replaced, a client will die from hemorrhaging and/or will not be able to stave off infection.

  a. Prerequisites—a closely matched donor; client must be in remission

  b. Administration—through central line, similar to blood transfusion

  c. Until engraftment—infection and severe thrombocytopenia

  d. Complications—failure to engraft, graft vs. host disease

NURSING CARE

A. Client comfort
   1. **Nausea**
      a. Progressive relaxation, imagery, and antiemetic medications are helpful.
      b. Antiemetics should be administered before administration of chemotherapy.
      c. Clients who are on chemotherapy drugs that cause nausea and have a long half-life should be given around-the-clock medications for up to four days after treatment has ended.
   2. **Pain**
      a. Pain medications are best given around the clock. Waiting until a client requests it is too late for continuing effectiveness.
      b. Pain medications should be given before invasive procedures.
      c. Clients on high doses of narcotics for extended periods of time may develop tolerance and need higher doses than clients who are receiving periodic therapy.

B. Client support
   1. Provide emotional support by talking with the client about fears or questions.
   2. Always be honest with the client so that he or she may discuss things openly.
   3. Support the client's family members as they go through the grieving process.
   4. Times of increased stress are when the client is diagnosed, he or she enters the hospital, and upon release from the hospital.
   5. Denial is a common initial reaction to a cancer diagnosis. It is a defense mechanism that gives the client time to prepare to confront the implications of the diagnosis.

EXERCISES: ONCOLOGY

1. Two weeks after receiving chemotherapy, Mrs. Constant develops sores in her mouth, has hair loss, and complains of being extremely tired. She asks what is happening to her. Your best answer is

    (1) "The chemotherapy is designed to attack rapidly multiplying cells but doesn't distinguish between cancer cells and normal cells."

    (2) "Chemotherapy is very toxic, and I told you that you would experience side effects before the therapy was started."

    (3) "These are normal side effects, and they will go away after awhile."

    (4) "Here is a booklet you can read. Your doctor will answer all your questions."

2. Tumors that have broken off from the original malignant site are referred to as

    (1) infectious.

    (2) cancerous.

    (3) sarcomas.

    (4) metastatic.

3. Which of the following are treatment modalities for various forms of cancer? **Select all that apply.**

    ☐ **(1)** Radiation therapy and surgery

    ☐ **(2)** Behavior modification and chemotherapy

    ☐ **(3)** Use of hormones and antimetabolites

    ☐ **(4)** Chemotherapy and internal radiation

4. Celia Gatto is having radiation therapy for breast cancer. She asks how this treatment works. Your best response would be

    (1) "The radiation kills only the cancer cells."

    (2) "The radiation kills the cells by preventing their ability to reproduce."

    (3) "The radiation is much neater than surgery and kills all the cancer cells by dehydrating them."

    (4) "Please direct your questions to the physician."

5. You know Mr. Yard is receiving antineoplastic drugs in the outpatient oncology unit. He asks you what the goal is of this type of drug therapy. Your appropriate response is

    (1) "To slowng down the spread of the cancer cells in your body."

    (2) "To destroy all the malignant cells."

    (3) "To kill the cells at the primary site of the cancer."

    (4) "To shrink the cells at the primary site."

6. Mr. Mum has been diagnosed with bone cancer. You know this type of cancer is classified as

    (1) sarcoma.

    (2) lymphoma.

    (3) carcinoma.

    (4) melanoma.

7. You are teaching a cancer prevention class at a local high school. Which acronym would you suggest to help the students remember the warning signs of cancer?

    (1) ACE
    (2) CAUTION
    (3) DARE
    (4) LCTA

8. Brian Shatz is being treated with radiation for leukemia. To prevent excessive skin damage from this therapy, the nurse instructs him to do which of the following?

    (1) Sunbathe for short periods of time to help the skin heal.
    (2) Wash it thoroughly with soap and water after radiation.
    (3) Avoid applying cream and powders to the area.
    (4) Use a wet to dry dressing on affected areas.

exercises

ANSWER KEY AND EXPLANATIONS

1. 1	3. 1,3,4	5. 2	7. 2
2. 4	4. 2	6. 1	8. 3

1. **The correct answer is (1).** Chemotherapy destroys new growth of cells in hair follicles, mucus membranes of the GI tract, and bone marrow, while killing cancer cells.

2. **The correct answer is (4).** Tumors confined to one area are referred to as the primary site and generally have a better prognosis than metastatic disease.

3. **The correct answers are (1), (3), and (4).** Behavior modification is not a form of cancer treatment.

4. **The correct answer is (2).** Radiation causes cell destruction by projecting enormous energy into the chromosomes and breaking them. Without the chromosomes, cells cannot reproduce.

5. **The correct answer is (2).** The goal of cancer treatment is to rid the client of malignant cells. Chemotherapy in particular is designed to destroy all malignant cells, but it also kills healthy tissue in the process.

6. **The correct answer is (1).** Tumors that originate from bone, muscle, and other connective tissue are called sarcomas.

7. **The correct answer is (2).** CAUTION is taught by the American Cancer Society to list the seven warning signs for cancer. (See page 250, Early Detection.)

8. **The correct answer is (3).** Creams and powders should not be used on irradiated skin. None of the other measures—sunbathing, washing with soap and water, and the use of wet to dry dressings—is appropriate for a client being treated with radiation.

SUMMING IT UP

- Cancer is the second leading cause of death in the United States.
- Skin cancer is the most common type of cancer overall.
- Lung cancer has the highest mortality rate.
- The two most common cancers in men are cancer of the prostate and lungs.
- The two most common cancers in women are breast and lung cancer.

The Integumentary System

chapter 15

OVERVIEW

- Basic concepts
- Skin structure and function
- Skin assessment
- Integumentary system disorders
- Summing it up

BASIC CONCEPTS

The integumentary system is made up of skin, hair, nails, sensory organs for touch, and glands that help maintain homeostasis. The system makes up 15 percent of a person's body weight and its primary functions are protection, temperature regulation, sensation, and storage. Its appearance is a sensitive indicator of overall health. Preserving skin integrity is a major nursing function, as any break presents a significant portal of entry for infection.

SKIN STRUCTURE AND FUNCTION

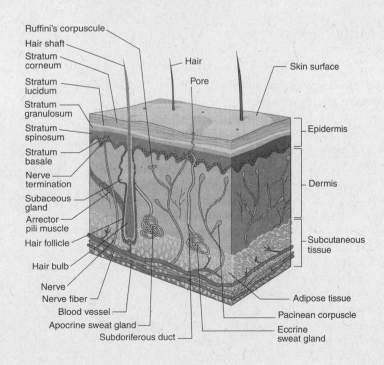

Ruffini's corpuscule
Hair shaft
Stratum corneum
Stratum lucidum
Stratum granulosum
Stratum spinosum
Stratum basale
Nerve termination
Subaceous gland
Arrector pili muscle
Hair follicle
Hair bulb
Nerve
Nerve fiber
Blood vessel
Apocrine sweat gland
Subdoriferous duct
Hair
Pore
Skin surface
Epidermis
Dermis
Subcutaneous tissue
Adipose tissue
Pacinean corpuscle
Eccrine sweat gland

A. **Anatomy**
1. **Epidermis**—outermost layer, contains the melanin pigment and dead cells that are constantly being replaced
2. **Dermis**—living cells underneath the epidermis that perform most of the skin functions
3. **Subcutaneous Tissue**—primarily fat cells that give skin a smooth appearance and act as a cushion; it also activates vitamin D for use by the body
4. **Nail**—hard layer of keratin growing from the root beneath the cuticle of the nail bed; may reflect systemic illnesses
   a. Clubbing—nail becomes convex due to chronic hypoxia as with cardiac or respiratory problems
   b. Beau's line—a transverse groove caused by a temporary halt in nail growth due to a systemic disorder
5. **Hair**—covers the entire body except for the palms of the hands and the soles of the feet
   a. Grows from hair follicles located in the dermis.
   b. Has a protective function.
   c. Hair growth is controlled by hormones and blood supply. Loss of hair is called alopecia.
6. **Glands**
   a. Sebaceous—oil glands stimulated by sex hormones
   b. Eccrine—sweat glands that regulate body temperature
   c. Apocrine—sweat glands in the axilla and pubic areas

B. **Skin Functions**
1. **Protection**—barrier to external agents such as bacteria and chemicals; prevents loss of fluid and electrolytes
2. **Thermoregulation**—cools by evaporation, radiant heat loss
3. **Sensory Perception**—touch, temperature, pressure, pain
4. **Excretion**—water and urea are excreted, water balance is maintained

SKIN ASSESSMENT

NOTE
Dermatologic Diagnostic Testing
Skin biopsy
Skin cultures
Skin testing for allergies
Wood's light exam

A. **Health History**
1. Presenting problem and symptoms
2. Lifestyle and health behaviors
3. Nutrition
4. Family medical history
5. Client's medical history
6. Medications

B. **Physical Exam**
1. **Inspection**
   a. Color—assess in good light and check mucous membranes to verify
      (1) Pallor (white)
      (2) Flushed (red)
      (3) Ashen (gray)
      (4) Cyanotic (blue)
      (5) Jaundiced (yellow)
   b. Discolorations
      (1) Ecchymosis—black and blue marks
      (2) Petechiae—red pinpoint hemorrhages

(3) Purpura—bruising, as above, usually due to a low platelet count (thrombocytopenia)
(4) Erythema—red area, as in sunburn
(5) Identify lesions if present (see chart, below)

2. Palpation
   a. Skin temperature—any changes in extremities, warmth from infection
   b. Skin turgor—ability to resume its original shape
   c. Pitting edema

Primary Skin Lesions

Lesion	Characteristics	Example
Macule	Flat area of color change	Freckle
Papule	Raised lesion, less than 1 cm in diameter	Wart
Vesicle	Small, fluid-filled lesion	Blister
Nodule	Hard, elevated, and solid lesion	Enlarged lymph node
Bulla	Vesicle larger than 1 cm	Poison Ivy
Pustule	A vesicle or bulla containing pus	Acne
Wheal	Raised, irregular lesions that may itch	Mosquito bite

INTEGUMENTARY SYSTEM DISORDERS

A. Contact Dermatitis—an inflammatory skin response that includes redness, edema, skin thickening, and frequent scaling. There may also be vesicles and papules. It is due to direct contact with an allergen.
1. **Assessment**
   a. Erythema and itching
   b. History of direct contact with an agent to which the client is sensitive
2. **Medical Treatment**
   a. Allergy testing
   b. Systemic medication: antihistamines, antipruritics, and corticosteroids
3. **Nursing Interventions**
   a. Prevent scratching.
   b. Instruct client to keep fingernails short.
   c. Administer medications as ordered.
   d. Tepid bath or wet compresses for itching, if helpful.

B. Eczema or Atopic Dermatitis—an inflammatory skin disorder, which primarily involves the epidermis. Local eruptions that tend to recur. There is frequently a family history of sensitivity.
1. **Assessment**
   a. Intense itching
   b. Papules and vesicles—area may be eroded, weeping, and/or crusted
2. **Medical Treatment**
   a. Allergy testing and identification of cause
   b. Symptomatic
3. **Nursing Interventions**
   a. Provide wet dressings or baths for comfort.
   b. Instruct client not to scratch.
   c. Suggest use of calamine lotion.

C. Psoriasis—a chronic dermatitis that involves increased turnover rate of epidermal cells. May be familial and is precipitated by stress, illness, or trauma.
1. **Assessment**
   a. Mild itching
   b. Circumscribed scaling plaques on knees, elbows, scalp
2. **Medical Treatment**
   a. Topical corticosteroids
   b. Ultraviolet light
   c. Coal tar preparations
3. **Nursing Interventions**
   a. Administer medications as ordered.
   b. Educate client about appearance of skin, importance of adhering to treatment plan.

D. Acne Vulgaris—a skin disorder involving eruption of papules or pustules due to increased production of sebum that may be caused by adolescent hormone changes, especially increasing androgen levels
1. **Assessment**
   a. Non-inflammatory—whiteheads and blackheads
   b. Inflammatory—acne pustules, scarring is possible
2. **Medical Treatment**
   a. Birth control pills
   b. Preparations that dry and peel squamous cells of the skin, allowing free flow of sebum
   c. Oral Accutane (for cystic acne)—causes birth defects
   d. Tetracycline or topical antibiotics
   e. Retin-A cream, which reduces acne scarring
3. **Nursing Interventions**
   a. Instruct in good skin care, including avoidance of greasy creams.
   b. Squeezing or picking at acne may cause infection and increased chance of scarring.
   c. Encourage rest, sunlight, and stress management.
   d. Support client in maintaining positive body image despite skin problems.

E. Cellulitis—infection of the dermis or subcutaneous tissue caused by streptococcus or staphylococcus; may be a wound infection
1. **Assessment**
   a. Pain, itching, swelling, erythema
   b. Increased number of leukocytes
2. **Medical Treatment**
   a. Systemic antibiotics
3. **Nursing Interventions**
   a. Administer antibiotics as ordered.
   b. If extremity is involved, keep it elevated and apply heat.
   c. Encourage client to rest.
   d. Provide support and teaching about home follow-up care.

F. Skin Malignancies
1. **Basal Cell Carcinoma**—tumor arising from the basal layer of the epidermis; small, smooth papule

a. **Assessment**
  (1) Starts as a papule and grows slowly. Center of lesion may become depressed and ulcerated.
  (2) Invasive locally, does not usually metastasize.
b. **Medical Treatment**
  (1) Surgical removal.
  (2) If lesion is on eye or nose, radiation therapy.
  (3) Monitor closely for recurrences.
c. **Nursing Interventions**
  (1) Educate client about avoiding sunlight and using sunscreen.
  (2) Stress the need for ongoing follow-up for other possible malignancies.

2. **Squamous Cell Carcinoma**—epidermal tumor that usually occurs on areas exposed to the sun. It starts out as a papule, plaque, or nodule and evolves to an eroded, crusty tumor. Faster growing than basal cell cancer.
  a. **Assessment**
    (1) Tumor with scaling plaque or ulceration
    (2) Adenopathy may be present in larger tumors
  b. **Medical Treatment**
    (1) Biopsy to confirm type.
    (2) Tumor should be removed with an approximately 5 mm margin.
    (3) If tumor is poorly differentiated, refer for Moh's technique, which is microscopically controlled surgery that can more precisely delineate affected tissue.
    (4) Radiation is usually employed.
  c. **Nursing Interventions**
    (1) Teach client the importance of follow-up.
    (2) Emphasize the role of sun exposure in developing this disease. Demonstrate measures to protect from the sun.
    (3) Teach self-examination and signs of possible developing cancers.

3. **Melanoma**—pigmented tumor that arises out of melanocytes and is frequently fatal. May develop from what appears to be a blue-black mole.
  a. **Assessment**
    (1) May appear from pre-existing moles
    (2) Frequently appears on back and legs

Characteristics of Melanomas
A—Asymmetry
B—Border irregularity
C—Color variations
D—Diameter greater than 6 mm

  b. **Medical Treatment**
    (1) Surgical excision, cryosurgery, electrodessication, and curettage
    (2) X-ray therapy
    (3) Topical chemotherapy (fluorouracil − 5-FU)
  c. **Nursing Interventions**
    (1) Stress the importance of avoiding sunlight.
    (2) Teach the warning signs of cancer.
    (3) Suggest removal of moles in areas that are repeatedly irritated.
    (4) Support client by pointing out coping strengths and allowing verbalization of fears.

G. Pressure Ulcers—also called decubitous ulcer or bedsore. They start as local areas of redness, that do not blanch when pressed, and progress to skin breakdown that can expose the bone.

1. **Assessment**
   a. Risk factors—immobility, poor nutrition, infection, skin dryness or excessive moisture, elderly client. Equipment that immobilizes the client such as casts, restraints, etc., are also risk factors.
   b. Clinical indications—reddened area that will not blanch, progression through four stages.

Stages of Pressure Ulcers

Stage I: Intact skin, but areas that will not blanch with external pressure.

Stage II: Partial thickness skin loss with a superficial ulcer that looks like an abrasion, blister, or shallow crater.

Stage III: Full thickness skin breakdown; necrosis or damage of tissue extends to the fascia. Ulcer presents as a deep crater.

Stage IV: Full thickness skin loss and extensive tissue destruction, necrosis, or damage to muscle and/or bone.

---

2. **Medical Treatment**
   a. Debridement to remove dying tissue
   b. Wound cleaning, which is usually with sterile saline
   c. Dressings—usually wet to dry, but newer hydrocolloid dressings are becoming popular
   d. Diet should include increased protein, carbohydrates, vitamin C, and zinc
3. **Nursing Interventions**—prevention
   a. Keep the tissue of the ulcer moist, but make sure the surrounding tissue is dry.
   b. Change position—turn client every 2 hours.
   c. Special beds that continually change pressure, or eggcrate mattress.
   d. Active and passive range of motion and gentle massage (not over bony prominences) to maintain circulation.
   e. Inspect skin frequently—especially pressure points such as bony prominences.
4. **Nursing Interventions**—promote healing
   a. Decrease amount of pressure and time pressure is maintained on any body part.
   b. Keep the skin clean and dry.
   c. Position the ulcer so it is exposed to air.
   d. Observe the ulcer for signs of infection (debridement will be necessary if this occurs).

H. Herpes Simplex Types I and II—a recurrent viral infection that spreads by direct contact. Type I primarily affects the skin and mucous membranes (cold sores) and type II, or genital herpes, affects the genital area. After a primary infection, which causes systemic malaise, the virus becomes latent and resides in the nerve fibers. Subsequent outbreaks are usually in the same place and are often associated with illness, sunburn, or stress. Type II may occur above the waist and type I on the genitalia.

1. **Assessment**
   a. Clusters of vesicles and local erythema.
   b. After prodromal burning or stinging sensation, the lesions appear and are quite painful. Viral shedding usually (but not always) occurs during outbreaks, so it is most contagious at that time.
   c. Adenopathy (enlarged lymph nodes) is often present.

2. **Medical Treatment**
   a. Diagnosis is confirmed by swabbing an open lesion and doing a Tzanck smear.
   b. Usually symptomatic, soothing compresses and analgesics.
   c. Antiviral agents (Zoviran and Famvir) are also used, both to control and prevent outbreaks.
3. **Nursing Interventions**
   a. Antihistamines for itching and analgesics for pain.
   b. Teach client about transmission of disease and the importance of careful handwashing and other hygiene measures, such as not sharing towels.
   c. Educate client about precipitating factors and to avoid sunbathing and other triggers.

I. **Herpes Zoster (shingles)**—is a reactivation of varicella, the chicken pox virus, in a client with a history of prior varicella infection. The virus had remained latent in the nerve root ganglia. It is contagious to anyone who is not immune to varicella. Most cases occur in clients over 50. It is quite painful, and the pain may persist well after the lesions have healed as a postherpetic neuralgia.
   1. **Assessment**
      a. Presence of grouped vesicles on an erythematous base, following a dermatome in distribution.
      b. Disease is often on one side (unilateral), and a history of previous varicella infection is typical.
      c. A Tzanck smear reveals multinucleated giant cells.
      d. Rash often appears on the trunk but may be on the face. It is often accompanied by myalgia and fever.
   2. **Medical Treatment**
      a. Antivirals as for HSV I and II
      b. Analgesics
      c. Antibiotic ointments to prevent secondary infection
      d. Pain clinic referral may be needed for severe neuralgia
   3. **Nursing Interventions**
      a. Monitor for complications as well as secondary infections.
      b. Teach clients about the possibility of infecting nonimmune or immunocompromised clients. Instruct to carefully wash hands and avoid sharing towels.
      c. Administer antivirals as ordered.

J. **Systemic Lupus Erythematosus**—a chronic connective tissue disease that involves multiple organs, and primarily affects young women. It is thought to be caused by immune, genetic, or possible viral factors. The body produces autoantibodies that cause problems in the kidney, heart, central nervous system, etc.
   1. **Assessment**
      a. Fatigue, malaise, fever, joint pain with morning stiffness
      b. Characterized by remissions and exacerbations
      c. "Butterfly" rash over nose and cheeks, photosensitivity
      d. Often oral or nasopharyngeal lesions
      e. Labs: elevated ESR, anemia, ANA positive, chronic false-positive test for syphilis
   2. **Medical Treatment**
      a. Drug therapy: NSAIDs to relieve mild symptoms
      b. Corticosteroids to relieve the acute inflammatory stages
      c. Immunosuppressive agents to suppress the autoimmune response when client is unresponsive to other therapies

3. **Nursing Interventions**
   a. Administer medications as ordered.
   b. Provide teaching and discharge planning concerning disease process, medication regimen, importance of sufficient rest.
   c. Need to follow daily exercises and treatments for arthritis.
   d. Suggest trying to avoid stress as much as possible, and avoid exposure to sunlight.
   e. Inform client of community agencies that can help.

K. **Burns**—destruction of skin layers by fire, chemical agents, thermal heat, electrical current, and smoke inhalation. They destroy the skin, and therefore the problems encountered are because of the loss of its protective functions, such as those of infection and fluid loss.

   1. **Assessment**
      a. The first priority in assessing a burn victim is determining if there is a patent airway and then estimating the severity of the burn. Severity is determined by both the depth of the burn and the percent of the total body surface burned.

Depth of Burn

Type of Burn	Skin injury	Description
First Degree	Epidermis	Skin reddened, painful, no blistering
Second Degree	Dermis and Epidermis	Blistered, underlying skin erythematous
Third Degree	Dermis and Subcutaneous	Skin destroyed. Dry, charred appearance—will require skin grafting to cover.
Fourth Degree	Full Thickness	Bones, muscles, nerves destroyed. No pain.

   2. **Medical Treatment**
      a. Goals
         (1) Preserving body function
         (2) Preventing infection
         (3) Providing support and comfort
         (4) Restoring ability to live normally
      b. Treatment Stages
         (1) Emergent phase—remove from source of burn; assess extent of burn; check airway, breathing, and circulation; provide IV route if possible; transport.
         (2) Shock phase—plasma to interstitial fluid shift and third spacing (fluid moving to areas that normally do not have fluid), result in hypovolemia. This results in dehydration, increased pulse, and decreased urine output and thirst.
         (3) Fluid remobilization or diuretic phase (two to five days after burn)—interstitial fluid returns to blood vessels. Blood pressure and urine output increase.
         (4) Convalescent phase—begins when diuresis is ended and healing has begun. Appearance of full thickness burn changes from dry and waxy-white to dark brown, wet and shiny. A serous exudate will be evident in partial thickness burns.

3. **Nursing Interventions**
   a. Adminster analgesics, narcotics for pain relief and 30 minutes before treatments.
   b. Monitor alterations in fluid and electrolytes—hourly Foley catheter output (urine output should be at least 30–50 cc/hour), daily weights, administer IV fluids as needed.
   c. Provide high-calorie, high-protein, high-carbohydrate diet. Frequent, small portions are best.
   d. Schedule wound care, other treatments 1 hour before meals.
   e. Prevent wound infection—controlled sterile environment, apply Sulfamylon and Silvadene as ordered.
   f. Provide client teaching and discharge planning—care of healed wound, prevention of injury to area, signs of infection. Discuss alterations in body image, suggestions for coping and referral to community resources.

Skin Changes in Older Adults

Skin becomes more fragile and transparent—more susceptible to breakdown.

Less active oil and sweat glands, so decrease frequency of skin cleansing.

Bruise easily due to a decrease in subcutaneous tissue and loss of skin elasticity.

Nails become thick and brittle—may need to be cared for by a nurse or podiatrist.

Brown spots, skin tags, and other changes in older skin make it important to monitor changes closely.

NOTE

Pediculosis, scabies, ringworm, and impetigo are discussed in Chapter 6.

EXERCISES: THE INTEGUMENTARY SYSTEM

1. When caring for her client on restraints, the nurse knows to assess the client frequently, at least as often as agency protocol dictates. Which of these assessments would *not* be related to use of restraints?

   (1) Skin integrity under the restraint

   (2) Adequate circulation in the restrained body part

   (3) Need for continued use of restraints

   (4) Adequate urinary output

2. After changing the incision dressing on his older client, the nurse reports the following findings. Which is *not* consistent with the presence of an infection?

   (1) Redness observed on the skin surrounding the incision

   (2) Skin warmth felt around the incision

   (3) Client reporting increased incisional pain

   (4) Client complaining of nausea

3. A nurse gives 90-year-old Henry T. meticulous skin care and is careful to turn him every 2 hours. During Henry's daughter's visit, the nurse explains why elderly skin changes require extra precautions. Which of the following contribute to skin breakdown in the elderly?
   Select all that apply.

   ☐ (1) The skin becomes increasingly fragile and transparent.

   ☐ (2) Oil and sweat glands become less active.

   ☐ (3) Subcutaneous tissue decreases and bruising may increase.

   ☐ (4) The skin becomes more susceptible to allergic lesions.

4. Mr. Bummel's hematology reports indicate that he is thrombocytopenic. Which of the following symptoms might the nurse observe during the assessment?

   (1) Headache and hypertension

   (2) Ecchymosis and hypertension

   (3) Purpura and petechiae

   (4) Enlarged lymph nodes

5. Miss Cope is on bed rest and has developed a reddened area on her buttocks. Which of the following would be the most effective nursing intervention?

   (1) Sit her on a pillow.

   (2) Increase her fluid intake.

   (3) Turn and position her at least every 2 hours.

   (4) Get her bed rest order changed.

6. The most important focus when assessing a burn victim is:

   (1) Maintaining a sterile field to prevent infection

   (2) Determining if there is a patent airway and estimating the extent of the injury

   (3) Determining fluid and electrolyte losses and evaluating replacement therapy

   (4) Determining circulation to burned extremities that may need escharotomies

7. Marcia, a Haitian woman, has been complaining of chronic fatigue. You want to assess her for pallor, so the best place for you to check is the

   (1) sclera.

   (2) mucous membranes of the mouth.

   (3) toenail beds.

   (4) scalp.

8. A 22-year-old female is presenting symptoms of systemic lupus erythematosus. Lab results show that she is ANA positive and has elevated ESR and anemia—all indicators of the disease. The nurse on her case reviews the possible progression of the disease with the client. Place the following symptoms in the likely chronological progression of the disease.

   (1) Inflammation of lining around various organs, such as heart, lungs, brain, liver, and kidneys _____

   (2) Muscle aches and arthritis, often severe _____

   (3) Renal failure _____

   (4) "Butterfly" rash on cheeks and nose accompanied by fatigue and photosensitivity _____

9. Frank, a client with shingles (herpes zoster), asks the nurse whether his disorder is contagious. She correctly replies:

   (1) "No."

   (2) "No, except for persons who are immunocompromised."

   (3) "Yes, any person who comes in contact with you is susceptible to infection."

   (4) "Yes, those who have a compromised immune system and/or those who are not immune from a previous infection with varicella (chicken pox) can be infected."

10. A young man is being treated for skin cancer at the clinic. He is very anxious, and the nurse reassures him that his form of skin cancer is least likely to metastasize, although he should continue to monitor his skin carefully and stay out of the sun. The man's cancer is called:

    (1) Squamous cell carcinoma

    (2) Melanoma

    (3) Teratoma

    (4) Basal Cell Carcinoma

11. The nurse is caring for a severely burned client and monitoring her hourly urine output. At the end of her 8-hour shift, the client's total output is 250 cc. What would be the most appropriate action for the nurse to take?

    (1) Chart the output and notify the RN that it is low.

    (2) Increase the rate of the IV fluids to give the client a fluid challenge.

    (3) Notify the oncoming nurse of the output and suggest she notify the RN and provider if it doesn't increase.

    (4) Chart the output and inform the oncoming nurse. Since this is a normal finding, it is not necessary to report it to the RN.

12. An 88-year-old woman is transferred from an extended-care facility to the hospital. She is presenting a Stage III pressure ulcer. Identify with an "X" on the diagram the deepest layer of tissue involved in this complication.

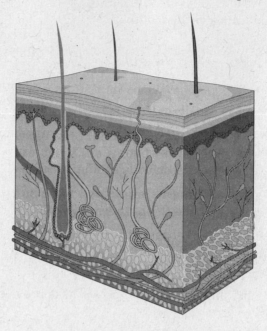

ANSWER KEY AND EXPLANATIONS

1. 4	4. 3	7. 2	10. 4
2. 4	5. 3	8. 4,2,1,3	11. 4
3. 1,2,3	6. 2	9. 4	12. subcutaneous tissue level

1. **The correct answer is (4).** Answers (1), (2), and (3) are important assessments for the client on restraints. Urinary output (4) is unrelated to this intervention.

2. **The correct answer is (4).** Nausea is unrelated to the presence of an infection. However, redness (1), warmth (2), and pain (3) are all classic signs of infection.

3. **The correct answers are (1), (2), and (3).** The skin of the older individuals becomes increasingly fragile (1), with less active oil and sweat glands (2), and less subcutaneous tissue (3), all of which lead to increased likelihood of skin breakdown. Allergic lesions, however, are not more common in the elderly.

4. **The correct answer is (3).** Low levels of thrombocytes (platelets) predispose a client to spontaneous bleeding.

5. **The correct answer is (3).** The best way to prevent skin breakdown and pressure ulcers is to move the client onto different areas of the body at frequent scheduled intervals.

6. **The correct answer is (2).** All burn victims need to be initially assessed for a patent airway. There are usually no burns evident around the nose and mouth, but damage through inhalation or restriction of the trachea from burns on the neck may suffocate a burn victim. All the answers are correct, but the airway is the most important initially.

7. **The correct answer is (2).** Pallor of the mucous membranes of the mouth is the best indicator of decreased amounts of oxyhemoglobin.

8. **The correct order of answers is (4), (2), (1), (3).** Most commonly, systemic lupus erythematosus is a chronic, lifelong disease, alternating between periods of symptom relapse or flares, and remission. The disease may not always follow a predictable pattern, but in general the initial symptoms of lupus include a telltale "butterfly" rash on the face, photosensitivity, and bouts of extreme fatigue. The onset of arthritis is a common symptom of lupus, and it may present early on. More serious cases of the disease progress to affect the lining of vital organs, and in the most severe cases complications may result in renal failure and death.

9. **The correct answer is (4).** Herpes zoster is a recurrence of the varicella virus in someone who has a history of infection. It consists of painful blisters, often on the trunk, along a dermatone. People with normal immune systems who have had chicken pox are immune to contagion.

10. **The correct answer is (4).** Basal cell carcinoma is the most common form of skin cancer in the United States. It is usually slow-growing and is considered the skin cancer that is least likely to metastasize.

11. **The correct answer is (4).** The desirable output for the client is 30–50 cc/hr, which would be between 240 and 400 cc over an 8-hour shift.

12. **The correct answer is the subcutaneous tissue level.** A Stage III pressure ulcer is full-thickness skin loss, so the deepest layer involved is the subcutaneous tissue. A pressure ulcer (or bedsore) that progresses to Stage III presents as a deep crater extending to the fascia.

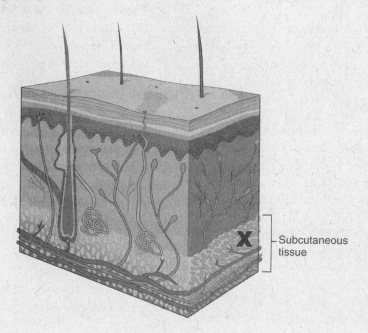

Subcutaneous tissue

SUMMING IT UP

- The integumentary system is made up of skin, hair, nails, sensory organs for touch, and glands that help maintain homeostasis.

- The integumentary system is 15 percent of a person's body weight.

- Its primary functions are protection, temperature regulation, sensation, and storage.

- Preserving skin integrity is a major nursing function.

The Respiratory System

OVERVIEW

- Basic concepts
- Anatomy and physiology
- Diagnostic tests for respiratory function
- Respiratory system disorders
- Summing it up

BASIC CONCEPTS

All cells in the body rely on adequate oxygenation and removal of carbon dioxide to function. The central nervous system regulates the respiratory system, and the oxygen is supplied by the blood via the cardiovascular system. Respiratory problems may occur alone or as part of another disorder.

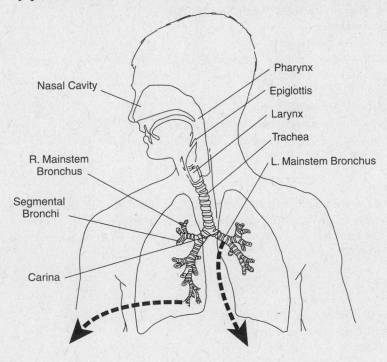

Nasal Cavity

Pharynx

Epiglottis

Larynx

Trachea

R. Mainstem Bronchus

L. Mainstem Bronchus

Segmental Bronchi

Carina

chapter 16

ANATOMY AND PHYSIOLOGY

A. Nose
1. **Structure**
   a. Nasal septum and four pairs of sinuses
   b. Cavities lined with ciliated mucous membrane
2. **Function**
   a. Air passage
   b. Filters, warms, moistens air
   c. Organ of smell

B. Pharynx
1. **Structure**
   a. Tubelike structure lined with ciliated mucous membrane
   b. Subdivided
   c. Nasopharynx—prevents food from entering trachea when swallowing
   d. Oropharynx—palatine tonsils on either side
   e. Laryngopharynx—lower portion of pharynx
2. **Function**
   a. Passage for food and air
   b. Aids in speech

C. Larynx
1. **Structure**
   a. Cartilage
      (1) Thyroid cartilage (Adam's apple)
      (2) Epiglottis
      (3) Cricoid cartilage
   b. Glottis—opening of the vocal cords and narrowest portion of larynx
   c. Epiglottis—area above the glottis
2. **Function**
   a. Controls flow of air
   b. Stops foreign objects from entering lungs
   c. Production of sound (glottis)

D. Trachea
1. **Structure**
   a. Tube shaped with walls of smooth muscle and C-shaped cartilage rings
   b. Lower end divides into right and left mainstem bronchi
   c. Right bronchus is wider—aspirated objects more likely to enter right lung
2. **Function**—Air passage

E. Lungs
1. **Structure**
   a. Located in thoracic cavity divided by the mediastinum
   b. Right lung has three lobes
   c. Left lung has two lobes
   d. Pleura
      (1) Visceral—on surface of the lung
      (2) Parietal—covers inside of chest wall

2. **Function**
   a. Distribute air to the alveoli at the end of each terminal respiratory bronchiole.
   b. Alveoli are the site of air exchange—CO_2 for O_2.
   c. Alveoli produce surfactant that allows them to expand and prevents collapse. (Premature infants often have insufficient surfactant that makes breathing difficult)
   d. Bronchial arteries bring nutrients to the lung tissue, but aren't involved in gas exchange.

F. Respiratory Physiology

1. **Inspiration and expiration**—two phases of breathing
   a. Inspiration (voluntary)
   b. Expiration (passive)
2. **Respiratory center**—controls breathing
   a. Located in the medulla oblongata
   b. Chemoreceptors that are sensitive to rising CO_2 levels in the blood stimulate breathing
3. **Compliance**
   a. Elasticity of the lung
   b. Decreased compliance makes breathing difficult
   c. Conditions that reduce compliance are pulmonary fibrosis, pneumonia, pulmonary edema, and others
4. **Carotid and aortic baroreceptors**
   a. Monitor arterial O_2 levels
   b. Stimulate breathing if O_2 levels fall below 60 mmHg pressure
   c. COPD clients and others used to high CO_2 levels use this mechanism (hypoxia) to breathe

G. Assessment

1. **Objective data (observable)**
   a. Respiratory rate and depth
   b. Symptoms of hypoxia
   c. Cough and associated symptoms
   d. Breath sounds, such as crackles, wheezes, or a friction rub
   e. Sputum characteristics, if applicable
   f. Skin color and temperature
   g. Vital signs
2. **Subjective data (reported by client)**
   a. Cough, sputum
   b. Pain or difficulty breathing
   c. Fatigue/weakness
3. **History**
   a. Dyspnea or need for extra pillows at night
   b. Respiratory illness
   c. Injuries
   d. Smoking
   e. Medications or respiratory equipment
   f. Seasonal allergies
   g. Occupation and environmental factors

DIAGNOSTIC TESTS FOR RESPIRATORY FUNCTION

Diagnostic Tests

Chest X-ray: Used to diagnose many conditions by showing changes caused by disease.

Bronchoscopy: Inspection of the trachea and bronchi through a tube inserted through the nose or mouth. May remove specimens for biopsy or foreign bodies. Nurse prepares as for surgery, sedative given, npo after until gag reflex returns.

Pulmonary Function Tests: Evaluates lung capacity and function. Assesses arterial O_2 and CO_2. Measures air flow, including vital capacity, timed vital capacity, and tidal volume.

Thoracentesis: Removal of fluid from the chest by a needle using local anesthetic. May be used to diagnose a disease or to remove excessive fluid.

Sputum Analysis: Used to determine presence of acid-fast bacillus (TB) or for cytology to detect lung carcinoma.

Arterial Blood Gas: Measures partial pressure of O_2 and CO_2 (pO_2 and pCO_2) as well as pH, which measures blood acidity (present with hypoxia). Bicarbonate—HCO_3—is used to buffer acid in the body and is elevated if the blood is acidic. Nurse should document vital signs and use of O_2 prior to test, apply pressure to area after.

Normal ABG Values

paO_2 — 80–100 mmHg
pH — 7.35–7.45
pCO_2 — 35–45 mmHg
HCO_3 — 22–28 mEq/L

RESPIRATORY SYSTEM DISORDERS

NOTE

Croup, asthma, and pneumonia are discussed in Chapter 6.

A. **Chronic Obstructive Pulmonary Disease (COPD)**—Asthma, chronic bronchitis, emphysema, and other often progressive disorders that affect expiratory air flow
    1. **Asthma** (see Chapter 6)
    2. **Chronic bronchitis**—progressive disorder caused by infection or irritant that leads to excessive mucus production, narrowing of small airways, and impaired airway clearance
        a. Assessment
           (1) Productive cough with gray sputum
           (2) Dyspnea
           (3) Wheezing
        b. Medical Diagnosis
           (1) Chest X-ray
           (2) Pulmonary function tests
           (3) ABGs

   c. Medical Treatment
     (1) Rest and increased fluid intake
     (2) Protection from infection
     (3) Oxygen and medications for relief of symptoms
   d. Nursing Interventions
     (1) If client smokes, encourage quitting.
     (2) Provide oxygen therapy, if needed.
     (3) Promote respiratory function by breathing exercises, increased fluid intake, and rest.

Abnormal Respiration

Dyspnea: Labored or difficult breathing

Hyperventilation: Increased rate and depth of breathing ($\rightarrow$ loss of CO_2)

Tachypnea: Rapid shallow breathing (possible $CO_2 \uparrow$)

Bradypnea: Slow but regular breathing, possibly due to drugs

Cheyne-Stokes: Episodes of apnea alternating with hyperventilation (heart failure, brain damage)

Kussmaul's: Deep rapid breathing associated with diabetic ketoacidosis

Good Health Practices for Clients with COPD

- Stop smoking.
- Get the recommended immunizations.
- Follow the recommended diet.
- Avoid spicy foods.
- Avoid very hot or very cold.
- Avoid gas-producing foods.
- Alternate periods of rest and activity.
- Avoid temperature extremes.
- Avoid environmental allergens such as feather pillows and pet dander.
- Use a wet cloth to dust.

 3. **Emphysema**—chronic progressive disorder in which the alveoli (air sacs) distend and rupture, trapping air in the lungs, which impedes air exchange
   a. Assessment
     (1) Respiratory symptoms as with bronchitis
     (2) Barrel (rounded) chest
     (3) Other respiratory symptoms, such as difficulty talking, pursed lip breathing, or use of accessory muscles on inspiration; medical diagnosis (as with chronic bronchitis)
   b. Medical Treatment
     (1) Medications to relieve symptoms
     (2) Oxygen
   c. Nursing Interventions
     (1) See chronic bronchitis.
     (2) Administer diuretics, bronchidilators, or steroids as ordered.
     (3) Monitor respiratory status.
     (4) Administer oxygen as ordered.

B. Tuberculosis—an acute or chronic respiratory infection that causes lung inflammation progressing to encapsulated lesions. It is transmitted by inhaled droplets, and once infected, a person will always have a positive PPD skin test.

1. **Assessment**
   a. Anorexia, weight loss
   b. Fever and night sweats
   c. Fatigue
   d. Cough and possible hemoptysis (spitting up blood)

2. **Medical Diagnosis**
   a. Positive tine or Mountoux tuberculin skin test
   b. Chest X-ray
   c. Sputum containing acid-fast bacilli

3. **Medical Treatment**
   a. Give antituberculin drugs for six to twenty-four months.
   b. Rest, nutritious diet.
   c. Respiratory precautions including a negative pressure room and masks to prevent transmission. Client is infectious until two to four weeks of drug treatment.

4. **Nursing Interventions**
   a. Educate about need for long-term treatment and possible initiation of directly observed drug treatment (compliance problems have led to resistant organisms).
   b. Reportable disease. Public health problem associated with malnutrition, crowded living conditions, and immunocompromised clients.
   c. Advise client that close contacts should be tested and inform about possible prophylactic treatment.
   d. Administer anti-tuberculin drugs, including rifampin, isoniazid, and ethambutol; multiple drug therapy decreases the emergence of resistant bacteria.
   e. Instruct about prevention of transmission by ensuring proper respiratory isolation, including HEPA filter masks and negative pressure room.

C. Influenza—acute, frequently epidemic, infectious disease caused by a virus

1. **Assessment**
   a. Sudden onset with variable symptoms
   b. Headache, muscle aches
   c. Coughing, sneezing, nasal discharge
   d. Nausea and vomiting
   e. Malaise

2. **Medical Diagnosis** (client history and physical assessment)

3. **Medical Treatment**
   a. Prevention with yearly influenza vaccine
   b. Symptomatic

4. **Nursing Interventions**
   a. Provide rest, fluids, and antipyretics if needed.
   b. Offer supportive care.

D. Cancer of the Larynx—most common in men over 50, associated with heavy alcohol use and smoking

1. **Assessment**
   a. Only early symptom is hoarseness
   b. Later symptoms include pain, dysphagia, and enlarged lymph nodes
   c. Feeling of "lump in the throat"

2. **Medical Diagnosis**
   a. History, physical exam
   b. CT scan of neck

      c. Biopsy
- 3. **Medical Treatment**
  - a. Radiation, chemotherapy
  - b. Surgery
    - (1) Laryngectomy—may be partial or complete
    - (2) Radical neck dissection—removal of epiglottis, thyroid cartilage, lymph nodes; a permanent tracheostomy is needed
- 4. **Nursing Interventions**
  - a. Remember that patent airway is most important postoperative consideration.
  - b. Help client communicate.
  - c. Provide emotional support.

E. Lung Cancer—usually associated with smoking and one of the leading causes of cancer death
- 1. **Assessment**
  - a. Usually asymptomatic in early stages
  - b. Later cough, chest pain, hemoptysis
- 2. **Medical Diagnosis**
  - a. Sputum cell analysis
  - b. Chest X-ray
  - c. Bronchoscopy and biopsy
- 3. **Medical Treatment**—poor prognosis unless early detection and treatment
  - a. Radiation
  - b. Chemotherapy
  - c. Surgery
    - (1) Lobectomy—removal of a lobe of the lung
    - (2) Pneumectomy—removal of the entire lung
- 4. **Nursing Interventions**
  - a. Preoperative and postoperative care, including careful monitoring of respiratory status
  - b. Chest tube (or Pleurevac) if needed
    - (1) Purpose of water-sealed chest drainage is to maintain negative pressure in the pleural cavity to promote lung re-expansion.
    - (2) Nurse is responsible for monitoring and documenting amount and characteristics of drainage and monitoring for patency and proper functioning of chest tubes
      - (a) Full drainage bottle should not be emptied—notify provider.
      - (b) Chest tubes from client must not be exposed to air.
      - (c) Constant bubbling of fluid in water seal chamber indicates a leak.
      - (d) Tubing should not be clamped during transportation or ambulation.
      - (e) If system is damaged or disconnected, cover opening immediately to maintain seal, remain with the client, and call for help.
    - (3) Position the pneumonectomy client on the operative side to promote drainage and full expansion of remaining lung
      - (a) Provide support to client and family to help cope with possibly terminal illness.

F. Pneumothorax or Hemothorax—pneumothorax is accumulation of air in the pleural space; hemothorax is an accumulation of blood
- 1. **Assessment**
  - a. Sudden, sharp chest pain
  - b. Diminished breath sounds
  - c. Dyspnea, tachycardia
  - d. Shift of trachea toward unaffected side

NOTE

Know positioning of client after lung surgery, nursing responsibilities with chest tubes, and closed drainage systems.

2. **Medical Diagnosis**
   a. Clinical signs and symptoms
   b. Chest X-ray

3. **Medical Treatment**
   a. Chest tubes or thoracentesis
   b. Oxygen as needed

4. **Nursing Interventions**
   a. Maintain ongoing respiratory and cardiovascular assessment.
   b. Administer oxygen therapy.
   c. Monitor chest tube status.
   d. Assist with turning, coughing, deep breathing, and incentive spirometry to enhance mobilizaton of secretions.

G. **Pulmonary Embolus**—obstruction of a pulmonary blood vessel by fat, air, or a mobilized thrombus (clot). Risk factors include obesity, immobility, abdominal surgery, and birth control pills.

1. **Assessment**
   a. Dyspnea
   b. Sudden, sharp chest pain
   c. Cyanosis
   d. Anxiety, tachycardia
   e. May result in sudden death if a large pulmonary vessel is involved

2. **Medical Diagnosis**
   a. Pulmonary angiogram
   b. Lung scan
   c. ABGs

3. **Medical Treatment**
   a. Anticoagulant administration—heparin or warfarin (Coumadin) to treat and prevent blood clots
   b. Fibrinolytics—streptokinase or urokinase to help dissolve the clot
   c. Bed rest and oxygen

4. **Nursing Interventions**
   a. Administer oxygen as indicated.
   b. Position dyspneic client in semi-Fowler's if not contraindicated to promote chest expansion and ventilation.
   c. Monitor laboratory clotting studies: PTT and PT to titrate anticoagulants and antifibrolytics.
   d. Record intake and output to detect fluid overload.
   e. Assess for a positive Homan's sign (leg pain on dorsiflexion of the foot) to detect possible formation of thrombophlebitis.

Oxygen Administration

Used to treat hypoxemia (low blood oxygen).

Ordered in liters per minute (L/minute).

Oxygen must always be humidified.

Higher concentrations are delivered by masks and ventilators; lower concentrations by nasal cannula.

Signs to prohibit smoking should be posted, since oxygen promotes combustion.

High levels of oxygen over a long period of time can cause damage to the retina and cornea.

Caution should be used in COPD clients, since oxygen may depress their respiratory drive and result in respiratory arrest.

An oxygen analyzer is used to monitor levels of O_2. It is calibrated using room air, which is approximately 20 percent oxygen.

EXERCISES: THE RESPIRATORY SYSTEM

1. Paula is admitted to the unit with pulmonary emphysema. As her nurse, you know that the oxygen must be delivered

   (1) by a mask that will maintain a high O_2 concentration.

   (2) at 10 L/minute or more.

   (3) only at night.

   (4) in low concentrations.

2. A client who is being evaluated for pulmonary tuberculosis is being admitted to the med surg floor. The *primary* consideration in her room placement will be which of the following?

   (1) She can only be put with another client who has a respiratory disorder.

   (2) She must be admitted to a negative pressure room.

   (3) She must be placed near the nursing station in case of an emergency.

   (4) She must be in a room with another woman who is close to her in age.

3. The nurse is caring for a client who is receiving 90 percent oxygen. Before putting the mask on, he checks the oxygen analyzer to determine that it is delivering the correct amount. What percentage of oxygen should the analyzer indicate when it is in room air?

   (1) 20 percent

   (2) 90 percent

   (3) 50 percent

   (4) 8 percent

4. A client is admitted to the hospital with chronic obstructive pulmonary disease (COPD). What are some of the signs and symptoms of COPD?
   Select all that apply.

   ☐ (1) Dyspnea on exertion

   ☐ (2) Clubbed fingers and toes

   ☐ (3) Shortened expiratory phase

   ☐ (4) Excessive mucus production

5. When checking the apical pulse of a client who has suddenly developed respiratory distress, the nurse notes that the point of maximal impulse has shifted to the left. What disorder does the client probably have?

   (1) Pneumothorax

   (2) Pleurisy

   (3) Emphysema

   (4) Pulmonary embolus

6. As the postoperative client begins to wake up, she rolls over and manages to pull out one of her chest tubes. The nurse's first action will be to

   (1) call for help.

   (2) reinsert and tape the tube.

   (3) check the client's respiratory status.

   (4) cover the opening to maintain the seal.

7. A nurse is caring for Tom C., a second-day postop laryngectomy client. During his assessment, he told the nurse he drank "a few beers" most evenings to relax. He had trouble sleeping last night, and he appears to be getting increasingly agitated. He is also tremulous, and his pulse and blood pressure are elevated. A life-threatening complication he may have is

   (1) hemothorax.
   (2) delirium tremens.
   (3) hypoxia.
   (4) pleurisy.

8. Maria S., a 48-year-old woman, is about to have a hysterectomy. She weighs 194 pounds, and the only medication she takes is Ortho Tri-Cyclen to help regulate her period and ease perimenopausal symptoms. In light of this information, what intervention will be extremely important postoperatively?

   (1) Early ambulation
   (2) Incentive spirometry
   (3) Monitoring closely for bleeding problems
   (4) Adequate pain management

ANSWER KEY AND EXPLANATIONS

1. 4	3. 1	5. 1	7. 2
2. 2	4. 1,2,4	6. 4	8. 1

1. **The correct answer is (4).** Clients with emphysema rely on low oxygen levels to stimulate respiration. High levels will depress the respiratory drive and cause respiratory depression and arrest.

2. **The correct answer is (2).** A possible tuberculosis client must be placed on respiratory isolation in a negative pressure room.

3. **The correct answer is (1).** An oxygen analyzer is used to monitor levels of O_2. It is calibrated using room air, which is approximately 20 percent oxygen.

4. **The correct answers are (1), (2), and (4).** Typical findings in clients with COPD include dyspnea (labored breathing) on exertion (1) and excessive mucous production (4). Another sign of COPD that can be caused by chronic hypoxia is clubbed fingers and toes (2). Clients with COPD typically have a prolonged expiratory phase.

5. **The correct answer is (1).** A pneumothorax is due to air in the pleural space that causes the complete or partial collapse of the lung. The unaffected lung will then expand, shifting the mediastinum to the opposite side.

6. **The correct answer is (4).** The chest tube maintains negative pressure in the pleural cavity, and this allows the lungs to expand. When the negative pressure is stopped, air rushes in and the lung will collapse. Covering the opening will help to prevent this.

7. **The correct answer is (2).** A laryngectomy is surgery performed on clients with cancer of the larynx. This cancer is associated with smoking and heavy alcohol use, so the mention of drinking in his assessment as well as his current symptoms suggest it might be possible that he abuses alcohol.

8. **The correct answer is (1).** Because of her scheduled abdominal surgery, excess weight, and birth control medication, Maria is at very high risk for DVT (deep vein thrombosis). Early ambulation is the best intervention to prevent venous stasis and reduce the risk.

SUMMING IT UP

- All cells in the body rely on adequate oxygenation and the removal of carbon dioxide to function.

- The central nervous system regulates the respiratory system and the oxygen is supplied by the blood via the cardiovascular system.

- Respiratory problems may occur on their own or as part of another disorder.

The Reproductive System

chapter 17

OVERVIEW

- Basic concepts
- The male reproductive system
- The female reproductive system
- Client assessment
- Male reproductive system disorders
- Female reproductive system disorders
- Other reproductive disorders
- Summing it up

BASIC CONCEPTS

The male and female reproductive systems influence the functioning of the genitourinary system. The hormones they produce have wide ranging psychological and physical effects on the body. Reproductive function involves not only the ability to have children, but also the social functioning, self-esteem, and comfort of clients.

THE MALE REPRODUCTIVE SYSTEM

A. External
1. **Penis**—erectile tissue, consists of the shaft and glans; outlet for urine and sperm
2. **Scrotum**—skin-covered pouch holding the testes, epididymis, and lower part of the vas deferens; located outside of the body to protect the sperm from high temperatures

B. Internal
1. **Testes**—small oval glands in testes that produce sperm and testosterone
2. **Epididymis**—narrow coiled tubes out of testes, which temporarily store the immature sperm
3. **Vas Deferens**—two short tubular structures extending from the epididymis through the inguinal canal to the ejaculatory ducts
4. **Ejaculatory Ducts**—pass through the prostate; conduct semen and seminal fluid through the penis to be ejaculated

C. Accessory Glands
   1. **Seminal Vesicles**—produce a fluid that increases sperm motility and metabolism
   2. **Prostate Gland**—produces a fluid that helps sperm motility and lubricates the urethra during sex
   3. **Bulbourethral (Cowper's) Gland**—produces an alkaline lubricating fluid that neutralizes acidic secretions in the female reproductive tract, thus prolonging sperm life

D. Semen
   1. Fluid discharged at ejaculation that carries sperm and ejaculate

E. Sperm
   1. Male germ cell

THE FEMALE REPRODUCTIVE SYSTEM

(See section in Chapter 5 for complete discussion.)

A. **External Genitalia (vulva)**
   1. **Mons Pubis**
   2. **Labia Majora**
   3. **Labia Minora**

B. **Internal Genitalia**
   1. **Ovaries**
   2. **Fallopian Tubes**
   3. **Uterus**
   4. **Cervix**
   5. **Vagina**

C. **Breasts**

D. **Menstrual Cycle Phases**
   1. **Menstrual**
   2. **Proliferative**
   3. **Secretory**
   4. **Ischemic**

E. **Ovarian Cycle Phases**
   1. **Follicular**
   2. **Luteal**

CLIENT ASSESSMENT

A. **History**
   1. **Urinary**
      a. Urgency, frequency, burning
      b. Difficulty voiding, hesitancy
      c. Incontinence
      d. Urinary retention
      e. Hematuria
   2. **Reproductive**
      a. Sexual and contraceptive history
      b. Problem description, onset and associated symptoms

      c. Female obstetrical and menstrual history

      d. Treatments and outcome

   3. **Change in Sexual Function**

      a. Problems with intercourse

        (1) Nurses should know that many medications, such as anti-hypertensives, antidepressants (especially many of the SSRIs—selective serotonin reuptake inhibitors) like Prozac, and antipsychotic medications have the effect of decreasing sexual response.

      b. Sexually transmitted diseases

B. Physical Assessment

   1. **Vital Signs**

   2. **Assessment**

      a. Inspection of external genitalia

      b. Female pelvic exam

      c. Rectal exam

      d. Diagnostic tests as indicated

MALE REPRODUCTIVE SYSTEM DISORDERS

A. Benign Prostatic Hypertrophy (BPH)—gradual obstruction of urine outflow by enlarged prostate

   1. **Assessment**

      a. Nocturia (often first symptom), dysuria, frequency, urgency, decreased flow of stream

      b. Urinary retention

      c. Urinary tract infection

   2. **Medical Diagnosis**

      a. History

      b. Examination, including rectal palpation of prostate

      c. IVP, cystoscopy, retrograde pyelography

      d. Urine culture

      e. BUN, creatinine

   3. **Medical Treatment**

      a. Symptomatic

        (1) Bladder drainage by catheter

        (2) Decompression

        (3) Antibiotics as needed

      b. Surgery

        (1) Transurethral resection of the prostate (TURP)

          (a) Removal of prostatic tissue using a resectoscope; small pieces of gland are removed under direct visualiation. This is the primary treatment for BPH. Postoperative bleeding is a common problem.

          (b) Suprapubic prostatectomy—removal of the prostate through a lower midline abdominal incision through the bladder. Continuous bladder irrigation is done postoperatively through a cystotomy tube and Foley catheter.

          (c) Retropubic prostatectomy—a low abdominal incision into the prostate gland that bypasses the bladder.

          (d) Perineal prostatectomy—incision through the scrotum and anus. Usually used for prostate cancer. Often results in impotence and urinary incontinence.

  c. Non-Surgical

    (1) Finasteride (Proscar), an androgen hormone inhibitor; may arrest prostate enlargement

    (2) TUIP—transurethral incision at bladder neck

    (3) Transcystoscopic urethroplasty—balloon dilatation of the urethra

4. **Nursing Interventions**

  a. Preoperative

    (1) Assess for adequate bladder emptying, symptoms of UTI.

    (2) Encourage increased fluid intake.

    (3) Help client discuss concerns about the surgery and its possible effect on sexual functioning.

    (4) Note any anticholinergic medications that can cause urinary retention as a side effect. May increase difficulty voiding post-surgery. Atropine is an example of a common preoperative drug that is anticholinergic.

  b. Postoperative

    (1) Continuous bladder irrigation with sterile isotonic irrigating solution

      (a) Use a triple lumen catheter—one for balloon, one for urine outflow, and one for irrigating solution being instilled.

      (b) Irrigation fluid helps prevent infection and rid the bladder of tissue and clots following TURP.

      (c) Blood clots are normal for the first 24–36 hours. Increase flow of irrigating fluid if blood clots or bright red drainage is present; slow to approximately 40 gtt/min after drainage clears. Report excessive bleeding. If it occurs, the size of the indwelling catheter balloon may need to be increased to place pressure on the area of bleeding.

      (d) It is important to prevent overdistention of the bladder due to obstruction of the drainage by clots. If client complains of pain, make sure drainage system is patent.

    (2) Bladder spasms may occur. Administer antispasmodica, analgesics as ordered.

    (3) Provide sitz bath PRN for pain and inflammation.

    (4) Have client avoid constipation and straining. Encourage increased fluids, fiber, and administer laxatives as ordered.

    (5) Use an oral thermometer, not rectal.

    (6) Teach client to contract the perineal muscles to start and stop the flow of urine.

    (7) Prior to discharge, evaluate client's ability to empty the bladder completely, and note if there is any dribbling.

    (8) Administer urinary antiseptics or antibiotics to prevent infection. Epididymitis is the most frequent complication.

NOTE

For more on cancer care, see Chapter 14.

B. Prostate Cancer—common in men over 50; survival rate is 70 percent if treated while localized

1. **Assessment**

  a. Hematuria

  b. Decreased size and force of urine stream

  c. Difficulty urinating, retention

2. **Medical Diagnosis**

  a. Prostate nodule or diffused induration palpated during digital rectal exam

  b. Increased serum phosphatase

  c. Prostate Specific Antigen (PSA) is increased

  d. Transurethral ultrasound

  e. Biopsy of prostate

3. **Medical Treatment**
    a. Surgery: TURP, Radical perineal prostatectomy
    b. Estrogen therapy
    c. Radiation (external, seed implants)
4. **Nursing Interventions**
    a. See BPH, page 291
    b. Provide support concerning fears about surgery and feminization from estrogens.

C. **Undescended Testes (Cryptorchidism)**
    1. **Assessment**
        a. Inability to palpate testes in scrotal sac
        b. Often accompanied by inguinal hernia
    2. **Medical Diagnosis**—by exam (above)
    3. **Medical Treatment**
        a. Surgery (Orchiopexy)
            (1) Usually at approximately two years
            (2) Outpatient
            (3) Testes sutured to inner wall of scrotum
        b. Long-term follow-up for fertility. However, since it usually only affects one testis, it does not rule out fatherhood.
    4. **Nursing Interventions**
        a. Keep scrotal area clean of urine and stool.
        b. Instruct parents that there is an increased risk of testicular cancer. Child to be taught self-exam when older.

D. **Testicular Cancer**—most common cancer in men ages 15–35, usually unilateral
    1. **Assessment**
        a. Palpation of a mass in the scrotum
        b. Frequently have a sensation of heaviness in the scrotum
        c. Backache, abdominal pain, weight loss if metasteses
    2. **Medical Diagnosis**
        a. Transillumination can distinguish cancer from hydrocele (fluid-filled cystic mass in testicle)
        b. CT scan to detect metastases
    3. **Medical Treatment**
        a. Surgery—orchiectomy (removal of the testis)
        b. Radiation and chemotherapy
    4. **Nursing Interventions**
        a. Teach clients monthly testicular examination to be done while showering or bathing to detect a mass.
        b. Emphasize follow-up to a client with a history of an undescended testicle or previous mass.

FEMALE REPRODUCTIVE SYSTEM DISORDERS

A. **Menstrual Abnormalities**
    1. **Amenorrhea**—absence of menstrual periods
        a. Assessment
            (1) History may indicate cause: diabetes, anorexia, excessive exercise, obesity, anxiety, endocrine problems
            (2) Absence of menses by age 17 (primary amenorrhea)
            (3) Failure of a menstrual period (secondary amenorrhea)

b. Medical Diagnosis
   (1) Pelvic exam
   (2) LH level
   (3) FSH level
   (4) Thyroid function test
   (5) Adrenal function test
   (6) Progestin challenge test to assess for withdrawal bleed
c. Medical Treatment
   (1) Varies with diagnosis
   (2) Outflow obstruction—surgery
   (3) Failure of GnRH from the hypothalamus to stimulate FSH or LH release—lifestyle problems such as exercise, weight, stress; neoplasm such as pituitary tumor; drug induced, as by marijuana or tranquilizers; treatment of cause
   (4) Ovarian failure—estrogen replacement
d. Determination of cause and addressing it
e. Nursing Interventions
   (1) Encourage client to comply with prescribed regimen.
   (2) Help client to understand cause of disorder to relieve anxiety.

2. **Menorrhagia (Hypermenorrhea)**—excessive menstrual flow
   a. Assessment
      (1) Feeling of pelvic heaviness
      (2) Fatigue
      (3) Profuse menstrual bleeding with clots
   b. Medical Diagnosis
      (1) Pelvic exam—possible fibroid
      (2) FSH and LH, thyroid levels, adrenal function test—endocrine disturbance
      (3) Pap smear
      (4) RBC count
   c. Medical Treatment—address cause
   d. Nursing Interventions
      (1) Help teach the client how to keep accurate records of menstrual flow.
      (2) Encourage continued follow-up, especially if there are cervical changes associated with cancer.

3. **Metrorrhagia**—bleeding between menstrual intervals
   a. Assessment
      (1) Feeling of pelvic heaviness
      (2) Fatigue
      (3) Spotting between menstrual periods
   b. Medical Diagnosis
      (1) Pelvic exam
      (2) LH, FSH, thyroid function, adrenal function
      (3) RBC count
      (4) Pap smear (may be an early symptom of cervical cancer)
   c. Medical Treatment—address cause
   d. Nursing interventions
      (1) Help the client maintain records of menstrual bleeding.
      (2) Encourage medical follow-up because of possible association with cervical cancer.

B. Vaginal Inflammatory Disorders
   1. **Risk Factors**—circumstances that promote bacterial growth or disrupt natural vaginal flora

ALERT!

Vaginal bleeding after menopause or surgical hysterectomy indicates a problem that should be evaluated.

    a. Medications

       (1) Oral contraceptives

       (2) Antibiotics (wipe out normal vaginal flora)

       (3) Steroids

    b. Health habits or conditions

       (1) Diabetes

       (2) Stress

       (3) Tight clothing and panty hose

2. **Inflammatory Conditions**

    a. Bacterial Vaginosis—sex partner not treated

       (1) Cause: Gardnerella vaginalis

       (2) Malodorous, gray-white vaginal discharge—"fishy" smell

       (3) Vulvar pruritis, dysuria

       (4) Treatment: Metronidazole (Flagyl)

    b. Candidiasis—sex partner not treated

       (1) Cause: Candida albicans

       (2) Internal itching, beefy red irritation, pruritis

       (3) White, cottage-cheese-like discharge

       (4) Treatment: Antifungal such as Terazole or other "azole"

    c. Trichomonas—sex partner should be treated due to cross-infection; men are often asymptomatic

       (1) Organism: Trichomonas vaginalis (protozoan)

       (2) Yellow-green, frothy discharge

       (3) "Fishy" smell may be present

       (4) Treatment: Metronidazole (Flagyl)

    d. Atrophic Vaginitis—caused by lack of estrogen

       (1) Itching and burning

       (2) Dyspareunia—painful intercourse

       (3) Treatment: local or systemic estrogen replacement

3. **Nursing Interventions**

    a. Client education to help prevent infections

       (1) Frequent tampon changes during menstruation.

       (2) No douching—washes out protective bacteria.

       (3) Partner treatment should be considered for chronic infections.

       (4) Avoid tight clothing and panty hose—cotton is best for underwear.

       (5) Avoid feminine hygiene sprays.

    b. Teaching about medication

       (1) Stress importance of handwashing before and after insertion of a vaginal suppository or cream.

       (2) Suggest client lie down for 30 minutes after application to allow absorption.

       (3) Offer client perineal pads to help prevent soiling clothes with the discharge of the ointment.

C. **Sexually Transmitted Diseases**—transmitted by sexual activity. All sex partners need to be treated. Nurses need to be able to instruct client on mode of transmission, prevention of transmission, importance of notifying and treating contacts. Interactions should be accepting and nonjudgmental.

1. **Syphilis**

    a. Transmission— caused by a spirochete, *treponema pallidum*

       (1) Average incubation period is approximately three weeks (can be ten to ninety days).

       (2) Transmission is by direct contact with a primary chancre lesion, body secretions, and through placenta to fetus.

(3) Highly infectious during the primary stage. Blood is infectious during the secondary stage. Usually noninfectious after one year in the latent stage. Tertiary phase is noninfectious.

b. Stages

(1) *Primary Stage:* After incubation period (usually three weeks) with no symptoms, a chancre appears at the site of infection. It is highly infectious. Mild localized or general symptoms may occur, such as lymph node enlargement or headache. Chancre heals in three weeks without treatment.

(2) *Secondary stage:* Three weeks after primary stage a mild rash develops on the skin (usually palms and feet) and as papules on mucous membranes. Lesions are highly contagious. Mild or generalized symptoms are possible—bone pain, sore throat, patchy hair loss. After a few weeks, the disease becomes dormant.

(3) *Tertiary (latent) stage:* Ten to thirty years later, the spirochetes, now in the tissues and organs, are in lesions (gummas). These destroy the tissue. Often are in the CNS, eyes, and aorta. Signs and symptoms relate to the organ involved.

c. Diagnostic Tests

(1) *Primary stage:* microscopic examination of smear, using darkfield.

(2) *Second and third stages:* blood serum tests (e.g., VDRL and Wasserman).

(3) *All stages:* Flourescent treponemal antibody absorption test. Most sensitive test—reactive within two weeks of primary lesion. Once positive, it is permanently so.

d. Medical Treatment

(1) Penicillin G. Benzathine

(2) Tetracycline or Erythromycin if allergic to penicillin

e. Nursing Interventions

(1) Use standard precautions to prevent infection.

(2) Urge clients to seek VDRL testing after three, six, and twelve months to detect possible relapse.

(3) Syphilis is a reportable illness, and all cases must be reported to the public health authorities.

(4) Encourage the client to inform his or her sexual partners.

(5) Refer the client and partner for HIV testing, since high-risk behaviors that gave them syphilis are likely to place the client at risk for HIV.

(6) Teach client about safer sex, and inform client about importance of completing therapy even if symptoms subside.

2. **Gonorrhea**—caused by Neisseria gonorrhoeae, highly infectious, starts as inflammation of the urethra and spreads to other organs of the genital tract; incubation three to four days

a. Assessment

(1) Female clients—no symptoms or purulent vaginal discharge, dysuria, urgency. If untreated, can spread and cause PID (pelvic inflammatory disease).

(2) Male clients have a purulent urethral discharge and burning on urination.

b. Medical Diagnosis

(1) Client history and physical

(2) Smear or culture

c. Medical Treatment

(1) Ceftriaxone, 125 mg IM × 1, or an oral dose of a cephalosporin such as Cefixine 400 mg × 1

(2) In addition, the client should be given a medication against chlamydia, such as azithromycin, 1 g po × 1

   d. Nursing Interventions
     (1) Teach safer sex.
     (2) Instruct regarding medication regimen.
     (3) Teach importance of abstinence from sexual intercourse until diagnostics are negative.
     (4) Urge client to inform sexual partners so they may be treated.

3. **Herpes simplex**—HSV I, usually above the waist, causing cold sores; HSV II, usually below the waist—genital area, transmitted by sexual contact. Cross-contamination can occur with oral/genital sex. Transmission of HSV I by oral or respiratory secretions. HSV II is transmitted by sexual contact.

   a. Assessment
     (1) Primary infection
       (a) Appetite loss
       (b) Blisters on mouth with erythematous skin
       (c) Conjunctivitis
       (d) Fever, increased salivation
       (e) Swelling of nodes under the jaw
     (2) HSV II causes
       (a) Fever, swollen lymph nodes
       (b) Fluid-filled blisters
       (c) Painful urination

   b. Diagnosis
     (1) Virus is isolated from lesions—histological biopsy
     (2) Blood studies show a rise in antibodies and moderate leukocytosis

   c. Medical Treatment
     (1) First episode—Acyclovir 200 mg po, 5x/day, seven to ten days
     (2) Daily suppressive therapy for frequent recurrences (26x/yr.)—Acyclovir 400 mg po bid

   d. Nursing Interventions
     (1) Use standard precautions. If extensive cutaneous, oral, or genital lesions, use contact precautions to prevent the spread of infection.
     (2) Administer pain medications and antiviral agents as prescribed.
     (3) Provide supportive care such as oral hygiene, nutritional supplementation, and antipyretics.
     (4) Nurses with a herpetic whitlow (an HSV finger infection) should abstain from client contact.
     (5) Teach client self-care during an outbreak
     (6) Encourage HSV clients to have an annual pap test.
     (7) Instruct client to avoid kissing those with open sores, such as eczema, if a cold sore is present.

4. **Chlamydia**—most common STD in the United States, causes symptoms similar to gonorrhea; organism: Chlamydia trachomatis

   a. Assessment
     (1) Men: urethritis, dysuria, frequency, watery mucoid discharge
     (2) Women: often asymptomatic; mucopurulent cervicitis, dysuria, frequency, local soreness; complications include PID

   b. Medical Diagnosis
     (1) Urogenital smear analysis—detect antigen
     (2) Tissue cell cultures

   c. Medical Treatment
     (1) Doxycycline or azithromycin (Zithromax)
     (2) Pregnant women should receive axithromycin in a single 1-gram dose

      d. Nursing Interventions
         (1) Use standard precautions.
         (2) Explain medication regimen.
         (3) Report cases to health department if required in your state.
         (4) Suggest HIV testing due to unsafe sex.
         (5) Evaluate newborns of infected mothers for signs of chlamydial infection.

5. **Human Papilloma Virus (Genital Warts)**
    a. Assessment
        (1) Women: clusters of warts on the vulva, vagina, and/or cervix
        (2) Men: clusters of warts on the glans penis or in the urethra
    b. Medical Diagnosis
        (1) Inspection of lesions
        (2) Culture and biopsy
    c. Medical Treatment
        (1) Cryotherapy
        (2) Acid treatments
        (3) Surgery
    d. Nursing Interventions
        (1) Educate about transmission (by direct contact) and increased chance of cervical cancer.
        (2) Instruct women to continue to follow up with pap smears.

OTHER REPRODUCTIVE DISORDERS

A. Pelvic Inflammatory Disease—an infection of the pelvic cavity involving the fallopian tubes, ovaries, or the peritoneum
    1. **Background**
        a. Can occur following abortion, pelvic surgery, childbirth; IUDs are associated with an increased risk of PID
        b. Often an ascending infection following gonorrhea or chlamydia
        c. Consequences: 10 times an increased chance in ectopic pregnancies; four times an increase in pelvic pain, sterility
    2. **Medical Diagnosis**
        a. Malaise, fever, nausea, and vomiting
        b. Leukocytosis
        c. Cervical motion tenderness, adnexal tenderness (ovaries); lower abdominal pain
        d. Evidence of presence of N. gonorrhea and/or C. trachomatis in the endocervix
    3. **Medical Treatment**
        a. Antibiotics and analgesics; antibiotics will treat gonorrhea and chlamydia
        b. May be inpatient and will be given the same or similar medications by IV
        c. Surgery—incision and drainage of abscesses
    4. **Nursing Interventions**
        a. Semi-Fowler's position may decrease tendency of infection to ascend.
        b. Excellent hygiene and good hand washing before and after voiding.
        c. Frequent perineal care.
        d. Encourage oral fluids.
        e. Client should avoid sexual intercourse until advised by health-care provider.

B. Endometriosis—presence of endometrial tissue outside the uterus. It will respond to hormonal stimulation during the menstrual cycle and bleed into areas within the pelvis, leading to pain and adhesions.

1. **Assessment**
   a. Dysmenorrhea; aching pain in lower abdomen, vagina, posterior pelvis, and back prior to menses
   b. Excessive uterine bleeding and painful intercourse
   c. Pain or difficulty in defecation
2. **Medical Diagnosis**
   a. Culdoscopy and laporoscopy
   b. Client history and symptoms
3. **Medical Treatment**
   a. Oral contraceptives or hormones to decrease tissue expansion
   b. Surgery—removing endometrial tissue in extrauterine area
4. **Nursing Interventions**
   a. Teach client about disease process and postoperative care.
   b. Reassure that sexual activity will be normal, but reproductive ability and menses will be gone.
   c. Educate about hormone replacement therapy if applicable.
   d. Tell client to avoid prolonged sitting or standing, which increase pelvic congestion.
   e. Provide support for client to discuss body image changes.

C. **Cervical Cancer**—a progressive disease, which is typically diagnosed in a woman between ages 43 and 48. Risk factors include smoking, multiple sex partners, early onset of sexual activity. Barrier contraceptives are protective.
   1. **Assessment**
      a. May be asymptomatic
      b. Leukorrhea, painless vaginal discharge between periods; becomes dark and foul smelling as the disease progresses
      c. Bleeding after intercourse
      d. Menstrual disturbances or postmenopausal bleeding
      e. Suspicious pap smear result
   2. **Medical Diagnosis**
      a. Annual pap smear should begin at 18 or when a woman becomes sexually active and should be continued after menopause or a hysterectomy
      b. Cervical biopsy
      c. Colposcop
      d. Schiller's test
      e. Cryotherapy
      f. Conization
   3. **Medical Treatment**
      a. Panhysterectomy (excision of uterus and cervix)
      b. Radiation
      c. Chemotherapy
   4. **Nursing Interventions**
      a. Preoperative and postoperative care—monitor for urinary output, difficulty voiding, vaginal hemorrhage.
      b. Radiation therapy—advise visitors to limit time with client. Maintain high fluid intake.
      c. Administer antiemetics as ordered.
      d. Support client with pelvic exenteration, who will have lost her vagina and undergone surgical menopause. There will also be a colostomy.

NOTE

For more on the urinary and renal systems, see Chapter 12.

D. Cystocele and Rectocele

1. **Assessment**—due to weakened support muscles and ligaments of the pelvis, often due to childbirth injuries or multiple pregnancies
   a. Cystocele: abnormal protrusion of the bladder against the vaginal wall; causes stress, incontinence, frequency, and urgency
   b. Rectocele: abnormal protrusion of part of the rectum against the vaginal wall; causes constipation, incontinence of gas or liquid feces
   c. Pelvic pressure, backache
   d. Residual urine after voiding (cystocele); hemorrhoids (rectocele)

2. **Medical Diagnosis**
   a. Signs and symptoms
   b. Pelvic exam

3. **Medical Treatment**
   a. Surgery
   b. Anterior and posterior colporrhaphy—"A & P repair"

4. **Nursing Interventions**
   a. Postoperative—catheter care, perineal care. Heat lamp, ice packs, or anesthetic spray to relieve discomfort.
   b. Teach client to avoid heavy lifting and prolonged standing and sitting.
   c. Alert client to avoid sexual intercourse until approved by provider.
   d. Instruct client in pelvic floor exercises (Kegels).

E. Breast Cancer—risk factors include age (women over 50), a family history of breast cancer; no children or first child after age 30. Early menstruation and late menopause are also associated with increased risk. Ovary removal prior to age 40 decreases risk. Recurrence rate is almost 25 percent.

1. **Assessment**
   a. Breast asymmetry
   b. Skin dimpling, nipple retraction
   c. Nipple discharge
   d. Painless, nontender, fixed mass—usually in upper outer quadrant of breast

2. **Medical Diagnosis**
   a. Mammogram
   b. Biopsy

3. **Medical Treatment**
   a. Surgical
      (1) Lumpectomy—removal of the mass plus some normal surrounding tissue
      (2) Axillary node dissection—may be done to stage the malignancy
      (3) Simple mastectomy—removal of the breast
      (4) Modified radical mastectomy—removal of all breast tissue, axillary nodes, and overlying skin
      (5) Radical mastectomy—removal of the breast, pectoral muscles, pectoral fascia, and nodes
   b. Radiation—early-stage treatment may include this as well as a lumpectomy and an axillary node resection
   c. Hormonal therapy
   d. Chemotherapy

4. **Nursing Interventions**
   a. Educate women about risk factors, breast self-exam.
   b. Recommend that women over 40 have a mammogram every one to two years, women over 50 every year.
   c. Assist client with side effects of radiation or chemotherapy.
   d. Anticipate concerns about sexuality and fear of rejection by her husband or sex partner.

e. The arm on the affected side will be at increased risk of edema and infection due to the removal of the axillary lymph node tissue. Avoid procedures that impair skin integrity or hamper circulation.

f. Teach client arm exercises and squeezing a ball for early exercise. After two to three weeks, more active rehabilitative exercises are started.

g. Educate client about the need for continued follow-up assessments by her provider to monitor for recurrence.

h. Promote a positive self-image. Encourage her to participate in the Reach for Recovery or Look Good, Feel Better programs through the American Cancer Society.

EXERCISES: THE REPRODUCTIVE SYSTEM

1. Marcia asks about the risks she faces after having had pelvic inflammatory disease (PID). The nurse correctly informs her that

    (1) as long as she doesn't douche, there will be no problem.

    (2) ectopic pregnancies and infertility related to tubal problems are related to PID.

    (3) she may no longer use an IUD for contraception.

    (4) it is possible that she may have a greater chance of having multiple births.

2. Mr. Klein has been admitted to the med surg floor after a TURP (transurethral prostatectomy). You are doing the second set of vitals and make the following observations. Which of these findings should be reported to the RN?

    (1) Bloody drainage and some clots in the irrigation tubing.

    (2) Mr. Klein asks if he will be able to have sex again.

    (3) Mr. Klein states that he feels as if he needs to urinate even though the catheter is in.

    (4) Mr. Klein says that he has bladder pain.

3. Melanie, a 25-year-old woman who is being treated with Zoloft for depression, tells the nurse that she has not been enjoying sex as much as she had before starting on the drug. Aware of the side effects of this medication, the nurse replies that SSRI antidepressants and some of the following types of drugs can affect sexual function in men and women. Which of the following medications may have this effect?
Select all that apply.

    ☐ (1) Antihypertensives

    ☐ (2) Phenothiazines

    ☐ (3) Nonsteroidal anti-inflammatory drugs (NSAIDs)

    ☐ (4) Antipsychotic medications

4. A 62-year-old male, Tom Miller, underwent surgery last week for prostate cancer. The procedure was a perineal prostatectomy, which often causes impotence and urinary incontinence. The nurse can teach the client Kegel exercises to help improve his ability to control the flow of urine. To help promote positive sexual expression, the nurse can *best* help the client by

    (1) initiating a discussion with the client and his partner about potential sexual problems and possible ways to deal with them.

    (2) refraining from discussing the matter, since it may upset him.

    (3) emphasizing the importance of the emotional bond with his partner.

    (4) maintaining an optimistic attitude that there will be no problems.

5. The nurse is teaching the gynecological client about cervical cancer. The nurse states that it is more common among smokers and women who have had human papilloma virus (genital warts), and it is also associated with

    (1) the use of an IUD or a cervical cap.

    (2) frequent intercourse.

    (3) PMS and other difficulties with menstruation.

    (4) early onset of intercourse and multiple partners.

6. Bridget has been diagnosed with AIDS. You are teaching her the three most common routes of transmission, which are

    (1) saliva, blood, and cerebrospinal fluid.

    (2) urine, vaginal secretions, and feces.

    (3) tears, respiratory secretions, and urine.

    (4) sexual intercourse, placental transmission, and blood.

7. The nurse is admitting a 65-year-old man with congestive heart failure. Aware that men over 50 are at risk for benign prostatic hypertrophy, the nurse suspects this condition when the client says,

    (1) "I seem to get cold very easily, especially my feet."

    (2) "I have to get up several times a night to urinate, and then I have trouble starting to go."

    (3) "My ankles are swollen."

    (4) "My hand trembles when I try to pick up something."

8. Adele Franklin, an 80-year-old woman in the hospital for a broken hip, has had a long-standing problem with urinary retention. Which of the following assessments would the nurse be sure to include when she checks this client?

    (1) Ask her if she has problems with frequency, urgency, or burning with urination.

    (2) Assess the color of her urinary output.

    (3) Determine the specific gravity of her urine.

    (4) Ask about her bowel habits.

9. Tom and Kirsten married a year ago. They are very upset about Tom's diagnosis of testicular cancer and are talking to the nurse about it. Kirsten says that they were about to start a family and are fearful this will not be possible now. The nurse correctly replies,

    (1) "Testicular cancer is almost always unilateral, so Tom may still be able to be a father."

    (2) "There are many new technologies available now. I'm sure you could use donor sperm."

    (3) "It is too early to think of that. You'll be lucky if you still have a husband."

    (4) "Only a specialist can answer that question."

10. An RN in an OB/GYN's office is instructing a PN student about the order of events in the menstrual cycle. Arrange the items below in order as they occur in the progression of the menstrual cycle from Day 1 to Day 28.

    (1) Estrogen levels drop sharply and progesterone dominates.   _____

    (2) Estrogen levels are low and the endometrium is shed.   _____

    (3) Progesterone levels decrease, blood vessels rupture, and blood escapes into cells of the uterus.   _____

    (4) Endometrium thickens, estrogen level rises and peaks, and ovum is released.   _____

exercises

ANSWER KEY AND EXPLANATIONS

1. 2	3. 1,2,4	5. 4	7. 2	9. 1
2. 4	4. 1	6. 4	8. 1	10. 2,4,1,3

1. **The correct answer is (2).** Pelvic inflammatory disease affects the fallopian tubes and can affect transport of the fertilized egg through the tubes, causing either a tubal pregnancy or infertility.

2. **The correct answer is (4).** Bladder pain may be an indication of an obstruction in the tubing that could cause overdistention of the bladder. The RN must be informed, and the tubing must be cleared.

3. **The correct answers are (1), (2), and (4).** Antihypertensives, phenothiazines, and many antipsychotic medications have effects on sexual functioning. NSAIDs do not.

4. **The correct answer is (1).** Frank discussion of the possible sexual problems related to this surgery and ways to manage them can help clients begin to adjust.

5. **The correct answer is (4).** Factors related to cervical cancer are early onset of sex, multiple partners, cigarette smoking, human papilloma virus, immunodeficiency, and a male partner who has had previous partners with the disease.

6. **The correct answer is (4).** HIV, which causes AIDS, has been isolated in most body fluids, but the primary routes of transmission are through intercourse, placental transmission, and blood contact.

7. **The correct answer is (2).** Nocturia and hesitancy are symptoms of benign prostatic hypertrophy, in which the prostate gland enlarges and partially blocks the urethra. The other symptoms are unrelated to this condition.

8. **The correct answer is (1).** Urinary retention results in stasis of the urine in the bladder, providing a chance for bacteria to grow and lead to a UTI.

9. **The correct answer is (1).** It is still possible to father a child after testicular cancer since only one testis is usually involved.

10. **The correct order of answers is (2), (4), (1), (3).** As the menstrual phase begins (Days 1 to 6), estrogen levels are low and the endometrial lining of the uterus is shed. This is the time of the cycle that women typically refer to as their "period." During the proliferative phase, Days 7 to 14, the endometrium thickens again, estrogen levels peak, and ovulation occurs. Days 15 to 26 are the secretory phase, in which the uterus prepares for implantation. Estrogen levels drop sharply and progesterone is dominant. The ischemic phase is the final phase of the cycle (Days 27 and 28), in which progesterone levels decrease, blood vessels rupture, and blood escapes into the cells of the uterus in preparation for the cycle to begin again.

SUMMING IT UP

- The male and female reproductive systems influence the functioning of the genitourinary system, and the hormones they produce have wide-ranging psychological and physical effects on the body.

- Reproductive function involves not only the ability to have children, but also the social functioning, self-esteem, and comfort of clients.

The Cardiovascular System

BASIC CONCEPTS

Cardiovascular problems are the leading cause of death and disability in the United States. Modifying risk factors and managing cardiovascular health is increasingly important. If a problem arises, early identification and ongoing treatment with medications can often control disease progression and improve quality of life.

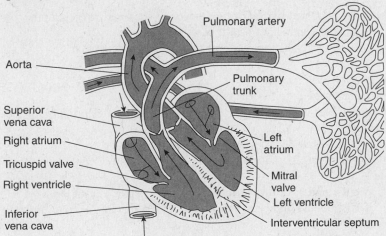

Aorta

Pulmonary artery

Pulmonary trunk

Superior vena cava

Right atrium

Tricuspid valve

Right ventricle

Inferior vena cava

Left atrium

Mitral valve

Left ventricle

Interventricular septum

chapter 18

307

CARDIOVASCULAR ANATOMY

A. **Heart**
1. Muscular organ separated into right (venous) and left (arterial) chambers
2. **Layers of the Heart**
   a. Pericardium—fibrous outer sac and serous inner surface that allows for movement
   b. Epicardium—covers surface of heart and great vessels
   c. Myocardium—muscular portion of the heart
   d. Endocardium—tissue that lines cardiac chambers
3. **Chambers**
   a. Right atrium (RA)—collects venous blood from the body through the coronary sinus, superior and inferior vena cava
   b. Right ventricle (RV)—receives blood from right atrium and pumps it into the lungs
   c. Left atrium (LA)—receives oxygenated blood from the lungs
   d. Left ventricle (LV)—pumps blood through the aorta to the rest of the body
4. **Valves**—permit flow of blood in one direction
   a. Types
      (1) Atrioventricular—between atria and ventricles (prevent blood from backing up into atria during systole)
         (a) Tricuspid—between the right atrium and right ventricle
         (b) Mitral—between the left atrium and left ventricle
      (2) Semilunar valves—located where blood leaves the heart to the pulmonary artery and aorta prevents backflow from these arteries
         (a) Pulmonic
         (b) Aortic
         (c) Heart
5. **Coronary Circulation**
   a. Arteries
      (1) Right and left coronary artery supply the myocardium
      (2) Blood flow is regulated by the oxygen needs of the heart myocardium
         (a) Systole is the contraction of the heart
         (b) Diastole is the relaxation phase of the heart
   b. Veins
      (1) Empty into coronary sinus
      (2) Coronary sinus leads into the right atrium
6. **Conduction System**—heart has specialized muscle that transmits electrical impulses
   a. Sinoatrial Node
      (1) Generates impulses at 60–100 beats per minute
         (a) The parasympathetic and sympathetic nervous system control the heart rate
      (2) Atrioventricular node—allows atrium to contract before ventricle
      (3) Bundle of His, bundle branches, Purkinje fibers—conduct impulses through the ventricles

B. **Vascular System**
1. **Arteries**—take blood away from the heart to the rest of the body
   a. Rapid flow—due to closed system and adequate blood volume; flow may decrease if there is too much resistance or too little blood
2. **Capillaries**—tiny blood vessels that form a bridge between arteries and veins and the place where blood and tissue fluid are exchanged
3. **Veins**—transport blood from the rest of the body back to the heart
   a. Thin walls capable of expanding if needed to store blood

    b. Valves prevent backflow of blood
    c. The amount and force of venous blood returning to the heart is due to an interplay of factors
       (1) Blood volume—the less there is, the slower it moves
       (2) Activity that causes muscle contractions speeds the blood
       (3) Increased resistance from the right side of the heart slows the blood return

CARDIAC PHYSIOLOGY

A. Heartbeat
    1. **Systole (contraction)**—atria and then ventricles contract and pump out the blood
    2. **Diastole (relaxation)**—valves close and the heart fills

B. Amount of Blood Pumped
    1. **Cardiac Output (CO)**—the amount of blood ejected from each ventricle in one minute
    2. **Stroke Volume (SV)**—the amount of blood ejected from each ventricle with each contraction
    3. **Cardiac Output**—Stroke volume × heart rate = cardiac output

C. Changes in the Amount of Blood Pumped
    1. **Force of Contraction**—the heart will adapt to larger amounts of blood by contracting with greater force (up to its physiological limit)
    2. **Cardiac Reserve**—the difference between the amount of work being done and the maximum the heart can do; a normal heart can increase its output four to six times
    3. **Heart Rate**—will increase in response to greater oxygen needs

D. Pulse
    1. Dilation of an artery in response to heartbeat
    2. Can be palpated over any large artery close to the skin
    3. Pulse deficit—the apical pulse (heard by the apex of the heart) minus the radial pulse (palpated at the wrist); a difference is due to a weak or ineffective heart

E. Blood Pressure
    1. **Pulse Pressure**—difference between the systolic and diastolic pressures

$$\left(BP \ \frac{120}{80} = 40 \text{ pulse pressure}\right)$$

    2. **Blood pressure is changed by**
       a. The force of heart contractions—more force means a higher blood pressure
       b. The volume of blood (as with hemorrhage)—less blood will mean a lower blood pressure
       c. The diameter and elasticity of blood vessels—this is the amount of resistance to blood flow; the more resistance, the higher the pressure needed to overcome it
       d. Blood viscosity or thickness (as with an abnormal amount of red blood cells, polycythemia); thicker blood needs more pressure to move it

F. Control of Blood Flow
    1. **Sympathetic Nervous System**
       a. Secretes epinephrine and norepinephrine
       b. Increases force and rate of heart contractions
       c. Constricts blood vessels
       d. Dilates arteries that supply the heart

2. **Parasympathetic Nervous System**
   a. Secretes acetylcholine
   b. Slows the heart rate and decreases the force of contractions
   c. Vasodilates blood vessels
   d. Has little effect on coronary arteries

BLOOD COMPOSITION

A. **Plasma**—the watery, colorless fluid part of the blood
   a. Makes up 55 percent of blood volume
   b. Primarily consists of water (92 percent), also some protein and dissolved organic substances

B. **Cellular Components of the Blood**
   1. **Erythrocytes (red blood cells)**
      a. Average life span is 90–120 days
      b. Contain hemoglobin, which carries oxygen to the tissues and carbon dioxide out to the lungs
      c. Produced in the bone marrow, stored in the spleen
      d. Male RBC count = 4.6–6.2 million cells
      e. Female RBC count = 4.2–5.4 million cells
   2. **Leukocytes (white blood cells)**
      a. Normal adult count is 4,500 to 11,000 cells per cu. mm of blood
      b. Primary defense against infection
      c. Leukocyte types
         (1) Neutrophils—phagocytes (can engulf and destroy bacteria)
         (2) Lymphocytes—part of immunological responses
         (3) Monocytes—the largest WBCs
   3. **Platelets (thrombocytes)**
      a. Normal platelet count is 150,000 to 400,000 per cu. mm of blood
      b. Needed for blood coagulation
      c. A low platelet count leads to problems with bleeding

C. **Spleen**
   1. Stores blood and removes waste and infectious organisms
   2. A primary source of antibodies for infants and children
   3. Produces lymphocytes, plasma cells, and antibodies in adults
   4. Destroys worn-out red blood cells

ASSESSMENT OF THE CARDIOVASCULAR SYSTEM

A. **History**
   1. **Identify Presence of Risk Factors for Heart Disease**
      a. Risk factors that may be modified
         (1) Smoking
         (2) Obesity
         (3) Inactivity
         (4) Hypertension
         (5) High cholesterol
         (6) Diabetes

  b. Risk factors that cannot be changed
   (1) Family history of heart disease
   (2) Age—more common in older adults
   (3) Sex—more common in men until women reach the age of menopause
 2. **Respiratory Problems**
  a. Asthma, COPD, and other respiratory problem
  b. Medications
  c. Activity level and exercise tolerance
 3. **Circulation**
  a. History of angina
  b. Edema, weight gain
  c. Episodes of loss of consciousness, feeling faint
  d. Medications for cardiac problems, hypertension

B. **Physical Assessment**
 1. **Appearance**—respiratory, cardiac problems, mental status
 2. **Vital Signs**—especially blood pressure, pulse pressure, postural hypotension, characteristics of pulse, respirations, assess peripheral pulses
 3. **Weight**—a gain of 3 pounds in 24 hours is fluid
 4. **Chest Pain**—onset, characteristics, location, precipitating, and relieving factors
 5. **Respiratory**—number of blocks client can walk comfortably or number of stairs can climb
 6. **Cough**—hemoptysis or nocturnal cough

DIAGNOSTIC TESTS FOR CARDIOVASCULAR ASSESSMENT

A. **Electrocardiogram (ECG)**
 1. A written record of the electrical activity of the heart.
 2. Used to identify abnormal rhythms or patterns of conduction, also identifies cardiac ischemia.
 3. The nurse should interpret ECG changes and reassure clients that electrical shock will not occur.

B. **Holter Monitor**
 1. Portable monitor used to record a client's heart activity during a 24-hour period. The client is supposed to keep a log of activities that can then be compared to the recording.
 2. Nurse should instruct client in use of monitor, recording of log. Teach client not to bathe or shower, use a microwave oven, or an electric shaver.

C. **Cardiac Catheterization and Arteriography (angiography)**
 1. An injection of contrast medium into the artery allows visualization of the coronary arteries with a flouroscope. Pressures, cardiac output, and oxygenation are also measured.
 2. Prior to the procedure the client should be npo. A consent is needed. Note the client's allergies to seafood, iodine, or radiopaque dyes. Monitor vital signs after procedure, and apply pressure to puncture site. Maintain a pressure dressing and bedrest for 8 hours after the procedure.

D. **Echocardiography**
 1. Sound waves are used to study cardiac structures and the direction of blood flow.
 2. The nurse should explain the procedure to the client.

E. Stress Test
1. An ECG done while the client performs increasing levels of exercise.
2. The nurse explains the procedure and informs the client to report shortness of breath, dizziness, or distress immediately.

F. Radionucleide Studies
1. Tracing material is injected, and a monitor is used to read levels of myocardial perfusion and cardiac circulation.
2. The nurse explains the procedure to the client and checks the site for bleeding afterward.

G. Doppler Ultrasound
1. Used to examine blood flow in peripheral circulation.
2. The nurse explains the procedure and may mark the site where peripheral pulses were identified.

H. Pulse Oximetry
1. Infrared light is used to measure arterial oxygen saturation.
2. The nurse attaches the monitor to a fingertip, ear lobe, or toe. Artificial nails, nail polish, and nail tips may interfere with reading on a fingertip. Protect the sensor from bright light.

I. Arterial Blood Gas
1. Blood test to assess for tissue oxygenation, acid-base status.
2. The nurse should document the client's vital signs and use of supplemental oxygen prior to the procedure. After the procedure, pressure should be applied to the puncture site.

J. Hemodynamic Monitoring
1. A pulmonary artery catheter is used to measure intracardiac pressures and cardiac output.
2. The nurse should explain the procedure, ensure that written consent has been obtained, monitor for complications, and check the insertion site for signs of infection.

K. Magnetic Resonance Imaging (MRI)
1. Use of a magnetic field and radiowaves to determine healthy and diseased tissue.
2. The nurse should explain the procedure and make sure the client does not have any metal on his or her body. Clients with implanted metal devices, such as pacemakers, are not candidates for an MRI.

L. Cardiac Enzymes
1. A blood test used to determine the status of enzymes that are associated with cardiac damage. Increased levels of CPK are the most significant, but the rapid onset and quick decline of this enzyme elevation means it may be missed. CPK-MB increases within 4–6 hours after an MI, peaks at 18–24 hours, and returns to normal in three to four days. Troponin rises within 4–6 hours and peaks within 10–24 hours.
2. The nurse should explain what is being tested and determine if the client has had a recent IM injection, tissue injury, or any other disease that could affect enzyme changes.

CARDIOVASCULAR SYSTEM DISORDERS

A. **Coronary Artery Disease**—narrowing of the coronary arteries, which results from the gradual deposit of plaque on the arterial walls. There may be few symptoms of the disease until a major obstruction resulting in a myocardial infarction (MI).
   1. **Assessment**
      a. Risk factor presence
         (1) Obesity, hypertension, smoking, stress, and inactivity—modifiable
         (2) Family history and age
      b. Other contributing disorders, such as diabetes, may be present
      c. Clinical signs and symptoms
         (1) Chest pain, often precipitated by exertion or excitement
            (a) Angina, burning, squeezing, substernal tightness or over precordial area
            (b) Pain may radiate down arms
         (2) Nausea/vomiting
         (3) Increased perspiration, cool extremities
   2. **Medical Diagnosis**
      a. ECG indicates ST-segment changes and T-wave inversion during episode of angina
      b. Coronary arteriography shows plaque formation
   3. **Medical Treatment**
      a. Lifestyle changes—weight loss, program of increased activity, low-sodium and low-fat diet
      b. Angioplasty
      c. Morphine sulfate IV
      d. Anticoagulant—heparin
      e. Antilipidemic medication such as cholestyramine (Questran) or lovastatin (Mevacor)
      f. Beta blockers—metropolol (Lopressor), propanolol (Inderal)
      g. Calcium channel blockers—nifedipine (Procardia), verapamil (Calan), diltiazem (Cardizem)
      h. Low-dose aspirin therapy
      i. Nitrates—nitroglycerin (Nitro-Bid), isosorbide dinitrate (Isordil)
   4. **Nursing Interventions**
      a. Administer medications as ordered.
      b. Encourage and counsel on lifestyle changes.
      c. Refer to support groups such as the American Heart Association as needed.
      d. Teach regarding medication use.

Nitroglycerin Use

Keep in a closed, dark glass container.
Bring a supply with you wherever you travel.
Replace after four to six months.
Take to avoid pain if anticipated.
Take when pain starts, and then rest.
Repeat in 3 minutes if still needed.
May repeat only a third time.
If no relief after three tablets, get medical help.
Side effects—headache, dizziness, and flushing.

B. Hypertension
    1. **Assessment**
        a. Persistent elevation of blood pressure
           (1) Systolic pressure over 140 mmHg
           (2) Diastolic pressure over 90 mmHg
        b. Primary hypertension—in which the cause is unknown (most common)
        c. Secondary hypertension—high blood pressure associated with another disease state
           (1) Kidney disease
           (2) Preeclampsia
           (3) Adrenal dysfunction
        d. Risk factors as for coronary artery disease
        e. African Americans have twice the incidence of Caucasians
        f. Birth control pills and estrogen may elevate pressure
    2. **Medical Diagnosis**
        a. Blood pressure over 140/90 on at least three occasions
        b. Lipid profile
        c. Urinalysis, BUN, and serum creatinine
        d. Blood sugar levels
        e. ECG, Holter monitoring
        f. Fundoscopic eye exam (to assess for retinal damage)
    3. **Medical Treatment**
        a. Antihypertensive medications
        b. Sodium-restricted diet
        c. Low-saturated-fat diet
        d. Weight management
        e. Stress management
        f. Smoking cessation
        g. Planned exercise
    4. **Nursing Interventions**
        a. Administer prescribed medications.
        b. Assess for drug side effects and report.
        c. Monitor weight q day.
        d. Monitor intake and output.
        e. Provide prescribed diet.
        f. Educate client regarding continuing drug therapy and maintaining lifestyle changes.

C. Myocardial Infarction (heart attack)—the obstruction of a coronary artery, after which there is myocardial ischemia and, later, necrosis of the heart muscle. The most common site for an MI is the left ventricle. The danger of death is greatest during the first 24–48 hours and still high for the first two weeks.
    1. **Assessment**
        a. May be precipitated by exercise, but often is not
        b. Severe, crushing, substernal pain unrelieved by nitroglycerin
        c. Frequently there is denial of the seriousness of the pain
        d. Dyspnea, diaphoresis
        e. Nausea, vomiting, weakness
        f. Hypotension
        g. Dysrhythmias—tachycardia, premature ventricular contractions
    2. **Medical Diagnosis** (see "Diagnostic Tests for Cardiovascular Assessment")
    3. **Medical Treatment**—complications of an MI include cardiogenic shock (hypotension, pulmonary edema, increasing ischemia), congestive heart failure, and dysrhythmias)

a. Thrombolytic drugs (streptokinase, tPA-tissue plasminogen activator) to help dissolve clot (if started within the first 3–6 hours of the MI)

b. Lidocaine for life-threatening arrhythmias; continuous cardiac monitoring

c. Oxygen; morphine sulfate for pain

d. Medications—nitrates, beta blockers, calcium channel blockers to stabilize blood pressure, maximize oxygenation of myocardium

e. Heart surgery for revascularization

f. Frequent monitoring of I and O; cardiac, respiratory, and peripheral circulation assessments

g. Give client and family emotional support and help decrease anxiety

h. Provide education and information on self-care and home follow-up

i. Instruct client to call physician for pain not controlled by nitroglycerin, pulse rate changes, decreased activity tolerance, syncope, increase in dyspnea

D. Congestive Heart Failure—the heart is unable to pump enough blood to meet the needs of the body

Left-sided failure—congestion is mainly in the lungs because of inadequate pumping of the blood into the systemic circulation

Right-sided failure—symptoms are primarily systemic; the heart is unable to pump the blood adequately from the body into the lungs

1. **History**
   a. Client has atherosclerosis, hypertension, MI, cardiac conduction defects—left-sided failure
   b. COPD, fluid overload, pulmonary hypertension, valvular problems—right-sided failure
   c. Problem starts as primarily one-sided; majority of clients have failure on both sides

2. **Assessment**
   a. Heart enlargement due to hypertrophy, dilatation
   b. Pulmonary symptoms (left-sided failure)
      (1) Dyspnea and moist cough; possible blood-tinged, frothy sputum
      (2) Fatigue, anxiety, irritability, and restlessness
      (3) Cyanosis or pallor
      (4) Palpitations, diaphoresis, arrhythmias
   c. Systemic symptoms (right-sided failure)
      (1) Dependent pitting edema (feet and legs)
      (2) Fatigue, liver congestion and ascites, nausea
      (3) Increased central venous pressure, jugular vein distention
      (4) Daytime oliguria; nighttime polyuria

3. **Medical Diagnosis**
   a. Left-sided failure
      (1) ABGs show hypoxemia and hypercapnia
      (2) Blood chemistry show decreased potassium and decreased sodium levels, increased BUN, and increased creatinine levels
      (3) ECG shows left ventricular hypertrophy; chest X-ray shows pulmonary congestion and left ventricular hypertrophy
   b. Right-sided failure
      (1) Lab results: ABGs, blood chemistry findings are the same
      (2) Chest X-ray shows pulmonary congestion, cardiomegaly, pleural effusions
      (3) ECG—left and right ventricular hypertrophy
      (4) Echocardiogram shows increased chamber size and decreased wall motion

4. **Medical Treatment**—treat underlying cause
   a. Morphine to reduce pain and anxiety, rest
   b. Angiotensin-converting enzyme (ACE) inhibitors—capoten (Captopril), enalapril (Vasotec)
   c. Oxygen therapy—nasal cannula (client feels he or she can't breathe already)
   d. Reduce sodium and water retention: diuretics, restricted fluid intake, moderate sodium restriction (1.5 to 2 gm)
   e. Digitalis—increases contraction strength and decreases rate

5. **Nursing Interventions**
   a. Assist client in bed rest in Fowler's position.
   b. Measure I and O, weigh daily (0.5–1 kg/day=water retention). Measure abdominal girth daily.
   c. Maintain proper skin care to edematous areas.
   d. Monitor for digitalis toxicity—has a cumulative effect.
   e. Observe for arrhythmias.
   f. Provide emotional support and client education regarding care.

6. **Possible Complications**
   a. Digitalis toxicity can be due to electrolyte imbalance; potassium loss from diuretics can lead to hypokalemia, which potentiates the effects of digitalis
      (1) Symptoms of digitalis toxicity include
         (a) Headache and visual disturbances
         (b) Nausea and vomiting
         (c) Bradycardia
         (d) The first symptom is often anorexia
      (2) Foods high in potassium are
         (a) Bananas
         (b) Potatoes and tomatoes
         (c) Orange juice
   b. Pulmonary embolism from bed rest
   c. Oxygen toxicity—especially COPD clients
   d. Acute pulmonary edema

NOTE

Monitor serum potassium level.

Heart Failure Management

Treatment focuses on increasing heart efficiency and decreasing workload

Increase cardiac efficiency:
1. Digitalis to increase the force of contractions
2. Oxygen to increase the O_2 saturation of the blood

Decrease workload:
1. Lower blood volume with diuretics, less salt
2. Decrease O_2 requirement with rest
3. Lower peripheral resistance with a vasodilator

E. **Inflammatory Heart Conditions**—disorders characterized by inflammation of the heart lining or valves caused by infection, trauma, or other inflammatory process
   1. **Pericarditis**—an inflammation pericardium, which is the fibrous sac that surrounds the heart
   2. **Myocarditis**—an inflammation of the heart muscle
   3. **Endocarditis**—an inflammation of the lining of the heart
   4. **Rheumatic heart disease**—a generalized inflammatory process in the heart that results in chronic valve disease; the inflammation is caused by infection with rheumatic fever, which is associated with strep throat

5. **Assessment**
   a. Signs of infection—fever, chills, diaphoresis, fatigue
   b. Chest pain and dyspnea
   c. Tachycardia
6. **Medical Diagnosis**
   a. White blood count and erythrocyte sedimentation rate (both are elevated in infection)
   b. ECG
   c. Echocardiogram to visualize heart structures
7. **Medical Treatment**
   a. Identification of infectious organism and specific antibiotic therapy
   b. Rest and supportive treatments
8. **Nursing Interventions**
   a. Administer antibiotic therapy as ordered.
   b. Maintain client on bed rest.
   c. Monitor cardiac and respiratory status.
   d. Administer oxygen, antipyretics, pain medications as needed.
   e. Provide adequate nutrition.

F. **Congenital Heart Disorders**—See Chapter 6, Pediatric Nursing.

VASCULAR DISORDERS

A. **Thrombophlebitis or Deep Vein Thrombosis (DVT)**—phlebitis is the inflammation of a vein, and a thrombus is a clot in the vein. The inflammation causes the clot formation. The thrombus usually occurs in the deep veins of the legs and pelvis, and such a clot may form an embolus that travels to the lungs or other organs.
   1. **Assessment**
      a. Risk factors
         (1) Venous stasis due to pregnancy, obesity, surgery, or prolonged bed rest
         (2) Increased blood coagulability
         (3) Injury to a blood vessel wall
      b. Clinical signs
         (1) Area around the vein is warm, tender to the touch, and reddened
         (2) Swollen extremity
         (3) Positive Homan's sign (pain at the back of the knee or calf when the foot is slowly and gently dorsiflexed, or bent in a dorsal direction, decreasing the angle between the foot and the leg)
   2. **Medical Diagnosis**
      a. Signs and symptoms
      b. Doppler ultrasound
   3. **Medical Treatment**
      a. Bed rest with extremity elevated
      b. Anticoagulant
      c. Antiembolism stockings during ambulation on affected leg
      d. Warm, moist compresses
      e. Embolectomy—done to prevent pulmonary embolus
      f. Filter device in the vena cava
   4. **Nursing Interventions**
      a. Provide bed rest and elevate limb.
      b. Apply moist heat.
      c. Administer pain medications as ordered.
      d. Measure thigh and calf daily.

ALERT!

Risk factors for thrombophlebitis include congenital valve weakness, venous stasis due to pregnancy, and obesity.

    e. Monitor vital signs q 4 hours

    f. Don't massage the affected leg

B. Varicose Veins—dilated and twisted leg veins resulting from blood congestion due to incompetent valves in the blood vessels

  1. **Assessment**

    a. Leg fatigue and pain

    b. Dilated veins

    c. Ankle edema

  2. **Medical Diagnosis**

    a. Clinical signs

    b. Venogram

  3. **Medical Treatment**

    a. Surgery—vein stripping, ligation, vein sclerosing

    b. Support stockings (should be put on before getting out of bed in the morning)

    c. Avoid prolonged sitting, elevate legs, walk around every hour or so

    d. Don't cross legs when sitting

    e. Weight management if indicated

    f. Prevent injury to extremity

  4. **Nursing Interventions**

    a. Provide postsurgical care.

      (1) Rewrap elastic bandages every shift if ordered.

      (2) Elevate affected leg.

      (3) Frequent checks of toe circulation (color and temperature).

      (4) Monitor for sensory loss in leg, calf pain, fever.

    b. Teach and assist client in implementing the above measures to decrease venous stasis.

C. Peripheral Vascular Disease—narrowing of the arteries of the extremities due to atherosclerosis

  1. **Assessment**

    a. Intermittent claudication (pain with activity relieved by rest)

    b. Sparse hair on extremity

    c. Stasis ulcers

    d. Decreased or absent peripheral pulses

    e. Leg cramps, numbness, loss of sensation

    f. History of excessive alcohol use, diabetes, hypertension, thombophlebitis, smoking

  2. **Medical Diagnosis**

    a. Doppler ultrasonography—uses sound waves to measure the amount of blood flowing through a vessel

    b. Venography

    c. Clinical signs and symptoms

  3. **Medical Treatment**

    a. Vasodilating medications

    b. Endarterectomy—removal of plaque within the artery

    c. Bypass graft

    d. Diet, exercise, and other lifestyle changes to reduce cardiac risk factors

  4. **Nursing Interventions**

    a. Encourage exercise program.

    b. Maintain constant warm temperature.

    c. Instruct client to avoid pressure on the back of the knee.

    d. Teach client to avoid vasoconstrictors—caffeine, smoking, cold temperatures.

    e. Check pulses of extremities every 15 minutes after surgery.

    f. Assess client's response to anticoagulants.

    g. Teach proper foot care.

    h. Encourage ambulation and movement of extremities.

D. Aneurysm—the enlargement or ballooning of an artery

  1. **Assessment**

    a. Abdominal

      (1) Increased blood pressure

      (2) Visible pulsating mass

      (3) Abdominal pain or tenderness

    b. Thoracic

      (1) Dyspnea

      (2) Severe chest pain

      (3) Dysphagia

      (4) Hoarseness or cough

    c. Ruptured aneurysm

      (1) Anxiety and restlessness

      (2) Pain

      (3) Diminished pulses

      (4) Shock

      (5) Sudden death

  2. **Medical Diagnosis**

    a. History and physical exam

    b. X-ray

    c. Ultrasound

    d. Angiography, arteriography

  3. **Medical Treatment**

    a. Drug therapy—antihypertensives, pain relievers

    b. Surgery to prevent rupture—surgical resection of the aneurysm

  4. **Nursing Interventions**

    a. Frequent check of vital signs.

    b. IV fluids and blood components if indicated.

    c. Evaluate of the presence and quality of the peripheral pulses in the lower extremities.

    d. Note hourly urine output (indicates renal perfusion).

    e. Assess for temperature.

    f. Administer prophylactic antibiotics as ordered.

E. Pulmonary Embolus—See Chapter 16.

TIP

The cause of an aneurysm is usually arteriosclerosis, but other causes include injury, congenital factors, infections, and hypertension.

EXERCISES: THE CARDIOVASCULAR SYSTEM

1. You enter the clinic waiting room to invite Mrs. Rosiclair in for her check-up. You notice edema in her left leg, and she states that the back of her leg hurts and has been swollen. Which nursing measure would be helpful for determining the cause of this problem?

   (1) See if she can stand on one leg at a time.
   (2) Check the Homan's sign.
   (3) Apply a cold compress and massage the area.
   (4) Measure both legs and compare the size.

TIP

Remember to read every question carefully to avoid selecting the wrong answer choice(s). For example, Question 4 asks for the *best* information—so you can assume that at least two of the answer choices will be correct in some way. You want to select the one that most completely and accurately answers the question.

2. Mr. Graham is scheduled for an ECG. The *best* way to describe this test to him is,

   (1) "It won't hurt and just be very still."
   (2) "It is a test that measures the electrical activity of your heart."
   (3) "It is a diagnostic procedure that will record impulses from the SA node through the electrical pathway throughout the cardiac tissue."
   (4) "It is a necessary test that will help the doctor determine how to take care of your heart."

3. Two ways to increase oxygenation to the myocardium are by administering

   (1) nitroglycerin and providing nasal O_2.
   (2) O_2 and performing CPR.
   (3) digoxin.
   (4) O_2 through a venti mask and administering Lidocaine.

4. Fluid retention has become a problem for a client with coronary artery disease. What is the *best* information to include in her teaching plan?

   (1) Take a walk for 10 minutes every day.
   (2) Report any chest pain to the doctor immediately.
   (3) Take your diuretic on schedule and eat a banana every day.
   (4) Don't drink any water during meals.

5. Peripheral vascular disease is *most* common in clients with

   (1) an aneurysm.
   (2) viral pneumonia.
   (3) leukemia.
   (4) diabetes mellitus.

6. Mrs. Brown has had a history of deep vein thrombosis and is admitted for insertion of a Greenfield filter. She states she doesn't understand what her physician has explained to her and asks you to repeat the explanation. You tell her it is a

   (1) filter placed in the large vein entering her heart that will catch all the clots before they enter her heart and lungs.
   (2) device to prevent her blood from clotting.
   (3) special filter that will keep any clots that form in her legs from leaving the peripheral circulation.
   (4) device that prevents platelet aggregation.

7. The nurse is preparing to instruct a client who has angina and is taking digitalis about how to care for herself. Which of the following points should the nurse include in the instruction?
Select all that apply.

☐ **(1)** The need to keep nitroglycerin in a clear plastic or glass container

☐ **(2)** How to modify risk factors, such as obesity and smoking

☐ **(3)** The prophylactic use of nitroglycerin

☐ **(4)** How to indentify factors that precipitate angina

8. The nurse is planning a diet for a client on digitalis and Lasix. What foods would she be sure to include in the client's meals?

(1) Bananas, orange juice, tomatoes, and potatoes

(2) Milk, cheese, and yogurt

(3) Beef, pork, and lamb

(4) Fish, chicken, beans, and soy products

9. The 67-year-old man is transferred to the unit for management of congestive heart failure. The nurse asks him to describe his symptoms, and the client replies that he is often short of breath when he tries to walk, has a frequent cough, and sometimes has heart palpitations. The nurse knows that these symptoms are characteristic of

(1) left-sided heart failure.

(2) right-sided heart failure.

(3) complications caused by coronary artery disease.

(4) hospital acquired pneumonia.

10. The nurse is treating an overweight post–cesarean section client with varicose veins. It is *especially important* that she check for the following when assessing this client.

(1) Integrity of the incision

(2) Positive Homan's sign

(3) Clear lung sounds

(4) Bowel sounds in all four quadrants

ANSWER KEY AND EXPLANATIONS

1. 2	3. 1	5. 4	7. 2,3,4	9. 1
2. 2	4. 3	6. 1	8. 1	10. 2

1. **The correct answer is (2).** A positive Homan's sign is helpful in identifying a DVT. Never massage the leg when DVT is suspected, as a clot may be dislodged.

2. **The correct answer is (2).** Provide the client with information he can understand and that is descriptive of the procedure.

3. **The correct answer is (1).** Administration of O_2 and vasodilatation of the coronary arteries are the only ways to increase oxygen supply to the myocardium.

4. **The correct answer is (3).** Diuretics will decrease the fluid overload but will drain potassium as well. Bananas are rich in potassium.

5. **The correct answer is (4).** Clients with diabetes frequently have peripheral vascular disease as a complication.

6. **The correct answer is (1).** The inferior vena cava filter is designed to trap emboli before they enter the left atrium. Anticoagulant therapy is administered to dissolve these clots in the filter.

7. **The correct answers are (2), (3), and (4).** Nitroglycerine must be kept in a light-resistant container, not in a clear plastic or glass container.

8. **The correct answer is (1).** Bananas, orange juice, tomatoes, and potatoes are all high in potassium, which tends to be depleted with diuretic use. Low potassium can cause digitalis toxicity.

9. **The correct answer is (1).** Left-sided heart failure is characterized by dyspnea on exertion and a moist cough, as well as cyanosis or pallor, fatigue, irritability, and palpitations.

10. **The correct answer is (2).** Although all of these assessments are made on a postpartum C/S client, an overweight woman with varicose veins is particularly at risk for phlebitis. A positive Homan's sign is a symptom of this disorder.

SUMMING IT UP

- Cardiovascular problems are the leading cause of death and disability in the United States.
- Early identification and ongoing treatment with medications can often control disease progression and improve quality of life.

The Musculoskeletal System

OVERVIEW

- Basic concepts
- Skeleton
- Joints and connective tissue
- Muscular system
- Musculoskeletal system disorders
- Summing it up

BASIC CONCEPTS

The skeleton protects and supports the body, while the muscles and connective tissue add additional support and allow movement. The bones also store and release vital minerals, and the bone marrow produces erythrocytes (red blood cells) and thrombocytes (platelets).

SKELETON

A. **Bone Structure**
   1. The cells of the bone are called osteocytes, which are embedded in a matrix of a calcified intercellular substance composed of calcium phosphate and other inorganic mineral salts.
   2. Each bone is composed of cylindrical layers, and the outside layer is called the periosteum.
   3. A central canal contains bone marrow. There are also fine branching canals (the Haversian system) through which blood vessels and lymphatics run.

B. **Bone Development**
   1. Young children's bones are primarily cartilage.
   2. Bones develop through the calcification of this cartilage by layers: first cartilage, then calcification, then another layer of cartilage, etc.
   3. The epiphysis is a cartilage area on the ends of children's bones that provides for longitudinal bone growth.
   4. The thyroid and parathyroid control the deposition and reabsorption of calcium from blood to bone.

C. **Bone Maintenance**—formation and reabsorption of bone are controlled by the following:
   1. Weight-bearing stress stimulates bone formation and calcium formation on the bone.

chapter 19

2. Immobility, in contrast, allows mobilization of calcium from the bone to the blood.
3. Vitamin D promotes the absorption of calcium.

D. Classification of Bones (by shape)
   1. **Long Bones**—made up of a long shaft and flared end; include radius and femur
   2. **Short Bones**—include carpals and tarsals
   3. **Flat Bones**—ribs and skull
   4. **Irregular bones**—vertebrae

JOINTS AND CONNECTIVE TISSUE

A. Joints—serve to provide flexibility
   1. **Articulation is the joining of two bones**
   2. **Classification of Joints**
      a. Diarthroses (synovial)—freely movable joints
         (1) Hinge type—elbows and knees
         (2) Ball-and-socket type—hip
         (3) Saddle type (multidirectional movement)—thumb
         (4) Pivot type (rotary movement)—radius and ulna
         (5) Gliding type (sliding)— wrist, ankle, intervertebral joints
         (6) Condyloid—wrist
      b. Synarthroses—immovable joints
   3. **Suture Lines of Skull**
      a. Amphiarthroses—joints with slight movement
   4. **Types of Joint Movements**
      a. Flexion—bending of a joint with a decreased angle between two bones
      b. Extension—bending of a joint with an increased angle between two bones
      c. Hyperextension—bending leading to an increased angle greater than 180 degrees
      d. Abduction—movement of a part away from midline
      e. Adduction—movement of a part toward midline
      f. Rotation—movement around an axis
      g. Eversion—turn joint outward
      h. Inversion—turn joint inward
      i. Pronation—moving palm downward or sole outward
      j. Supination—moving palm upward or sole inward

B. Ligaments and Tendons
   1. Tendons attach muscles to bones; ligaments attach bones to bones at joints
   2. Composed of dense, fibrous connective tissue
   3. Relatively poor blood supply; therefore, healing—as with a sprain—can be slow

C. Fascia—strong connective tissue separating or binding together muscles and organs
   1. **Types**
      a. *Superficial fascia:* loose connective tissue directly under the skin
      b. *Deep fascia:* fibrous connective tissue surrounding and separating muscles and binding blood vessels and nerves together
      c. *Visceral fascia:* suspends organs within their cavities and wraps them in layers of connective tissue membranes
   2. **Function**
      a. Allows independent muscle action and gliding of one muscle over another
      b. Strengthens muscle tissue

D. Bursae
   1. Sacs of connective tissue lined and filled with synovial fluid
   2. Located at joints to prevent friction where one body part moves on another

MUSCULAR SYSTEM

A. Muscles
   1. **Functions**
      a. Provide heat and energy
      b. Support for maintaining posture
      c. Cause movement by contracting
   2. **Characteristics**
      a. Stimulation → contraction → movement by pulling on bones
      b. Each muscle has a point of origin and a point of insertion (insertion point usually moves)
      c. Ligaments hold bones together and tendons hold muscles to bones
   3. **Muscle Changes**
      a. Hypertrophy—increased muscle mass caused by exercise
      b. Atrophy—decreased muscle mass results from disuse

B. Assessment
   1. **History**
      a. Previous injuries, neuromuscular problems, inflammatory/metabolic/endocrine disorders affecting the musculoskeletal system
      b. Family history of problems
      c. Normal activity, exercise
   2. **Physical Assessment**
      a. Inspect for deformities.
      b. Evaluate nutritional status.
      c. Assess joint movement, tenderness.
      d. Observe client's gait and posture.
      e. Assess peripheral circulation.
      f. Evaluate for presence and characteristics of pain.
   3. **Musculoskeletal Changes with Aging**
      a. Osteoporosis and increased likelihood of fracture
      b. Less subcutaneous tissue over bone
      c. Decreased range of motion
      d. Slower movement and less muscle strength

MUSCULOSKELETAL SYSTEM DISORDERS

Fractures, congenital dislocation of the hip (congenital hip dysplasia), scoliosis, club foot, and cerebral palsy are discussed in Chapter 6.

Common Fractures

Colle's: Fracture of distal radius (common while protecting with hand in fall)
Pelvic: Common in elderly due to falls
Hip: Common in women over 60 due to osteoporosis

Important Points About Fractures:
1. Assess for compartmental syndrome (caused by pressure on blood vessels).
2. Don't apply heat to a cast.
3. Don't get a cast wet.
4. Don't allow the client to bear weight on the casted area until instructed by provider to do so.
5. A fractured hip should be maintained in an abducted position with neutral rotation (use pillows).
6. Monitor for complications related to immobility.
7. Help client learn the use of assistive devices.
8. A fat embolism occurs primarily with long bone fractures. It is a life-threatening complication that causes shortness of breath and could lead to shock and possibly death.

A. **Total Hip Replacement**—used to alleviate pain and restore movement for clients with arthritis or a fracture
   1. **Preoperative**
      a. Teach crutch walking or use of a walker.
      b. Teach proper positioning with pillows to maintain abduction postoperatively.
   2. **Postoperative**
      a. Encourage prescribed exercise.
      b. Do not allow hip flexion greater than 90 degrees.
      c. Maintain abduction and internal rotation of extremity.
      d. Frequently assess circulation.

B. **Amputation**—surgical removal of part or all of an extremity
   1. Elevate stump for approximately 24 hours, then keep the joint above the stump extended to prevent a flexion contracture.
   2. Provide analgesics and discuss phantom limb pain (is real to the client and should be treated).
   3. Provide wound care to stump.
   4. Encourage strengthening of unaffected extremities.
   5. A compression bandage or wrap will help prevent swelling and increase comfort.
   6. Prosthesis should be fitted and worn as soon as possible.
   7. Provide emotional support and monitor for depression.

C. **Herniated Disc**—stress on the disc causes the cartilage (nucleus pulposus) to herniate inward toward the spinal cord causing pain from compression of the spinal nerve root; lower back is usually affected
   1. **Assessment**
      a. Low back pain radiating down back of buttock and thigh—sciatic pain
      b. Raising the leg in a supine position causes pain

2. **Medical Diagnosis**
   a. MRI
   b. Myelogram
3. **Medical Treatment**
   a. Analgesics and muscle relaxants
   b. Heat and physical therapy
   c. Weight reduction, if appropriate
   d. Surgery—laminectomy
4. **Nursing Interventions**
   a. Instruct the client in proper body mechanics.
   b. Administer medications as ordered.
   c. Provide counseling in nutrition, if appropriate for weight loss.
   d. Laminectomy
      (1) Preoperative—practice of logrolling.
      (2) Evaluate bowel and bladder function.
      (3) Postoperative—position pillow between the legs when on the side.
      (4) Logroll client when turning.
      (5) Evaluate pain, extremity sensation, bowel and bladder function. (Client may have difficulty voiding postoperatively due to edema from surgery that may interfere with sensation).

D. **Osteomyelitis**—a bone infection, often caused by staphylococcus
   1. **Assessment**
      a. Symptoms of inflammation: pain, redness, warmth
      b. Drainage from infected site
      c. Fever, chills
   2. **Diagnosis**
      a. Wound culture
      b. Blood culture
   3. **Medical Treatment**
      a. IV antibiotics
      b. Immobilization of affected part
   4. **Nursing Interventions**
      a. Prevent contractures of extremity.
      b. Maintain isolation precautions if there is an open wound.
      c. Advise client that condition may recur.

E. **Rheumatoid Arthritis**—a systemic inflammatory disease, involving synovial (freely moving) bone joints
   1. **Assessment**
      a. Exacerbations and remissions
      b. Gradual onset
      c. Joints warm, red, painful
      d. Stiffness and pain that is worse in the morning
      e. Joint involvement is bilateral and symmetrical (e.g., both knees)
      f. Subcutaneous nodules on fingers
      g. Stress may make symptoms worse
      h. Deformities may develop
   2. **Medical Diagnosis**
      a. Increased ESR (erythrocyte sedimentation rate)—an index of inflammation
      b. Antinuclear antibody titer
      c. Positive serum rheumatoid factor
      d. Pattern of symptoms

3. **Medical Treatment**
   a. Anti-inflammatory medications
      (1) Nonsteroidal anti-inflammatory drugs (NSAIDS), such as aspirin
      (2) Steroids
   b. Heat and cold
   c. Joint replacement
4. **Nursing Interventions**—goal is to decrease pain and increase ability to move
   a. Apply warm or cold compresses.
   b. Teach exercises to maintain joint mobility.
   c. Have client take medications with food to avoid stomach upset.

F. **Osteoarthritis**—noninflammatory degenerative joint disease
   1. **Assessment**
      a. Usually involves weight-bearing joints, may be unilateral and occur as a result of stress
      b. Pain, swelling, and tenderness with weight bearing, movement
      c. Pain increased with activity
      d. Herberden's nodes—bony nodules on the distal finger joints
      e. Client is usually overweight
   2. **Medical Diagnosis**—X-ray to detect change in joint structure
   3. **Medical Treatment**
      a. NSAIDS (aspirin is more effective in rheumatoid arthritis)
      b. Cortisone injections to joint
      c. Physical therapy
      d. Joint replacement
      e. Weight reduction, if appropriate
   4. **Nursing Interventions**
      a. Rest and physical therapy.
      b. Warmth (to reduce stiffness) or cold compresses (to reduce inflammation).
      c. Brace joint to prevent movement.
      d. Exercise that does not stress joints.
      e. Discuss diet and nutrition; help client with weight loss.

G. **Osteoporosis**—age-related metabolic disease
   1. **Assessment**
      a. Loss of bone mass, resulting in fragile and porous bones and fractures
      b. Most frequent occurrence: hips, wrists, and vertebral column
      c. May result from postmenopausal changes, metabolic disorder, or calcium deficiency
   2. **Medical Diagnosis**—may be asymptomatic until fracture occurs
   3. **Medical Treatment**
      a. Calcitonin to prevent bone loss
      b. Estrogen or androgens to decrease bone resorption
      c. Calcium, vitamin D, phosphorus
      d. Diet rich in protein, calcium, vitamin C, vitamin D, iron
   4. **Nursing Intervention**
      a. Identify risk areas for accidents in the home.
      b. Advise exercises to strengthen back and abdominal muscles.
      c. Suggest use of a firm mattress.
      d. Recommend avoiding coffee and alcohol.
      e. Propose use of rails, a walker, a cane.

H. Gout—arthritis caused by uric acid crystals deposited in the joints and cartilage

1. **Assessment**
   a. Primarily involves men over 30
   b. Rapid onset of pain, swelling, and inflammation of great toe (usually); also ankles and knees
   c. Joint is swollen, warm, and red
   d. Tophi (lumps of uric acid crystals) around great toe and outer ear

2. **Medical Diagnosis**
   a. Increased serum uric acid
   b. Elevated WBC and ESR

3. **Medical Treatment**
   a. Low-purine diet (high-purine foods are liver, kidney, brain, sweetbreads, sardines, fish, poultry, nuts, beans, dried peas, oatmeal, and whole wheat)
   b. Medications to prevent and treat (see box below)
   c. Client should avoid aspirin, alcohol, and diuretics, which can cause an attack

4. **Nursing Interventions**
   a. Teach client to administer medications early in attack.
   b. Protect affected area: elevate, immobilize, and use cold packs for pain.
   c. Educate client about a low-purine diet.
   d. Encourage increased po fluids to flush out uric acid.

Medications for Gout

Medication	Action	Nursing Considerations
Colchicine	Reduce pain and swelling	Administer early in attack. Take with food, increase fluids.
Allopurinol (*Zyloprim*)	Inhibit uric acid formation	Administer with food. Caution if kidney problems.
Probenecid (*Benemid*)	Decrease urate deposits	Lifelong therapy usually needed. Can give with Colchicine: Colbenemid.

EXERCISES: THE MUSCULOSKELETAL SYSTEM

1. The nurse is ordering a meal for the new client with gout. Which of the following menus would be contraindicated for this condition?

    (1) Pizza with cheese, peppers and onions, iced tea, chocolate ice cream
    (2) Whole-wheat bean burrito, coffee, pecan pie
    (3) Cheeseburger, french fries, root beer, soft-serve yogurt
    (4) Vegetable lasagna, salad, milk, Italian pastry

2. The nurse is checking the client's lab results to see if they indicate any possibility of inflammation. Which finding would *not* be indicative of the presence of inflammation?

    (1) Increased white blood count
    (2) Increased erythrocyte sedimentation rate
    (3) Increased number of leukocytes
    (4) Decreased hemoglobin

3. The nurse is caring for a client with a total hip replacement and places a pillow between her knees. The purpose of this intervention is to prevent

    (1) abduction.
    (2) adduction.
    (3) flexion.
    (4) internal rotation.

4. A nursing home client has severe rheumatoid arthritis. Which of the following symptoms would the client's nurse expect to find?
    Select all that apply.

    ☐ (1) Symmetrical joint pain
    ☐ (2) Pain that is worse in the morning than later in the day
    ☐ (3) Swelling of the small joints
    ☐ (4) Asymmetrical joint pain

5. The nurse, who works on an orthopedic unit, finds that hip fractures typically occur in older clients who suffer from

    (1) Paget's disease.
    (2) osteoarthritis.
    (3) osteoporosis.
    (4) osteomyelitis.

6. Mrs. Smith, an overweight 45-year-old woman with osteoarthritis of the knee, asks the nurse what would help her to reduce the pain. The nurse replies that the most effective intervention for her would be

    (1) antispasmodics to decrease muscle spasms.
    (2) regular program of weight-bearing exercise.
    (3) steroid injections.
    (4) weight loss.

7. The nurse is caring for a client with an arm fracture. The client complains of numbness and tingling of the hand and pain unrelieved by analgesics, and the radial pulse is diminished. The nurse realizes the client may have the following complication, which requires prompt intervention:

    (1) Fat embolism

    (2) Infection

    (3) Compartmental syndrome

    (4) Venous stasis

8. A serious complication that occurs after bone fracture is fat embolism. Which is the first sign that this may have occurred?

    (1) Respiratory distress

    (2) Cardiogenic shock

    (3) Hypoactive bowel sounds

    (4) Positive Homan's sign

9. Which of the following *best* characterizes rheumatoid arthritis?

    (1) Infection of the bone

    (2) Bones that become porous

    (3) Joint degeneration

    (4) Chronic inflammation of the synovial membrane

ANSWER KEY AND EXPLANATIONS

1. 2	3. 2	5. 3	7. 3	9. 4
2. 4	4. 1,2,3	6. 4	8. 1	

1. **The correct answer is (2).** Whole wheat, beans, and nuts are high in purine, which breaks down to uric acid, the cause of the painful joint swelling.

2. **The correct answer is (4).** The white blood cell count (1) and the erythrocyte sedimentation rate (2) are increased in inflammation. Leukocytes (3) are white blood cells. The hemoglobin is not usually affected by inflammation.

3. **The correct answer is (2).** Keeping the hip in proper alignment helps prevent excessive pain. Pillows are kept between the knees to prevent adduction, and pillows are used to prevent external rotation.

4. **The correct answers are (1), (2), and (3).** Rheumatoid arthritis is a chronic systemic inflammatory disease that causes symmetrical pain in joints and is generally worse in the morning. It also causes swelling of the small joints. Osteoarthritis, in contrast, generally affects one weight-bearing joint, not both.

5. **The correct answer is (3).** Osteoporosis is a condition of decreased bone mass leading to bone fragility. Paget's disease (1) is a localized bone disorder that often leads to deformities. Osteoarthritis (2) is a degenerative joint disease, and osteomyelitis (4) is a bone inflammation caused by an infectious organism.

6. **The correct answer is (4).** Osteoarthritis is associated with aging, obesity, and joint trauma. Weight reduction is encouraged as a first-line treatment, along with NSAIDs.

7. **The correct answer is (3).** Compartmental syndrome is the increased pressure in a closed area resulting from edema. It causes pain and reduced circulation to the area as well as pressure on muscles that can result in permanent anesthesia and paralysis. Infection (2) would not cause these symptoms, venous stasis (4) would likely cause thrombosis, and a fat embolism (1) is usually pulmonary and causes shortness of breath and shock.

8. **The correct answer is (1).** The pulmonary circulation is often the site where fat emboli become obstructed, causing dyspnea, chest pain, coughing, tachycardia, and restlessness.

9. **The correct answer is (4).** Rheumatoid arthritis is diagnosed in freely movable (synovial) joints in which the synovial membrane is inflamed.

SUMMING IT UP

- The skeleton protects and supports the body, and the muscles and connective tissue add support and allow movement.
- The bones also store and release vital minerals, and the bone marrow produces erythrocytes and thrombocytes.

PART III

TWO PRACTICE TESTS

ANSWER SHEET PRACTICE TEST 1

1. ①②③④
2. ①②③④
3. ①②③④
4. ①②③④
5. _ _ _ _
6. ①②③④
7. ①②③④
8. ①②③④
9. ①②③④
10. ①②③④
11. ①②③④
12. ①②③④
13. _____
14. ①②③④
15. ①②③④

16. ①②③④
17. ①②③④
18. ①②③④
19. ①②③④
20. ①②③④
21. ①②③④
22. ①②③④
23. ①②③④
24. ①②③④
25. ①②③④
26. ①②③④
27. ①②③④
28. ①②③④
29. ①②③④
30. ①②③④

31. ①②③④
32. _ _ _ _
33. ①②③④
34. ①②③④
35. ①②③④
36. ①②③④
37. ①②③④
38. ①②③④
39. ①②③④
40. ①②③④
41. ①②③④
42. ①②③④
43. ①②③④
44. _____
45. ①②③④

46. ①②③④
47. ①②③④
48. ①②③④
49. ①②③④
50. ①②③④
51. ①②③④
52. ①②③④
53. ①②③④
54. ①②③④
55. ①②③④
56. ①②③④
57. ①②③④
58. ①②③④
59. ①②③④
60. ①②③④

61. ①②③④
62. ①②③④
63. ①②③④
64. ①②③④
65. ①②③④
66. ①②③④
67. ①②③④
68. ①②③④
69. ①②③④
70. ①②③④
71. ①②③④
72. ①②③④
73. ①②③④
74. _ _ _ _
75. ①②③④

answer sheet

Practice Test 1

Directions: Each question or incomplete statement below is followed by four suggested answers or completions. In each case, select the statement that best answers the question or completes the sentence.

1. When determining the readiness of a client to be advanced to a regular diet, the nurse knows that the most significant indication of return of bowel function is

   (1) normal bowel sounds.
   (2) lack of abdominal distention.
   (3) tolerance for clear fluids.
   (4) passing of flatus.

2. A nurse will be administering an enteral feeding to an older client who is unable to take foods orally. After the client is in a high-Fowler's position and prior to administering the feeding, the nurse *must*

   (1) provide free-flow oxygen to the client to assure adequate oxygenation during the procedure.
   (2) provide mouth care.
   (3) aspirate the stomach contents to check for proper placement and amount of gastric residual.
   (4) check the client's weight to determine the amount of feeding to be given.

3. The nurse is preparing to insert a nasograstic tube in the client being treated for paralytic ileus. Prior to insertion, the nurse measures the distance to insert the tube by using the tube to measure and mark the distance with tape from the

   (1) upper part of the nose to the left midclavicular line.
   (2) lower part of the earlobe to the nose to the lower part of the sternum.
   (3) epigastric area to the top of the nasal cartilage.
   (4) mid-sternum to the earlobe to the mouth.

4. Mr. Lee, who is in Buck's traction for a right hip fracture, complains his right foot is numb. Which is the most appropriate action for the nurse to take *first*?

   (1) Notify the RN and provider.

   (2) Massage the foot to help the return of circulation.

   (3) Tell the client that this is a common side effect that will pass.

   (4) Assess the client's body alignment as well as the placement and line of pull of the traction.

5. A client who has an IV complains of pain at the site of insertion. Assessment of the site reveals that the client is suffering from phlebitis. Place the actions that the nurse should take in chronological order, from the first action to the last.

   (1) Apply warm soaks to site.   _____

   (2) Check for skin sloughing.   _____

   (3) Discontinue IV and insert new catheter proximal to discontinued
       site or on opposite arm.

   (4) Document (nurse's) assessment, (nurse's) actions taken, and the
       client's response.   _____

6. When gathering data for a client who is hyperthyroid, the nurse is careful to include which of the following data?

   (1) Weight, temperature, mental status, pulse rate

   (2) Height, vision, deep tendon reflexes, balance

   (3) Oxygen saturation, blood sugar, peripheral pulses, capillary refill time

   (4) Waist to hip ratio, skin tone, hearing, CBC

7. The 62-year-old woman who is overweight and has a family history of diabetes presents to the nurse for her first follow-up visit after her diet and exercise plan has been put in place. Without checking the chart, the nurse knows that this client most likely has

   (1) type 1 diabetes.

   (2) type 2 diabetes.

   (3) gestational diabetes.

   (4) impaired glucose tolerance.

8. The antepartum client is being routinely screened for gestational diabetes by administering 50 mg of glucose and testing the woman's blood sugar in an hour. The client asks for the normal glucose values an hour after taking the glucose. The nurse replies:

   (1) "It should be less than 140 or we do further testing."

   (2) "Anything under 105 is acceptable."

   (3) "We like to see a result between 130 and 165."

   (4) "It is different for each individual."

9. The nurse is reinforcing the importance of proper foot care to a 76-year-old diabetic woman, who states that they surely must have something more important to discuss. The nurse correctly replies:

   (1) "Foot care as well as any other type of hygiene is always important."
   (2) "We can skip this if you prefer."
   (3) "All right, just remember that you will be more prone to foot odor."
   (4) "Diabetics can easily develop severe foot injury or infection without knowing it."

10. The diabetic client is demonstrating her knowledge of self care by discussing the diet that has been prescribed for her, the symptoms of hyper- and hypoglycemia, as well as the role of exercise in her treatment. Which comment would indicate the need for further teaching?

    (1) "If I decide not to eat bread at a meal, I can exchange it for one cup of rice."
    (2) "I am likely to get hyperglycemic if I eat too many simple carbohydrates at one time."
    (3) "I have always exercised—my husband and I bowl together at least once a week."
    (4) "I need to be especially careful about infections and will let my health provider know if I get one."

11. Mrs. Stevenson was diagnosed with Graves' disease (hyperthyroidism). The nurse on Mrs. Stevenson's case would expect which findings on assessment?

    (1) Decreased level of consciousness, irregular breathing, and hypotension
    (2) Dry skin, sensitivity to cold, weight gain, and decreased pulse pressure
    (3) Weight loss, increased activity, sensitivity to heat, and tachycardia
    (4) Diaphoresis, flushed skin, extreme fatigue, and decreased heart rate

12. In teaching the newly diagnosed diabetic about the exchange system, the nurse explains that potatoes would be considered a

    (1) vegetable exchange.
    (2) meat exchange.
    (3) starch-bread exchange.
    (4) fruit exchange.

practice test

13. A 56-year-old man with a history of arterial fibrillation is brought to the emergency department, where he is diagnosed with an embolic stroke. Identify the heart chamber in which the clot that caused the stroke was most likely formed, and mark that area with an "X."

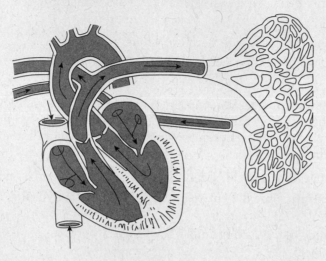

14. A nurse is counseling a 58-year-old man whose cholesterol reading was 250. She is instructing him in diet, exercise, and the avoidance of high-cholesterol foods. Which of the following food choices would indicate the need for further teaching?

    (1) Pasta primavera

    (2) Large salad with lowfat dressing

    (3) Turkey sandwich on whole grain bread

    (4) Cheese omelet

15. An African American adolescent came into the ambulatory clinic complaining of fatigue and occasional shortness of breath when playing sports. In order to assess for skin pallor, which might be a symptom of anemia, the nurse examines the

    (1) nail beds.

    (2) palms of the hands.

    (3) sclera.

    (4) buccal mucosa of the mouth.

16. John A. is on Coumadin therapy, which he takes because he has an artificial heart valve. Which meal plan would suggest the need for further teaching about the effects of diet on this medication?

    (1) Caesar salad with a spinach frittata

    (2) Steak, french fries, and a milkshake

    (3) Chicken tettrazini and fresh fruit salad

    (4) Chile con carne with garlic bread

17. A nurse has written his notes on the wrong client's chart. It is one of the first entries on the page. The best way for him to correct this is to:

    (1) discard the page with the incorrect entry and rewrite the notes.

    (2) move the page to the correct chart and change the client's name at the top.

    (3) cross out the wrong entry several times so that it cannot be read.

    (4) draw a line through the incorrect entry and initial it.

18. Frannie R., a young woman who was in an automobile accident, received a head injury and is being treated for increased intracranial pressure. Which of the following medications ordered for her would the nurse question?

    (1) Dexamethasone (Decadron)

    (2) Mannitol (Osmitrol)

    (3) Phenytoin (Dilantin)

    (4) Secobarbital (Seconal)

19. The CVA client the nurse is caring for has expressive aphasia and becomes irritable and frustrated when he wants something. What would be the *best* intervention for this problem?

    (1) Try to anticipate his needs so that he does not become frustrated.

    (2) Speak in slow, simple language to help him understand.

    (3) Discuss the problem with his family while caring for him.

    (4) Offer a communication board so the client can point to what he wants.

20. Mr. Fred S. is 80 years old and has Parkinson's disease. He has been put on levodopa (L-Dopa) 500 mg bid. Which of the following observations would indicate the medication was having the desired effect?

    (1) He is able to walk to the bathroom.

    (2) His sister states that he is more cheerful.

    (3) He exhibits a decrease in tremors.

    (4) He is able to eat soft food.

21. Sarah J. is admitted to the unit after a CVA that damaged the right side of her brain. The nurse knows to position her

    (1) on her right side with the head of the bed slightly elevated.

    (2) on her left side with the head of the bed slightly elevated.

    (3) in the prone position.

    (4) supine with the bed in trendelenberg.

22. The client in the E.R. was in a car accident, and while not seriously injured, he is exhibiting signs of the "fight or flight" sympathetic nervous system response. The nurse knows to expect the following findings:

    (1) Bradycardia

    (2) Cold hands

    (3) Pinpoint pupils

    (4) Diarrhea

23. What is the first nursing consideration for a client who has a stroke?

    (1) Maintaining a patent airway and preventing aspiration

    (2) Assessing the client's level of consciousness

    (3) Reassuring the client, who may be frightened and confused

    (4) Providing active and passive ROM to preserve function

24. Adequate fluids are necessary for surgical clients in the postoperative period in order to maintain

(1) peristalsis and range of motion.

(2) urine output and blood volume.

(3) wound healing.

(4) patent airway.

25. Caitlin Block brings her grandmother to the clinic for her routine cardiac checkup. While you are interviewing the older woman, you notice Caitlin has exophthalmus, a slight goiter, and mild tremors. You know these are definite symptoms of hyperthyroidism. You ask Caitlin if she has any other symptoms related to this disease such as

(1) thinning hair, weight loss, tachycardia, or oligomenorrhea.

(2) excessive sweating, weight gain, gastric reflux, or slurred speech.

(3) weight loss, bradycardia, dry mouth, or constipation.

(4) weight gain, dyspnea, blurred vision, or tachycardia.

26. Mrs. Farinella has been newly diagnosed with insulin-dependent diabetes mellitus. You must teach her the symptoms of hypoglycemia. Which would be the *best* description?

(1) Increased heart rate, hunger, sweating, tremors, and confusion

(2) Dry mouth, nausea, dizziness, and tremors

(3) Hunger, lethargy, difficulty breathing, and increased urine output

(4) Sweating, decreased heart rate, lethargy, and nausea

27. The nurse must follow specific steps to maintain sterility when inserting a Foley catheter into a client's bladder. Which series of steps is *best*?

(1) Establish a sterile field, don sterile gloves, check the balloon on the catheter, clean the urinary meatus, and insert the catheter.

(2) Clean the client, establish a sterile field, open all the necessary packages, don sterile gloves, and insert the catheter.

(3) Position the client, set up all the necessary equipment, don sterile gloves, clean the urinary meatus, and insert the catheter.

(4) Establish a sterile field, clean the urinary meatus, check the balloon on the catheter, and insert the catheter.

28. One of the most important functions to assess when caring for a client with myasthenia gravis is

(1) bowel activity.

(2) ability to see.

(3) cardiac status.

(4) respiratory rate and depth.

29. The wife of Paul H. asks you if her husband will be able to feed himself now that he has Parkinson's disease. Your best response is:

    (1) "You will have to assist him from now on."

    (2) "He may be able to continue to do things for himself for quite a while, depending on how fast the disease progresses."

    (3) "You should speak to his doctor about his prognosis."

    (4) "Most of his problems will be emotional rather than physical from now on."

30. The most important sign to watch a client with head injury is for

    (1) a widening pulse pressure and change in the level of consciousness.

    (2) sleeplessness.

    (3) nausea.

    (4) seizure.

31. Marie, a 62-year-old woman, is in the physician's office for a checkup. While talking to the nurse before her exam, Marie says that she and her husband have been having sex less frequently, because she has been experiencing discomfort when they had sex. The nurse explained that physiological changes of aging can affect certain aspects of sexual expression. One of the best interventions to assist these clients is for the nurse to

    (1) explain that decreasing interest in sex is normal, and that most older people do not miss it much.

    (2) tell Marie that even at his age, her husband might feel justified in "looking elsewhere" for sex, and that there are many more older women than men.

    (3) suggest that Marie get George a book to help him brush up on his technique so she can start enjoying sex more.

    (4) discuss with Marie the normal age-related changes in sexual function and possible methods to help alleviate her discomfort so it will not interfere with her sexual expression.

32. Arrange the following cognitive stages of development as defined by Piaget from youngest to oldest.

    (1) Preoperational thought, intuitive phase   ____

    (2) Concrete operations   ____

    (3) Sensorimotor   ____

    (4) Preoperational thought, preconceptual phase   ____

33. The nurse is treating a 16-year-old client who is in the hospital for a broken shoulder. When discussing his care, it is important for the nurse to remember that adolescents

    (1) can only understand information and examples that are concrete.

    (2) need an authority figure who will tell them what to do.

    (3) tend to plan and think about future consequences.

    (4) should be allowed to participate in treatment decisions.

34. The nurse is in the room as the new baby is delivered. The father asks when the APGAR score will be given. The nurse replies that the assessment is completed at

    (1) 5 and 10 minutes after birth.
    (2) 1 and 5 minutes after birth.
    (3) 15 minutes and 1 hour after birth.
    (4) the time of birth.

35. A nurse is assessing a third-day postpartum cesarean section client who is to be discharged later in the day. Which of the following findings would she report to her charge nurse?

    (1) Abdominal tenderness near the incision site
    (2) Client states breasts are swollen and uncomfortable
    (3) Abdominal distention, absent bowel sounds, client has not passed flatus
    (4) Scant lochia rubra

36. At her thirty-nine week checkup, the midwife informs the client that her baby's head is engaged. The client asks the nurse if she should be feeling any differently. The nurse explains that she may find that she has

    (1) leg cramps.
    (2) pedal edema.
    (3) an increased need to urinate.
    (4) more shortness of breath.

37. The young woman comes to the clinic with amenorrhea, urinary frequency, and nausea. The nurse explains that these are referred to as

    (1) presumptive signs of pregnancy.
    (2) probable signs of pregnancy.
    (3) diagnostic signs of pregnancy.
    (4) positive signs of pregnancy.

38. When providing teaching for the 85-year-old home-care client, the nurse knows to emphasize which of the following to help prevent a major cause of disability in older individuals?

    (1) Arrange for regular periods of rest to avoid becoming overtired.
    (2) Do regular stretching exercises to maintain flexibility.
    (3) Decrease caloric intake due to lower metabolic rate and tendency to gain weight.
    (4) Accident-prevention strategies such as using night lights and bathroom handrails.

39. A child comes to a pediatrician's office for a well visit. Based on the information on the child's chart, what is her age?

    (1) Three months

    (2) Five months

    (3) Six months

    (4) Nine months

DEVELOPMENT

Fine/Gross motor skills: Sits without support. Can self-feed a cracker or biscuit.

Speech/Social: Says "dada" and "mama." Shows signs of stranger activity.

Activities: Plays peek-a-boo and pat-a-cake. Likes to look at self in mirror.

VACCINES

Hep B	2/12/09 3/14/09 8/13/09
DTaP	4/14/09 6/12/09 8/13/09
Hib	4/14/09 6/12/09 8/13/09
Polio	4/14/09 6/12/09

HEIGHT/WEIGHT

Weight at birth: 7 lbs 10 oz
Length at birth: 21 in
Head circ. at birth: 13 in
Date: 8/13/09
Weight: 15 lbs 4 oz
Length: 25¼ in
Head circ.: 21 in

40. The second-time mother of a newborn and a 3-year-old daughter named Amanda confides to the nurse that Amanda, who has been toilet-trained and has been drinking from a cup for some time, now wants to wear a diaper and drink from a bottle on occasion. The nurse explains that Amanda is using a defense mechanism to deal with the stress of a new family member. This defense mechanism is called

    (1) compensation.

    (2) displacement.

    (3) regression.

    (4) sublimation.

41. The client states that her last menstrual period was on May 15, 2009, and asks the nurse when she can expect to deliver. Using Nagele's rule, the nurse calculates that her due date is

    (1) February 22, 2010.

    (2) February 8, 2010.

    (3) February 15, 2010.

    (4) Cannot be calculated without knowing the date of conception

42. When checking Willy's mother's history, the nurse notices that the amniotic membranes had ruptured 72 hours before the delivery. She realizes that this increases Willy's risk for

    (1) amnionitis.

    (2) jaundice.

    (3) hypoglycemia.

    (4) infection.

practice test

43. The newborn baby boy was staring intently at his father's face. His dad, Jack, asked the nurse if the baby could see. The nurse told Jack that the baby could see, and that the position Jack was holding him in was ideal for the baby to see most clearly. The distance Jack was holding the baby from his face was

    (1) 12–14 inches.

    (2) 4–6 inches.

    (3) 8–10 inches.

    (4) 18–22 inches.

44. A physician writes an order for a client to receive Pediazole, 4 mL p.o. every 12 hours. Pediazole is a suspension medication that contains 200 mg erythromycin and 600 mg sulfisoxazole per 5 mL. How many ml of erythromycin is the client receiving in a 24-hour period?

Answer _____ mg

45. The oncoming nurse is given the following facts about the postoperative client during the 3 p.m. change-of-shift report. Which aspect of the client's condition requires prompt follow-up?

    (1) "Pain rated 4 on a scale of 1 to 10."

    (2) "Out of bed to chair for 45 minutes."

    (3) "Dressing removed, small amount of serous drainage noted."

    (4) "Foley discontinued at 8 a.m., has not voided."

46. The nurse is about to prepare the client for insertion of a central line. Before the procedure is started, the nurse must

    (1) explain the benefits and risks of the procedure.

    (2) explain how the procedure is done.

    (3) discuss alternatives to the procedure if the client asks.

    (4) confirm that informed consent has been given.

47. The 87-year-old hospital client will be sent to an assisted living facility. He asks the nurse who is responsible for arranging his continued care. She replies that this is primarily the responsibility of

    (1) hospital discharge planning.

    (2) the client's family.

    (3) the primary physician.

    (4) Medicaid.

48. The physician orders the following for the Alzheimer's client whose daughter has signed a "do not resuscitate" order. Which order should the nurse question?

   (1) Xanax 0.50 mg p.o. q.i.d. prn for agitation

   (2) 1 can Ensure t.i.d. with meals

   (3) Ambu bag to be kept at bedside

   (4) Seconal 100 mg. p.o. h.s. prn

49. The nurse has been asked to prepare the monthly report for the unit's quality assurance program. Which would be the *best* subject for quality assurance analysis?

   (1) Number of admissions

   (2) Physician handwriting

   (3) Documentation of medication administration

   (4) Staffing

50. The elderly cardiac client informs the nurse that he does not want to "be hooked up to a bunch of machines" and does not want to have CPR or other aggressive treatments done to prolong his life. The nurse tells him that the *most effective* way for him to assure that he will not have treatments he doesn't want is to

   (1) inform the hospital chaplain of his wishes.

   (2) inform his primary physician.

   (3) discuss the matter with his family.

   (4) prepare a living will.

51. A young mother crying to the nurse states, "I can't get any rest here in the hospital because my family and friends keep visiting, and I haven't been to sleep since I've had the baby." The nurse offers to put a sign on the door to have visitors check at the desk before going in the client's room. This is an example of

   (1) risk management.

   (2) empathy.

   (3) client advocacy.

   (4) quality control.

52. The first-day postoperative client who has been started on clear liquids tells the nurse that she is afraid of needles when the nurse prepares to administer her Demerol shot. The nurse would be acting as a client advocate by

   (1) reassuring the client that it will only hurt for a second and she will feel better.

   (2) asking if the physician could change the pain medication to one that is p.o.

   (3) using alternative pain relief measures such as relaxation and deep breathing.

   (4) not telling the client when the shot was to be given, so she would not be fearful.

53. When given an assignment to care for a client with an infusion pump she is unfamiliar with, the *best* action by the nurse would be to

    (1) explain to her supervising RN why she cannot care for the client.

    (2) care for the client and figure out how the pump works.

    (3) care for the client but not use the pump while she is on duty.

    (4) ask her charge nurse to show her how to use the pump.

54. During a snowstorm, the nurses scheduled to come for the next shift have not arrived by 3:30 p.m. The nurse should

    (1) notify the supervisor, give a summary of the status of her clients, and leave.

    (2) leave, but write an incident report about the nurses' not reporting to duty.

    (3) instruct an aide on how to care for her clients until relief nurses arrive.

    (4) remain with her clients until relief nurses arrive.

55. The young resident physician wants to take a photograph of a client with an unusual congenital condition. As a client advocate, the nurse should

    (1) help the client look as attractive as possible.

    (2) document in the client's chart that a photograph has been taken.

    (3) notify medical records.

    (4) inform the resident that he needs to obtain the client's consent.

56. Working with dietary consultants to help ensure that a Jewish patient receives kosher meals is an example of which of the following?
Select all that apply.

    ☐ **(1)** Cultural competence

    ☐ **(2)** Client advocacy

    ☐ **(3)** Informed consent

    ☐ **(4)** Meeting nutritional needs

57. To meet the goal of providing continuity of care as specified in the Patient's Bill of Rights, which of the following interventions would be appropriate?

    (1) Allowing the client to have the same room when rehospitalized

    (2) Providing a consistent daily routine of care while in the hospital

    (3) Having items from home, such as pictures, in the client's room

    (4) Giving the home care nurse a full report on the hospitalization

58. The nurse makes sure that the client has signed the informed consent form before the sigmoidoscopy. The purpose of obtaining consent is to

    (1) let the client know what is going to happen to him.

    (2) save the doctor time by providing a form that explains the procedure.

    (3) allow the client the opportunity to participate in choosing the plan of care.

    (4) protect the hospital from liability if the client changes his or her mind.

59. Which of the following nursing activities would the PN expect to perform in the acute care setting?

(1) Take vital signs and collect data for the assessment of a client with a broken hip.

(2) Prepare a nursing care plan for a pediatric client with respiratory syncytial virus.

(3) Provide teaching to a newly diagnosed diabetic.

(4) Teach a client after a mastectomy.

60. On the nursing unit, the RN, PN, and unlicensed nursing assistant may each be responsible for certain tasks and responsibilities. Which of the following is an appropriate allocation of unit activities?

(1) The PN delegates the performance of vital signs to the nursing assistant.

(2) The PN supervises the performance of a procedure by the nursing assistant.

(3) The RN delegates a client admission and assessment to the PN.

(4) The RN assigns the unit assistant responsibility for caring for 6 clients.

61. The postpartum client tells the nurse that she does not want her brother to learn that her baby is receiving Ziduvodine because she is HIV positive. The nurse correctly replies:

(1) "I'll put a note on the chart not to inform him."

(2) "Can you describe him? I want to let the nursery know."

(3) "He will not be told since we don't inform anyone about a client's treatment."

(4) "We need to remove the medication sheet from the infant chart on the crib."

62. The client who has just been diagnosed with cancer states that she is not sure she will be able to cope with chemotherapy. The nurse can best help her by replying:

(1) "Don't say that. You'll be just fine."

(2) "I have a friend who just finished chemo, and she didn't have any problems."

(3) "You sound worried. Tell me about your concerns."

(4) "You have small children. You should be grateful for anything that may help. They need you."

63. The nurse is caring for the breast cancer client who states, "The worst part is my hair falling out. I don't want to look like Michael Jordan. My appearance is important to me." The nurse's *most helpful* response would be:

(1) "I don't think you look bad. You have pretty eyes."

(2) "Many people start getting their hair back within several weeks of treatment."

(3) "Your real friends love you for yourself, not your hair."

(4) "That bothers you a lot, doesn't it. Have you thought of talking to other people who have had the same problem?"

64. The nurse is discharging the 82-year-old man who has been hospitalized with complications from influenza. He informs the nurse that he has no family nearby and lives alone. Which of the following discharge instructions should receive *priority* for this client?

    (1) "You may take two tablets of acetaminophen p.o. prn for muscle aches or fever."

    (2) "Try not to overexert yourself until you have fully regained your strength."

    (3) "Make an appointment with the senior citizens center and call Meals on Wheels."

    (4) "Call your primary care provider if you have not fully recovered within two weeks."

65. The nurse's shift ends at 3 p.m. Which of these actions would be most likely to ensure continuity of care for the clients?

    (1) Inform the RN of any client problems.

    (2) Finish a progress note on each client.

    (3) Check to make sure the I & Os and assessments are completed.

    (4) Provide the oncoming nurse with a verbal or written report on each client.

66. The nurse is asked to participate in a case conference, along with the other health-care members treating the client. They plan to discuss how each discipline is handling the client's care and what are future plans for treatment. The main benefit to the client of such discussions is that they

    (1) promote continuity of care from his health-care team.

    (2) make him feel that people care about him.

    (3) prevent malpractice suits.

    (4) provide preventive care.

67. The hospital diabetes nurse-educator is coming to see the nurse's client, a newly diagnosed diabetic who is hard of hearing and nearsighted. The *best* way for the nurse to assist in the client's teaching would be to

    (1) provide privacy and uninterrupted time for the teaching session.

    (2) inform the educator of the client's sensory deficits, which are barriers to learning.

    (3) obtain the unit glucometer and glucose testing strips in case they're needed.

    (4) emphasize to the client's family the importance of good blood sugar control.

68. The unit manager has instituted a quality improvement program to improve documentation of medication administration. Which of the following outcomes would indicate that the program is successful?

    (1) Medication errors have decreased by 12 percent.

    (2) Drug costs for the unit have declined by 7 percent.

    (3) The site of IM injections is documented 25 percent more often than previously.

    (4) The pharmacy reports increased compliance with return of unused drugs.

69. Because of current health-care reimbursement practices, the home-care nurse finds that her client who definitely is in need of ongoing care no longer qualifies for Medicare reimbursement. The decision between complying with regulations and providing adequate care is *most accurately described* as a(n)

(1) opportunity to teach self-help measures.

(2) illustration of the need for community centers.

(3) ethical dilemma.

(4) matter of continuity of care.

70. The nurse finds the 83-year-old client on the floor with her restraints wrapped around her shoulders. After having a physician check to make sure she is unhurt and putting her back to bed, the nurse *must*

(1) notify biomedical engineering.

(2) have the client's medications adjusted so she is less agitated.

(3) complete an incident report.

(4) call the next of kin.

71. After the physician has explained the risks and benefits of a procedure, as well as any possible alternatives to a procedure, the nurse witnesses the client's signature permitting the procedure to be conducted. What is this process called?

(1) A contract

(2) A living will

(3) Informed consent

(4) Advocacy

72. The nurse is obtaining admission data on an older woman who has numerous bruises in varying states of healing on her back. When questioned by the nurse, she confides that her son-in-law has been hitting her. The nurse is legally required to

(1) fill out an incident report.

(2) report the abuse to the proper authorities.

(3) make sure the woman has a safe place to stay.

(4) file a criminal complaint against the son-in-law.

73. The nurse, who has been working exclusively with older clients, is asked to float to the nursery. She knows she is liable for charges of negligence if she makes a mistake performing functions she is not prepared or educated to handle. What would be the *best* solution to this problem?

(1) Refuse to float since she has not been trained to work with newborns.

(2) With her supervisor, decide on tasks she is capable of handling.

(3) Take the nursery assignment and do her best—they need the help.

(4) Go home since she cannot do the assigned work.

74. A nurse is working the evening shift at a continuing-care facility. During her shift, she smells smoke in the hallway. She follows the smell of smoke into a client's room and discovers that the client has fallen asleep in a chair and that there is a small fire in the wastebasket next to him. The nurse takes immediate action. Place the actions in chronological order beginning with the first priority.

(1) Extinguish the fire.　　　　　　　　　　　　　　　　　　　　　＿＿＿

(2) Rescue the patient.　　　　　　　　　　　　　　　　　　　　　＿＿＿

(3) Trigger the fire alarm.　　　　　　　　　　　　　　　　　　　＿＿＿

(4) Confine the fire.　　　　　　　　　　　　　　　　　　　　　　＿＿＿

75. Hemorrhoids, commonly called piles, affect which of the following structures?

(1) Pyloric sphincter

(2) Rectal sphincter

(3) Urethral orifice

(4) Mitral orifice

ANSWER KEY AND EXPLANATIONS

1. 4	16. 1	31. 4	46. 4	61. 3
2. 3	17. 4	32. 3,4,1,2	47. 1	62. 3
3. 2	18. 4	33. 4	48. 3	63. 4
4. 4	19. 4	34. 2	49. 3	64. 3
5. 3,2,1,4	20. 3	35. 3	50. 4	65. 4
6. 1	21. 2	36. 3	51. 3	66. 1
7. 2	22. 2	37. 1	52. 2	67. 2
8. 1	23. 1	38. 4	53. 4	68. 3
9. 4	24. 2	39. 3	54. 4	69. 3
10. 3	25. 1	40. 3	55. 4	70. 3
11. 3	26. 1	41. 1	56. 1,2,4	71. 3
12. 3	27. 1	42. 4	57. 4	72. 2
13. left ventricle	28. 4	43. 3	58. 3	73. 2
	29. 2	44. 240	59. 1	74. 2,3,4,1
14. 4	30. 1	45. 4	60. 2	75. 2
15. 4				

1. **The correct answer is (4).** Passing flatus is an important sign indicating normal bowel function.

2. **The correct answer is (3).** Aspirating to check for gastric residual not only determines if the previous feedings are being digested, but it confirms the correct placement of the tube.

3. **The correct answer is (2).** The usual way of measuring the length to insert a nasogastric tube is to measure from the earlobe to the nose to the lower part of the sternum.

4. **The correct answer is (4).** The nurse should assess for a problem in positioning or alignment which can readily be fixed before notifying the RN or provider. Massaging will not help, and it is incorrect to tell the client that this is a common side effect that will pass.

5. **The correct order of answers is (3), (2), (1), (4).** Redness, warmth, pain, and a hard, "cord-like" vein at the site of an IV insertion are signs of phlebitis. The nurse should first discontinue the IV and remove the line. He should then insert a new catheter proximal to the infected site or on the other arm. This will ensure that the new line does not contribute to the inflammation. Skin sloughing is associated with extravasation of certain toxic medications, and the nurse should include this in an assessment of the infection site. Warm soaks applied to the site will help reduce the inflammation. Finally, the nurse should document the complete assessment, including the actions he took and the client's response to the treatment.

6. **The correct answer is (1).** Weight loss, increased temperature, nervousness and irritability, as well as tachycardia, are signs of hyperthyroidism.

7. The correct answer is (2). Older, overweight clients typically suffer from type 2 diabetes, which tends to be familial, whereas type 1 diabetes is not.

8. The correct answer is (1). In the glucose challenge test, which is used to screen for diabetes in pregnancy, a reading of 140 or over should be followed by the glucose tolerance test. A glucose level less than 105 (2) is a good reading for a fasting blood glucose. A result between 130 and 165 (3) includes readings between 140 and 165, which are considered high. The blood sugar guidelines apply to all clients and are not different for each individual (4).

9. The correct answer is (4). Proper foot care is one of the most important things to teach diabetics, since they often cannot feel injuries to their feet, and neglected infections can and frequently do cause loss of a leg or death.

10. The correct answer is (3). Her answers (1), (2), and (4) are correct statements about diabetic care. However, bowling once a week is exercise that is not of sufficient intensity nor is it frequent enough to help in diabetic management.

11. The correct answer is (3). Graves' disease is characterized by an increased metabolic rate because of increased thyroid levels. The client is likely to feel excessively warm and to experience an increased heart rate, increased activity level, and weight loss.

12. The correct answer is (3). Potatoes are considered a starch exchange on the diabetic exchange system diet.

13. The correct answer is the left ventricle. Arterial fibrillation carries an increased risk of clot formation in the left ventricle of the heart because blood stagnates in this region. When a piece of the clot breaks loose and travels to the brain, a client experiences an embolic stroke.

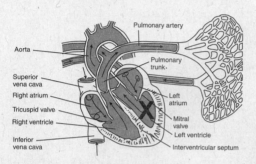

14. The correct answer is (4). A cheese omelet is made up of two extremely high-cholesterol foods: cheese and eggs. The other answer choices are examples of low-cholesterol foods.

15. The correct answer is (4). The buccal mucosa is considered to be the most accurate area of the body to assess skin pallor on those with dark skin.

16. The correct answer is (1). Caesar salad with spinach frittata would be a meal high in vitamin K, which is an antagonist to Coumadin. None of the other foods are high in this vitamin.

17. The correct answer is (4). Nurses' notes are legal documents and cannot be destroyed or obliterated. Transferring a page to another client's chart is not feasible because client information is stamped by addressograph on the upper right corner of each document page. Changing a name would still leave the other client's identifying information on the page.

18. **The correct answer is (4).** Secobarbital is a sedative agent and sleep medication. Sedatives and narcotics can mask symptoms of increased ICP and cause respiratory depression. Dexamethasone (1) is a glucocorticoid and anti-inflammatory that can decrease swelling. Mannitol (2) is an osmotic diuretic that promotes diuresis, which can decrease intracranial pressure. Phenytoin (3) is an anticonvulsant.

19. **The correct answer is (4).** A communication board can help this client communicate his needs. Anticipating his needs will not help him learn to communicate, speaking as if he were a child is demeaning, and discussing the client's problems in front of him as if he did not exist is rude.

20. **The correct answer is (3).** The characteristic problem in Parkinson's is tremors, and the medication for it is designed to reduce these.

21. **The correct answer is (2).** A client with a right-sided CVA would have left-sided paralysis, so having her lie on her left side leaves her functional side up. If she were lying on her right side, she would have no way to move. The prone and supine Trendelenburg positions both increase intracranial pressure.

22. **The correct answer is (2).** Cold hands are a symptom of peripheral vasoconstriction characteristic of a sympathetic nervous system response. Bradycardia, pinpoint pu-

pils, and diarrhea are all symptoms of parasympathetic dominance.

23. **The correct answer is (1).** After a stroke, the client is at high risk for aspiration and may have problems maintaining a patent airway because of paralysis.

24. **The correct answer is (2).** Fluids lost due to blood loss in surgery, npo, diaphoresis or other insensible loss, and urine all contribute to potential dehydration or hypovolemia.

25. **The correct answer is (1).** The increase in metabolic rate resulting from excessive thyroid hormones causes thinning hair, weight loss, tachycardia, and/or oligomenorrhea (abnormally light or infrequent menstruation).

26. **The correct answer is (1).** Hypoglycemia results from too much circulating insulin and not enough glucose. Visual disturbances and decreased urinary output can also be indicative of this problem.

27. **The correct answer is (1).** Every effort must be made to keep the urinary bladder free from microorganisms.

28. **The correct answer is (4).** Clients with myasthenia gravis often have upper-body muscle weakness, including the respiratory muscles.

29. **The correct answer is (2).** Manifestations of the disorder progress so slowly that years may go by before the client needs total physical care. Treatment is aimed at keeping the client independent as long as possible.

30. The correct answer is (1). After head injury the risk of intracranial injury is possible without any visible signs. These symptoms are the best indicators of increasing intracranial pressure.

31. The correct answer is (4). Age-related changes in sexual functioning can often be alleviated by the use of lubricants.

32. The correct order of answers are (3), (4), (1), (2). According to Jean Piaget, a child will develop in these stages:

0–2 years: Sensorimotor Period

2–4 years: Preoperational Thought—preconceptual phase using transductive reasoning

4–7 years: Preoperational Thought—intuitive phase using transductive reasoning

7–11 years: Concrete Operations using inductive reasoning and beginning logic

33. The correct answer is (4). Adolescents are seeking autonomy and want to make decisions for themselves as much as possible.

34. The correct answer is (2). The AP-GAR is completed at 1 minute to help identify intrauterine problems and at 5 minutes to evaluate the infant's adaptation to extrauterine life.

35. The correct answer is (3). These are signs of a possible ileus, and the client must be assessed further.

36. The correct answer is (3). When the baby's head drops farther into the pelvis, the mother can often breathe easier, but she may feel increased pelvic pressure and urinary frequency.

37. The correct answer is (1). The presumptive signs of pregnancy are amenorrhea, nausea and vomiting, breast sensitivity, urinary frequency, fatigue, weight gain, and quickening.

38. The correct answer is (4). Susceptibility to accidents in older individuals is increased by a number of factors, including a decline in sensory acuity, increased reflex time, confusion, and medications that may cause drowsiness.

39. The correct answer is (3). Based on all three charts, the child's age is about six months. Gross/fine motor skills, speech and social development, and activities are all consistent with those of a 6-month-old. The vaccination schedule is consistent with that of a 6-month-old child. Also, a healthy infant should double his/her weight by about six months, and the infant's head circumference should increase by about 2 inches per month for the first three months of life and about 1 inch per month for the next few months.

40. The correct answer is (3). Regression is coping with a stressor through actions and behaviors associated with an earlier developmental period.

41. The correct answer is (1). Nagele's rule is a way of determining a woman's due date by taking the first day of the last menstrual period, subtracting three months, and then adding seven days.

42. The correct answer is (4). Prolonged rupture of membranes allows for greater likelihood of an ascending infection, which can affect both the mother and infant. Amnionitis (1) is an infection of the amniotic fluid, jaundice (2) is a newborn condition due to increased levels of bilirubin, and hypoglycemia (3) is low blood sugar.

43. The correct answer is (3). Although newborns can see, they are nearsighted and can see most clearly at the distance parents instinctively hold their babies when facing them, 8–10 inches.

44. The correct answer is 240. This should be recorded as "240 mg" in a clinical setting. Solve for mL per dose using the following ratio:

$$\frac{200 \text{ mg}}{5 \text{ mL}} = \frac{x \text{ mg}}{4 \text{ mL}}$$

$$800 = 5x$$

$$x = \frac{800}{5}$$

$$x = 120 \text{ mg per dose}$$

To determine the amount given in a 24-hour period, multiply the mg per dose by the number of doses administered over 24 hours. One dose every 12 hours = 2 doses every 24 hours.

120 mg × 2 = 240 mg/24 hours

45. The correct answer is (4). A pain rating of 4 on a scale of 10 is not usually a cause for immediate action. Getting out of bed and the dressing change finding are both routine. A client who has not voided for 7 hours requires prompt assessment and intervention.

46. The correct answer is (4). Insertion of a central line is a procedure that requires informed consent, and the nurse is responsible for verifying that a signed consent form has been obtained.

47. The correct answer is (1). The individual or department that handles discharge planning is responsible for coordinating and implementing adequate arrangements for discharge from the acute-care facility. Input from the physician and family are important, but the responsibility remains with the hospital. Medicaid is involved with care reimbursement.

48. The correct answer is (3). Since the daughter has signed a "do not resuscitate" order, resuscitation equipment, such as the ambu bag, should not be kept by the client.

49. The correct answer is (3). Unit quality assurance programs are intended to monitor and improve practices and procedures that are handled by the unit, such as nursing documentation. Staffing, physician handwriting, and number of admissions are not controlled by the unit.

50. The correct answer is (4). A living will is the mechanism designed to communicate the client's preferences regarding end-of-life care and must be in the chart. The chaplain, family members, and even the physician may not be present when decisions must be made.

51. The correct answer is (3). Client advocacy by nurses involves the protection of their human and legal rights, including the right to sleep in this case.

52. The correct answer is (2). This client is saying that she is not happy with the medication choice, and the nurse would be acting as her advocate by seeking to change it. Since this is the first day postoperative, relaxation and breathing are unlikely to provide sufficient pain relief.

53. The correct answer is (4). Nurses should not work with unfamiliar equipment, especially pumps that can cause serious problems if they malfunction. Not using the pump or not caring for the client are not responsible alternatives; the nurse needs to get an inservice from her charge person.

54. The correct answer is (4). Once a nurse has accepted care of a client, she may not leave the client without transferring the responsibility to another caregiver.

55. The correct answer is (4). A photograph of a client may not be taken without his or her consent, and it is the nurse's responsibility to make sure that consent is obtained.

56. The correct answers are (1), (2), and (4). Care that is sensitive to and takes into account clients' cultural backgrounds is an expectation in today's diverse society.

57. The correct answer is (4). Continuity of care, which involves well-coordinated management of a client's care, necessitates excellent communication among members of the health-care team.

58. The correct answer is (3). The purpose of informed consent is part of the principle of autonomy for clients in that they should be allowed to make choices in their care and be an active partner in choices made.

59. The correct answer is (1). PNs provide direct care to stable clients under the direction of a registered nurse or physician. They may collect data for the nursing diagnosis (1). However, they usually do not prepare nursing care plans (2) or provide initial teaching to newly diagnosed or postsurgical clients (3) and (4).

60. The correct answer is (2). The PN may not delegate tasks to the nursing assistant (1), nor may the RN delegate a client admission to the PN (3), since delegation involves assigning responsibility for the task to another, and the RN must maintain responsibility for the clients. This is true in the case of assigning care to a unit assistant as well (4). However, the PN may supervise the performance of a procedure of a nursing assistant (2).

61. The correct answer is (3). As a matter of confidentiality, this information should not be given out to anyone.

62. The correct answer is (3). Giving advice or telling the client what to do prevents the client from arriving at conclusions independently and is considered to be a barrier to therapeutic communication. Using cliches or providing false reassurance also are nontherapeutic and leave the client feeling alone and misunderstood. Helping clients to clarify and focus their feelings can allow them to better understand and deal with their emotions.

63. **The correct answer is (4).** Minimizing the problem (1), offering false reassurance (2), or belittling her feelings (3) are not helpful. Clarifying and offering a suggestion may help (4).

64. **The correct answer is (3).** This client needs support and assistance in meeting his basic needs as he recovers. These organizations may be able to help improve his health and quality of life.

65. **The correct answer is (4).** A complete verbal or written report on each client is one of the best ways that nurses may communicate important information about their clients to the oncoming shift.

66. **The correct answer is (1).** Communication among different members of the health-care team allows the client to benefit from a coordinated effort. While it is possible that this may make the client feel cared for, prevent malpractice suits, or contribute to preventive care, it is not the primary intent.

67. **The correct answer is (2).** Addressing the client's barriers to learning—his hearing and sight problems—are critical to the success of the client teaching.

68. **The correct answer is (3).** To assess the success of a quality improvement program in a nursing unit, the change in the problem being addressed, in this case documentation, must be measured.

69. **The correct answer is (3).** Even though reimbursement has changed, client needs have not necessarily declined. Health-care providers today are faced with many ethical problems related to this issue.

70. **The correct answer is (3).** An incident report must be filled out whenever something happens that is inconsistent with normal hospital routine and the follow-up care provided.

71. **The correct answer is (3).** Informed consent is the process of explaining the risks and benefits of a procedure, as well as any alternative treatments, in order to allow the client to make an informed decision about his or her care.

72. **The correct answer is (2).** Nurses are required to report elder abuse as well as child abuse to the proper authorities.

73. **The correct answer is (2).** In order to protect herself from charges of negligence, the nurse should not perform tasks she is not trained to do. However, to show that she is trying to be as helpful as possible, working with her supervisor on appropriate tasks is usually the best solution.

74. **The correct order of answers is (2), (3), (4), (1).** Based on the RACE (Rescue, Alarm, Confine, Extinguish) mnemonic, the nurse's first priority is the client's safety. Next, the nurse should summon help with the alarm

and then attempt to confine and extinguish the fire if it is manageable.

75. The correct answer is (2). A hemorrhoid is a dilation of veins in the anal region. This can lead to an enlargement of tissue, especially the rectal sphincter, which is a ring-shaped muscle controlling the anal opening.

ANSWER SHEET PRACTICE TEST 2

1. ①②③④   16. ①②③④   31. ①②③④   46. ①②③④   61. ①②③④
2. ①②③④   17. ①②③④   32. ①②③④   47. ①②③④   62. ①②③④
3. ①②③④   18. ①②③④   33. ①②③④   48. ①②③④   63. ①②③④
4. ①②③④   19. ①②③④   34. ①②③④   49. ①②③④   64. ①②③④
5. ①②③④   20. _____   35. ①②③④   50. ①②③④   65. ①②③④
6. ①②③④   21. ①②③④   36. ①②③④   51. ①②③④   66. ①②③④
7. ①②③④   22. ①②③④   37. _____   52. ①②③④   67. ①②③④
8. _ _ _ _   23. ①②③④   38. ①②③④   53. ①②③④   68. ①②③④
9. ①②③④   24. ①②③④   39. ①②③④   54. ①②③④   69. ①②③④
10. ①②③④   25. ①②③④   40. ①②③④   55. ①②③④   70. ①②③④
11. ①②③④   26. ①②③④   41. ①②③④   56. ①②③④   71. ①②③④
12. ①②③④   27. ①②③④   42. ①②③④   57. ①②③④   72. ①②③④
13. ①②③④   28. ①②③④   43. ①②③④   58. ①②③④   73. ①②③④
14. ①②③④   29. ①②③④   44. ①②③④   59. ①②③④   74. ①②③④
15. ①②③④   30. ①②③④   45. ①②③④   60. ①②③④   75. ①②③④

answer sheet

Practice Test 2

Directions: Each question or incomplete statement below is followed by four suggested answers or completions. In each case, select the statement that best answers the question or completes the sentence.

1. The nurse is writing her notes after collecting data about her newly admitted client. Which information would be appropriate to document as the subjective portion of the note?

    (1) Temperature of 100.8 degrees Fahrenheit

    (2) Maculopapular rash on upper abdomen

    (3) Client says, "I have a sore throat."

    (4) Apical pulse, 84

2. A nurse is talking with a 54-year-old woman who has come to the clinic for an annual physical. The client starts to discuss her 25-year-old son, who has recently become engaged and also has been promoted at his engineering company. The nurse tells the woman that it sounds as though her son is doing well. The nurse knows that the son is dealing with the developmental tasks of young adults, which include which of the following?
   Select all that apply.

    ☐ (1) Gaining stability in employment

    ☐ (2) Beginning intimate relationships

    ☐ (3) Acceptance of body image changes

    ☐ (4) Settling into responsibility

3. The night nurse is unable to contact the physician, and she is concerned that her critically ill client's condition is getting worse. She is legally obligated to

    (1) document that the physician did not return her call.

    (2) provide whatever care is necessary to save the client.

    (3) notify the risk manager of the problem.

    (4) continue to go up the chain of command until her client receives medical attention.

4. The nurse is admitting a new client and performing the assessment phase of the nursing process. She is aware that the role of a practical nurse in assessing a client is to

   (1) assess the client and make nursing diagnoses for the care plan.

   (2) obtain the necessary documents so the client may be admitted.

   (3) collect the data base of information on the client's condition.

   (4) use therapeutic communication to orient and admit the client to the room.

5. Sandra L., who has been treated in the hospital for pneumonia, has decided to leave the hospital even though she has not been discharged. The *most important* obligation of the nurse or other medical provider is to

   (1) attempt to convince the client to remain in the hospital.

   (2) notify discharge planning.

   (3) advise the client of the risks of her decision.

   (4) inform the next of kin.

6. The registered nurse has delegated blood pressure checks to an unlicensed caregiver. The *primary* role of the practical nurse in relation to the unlicensed person is

   (1) making sure the person understands the task and performs it correctly.

   (2) determining which are the primary responsibilities of the unlicensed person.

   (3) informing the physician of problems in the performance of an unlicensed person.

   (4) deciding which tasks the unlicensed person can perform.

7. The nurse answers a call bell and finds a frightened mother whose child, the client, is having a seizure. Which of these actions should the nurse take?

   (1) The nurse should insert a padded tongue blade in the client's mouth to prevent the child from swallowing or choking on his tongue.

   (2) The nurse should help the mother restrain the child to prevent him from injuring himself.

   (3) The nurse should call the operator to page for seizure assistance.

   (4) The nurse should clear the area and position the client safely.

8. A nurse has just examined a client in a contact isolation room. Upon leaving the room, the nurse must be sure to remove her protective wear in the correct order. Place the following steps in the correct order from first piece to last.

   (1) Remove eyewear.   _____

   (2) Remove mask.   _____

   (3) Remove gloves.   _____

   (4) Remove gown.   _____

9. The nurse admits the antepartum client with ruptured membranes who is put on bed rest. The physician, in order to reduce the possibility of a prolapsed cord, orders her bed to be tilted with her head lower than her feet. The nurse correctly places her in the following position:

    (1) Sims
    (2) Lithotomy
    (3) Trendelenberg
    (4) Dorsal recumbent

10. An older client has been put in four-point restraints to protect herself from getting out of bed and falling. The nurse knows that an *essential* part of the care of a restrained client is to

    (1) notify the physician daily when a client is on restraints.
    (2) release and reapply the restraints at least every 2 hours
    (3) adequately sedate the client so he or she will not be agitated.
    (4) make sure the restraints are secure and will tighten if the client moves.

11. The nurse is assessing her new client, who states that she has a headache, dizziness, nausea, and fever. Which of the following would the nurse record as an *objective* finding?

    (1) Nausea after meals
    (2) Persistent frontal headache
    (3) Dizziness when standing
    (4) Temperature of 101.8 degrees Fahrenheit

12. In the client assessment of a woman complaining of lower extremity paresthesia, a diffuse papular rash, pedal edema, and an infected toe, which of her signs and symptoms should the nurse report as *subjective*?

    (1) Diffuse papular rash
    (2) Lower extremity paresthesia
    (3) Pedal edema
    (4) Toe infection

13. The nurse is preparing the room for a sterile procedure. She opens a sterile drape and places it over the top and sides of the table and carefully peels back the wrapping of several syringes and drops them on the table. She then pours 1–2 mL of sterile water into a waste receptacle and the remainder into a sterile bowl she has previously placed on the table. Some of the water splashes onto the table. The nurse, who is wearing a sterile gown and gloves, realizes that she may only touch which one of the following in order to maintain sterility?

    (1) The water in the bowl
    (2) The border of the sterile drape
    (3) The spot where the water splashed
    (4) The part of the drape covering the sides of the table

14. The nurse changes the dressing on the older client's decubitous ulcer. She notes that there is a quarter-sized area of clear watery drainage on the dressing. She would document this drainage as

   (1) sero-sanguinous.
   (2) purulent.
   (3) sanguinous.
   (4) serous.

15. The nurse is providing routine client care on her medical surgical unit. Which of the following actions is *essential* to prevent the spread of pathogens by reducing possible reservoirs of infection?

   (1) Changing soiled dressings
   (2) Making beds
   (3) Encouraging client ambulation
   (4) Administering intravenous fluids

16. In order to help provide a safe environment, the night nurse is careful to ensure that which of the following is done before leaving the room of a recently admitted client?

   (1) The light and TV are turned off.
   (2) Phone calls are diverted to the nurses' station for the night.
   (3) Visiting hours are explained.
   (4) The siderails are up and the call bell is within reach.

17. The nurse knows that client falls are a major cause of injury to older and confused clients. Since many falls occur when clients attempt to get out of bed to go to the bathroom, she makes sure to

   (1) leave a night light on for better vision.
   (2) insert a catheter so they won't have to get up.
   (3) restrain clients so they can't get up.
   (4) establish a regular schedule of toileting.

18. The nursing unit contains a number of hazardous materials. The nurse happens to spill one of them—a potentially flammable lubricant. She checks which of the following references to learn how best to dispose of this substance?

   (1) The unit MSDS book
   (2) The manual of nursing standards
   (3) The employee handbook
   (4) The nursing policy and procedure book

19. During the safety inspection, the nurse is asked for the location of the fire alarms and oxygen shut-off valves. She also knows to point out which other type of fire safety device located on the nursing unit?

   (1) Fire hoses
   (2) Escape ladders
   (3) Fire extinguishers
   (4) Smoke alarms

20. A nurse is caring for a client who is unable to swallow tablets. The attending physician orders an oral suspension of 40 mg/5 mL famotidine for the client. The client weighs 61 kg; the order states to administer 0.7 mg/kg/day divided twice daily. How many milliliters (to the nearest tenth) would the nurse pour into the medication cup for the first dose?
Round up to the nearest tenth.

Answer: _____ mL

21. Electrical safety is important both in the home and the hospital. Nurses are trained in yearly mandatory education sessions about ways to reduce the danger of electrical injury or fire. Which of the following would a nurse consider to be consistent with electrical safety?

(1) Frayed wires

(2) Overloaded outlets

(3) Using electrical appliances near water

(4) Grounded electrical equipment

22. The nurse finishes administering the intramuscular injection and drops the needle and syringe in the nearby sharps container. Needlestick injuries are a hazard for health-care workers, and so the nurse also takes which of the following precautions?

(1) Does not recap used needles

(2) Does not perform invasive procedures

(3) Does not draw blood

(4) Discontinues intravenous therapy

23. In maintaining infection-control precautions, a nurse is aware that there are three main types of infection control. Which of the following are elements of infection control?
Select all that apply.

☐ (1) Contact

☐ (2) Droplet

☐ (3) Respiratory

☐ (4) Airborne

24. The nurse is conscious of back safety when working, because back injuries are common in the health-care profession. Which of the following activities is consistent with back protection?

(1) Bending the knees and lifting objects by holding them close to the body

(2) Bending down with the knees straight

(3) Lowering the height of beds when they are being made

(4) Stretching and reaching whenever possible

25. The nurse is admitting a 65-year-old man with congestive heart failure. Aware that men over age 50 are at risk for benign prostatic hypertrophy, the nurse suspects this condition when the client says:

    (1) "I seem to get cold very easily, especially my feet."
    (2) "My hand trembles when I try to pick up something."
    (3) "My ankles are swollen."
    (4) "I have to get up several times at night to urinate."

26. A nurse is doing a mental status exam on the 90-year-old woman, who is oriented only to person. The woman is unsure of the date and does not know where she is. The nurse is careful to check the medical history for evidence that it might be due to a frequent cause of mental confusion in older individuals, which is

    (1) current medications.
    (2) lack of exercise.
    (3) damage to motor neurons.
    (4) parasympathetic reactivity.

27. The nurse placed an ice pack on her new client's perineum. The client asked when the episiotomy stitches would come out. The nurse answered that the stitches

    (1) would be removed at her six-week obstetrical visit.
    (2) would be removed and replaced with steri strips before discharge.
    (3) would remain as a permanent reinforcement to maintain vaginal tone.
    (4) were self-absorbing and would gradually dissolve.

28. The next day, the same client in the question above said her stitches were so sore she could not sit comfortably. Having already assessed her perineum and found it edematous but intact, the nurse should suggest which of the following as a comfort measure?

    (1) A warm sitz bath
    (2) Remaining on bed rest until she felt more comfortable
    (3) A perineal block
    (4) Nursing the baby to help ease the discomfort

29. At 1 and 5 minutes after birth, the nurse checks the baby's APGAR score. The newborn, born at 8:42 a.m., at 8:47 has a heart rate of 110, has a lusty cry, is active, and cries while being suctioned with the bulb syringe. The baby's hands and feet have a slightly blue undertone. What is her second APGAR score?

    (1) 10
    (2) 12
    (3) 9
    (4) 7

30. When the nurse checks her postpartum clients, she knows that thrombophlebitis is a potential complication after birth. In order to assess for this condition, she looks for calf redness, soreness, or edema. In addition, she dorsiflexes each foot to assess for pain. If it is present, she reports a positive

    (1) Chadwick's sign.
    (2) Homan's sign.
    (3) Goodell's sign.
    (4) McRobert's sign.

31. The nurse is assisting her obese two-day post C-section client, Ms. Johnson, out of bed. Ms. Johnson has been advised to ambulate due to gas pain and abdominal distention. As she starts to stand, she cries out and holds her abdomen. She says it feels as if her incision opened up. In addition to notifying the surgeon, the nurse should *immediately*

    (1) reinforce the incision with tape.
    (2) assist the client back to bed in semi-Fowler's position with knees flexed.
    (3) administer a dulcolax suppository.
    (4) wrap the abdomen tightly in a towel or blanket.

32. A newly delivered mother on postpartum, G5P5, has just had a 4,000-gram baby boy. Her uterus is soft and boggy and does not become firm with massage. Which of the following medications ordered for her would the nurse question?

    (1) Methergine
    (2) Oxytocin (pitocin)
    (3) Magnesium sulfate
    (4) Prostaglandin (hemabate)

33. The nurse learns that the delivery of a thirty-week gestation infant is imminent. In preparing to care for the infant, the nurse would be correct to assume that the condition that most frequently occurs in premature infants is

    (1) neonatal respiratory distress syndrome.
    (2) hypoglycemia.
    (3) hypospadius.
    (4) brachial plexus palsy.

34. Mrs. Connelly delivered her third child yesterday. This morning, when the infant's bloodwork results arrive, the nurse learns that the baby is Rh+. Since Mrs. Connelly is Rh−, the nurse anticipates the need to administer Rhogam within 72 hours of the delivery. The mother says, "I should know this, but what is the purpose of this shot?" The nurse correctly explains:

    (1) "It will prevent the next baby from developing hemolytic disease if it is Rh+."
    (2) "It will protect the baby from hyperbilirubinemia."
    (3) "It protects the mother from an adverse reaction to the baby's blood type."
    (4) "It protects the newborn from reacting to the mother's antibodies."

35. The nurse is assessing the newborn baby girl. The anxious mother is asking many questions about her baby's appearance. She is concerned that the baby has a clear mucous discharge from her vagina. The nurse, who is aware of the effects of maternal hormones on the newborn, reassures her that this is normal, as well as other newborn characteristics related to the mom's hormone levels, such as

(1) uric acid crystals.

(2) witch's milk.

(3) small amount of blood leaking from the nipples.

(4) cutis marmorata.

36. The nurse admits a thin young woman who is carrying a tissue with her to spit up secretions if she feels sick to her stomach. She is fourteen weeks' pregnant and has been nauseated and vomiting since the onset of her pregnancy. She is losing weight and is dehydrated. The physician decides to hospitalize her for hyperemesis gravidarum, and the nurse sets up the room expecting which of the following treatments?

(1) Intravenous fluid

(2) Gastric tube feedings

(3) Parenteral feeding through a central line

(4) Endoscopy

37. Matt C., a 17-year-old high school football player, was brought to the emergency department after being injured during a varsity game. He tells the nurse that he is sure that he tore his ACL, just like his favorite NFL quarterback recently did. An MRI shows that Matt has also dislocated his left patella. Identify the patella on the diagram below by placing an X on it.

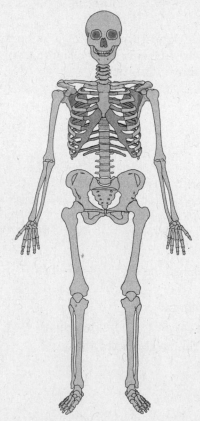

38. As the nurse is wheeling her client, Kim, down the hall towards labor and delivery, a gush of fluid leaks down Kim's leg onto the floor. The nurse notes the time the fluid leaked, its color, the amount, and, if present, any odor. When the nurse gets to the nursing station, she will check to verify that this is amniotic fluid. The first thing she does to determine if it was amniotic fluid leaking is

    (1) a sterile speculum exam to see if the amniotic sac is intact.

    (2) a nitrazine paper test.

    (3) send a stat sample of the fluid to the lab for analysis.

    (4) mix it with boric acid to see if a precipitate forms.

39. Pat is five months' pregnant and visiting the clinic for a glucose challenge test. While there, she tells the nurse she had a Cesarean section for fetal distress with her first baby and is wondering if she will need to have one this time. The nurse correctly replies:

    (1) "Once a Cesarean, always a Cesarean."

    (2) "You should be able to have a vaginal birth unless you develop a complication, such as with your last baby."

    (3) "You may try to have the baby vaginally, but it is unlikely you will succeed."

    (4) "I can guarantee you will be able to have your baby vaginally."

40. The nurse prepares to administer pitocin to the mother after the delivery. She knows that this medication is a synthetic form of the natural hormone oxytocin. Which observation would indicate that the medication has *not* been effective?

    (1) Blood pressure 100/68

    (2) Inability to void after delivery

    (3) Breast pain

    (4) Boggy uterus

41. The school nurse's office is responsible for periodically checking students for lateral curvature of the spine (scoliosis). The nurse examines each child for which of the following signs?
    Select all that apply.

    ☐ **(1)** Head and hip are not in vertical alignment.

    ☐ **(2)** Waistline is uneven.

    ☐ **(3)** When the child is bending forward, the shoulders are at different levels.

    ☐ **(4)** One leg is shorter than the other.

42. When planning care for the 80-year-old man scheduled to have hernia surgery, the nurse knows that because of his age, a priority in his care would include which of the following?

    (1) Strict monitoring of I & O after surgery

    (2) Evaluation of effectiveness of pain management

    (3) A history of current diseases and medications

    (4) Early ambulation and assessment for Homan's sign postoperatively

43. The twenty-eight-week pregnant client is visiting the physician's office for a sinus infection and cough. The doctor asks the nurse to call in several medications. Which of these would the nurse question?

   (1) Pseudoephedrine, 60 mg. p.o. q 4–6 hrs. prn
   (2) Tylenol with codeine, 1–2 tabs p.o. q 4–6 hrs. prn
   (3) Tetracycline Hydrochloride, 500 mg. p.o. qid
   (4) Dextromethorphan, 10 mg. p.o. q 4h prn

44. The nurse is assessing a woman at thirty-five weeks of gestation with pregnancy-induced hypertension. When checking her, the nurse can expect to find elevated blood pressure, proteinuria, as well as what other classic symptom of PIH?

   (1) Oligohydramnios
   (2) Decreased deep tendon reflexes
   (3) Edema
   (4) Thrombocytopenia

45. As the client progresses in labor to 7 cm dilation, the physician requests that the nurse give her an amniohook so she may perform an amniotomy. This procedure is done to help stimulate labor or to place an internal monitor on the baby. The nurse *must* chart which of the following information after the membranes are ruptured?

   (1) The time, color, amount, and odor of fluid
   (2) The purpose of the procedure and the client's response
   (3) A fetal movement count
   (4) The size of amniohook used and the type of sutures given to the physician

46. The second-day vaginal delivery client is preparing for discharge. The nurse is reinforcing discharge instructions and explaining the usual pattern of change in lochia postpartum. The flow will change from

   (1) rubra to serosa to alba.
   (2) rubra to alba to serosa.
   (3) alba to serosa to rubra.
   (4) serosa to rubra to alba.

47. The nurse is interviewing a pregnant client who has 3 children and once had a miscarriage at eighteen weeks' gestation. The nurse writes down

   (1) gravida 3, para 3.
   (2) gravida 4, para 3.
   (3) gravida 5, para 4.
   (4) gravida 5, para 3.

48. The new mother asks about how her older child will react to having a new baby in the household. The nurse cheerfully replies, "Don't worry, Kirsten will be so happy to have a new baby to play with." This nontherapeutic response is called

   (1) belittling.
   (2) rejecting.
   (3) giving advice.
   (4) false reassurance.

49. The nurse is working in an assisted living facility with older men and women. She knows that many of them feel depressed about their decreased ability to perform activities of daily living. In planning their care, a priority nursing diagnosis would be:

  (1) Disturbance in body image related to aging process and decreased mobility

  (2) Denial related to normal process of aging

  (3) Activity intolerance related to decreased functional capacity

  (4) Self-care deficit related to aging process

50. You notice Mrs. Green looking pale and fearful. When you touch her, she feels cold and clammy, and she doesn't recognize you when you call her name. Her pulse is 134, and her BP is 90/50. You realize she must be

  (1) having a myocardial infarction.

  (2) experiencing shock.

  (3) hypoglycemic.

  (4) fainting.

51. Mr. Albert, a 62-year-old salesman, is angry and frustrated over his limitations due to a recent CVA. He refuses to take his medications or cooperate with you during range-of-motion exercises. You understand that

  (1) he had better get used to this because he will probably never regain full use of his right arm or leg.

  (2) this must be extremely difficult for him to be so dependent on others for help, but he has no choice so he should learn to cooperate.

  (3) if he doesn't cooperate soon, his insurance company will deny him acute care, and he will have to go to a skilled nursing facility and won't get the rehab he needs.

  (4) this is typical behavior for a man who has lost his independence and needs assistance with accepting his current condition.

52. A 54-year-old woman was diagnosed with multiple sclerosis nine months ago and has had no symptoms during that time. She is admitted with muscle weakness in her legs. Your initial interaction should be to

  (1) inform her that she was lucky to have had nine months without symptoms.

  (2) allow her time to express her concerns and fears and to ask questions.

  (3) provide her with details of the disease process.

  (4) provide her with a teaching plan, focusing on the tests that will be done in the next two days.

53. Mr. Karas has never been a complainer, but today he is experiencing severe pain in his left foot. You observe his large toe and suspect he may have gout. Which of the following symptoms might you expect?

  (1) No palpable dorsal pedis pulse

  (2) Swelling, redness, immobility, and increased heat at the site

  (3) Cyanosis and cold to touch

  (4) Swelling, blotchy white patches, and increased heat

54. The client is scheduled to receive a 300 cc bolus feeding through a gastric feeding tube. You aspirate 125 cc of fluid from the stomach prior to giving the scheduled feeding. The most appropriate action would be to

(1) throw out the fluid you aspirated from the stomach and instill the new solution.

(2) replace the fluid you took out and put in the new solution as ordered.

(3) replace the fluid you took out and clamp the tube.

(4) throw out the fluid you aspirated from the stomach and clamp the tube.

55. You are teaching Mrs. Lewis to administer her own insulin injections. She has a combination of NPH and regular insulin ordered. Your instructions would include:

(1) Use two separate syringes when administering these two forms of insulin.

(2) Always draw from the regular insulin bottle first.

(3) Always draw from the NPH bottle first.

(4) It would not make any difference which insulin goes into the syringe first.

56. The M.D. order is written, "Titrate O_2 to keep Sat > 92%." You know that this means:

(1) Always keep the O_2 flow rate the same.

(2) Adjust the O_2 flow rate so that the Sat is always greater than or equal to 92%.

(3) The Respiratory Therapist must attend to this client, and the order has nothing to do with nursing.

(4) Adjust the O_2 flow rate so that the Sat is always less than 92%.

57. The nurse admits a client who has a head injury and is at risk for increased intracranial pressure. Which of the following interventions will she perform to help this client?

(1) Use the Glasgow Coma Scale to assess level of consciousness hourly.

(2) Assess pupils for size, movement, and response to light.

(3) Administer acetominophen q 3–4 hours for headache.

(4) Elevate the head of the bed approximately 30 degrees.

58. The nurse is assigned to report any sign of increased intracranial pressure on this client. What would most likely be the first sign of this?

(1) A decorticate posture

(2) A failure to respond to painful stimuli

(3) A widening pulse pressure

(4) An alteration in the level of consciousness

59. Mr. Bartlett is a 72-year-old client with chronic renal failure. Laboratory results indicate that he has hypocalcemia and hyperphosphatemia. When assessing the client, the nurse should be alert to which signs and symptoms?
Select all that apply.

☐ **(1)** Trousseau's sign
☐ **(2)** Constipation
☐ **(3)** Cardiac arrhythmia
☐ **(4)** Fractures

60. The nurse happens to be at the scene of an accident where a man who is unconscious and not breathing is lying next to a ladder. Suspecting a possible neck injury, the nurse initiates rescue breathing using the following maneuver:

(1) Jaw lift
(2) Head tilt
(3) Breathing through nose and mouth
(4) Tongue sweep

61. The nurse is assisting the anesthesiologist during the administration of epidural anesthesia. She helps to position the client

(1) lying prone with her arms extended.
(2) leaning over the side of the bed.
(3) on her side with her knees curled up to her chest.
(4) on her hands and knees.

62. What is the *first* nursing consideration when a client has a stroke?

(1) Maintaining a patent airway and preventing aspiration
(2) Assessing level of consciousness
(3) Reassuring client who may be frightened and confused
(4) Providing active and passive ROM to preserve function

63. Based on the chart below, what complication is this client experiencing after having given birth?

(1) Episiotomy
(2) Endometritis
(3) Postpartum hemorrhage
(4) Postpartum thyroiditis

04/04/09	Patient showing signs of labor at 634. Administered oxytocin at 840.
1305	Multiple birth delivery at 1238 and 1241. Placenta delivered at 1246. Assessment following delivery—Normal, BP—128/89, HR 62, Temp. 99.4, bleeding appears normal.
2030	Patient experiencing heavy bleeding. Soaking through 2 pads in 1 hour. Large clots (golf-ball sized) passing from uterus. Patient complaining of feeling faint and dizzy. This was patient's 4th full-term pregnancy. No complications after previous deliveries. First multiple birth. Estimate approximately 300 mL of blood lost in 7-hour period.

64. The expectant mother is complaining to the nurse that she feels sick to her stomach when she gets up in the morning and cannot bear the thought of breakfast. The nurse suggests that she should

(1) drink a glass of apple juice before bed.

(2) ignore it, as it will pass.

(3) increase fluid intake, especially with meals.

(4) have crackers by her bed to eat before she gets up.

65. The public health nurse is assessing the food intake of a low-income family and finds that it is protein deficient. Which of the following foods would provide a low-cost source of protein?

(1) Beans

(2) Bacon

(3) Rice

(4) Bananas

66. Diet pills on the market claim to reduce the amount of fat absorbed by 30 percent. The nurse explains to the young woman interested in taking them that they also reduce the amount of fat-soluble vitamins that are absorbed. These include:

(1) Vitamins B_1, B_6, and B_{12}

(2) Vitamins A, D, E, and K

(3) Vitamin C

(4) Calcium and iron

67. The 22-year-old first-time mother is asking about breastfeeding her baby. She wants to know how long she should continue nursing. The nurse replies:

(1) "Most people suggest that six weeks provides a good start for the baby."

(2) "If you can continue for three months, breastfeeding will be less important."

(3) "By six months, the baby will be taking a variety of solid foods, and this is a good time to wean."

(4) "Breastfeeding is recommended for the first year of life."

68. A client is recovering from abdominal surgery. The nurse notes that he exhibits several characteristics that put him at risk for thrombophlebitis. Which of the following is the client experiencing?
Select all that apply.

☐ (1) Prolonged bed rest

☐ (2) Obesity

☐ (3) Elevated Hgb and high platelet count

☐ (4) High cholesterol levels

69. When approaching a paranoid client, the nurse knows not to

(1) touch or invade the client's personal space.

(2) convey a calm, matter-of-fact attitude.

(3) establish trust and follow through on commitments.

(4) use a consistent approach.

70. A nurse is assigned to care for Mr. Lee, who is in Buck's traction for a right hip fracture. She knows the importance of making all of the following assessments EXCEPT

(1) peripheral pulses.

(2) capillary refill.

(3) skin pallor or coldness.

(4) level of consciousness.

71. The nurse on the medical floor walks into the diabetic client's room to find him unconscious. She is not sure when he ate last or when or if he took his insulin. The nurse's *best* response would be to

(1) inform the RN and prepare to give glucagon.

(2) obtain the glucometer and determine the client's blood sugar.

(3) call the lab to get a stat glucose on the client.

(4) check his vitals as well as his level of consciousness using the Glasgow coma scale.

72. A nurse is caring for Mr. Beecham, who has peptic ulcer disease. One of her most important nursing responsibilities is to assess for signs of hemorrhage that include which of the following?
Select all that apply.

☐ (1) Melena

☐ (2) Hematemesis

☐ (3) Rigid abdominal muscles

☐ (4) Tachychardia

73. A nurse is reviewing a client's laboratory values. Which of the following would indicate that the client probably has some type of infection?

(1) Hemoglobin: 16 g per dL

(2) White blood cells: 30,000 per mm^3

(3) Platelets: 200,000 per mm^3

(4) Glucose: 120 mg per 100 mL

74. The client is receiving instruction from the nurse about glucose monitoring. She asks how she will know if she is hypoglycemic. The nurse replies:

(1) "You will most likely have symptoms of low blood sugar, and your blood sugar reading will be less than 60."

(2) "Your blood sugar reading will be between 65 and 75, and you will most likely have blurred vision."

(3) "Your glucometer reading will be your 2-hour postprandial reading minus 40, and you will feel sleepy."

(4) "Your blood sugar will not register on the machine, and you will feel extremely lightheaded."

practice test

75. The client with a tibial fracture has been receiving ibuprofen, 600 mg qid prn for pain. Which of the following comments indicate the need for further teaching about the medication?

(1) "I always take the pill with food, so it won't irritate my stomach."

(2) "I will avoid the use of alcohol or aspirin while I am taking this medication."

(3) "I will limit fluids while taking this medication."

(4) "I will notify the provider if I develop swelling or high blood pressure."

ANSWER KEY AND EXPLANATIONS

1. 3	16. 4	31. 2	46. 1	61. 3
2. 1,2,4	17. 4	32. 3	47. 4	62. 1
3. 4	18. 1	33. 1	48. 4	63. 3
4. 3	19. 3	34. 1	49. 1	64. 4
5. 3	20. 2.7	35. 2	50. 2	65. 1
6. 1	21. 4	36. 1	51. 4	66. 2
7. 4	22. 1	37. kneecap	52. 2	67. 4
8. 1,3,2,4	23. 1,2,4	38. 2	53. 2	68. 1,2,3
9. 3	24. 1	39. 2	54. 3	69. 1
10. 2	25. 4	40. 4	55. 2	70. 4
11. 4	26. 1	41. 1,2,3	56. 2	71. 1
12. 2	27. 4	42. 3	57. 4	72. 1,2,4
13. 1	28. 1	43. 3	58. 4	73. 2
14. 4	29. 3	44. 3	59. 1,3,4	74. 1
15. 1	30. 2	45. 1	60. 1	75. 3

1. **The correct answer is (3).** The temperature, pulse rate, and the presence or absence of a rash can be objectively verified. Throat soreness is a client perception and would be noted as subjective information.

2. **The correct answers are (1), (2), and (4).** Young adults are initiating intimate relationships, establishing stable employment, and beginning to accept responsibilities. Generally, they have already adjusted to the body image changes of adolescence.

3. **The correct answer is (4).** In a 1977 decision, Utter v. United Hospital Center, Inc., nurses were charged with failing to activate the chain of command in exercising their "affirmative" duty to exercise independent judgment to prevent harm when caring for clients. Therefore, (1) and (3) are not satisfactory answers. Rather than attempting to care for the client by means not covered by her nurse practice act, the nurse must try to get in touch with the proper supervisory authority to advocate for her client.

4. **The correct answer is (3).** Answers (2) and (4) do not involve assessment. Although the practical nurse is able to make a list of client problems that need intervention, she is to assist the RN in making a nursing diagnosis (1). She is primarily responsible for collecting the database on the client's condition.

5. **The correct answer is (3).** The client has the right to refuse care, but it is the responsibility of the health-care provider to inform her of any risks involved in this decision. Convincing the client to remain (1) is not necessary, nor is notifying discharge planning (2), whose role has been bypassed. Once the client has left the hospital, the hospital is not responsible for informing the next of kin (4) unless the client has a guardian or legal representative.

6. **The correct answer is (1).** The primary role of the practical nurse in relation to the unlicensed assistant is to reinforce the directions of the RN about how to perform the tasks and to monitor the performance. The PN cannot determine the responsibilities (2) or what tasks (4) the unlicensed person may perform. The physician (3) is not involved in nursing responsibilities.

7. **The correct answer is (4).** The primary role of the nurse when a client has a seizure is to protect the client from harming him- or herself. Forcing an object into the client's mouth (1) could cause injury, as could restraining the client (2). Calling the operator for seizure assistance (3) is unnecessary, since the primary intervention is to protect the client from self-injury.

8. **The correct order of answers is (1), (3), (2), (4).** When leaving an isolation room, a health-care professional first removes eyewear. Then he or she unties the gown at the waist and removes the gloves without allowing hands to touch external surfaces. He or she then unties mask strings and removes and discards the mask. Finally, the health-care professional unties the gown neck strings, allows the gown to fall from the shoulders, and removes hands from the gown sleeves without touching the outside of the gown. He or she then holds the gown by the inside shoulder seams and discards it in a laundry bag.

9. **The correct answer is (3).** The Sims position (1) involves the client lying on her side with her upper leg flexed. The lithotomy position (2) is used for vaginal or rectal exams—the client lies on her back with her legs raised in stirrups. The dorsal recumbent position (4), primarily used for abdominal assessment, has the client lying on her back with her legs flexed at the knee. The Trendelenburg position (3), the correct answer, is a position in which the head is low and the body and legs are elevated.

10. **The correct answer is (2).** The physician is needed to order the restraints and should not merely be notified (1). Sedating the client so she will not be troublesome is not ethical (3); restraints that tighten when the client moves (4) are dangerous. Releasing and reapplying the restraints every 2 hours provides an opportunity to assess skin integrity and offer adequate circulation.

11. **The correct answer is (4).** Objective data are observations or measurements such as, in this case, client temperature taken by the data collector. Nausea, pain, and dizziness, answer choices (1), (2), and (3), are subjective, since they represent information that can only be provided by the client.

12. **The correct answer is (2).** Lower extremity paresthesia is a feeling reported by the client and thus is subjective data. A rash (1), pedal edema (2), and a toe infection (4) are all observable by the data collector and objective information.

13. **The correct answer is (1).** The water in the bowl is sterile, but the 1-inch border of the drape (2), the spot where the water splashed (3), and the sides of the table (4) are all

considered unsterile according to current practice guidelines.

14. **The correct answer is (4).** Serous drainage is clear, sero-sanguinous (1) is a combination of clear and bloody discharge, purulent discharge (2) contains white blood cells and bacteria, and sanguinous (3) drainage contains red blood cells and looks bloody.

15. **The correct answer is (1).** Soiled dressings are considered a possible reservoir of infection, because they may harbor bacteria. Bed making (2), encouraging ambulation (3), and giving IV fluids (4) are all nursing activities that do not involve reservoirs of infection.

16. **The correct answer is (4).** Before leaving a client, it is important for the nurse to make sure he or she can reach the call bell and to put the siderails on the bed up to avoid falls. The other actions, such as turning off the TV (1), diverting phone calls (2), and explaining visiting hours (3), are more for client comfort and convenience than for safety.

17. **The correct answer is (4).** By establishing a regular schedule of toileting older clients, they are less likely to need to go to the bathroom on their own. Inserting a catheter (2) is an infection-control risk, and restraining the client (3) is an unnecessary restriction of freedom for convenience. Since the clients are often confused, a night light (1) may not help much.

18. **The correct answer is (1).** The book containing the MSDS (Material Safety Data Sheets) lists information on all hazardous materials on the nursing unit, including protective gear needed, antidotes, and other safety information.

19. **The correct answer is (3).** Fire hoses (1) are not usually found on nursing units, nor are escape ladders (2), which would likely require more agility than that possessed by the average client. It is possible that smoke alarms (4) may be present, but they are not something the nurse is usually asked to know the location of since she does not use them. Fire extinguishers, however, are present on the unit and may be needed by the nurse to extinguish a fire.

20. **The correct answer is 2.7.** The full answer is 2.7 mL. Rationale: 0.7 mg/kg/day for a patient weighing 60 kg is: 0.7 mg/kg $\times$ 60 kg = 42 mg/day. The doses are administered twice daily, so each dose is:

$$\frac{42 \text{ mg/day}}{2 \text{ doses}} = 21 \text{ mg/dose}$$

Now use a ratio to determine the number of milliliters needed:

$$\frac{40 \text{ mg}}{5 \text{ mL}} = \frac{21 \text{ mg}}{x \text{ mL}}$$

$$40x = 105$$

$$x = 2.65 \text{ mL}$$

Rounding up to the nearest tenth: $x = 2.7$ mL

21. **The correct answer is (4).** Frayed wires (1), overloaded outlets (2), and using electrical appliances near water (3) are all electrical hazards, but grounded electrical equipment is a safe practice.

22. **The correct answer is (1).** The nurse doesn't recap needles in order to prevent a frequent cause of

needlestick injuries. Avoiding the procedures themselves [choices (2), (3), and (4)] is impractical and unsafe for clients.

23. **The correct answers are (1), (2), and (4).** The primary types of infection control in addition to standard precautions that apply to everyone are contact, droplet, and airborne. These categories classify precautions by mode of disease transmission. What are often considered respiratory illnesses can fall into any one of the three categories depending on how they are transmitted.

24. **The correct answer is (1).** Lifting objects by bending the knees and holding weight close to the body is an example of good body mechanics consistent with back safety. Bending with straight knees (2), making beds that are too low (3), and stretching and reaching (4) are all hard on the back and likely to lead to injury.

25. **The correct answer is (4).** Nocturia is one of the main symptoms of benign prostatic hypertrophy in which the prostate gland enlarges and partially blocks the urethra. The other symptoms are unrelated to this condition.

26. **The correct answer is (1).** Polypharmacy and vulnerability to adverse effects of medications make older individuals more susceptible to medication-induced confusion. Lack of exercise (2) over time may lead to more mental decline as well as other health problems, but this is a very gradual process. Motor neurons (3) are involved in movement. Parasympathetic reactivity (4) is an unknown process.

27. **The correct answer is (4).** Absorbable sutures are used to repair episiotomies.

28. **The correct answer is (1).** After cold has been applied for 24 hours, warmth may often be soothing to a sore perineum and can help the healing process by increasing blood flow to the area.

29. **The correct answer is (3).** The APGAR is computed by giving 0, 1, or 2 points for color, cry, reflexes, and muscle tone. This baby would get a 2 for the heart rate, a 2 for the cry, a 2 for muscle tone, a 2 for reflexes, and a 1 for color, because the hands and feet are blue.

30. **The correct answer is (2).** Chadwick's sign (1) is the bluish discoloration of the cervix, vagina, and vulva due to increased vascularity. Goodell's sign (3) is softening of the cervix at eight weeks of pregnancy. McRobert's *maneuver* is used to help deliver infants with shoulder dystocia.

31. **The correct answer is (2).** This complication is known as wound dehiscence, and the nurse should put the client in a semi-Fowler's position with flexed knees to reduce tension on the abdominal muscles. It is too late to attempt to administer a dulcolax laxative suppository (3) with the intent of relieving gas pain; it will only add to her problems. Attempting to reinforce the incision with tape or binding the abdomen with a towel [choices (1) and (4)] will only contaminate the wound and most likely will not hold the edges of the incision together.

32. **The correct answer is (3).** Methergine (1), oxytocin (2), and prostaglandin (hemabate) (4), are all used to treat postpartum hemorrhage. Magnesium sulfate, because it tends to block neuromuscular nerve transmission and cause muscle weakness, is a risk factor for postpartum hemorrhage and would not be used.

33. **The correct answer is (1).** Premature infants usually have insufficient lung surfactant, which makes it difficult for them to expand the lung alveoli, leading to respiratory distress syndrome. Hypoglycemia (2) may occur, but is not a first priority in treatment. Hypospadius (3) is no more common in premature infants than in term infants. Brachial plexus palsy (4) is usually related to shoulder dystocia, which is more common in large (macrosomic) infants.

34. **The correct answer is (1).** Rhogam, or Rho(4) immune globulin, prevents the Rh− mother from becoming "sensitized" to the red blood cells of the Rh+ fetus. This would cause her to produce antibodies to the next baby's red blood cells if it is Rh+, which could cause hemolysis of the red blood cells and lead to severe jaundice.

35. **The correct answer is (2).** Witch's milk (a folk term for the milk that sometimes comes from a newborn's breasts) is caused by the mother's hormones on the newborn's breast tissue. Uric acid crystals (1) are related to low fluid intake, and cutis marmorata (4) is marbling of newborn skin due to stress or overchilling. Blood does not usually leak from the newborn's nipples (3).

36. **The correct answer is (1).** Hyperemesis clients are typically treated with intravenous fluids to correct electrolyte imbalances, ketosis, and dehydration, while being maintained npo. Antiemetics or sedatives may be given if necessary.

37. **The correct answer is the kneecap.** A dislocated patella occurs when the kneecap (patella) "pops" from its normal position. This can occur as the result of force (as in a football or other sport injury), or it may be related to a developmental condition that leads to improper alignment of the kneecap with the femur (thigh bone). This is sometimes called "unstable kneecap."

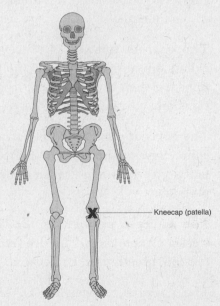

Kneecap (patella)

38. **The correct answer is (2).** A nitrazine paper test, which will turn blue in the presence of amniotic fluid and has a higher pH than urine, is a quick and noninvasive method of determining likely rupture of membranes. A speculum exam (1) will not reveal anything unless the cervix is dilated. Sending a stat sample to the lab (3) is unnecessary, and boric acid (4) is not used for this purpose.

39. **The correct answer is (2).** Assuming a low-transverse incision, which is almost universal in the United States, vaginal birth after Cesarean is commonly attempted and is approximately as likely to result in a nonsurgical delivery as any other birth when the reason for the first C/S (i.e., fetal distress) is nonrecurring.

40. **The correct answer is (4).** Pitocin is given to cause the uterine muscles to contract, so a boggy uterus would indicate that the drug was ineffective.

41. **The correct answers are (1), (2), and (3).** In scoliosis, the problem is curvature of the spine, not difference in limb length.

42. **The correct answer is (3).** Older clients are at high risk for complications related to preexisting conditions and current medications.

43. **The correct answer is (3).** Tetracycline causes discoloration of the infant's teeth when taken during pregnancy.

44. **The correct answer is (3).** The classic symptoms of PIH are hypertension, proteinuria, and edema.

45. **The correct answer is (1).** After the membranes are ruptured, the nurse charts the time (to assess how long membranes have been ruptured before birth), color (to check if meconium has been passed), amount (to determine how much fluid is present), and odor (in case of infection).

46. **The correct answer is (1).** The color of lochia will change from rubra to serosa to alba before subsiding.

47. **The correct answer is (4).** Gravida refers to any pregnancy regardless of the duration, including the present one. Para refers to past pregnancies that continue to the period of viability (usually considered to be 24–28 weeks).

48. **The correct answer is (4).** When a client has a realistic concern, false reassurance that there is nothing to worry about may discourage open communication.

49. **The correct answer is (1).** Older people may have problems coping with their decreasing physical capabilities, and interventions aimed toward helping them deal with these changes and providing the opportunity for them to remain as independent as possible can help them adjust.

50. **The correct answer is (2).** These symptoms, including decreased urinary output, are the classic symptoms of shock.

51. **The correct answer is (4).** Loss of independence is a serious adjustment for a middle-aged working man. Not only has he lost his physical independence, but his financial income has been compromised as well.

52. **The correct answer is (2).** Clients often have irrational fears concerning their disease processes. It is important to allow her to express any of these concerns, and then you may give her appropriate information.

53. **The correct answer is (2).** Gout reveals itself as an inflammation of the joints, typically in the toes. It is due to an accumulation of uric acid due to impaired excretion by the kidneys.

54. **The correct answer is (3).** Return the original stomach contents to maintain fluid and electrolyte balance, and hold the scheduled feeding. Delayed gastric emptying may be indicative of other problems, and the doctor should be notified.

55. **The correct answer is (2).** NPH insulin contains a protein that slows its absorption. You do not want to contaminate the pure form of regular insulin, which could affect its absorption time.

56. **The correct answer is (2).** Nursing has the responsibility of adjusting O_2 delivery rates based on the oxygen saturation level determined by the pulse oximeter.

57. **The correct answer is (4).** Choices (1) and (2) are assessments, not interventions. Acetominophen (3) would not help and could mask symptoms. Elevating the head of the bed can help reduce intracranial pressure by promoting venous drainage.

58. **The correct answer is (4).** The first sign of increased intracranial pressure is a change in the level of conciousness. Choices (1), (2), and (3) are later signs.

59. **The correct answers are (1), (3), and (4).** Hypocalcemia is a calcium deficiency that causes nerve fiber irritability and repetitive muscle spasms. Hypophosphatemia is a deficit in inorganic phosphorus. Signs and symptoms of hypophosphatemia include Trousseau's sign, cardiac arrhythmia, diarrhea, increased clotting times, anxiety, and irritability. A calcium-phosphorus imbalance leads to brittle bones and fractures.

60. **The correct answer is (1).** The jaw lift maneuver is used whenever there is a possibility of a neck injury.

61. **The correct answer is (3).** When the client is on her side with her knees curled up, her spine is extended, and it is easier to insert a needle between the vertebrae.

62. **The correct answer is (1).** After a stroke, the client is at high risk for aspiration and may have problems maintaining a patent airway due to the paralysis.

63. **The correct answer is (3).** A sign of postpartum hemorrhaging (PPH) is significant blood loss (more than 500 mL of blood in a 24-hour period following delivery), which is indicated by client's soaking through at least one sanitary pad in less than an hour. Passing large blood clots is also a sign of PPH, as is faintness or dizziness. Some causes of PPH include multiple birth, four or five previous deliveries, induced labor, and partial retention of the placenta.

64. **The correct answer is (4).** Low blood sugar is thought to play a role in morning sickness; therefore, the suggestion of dry crackers is good because they are generally well tolerated. Increased fluid intake may well make vomiting more likely, and

apple juice before bed not only increases fluid intake, it may also decrease the morning blood sugar. Ignoring morning sickness is not easy.

65. **The correct answer is (1).** Beans are a low-cost source of protein. Bacon is expensive and mostly fat, and rice and bananas are not good protein sources.

66. **The correct answer is (2).** A, D, E, and K are fat-soluble vitamins. The other vitamins are water soluble, and calcium and iron are minerals.

67. **The correct answer is (4).** The American Academy of Pediatrics, which sets health-care standards in pediatrics, suggests breastfeeding for the first year of life.

68. **The correct answers are (1), (2), and (3).** Thrombophlebitis is due to the formation of a blood clot, usually in a leg vein. Risk factors include surgery—especially abdominal—prolonged bed rest, elevated hemoglobin and high platelet count, both of which make the blood more prone to clotting. Cholesterol is not involved in clot formation.

69. **The correct answer is (1).** Paranoid clients feel easily threatened, and the most important point to remember when approaching such a client is to avoid touching him or her or getting too close physically.

70. **The correct answer is (4).** The most important assessments for a person in traction are neurovascular.

71. **The correct answer is (1).** If a diabetic client is unconscious, it is best to give a source of quick glucose, such as glucagon, since hypoglycemia can cause permanent brain damage. Glucose will not cause any permanent harm to the client suffering from coma due to diabetic ketoacidosis.

72. **The correct answers are (1), (2), and (4).** Melena is dark feces caused by blood; hematemesis is the vomiting of blood that occurs after bleeding into the UGI tract, indicating digested blood; and tachycardia is a compensation for decreased blood volume. Rigid abdominal muscles are a sign of peritonitis, not a peptic ulcer.

73. **The correct answer is (2).** An increased white blood count of 30,000 per mm^3 (normal is < 10,000) indicates the likelihood of an infectious process. Hemoglobin and platelets are not directly related to infections, and because glucose levels may drop during an infection, this is a normal glucose level.

74. **The correct answer is (1).** A blood sugar reading of less than 60 is hypoglycemic, and the symptoms of hypoglycemia (tremors, sweating, and tachycardia) typically accompany this finding.

75. **The correct answer is (3).** Adequate hydration is important since ibuprofen is eliminated through the kidneys. Taking the pill with food helps prevent stomach irritation; alcohol and aspirin should not be combined with ibuprofen. Swelling or hypertension are serious adverse effects of this medication.

APPENDIXES

State Boards of Nursing

Alabama
Alabama Board of Nursing
RSA Plaza
770 Washington Avenue, Suite 250
Montgomery, AL 36104
Phone: 334-242-4060
Fax: 334-242-4360
Web site: www.abn.state.al.us

Alaska
Alaska Board of Nursing
Robert B. Atwood Building
550 West 7th Avenue, Suite 1500
Anchorage, AK 99501-3567
Phone: 907-269-8161
Fax: 907-269-8196
Web site: www.dced.state.ak.us/occ/pnur.htm

Arizona*
Arizona State Board of Nursing
4747 N. 7th Street, Suite 200
Phoenix, AZ 85014-3653
Phone: 602-889-5150
Fax: 602-889-5155
Web site: www.azbn.gov

Arkansas*
Arkansas State Board of Nursing
University Tower Building
1123 South University Avenue, Suite 800
Little Rock, AR 72204-1619
Phone: 501-686-2700
Fax: 501-686-2714
Web site: www.arsbn.org

appendix A

*State participates in Nurse Licensure Compact (NLC).

California

California State Board of Registered Nursing
4625 North Market Boulevard, Suite N217
Sacramento, CA 95834-1924
Phone: 916-322-3850
Fax: 916-574-7697
Web site: www.rn.ca.gov

Colorado*

Colorado Board of Nursing
1560 Broadway, Suite 1350
Denver, CO 80202
Phone: 303-894-2430
Fax: 303-894-2821
Web site: www.dora.state.co.us/nursing

Connecticut

Connecticut Board of Examiners for Nursing
Department of Public Health
410 Capitol Avenue, MS#13PHO
Hartford, CT 06134-0328
Phone: 860-509-7624
Fax: 860-508-7553
Web site: www.ct.gov/dph/cwp/view.asp?a=3143&q=388910

Delaware*

Delaware Board of Nursing
Cannon Building
861 Silver Lake Blvd., Suite 203
Dover, DE 19904
Phone: 302-739-4500
Fax: 302-739-2711
Web site: http://dpr.delaware.gov/boards/nursing

District of Columbia

District of Columbia Board of Nursing
Department of Health
Health Professional Licensing Administration
717 14th Street, NW
Washington, DC 20005
Phone: 877-244-1689
Fax: 202-727-8471
Web site: http://hpla.doh.dc.gov/

*State participates in Nurse Licensure Compact (NLC).

Florida

Florida Board of Nursing
4052 Bald Cypress Way, BIN#A07
Tallahasee, FL 32399-1708
Phone: 850-245-4244
Web site: www.doh.state.fl.us/mqa/nursing

Georgia

Georgia Board of Nursing
237 Coliseum Drive
Macon, GA 31217-3858
Phone: 478-207-1650
Fax: 478-207-1660
Web site: http://sos.georgia.gov/plb/rn

Hawaii

Hawaii Board of Nursing
Professional and Vocational Licensing Division
P.O. Box 3469
Honolulu, HI 96801
Phone: 808-596-3000
Fax: 808-586-2689
Web site: http://hawaii.gov/dcca/areas/pvi/boards/nursing

Idaho*

Idaho Board of Nursing
280 North 8th Street, Suite 210
Boise, ID 83720-0061
Phone: 208-334-3110
Fax: 208-334-3262
Web site: www2.state.id.us/ibn/index.htm

Illinois

Department of Professional Regulation
James R. Thompson Center
100 West Randolph, Suite 9-300
Chicago, IL 60601
Phone: 312-814-4500
Fax: 217-782-7645
Web site: www.idfpr.com/dpr/WHO/nurs.asp

Indiana

Indiana State Board of Nursing
Health Professions Bureau
402 West Washington Street, Room W072
Indianapolis, IN 46204
Phone: 317-234-2043
Fax: 317-233-4236
Web site: www.in.gov/pla/nursing.htm

*State participates in Nurse Licensure Compact (NLC).

Iowa*

Iowa Board of Nursing
RiverPoint Business Park
400 S.W. 8th Street, Suite B
Des Moines, IA 50309-4685
Phone: 515-281-3255
Fax: 515-281-4825
Web site: www.state.ia.us/government/nursing/

Kansas

Kansas State Board of Nursing
Landon State Office Building
900 SW Jackson Street, Suite 5518
Topeka, KS 66612-1230
Phone: 785-296-4929
Fax: 785-296-3929
Web site: www.ksbn.org

Kentucky*

Kentucky Board of Nursing
312 Whittington Parkway, Suite 300
Louisville, KY 40222
Phone: 502-329-7000
Fax: 502-329-7011
Web site: http://kbn.ky.gov

Louisiana

Louisiana State Board of Nursing
17373 Perkins Road
Baton Rouge, LA 70810
Phone: 225-755-7500
Fax: 225-755-7584
Web site: www.lsbn.state.la.us

Maine*

Maine State Board of Nursing
161 Capitol Street
158 State House Station
Augusta, ME 04333-0158
Phone: 207-287-1133
Fax: 207-287-1149
Web site: www.maine.gov/boardofnursing/

*State participates in Nurse Licensure Compact (NLC).

Maryland*

Maryland Board of Nursing
4140 Patterson Avenue
Baltimore, MD 21215-2254
Phone: 410-585-1900
Fax: 410-358-3530
Web site: www.mbon.org

Massachusetts

Massachusetts Nursing State Board
Commonwealth of Massachusetts
239 Causeway Street, Suite 500
Boston, MA 02114
Phone: 617-973-0300
Fax: 617-727-1630
Web site: http://mass.gov/dph/boards/rn

Michigan

Office of Health Services
Michigan Department of Consumer and Industry Services
Ottawa Towers North
611 West Ottawa Street
Lansing, MI 48933
Phone: 517-373-9102
Fax: 517-373-2179
Web site: www.michigan.gov/healthlicense

Minnesota

Minnesota Board of Nursing
2829 University Avenue SE, Suite 500
Minneapolis, MN 55414
Phone: 612-617-2270
Fax: 612-617-2190
Web site: www.nursingboard.state.mn.us

Mississippi*

Mississippi Board of Nursing
1935 Lakeland Drive, Suite B
Jackson, MS 39216-5014
Phone: 601-987-4188
Fax: 601-364-2352
Web site: www.msbn.state.ms.us

*State participates in Nurse Licensure Compact (NLC).

Missouri

Missouri State Board of Nursing
3605 Missouri Boulevard
P.O. Box 656
Jefferson City, MO 65102-0656
Phone: 573-751-0681
Fax: 573-751-0075
Web site: http://pr.mo.gov/nursing.asp

Montana

Montana State Board of Nursing
P.O. Box 200513
Helena, MT 59620-0513
Phone: 406-841-2345
Fax: 406-841-2305
Web site: http://mt.gov/dli/bsd/license/bsd_boards/nur_board/board_page.asp

Nebraska*

Nebraska Health and Human Services System
Department of Regulation and Licensure, Nursing Section
301 Centennial Mall South
Lincoln, NE 68509-4986
Phone: 402-471-4376
Fax: 402-471-3577
Web site: www.hhs.state.ne.us/crl/nursing/nursingindex.htm

Nevada

Nevada State Board of Nursing
License Certification and Education
4330 South Valley View Blvd., Suite 106
Las Vegas, NV 89103
Phone: 702-486-5800
Fax: 702-486-5803
Web site: www.nursingboard.state.nv.us

New Hampshire*

New Hampshire Board of Nursing
78 Regional Drive, Building B
P.O. Box 3898
Concord, NH 03302-3898
Phone: 603-271-2323
Fax: 603-271-6605
Web site: www.nh.gov/nursing

*State participates in Nurse Licensure Compact (NLC).

New Jersey

New Jersey Board of Nursing
124 Halsey Street, 6th Floor
Newark, NJ 07101
Phone: 973-504-6586
Fax: 973-648-3481
Web site: www.state.nj.us/lps/ca/medical/nursing.htm

New Mexico*

New Mexico Board of Nursing
6301 Indian School Road NE, Suite 700
Albuquerque, NM 87110
Phone: 505-841-8340
Fax: 505-841-8347
Web site: www.bon.state.nm.us

New York

New York State Board of Nursing
Education Building
89 Washington Avenue
Albany, NY 12234
Phone: 518-474-3817, Ext. 120
Fax: 518-474-3706
Web site: www.op.nysed.gov/nurse.htm

North Carolina*

North Carolina Board of Nursing
3724 National Drive, Suite 201
Raleigh, NC 27612
Phone: 919-782-3211
Fax: 919-781-9461
Web site: www.ncbon.com

North Dakota*

North Dakota Board of Nursing
919 South 7th Street, Suite 504
Bismarck, ND 58504
Phone: 701-328-9777
Fax: 701-328-9785
Web site: www.ndbon.org

Ohio

Ohio Board of Nursing
17 South High Street, Suite 400
Columbus, OH 43215-3413
Phone: 614-466-3947
Fax: 614-466-0388
Web site: www.nursing.ohio.gov

*State participates in Nurse Licensure Compact (NLC).

Oklahoma

Oklahoma Board of Nursing
2915 North Classen Boulevard, Suite 524
Oklahoma City, OK 73106
Phone: 405-962-1800
Fax: 405-962-1821
Web site: www.ok.gov/nursing

Oregon

Oregon State Board of Nursing
800 NE Oregon Street, Box 25
Portland, OR 97232
Phone: 503-731-4745
Fax: 503-731-4755
Web site: www.osbn.state.or.us

Pennsylvania

Pennsylvania State Board of Nursing
P.O. Box 2649
Harrisburg, PA 17105-2649
Phone: 717-783-7142
Fax: 717-783-0822
Web site: www.dos.state.pa.us/bpoa/site/default.asp

Rhode Island*

Rhode Island Board of Nurse Registration and Nursing Education
Three Capitol Hill
105 Cannon Building
Providence, RI 02908
Phone: 401-222-5700
Fax: 401-222-3352
Web site: www.health.ri.org/hsr/professions/nurses.php

South Carolina*

South Carolina State Board of Nursing
110 Centerview Drive, Suite 202
Columbia, SC 29210
Phone: 803-896-4550
Fax: 803-896-4525
Web site: www.llr.state.sc.us/pol/nursing

South Dakota*

South Dakota Board of Nursing
4300 South Louise Avenue, Suite C-1
Sioux Falls, SD 57106-3124
Phone: 605-362-2760
Fax: 605-362-2768
Web site: http://doh.sd.gov/boards/nursing

*State participates in Nurse Licensure Compact (NLC).

Tennessee*

Tennessee Board of Nursing
227 French Landing, Suite 300
Nashville, TN 37243
Phone: 615-532-3202
Web site: http://health.state.tn.us/Boards/nursing

Texas*

Texas Board of Nurse Examiners
333 Guadalupe, Suite 3-460
Austin, TX 78701
Phone: 512-305-7400
Fax: 512-305-7401
Web site: www.bne.state.tx.us/

Utah*

Utah State Board of Nursing
Heber M. Wells Building, 4th Floor
160 East 300 South
Salt Lake City, UT 84111
Phone: 801-530-6628
Fax: 801-530-6511
Web site: www.dopl.utah.gov/licensing.nursing.html

Vermont

Vermont State Board of Nursing
Office of Professional Regulation
National Life Building, North Floor 2
Montpelier, VT 05620-3402
Phone: 802-828-2396
Fax: 802-828-2484
Web site: www.vtprofessionals.org/opr1/nurses/

Virginia*

Virginia Board of Nursing
Perimeter Center
9960 Mayland Drive, Suite 300
Richmond, VA 23233-1463
Phone: 804-367-4515
Fax: 804-527-4455
Web site: www.dhp.state.va.us/nursing

*State participates in Nurse Licensure Compact (NLC).

Washington

Washington State Department of Health
Nursing Care Quality Assurance Commission
P.O. Box 47865
Olympia, WA 98504-7865
Phone: 360-236-4700
Fax: 360-236-4818
Web site: www.doh.wa.gov/hsqa/Professions/hpqalinks.htm#n

West Virginia

West Virginia Board of Examiners for Registered Professional Nurses
101 Dee Drive, Suite 102
Charleston, WV 25311-1620
Phone: 304-558-3596
Fax: 304-558-3666
Web site: www.wvrnboard.com

Wisconsin

Wisconsin Department of Regulation and Licensing
P.O. Box 8935
Madison, WI 53708
Phone: 608-266-2112
Fax: 608-267-7083
Web site: www.drl.wi.gov/index.htm

Wyoming

Wyoming State Board of Nursing
1810 Pioneer Avenue
Cheyenne, WY 82002
Phone: 307-777-7601
Fax: 307-777-3519
Web site: http://nursing.state.wy.us/

*State participates in Nurse Licensure Compact (NLC).

PN/VN Organizations

These organizations have been formed to help promote continuing education, publish practical nursing journals, and to establish nursing standards. In addition, they provide a means for PNs and VNs to communicate with each other.

NATIONAL ASSOCIATION OF PRACTICAL NURSE EDUCATION AND SERVICE, INC. (NAPNES)

1. Publishes the *Journal of Practical Nursing,* a quarterly, peer-reviewed professional publication.
2. Membership includes anyone with an interest in practical nurse education and practice.
3. Publishes *The Directory of State-Approved Programs of Practical / Vocational Nurses.*

> NAPNES
> 8607 2nd Avenue, Suite 404A
> Silver Spring, MD 20910
> *Phone:* 301-588-2491
> *Fax:* 301-588-2839
> *Web site:* www.napnes.org

NATIONAL FEDERATION OF LICENSED PRATICAL NURSES, INC. (NFLPN)

1. Publishes on a quarterly basis (with affiliate partner, ADVANCE for LPNs), *NFLPN Extra!,* featuring articles on clinical skills improvement, new product reviews, health industry trends, legislative notes, continuing education opportunities, and more.
2. Purpose is to keep PNs informed about nursing issues and trends in health care and provide information about practical practice standards and guidelines for continuing education.

> NFLPN
> 605 Pode Drive
> Garner, NC 27529
> *Phone:* 919-779-0046
> *Fax:* 919-779-5642
> *Web site:* www.nflPN.org

NATIONAL LEAGUE FOR NURSING (NLN)

1. Publishes a variety of journals, newsletters, and books (http://www.nln.org/publications).
2. Publishes professional directories.
3. Prepares and scores selection and achievement tests.
4. Accredits schools of practical and registered nursing.
5. Provides for continuing education.

NLN
61 Broadway, 33rd Floor
New York, NY 10006
Phone: 212-363-5555
Fax: 212-812-0393
E-mail: generalinfonln.org
Web site: www.nln.org

Web Sites of Interest

WEB SITES OF INTEREST

www.nfPN.org

This is the home page for the National Federation of Practical Nurses. It includes membership information, job information, and an online discussion center. The organization publishes the *American Journal of Practical Nursing*.

www.nln.org

This is the Web site for the National League for Nursing and includes site information on testing and nursing education for PNs, VNs, and RNs.

www.allnurses.com

This is an online network of nurses. It features health care and nursing news, a career center, clinical references, and continuing education.

www.napnes.org

The National Association for Practical Nurse Education and Service is a professional organization of PNs. It develops curricula for practical nursing education programs, continuing education programs, and has a library with nursing and health education materials. The *Journal of Practical Nursing* and *Directory of State-Approved Programs of Practical/Vocational Nurses* are published by NAPNES.

www.mdconsult.com

A Web site offering information on diseases, medical news, and drug information. Includes information on speciality areas, such as Hematology-Oncology, Pediatric, and Pediontics.

www.clinicaltrials.gov

A U.S. listing by the National Library of Medicine that lists all ongoing clinical trials in the U.S. involving treatments for serious illnesses.

www.nurses.com

A Web site offering the latest information about the nursing industry as well as resources for medical news, suppliers, and more. Also includes newsletters, job searches, and a free consultant locator.

www.ec-online.net

An information database on rehabilitation providers, retirement communities, and long-term nursing care facilities. Useful for patients as well as hospitals and health-care providers.

www.mysurgery.com

Although this site is designed for clients, it provides an excellent refresher for health-care professionals. There are clear descriptions of many types of surgery, including diagrams and photographs. It also features video clips for those with Apple computers.

www.4woman.gov

This Web site provides answers to frequently asked questions about pregnancy and women's health. There is a section for health-care professionals with many links to other useful sites for professionals.

www.nursingnet.org

This is a Web site run by nurses that features chat rooms and clinical information. There is a PN Employment Board with many job openings listed.

www.afscme.org

The Web site of the United Nurses of America, which is part of AFSCME, a union of health-care employees. The United Nurses of America includes 76,000 RNs and PNs. The site includes clinical news, legal issues, and union activities. There is also a Spanish version.

www.nurse.com

This is a Web site created by nursing students for nursing students. It offers career information, drug data, a message board, and study aids.

www.oncolink.upenn.edu

Useful for patients and professionals, this site offers a great deal of cancer information and resources. It is useful for both patients and professionals.

www.ama-assn.org

This is a Web site for physicians and clients. It lists almost every MD in the United States and also contains journal information, women's health, and other features.

www.altmedicine.com

Covers major topics including homeopathy, hypnosis, and biofeedback. It also provides links to sites such as the Herb Research Foundation. The alternative health news is covered in the news bulletin.

www.thebreastclinic.com

Information on cysts, cancer, fibrocystic disease, and many other topics. It provides discussion forums and links for additional information.

Sites with PN/VN Job Postings

www.medhunters.com

www.hotnursejobs.com

www.hospitaljobsonline.com

www.healthdirection.com

www.nursingjobs.com

www.nurses123.com

www.hospitalsoup.com

www.nursejobs.com

www.degreehunter.com/nursing_jobs.html

www.healthjobsite.com

www.nursejobsrus.com

NOTES

NOTES

NOTES

NOTES

NOTES

NOTES

NOTES

NOTES

NOTES

Peterson's
Book Satisfaction Survey

Give Us Your Feedback

Thank you for choosing Peterson's as your source for personalized solutions for your education and career achievement. Please take a few minutes to answer the following questions. Your answers will go a long way in helping us to produce the most user-friendly and comprehensive resources to meet your individual needs.

When completed, please tear out this page and mail it to us at:

Publishing Department
Peterson's, a Nelnet company
2000 Lenox Drive
Lawrenceville, NJ 08648

You can also complete this survey online at **www.petersons.com/booksurvey**.

1. **What is the ISBN of the book you have purchased? (The ISBN can be found on the book's back cover in the lower right-hand corner.)** _____

2. **Where did you purchase this book?**
   ❑ Retailer, such as Barnes & Noble
   ❑ Online reseller, such as Amazon.com
   ❑ Petersons.com
   ❑ Other (please specify) _____

3. **If you purchased this book on Petersons.com, please rate the following aspects of your online purchasing experience on a scale of 4 to 1 (4 = Excellent and 1 = Poor).**

	4	3	2	1
Comprehensiveness of Peterson's Online Bookstore page	❑	❑	❑	❑
Overall online customer experience	❑	❑	❑	❑

4. **Which category best describes you?**

   ❑ High school student
   ❑ Parent of high school student
   ❑ College student
   ❑ Graduate/professional student
   ❑ Returning adult student

   ❑ Teacher
   ❑ Counselor
   ❑ Working professional/military
   ❑ Other (please specify) _____

5. **Rate your overall satisfaction with this book.**

Extremely Satisfied	Satisfied	Not Satisfied
❑	❑	❑

6. Rate each of the following aspects of this book on a scale of 4 to 1 (4 = Excellent and 1 = Poor).

	4	3	2	1
Comprehensiveness of the information	❑	❑	❑	❑
Accuracy of the information	❑	❑	❑	❑
Usability	❑	❑	❑	❑
Cover design	❑	❑	❑	❑
Book layout	❑	❑	❑	❑
Special features (e.g., CD, flashcards, charts, etc.)	❑	❑	❑	❑
Value for the money	❑	❑	❑	❑

7. This book was recommended by:
- ❑ Guidance counselor
- ❑ Parent/guardian
- ❑ Family member/relative
- ❑ Friend
- ❑ Teacher
- ❑ Not recommended by anyone—I found the book on my own
- ❑ Other (please specify) _____

8. Would you recommend this book to others?

Yes	Not Sure	No
❑	❑	❑

9. Please provide any additional comments.

_____

_____

_____

_____

_____

Remember, you can tear out this page and mail it to us at:

Publishing Department
Peterson's, a Nelnet company
2000 Lenox Drive
Lawrenceville, NJ 08648

or you can complete the survey online at **www.petersons.com/booksurvey.**

Your feedback is important to us at Peterson's, and we thank you for your time!

If you would like us to keep in touch with you about new products and services, please include your e-mail address here: _____